# GOING

#

# GROWING

## RICHARD JACKSON

# INTERNATIONAL TRAINING CENTRE (CCITC)

## RESPONDING TO A GOD-GIVEN VISION

# A REFLECTIVE HISTORY OF PIONEERING PARTNERSHIPS

DESCRIBING
TRAINING PROJECTS FOR MINISTRY AND MISSION
(2001-14)
SHARED WITH THE

CHRISTIAN COUNCIL OF SIERRA LEONE (CCSL)
(2002-4)
& METHODIST CHURCH SIERRA LEONE (MCSL)
(2005-6; 2009; 2012-14)
&
METHODIST CHURCH CUBA (MCC)
(2005)
&
METHODIST CHURCH NIGERIA (MCN)
(2006-8; 2008-10; 2010-12; 2012-14)
&
METHODIST CHURCH UGANDA (MCU)
(2014)

**CLIFF COLLEGE INTERNATIONAL TRAINING CENTRE:
IN POST-CONFLICT SIERRA LEONE**

**Further information about the CCITC Programme is available from:**

The CCITC Coordinator: Revd Richard Jackson MA BD
Tel: +44 (0) 1617182548
2 Almond Drive, Sale, Cheshire, M33 5QZ
Email: Rev.rj@ntlworld.com

or

The CCITC Director, Revd Dr Stephen Skuce BD MPhil
Tel: +44 (0) 1246584215
Cliff College, Calver, Hope Valley, Derbyshire S32 3XG
Email: s.skuce@cliffcollege.ac.uk

Web site: www.cliffcollege.ac.uk

# TABLE OF CONTENTS

The year 2001 began with the author, employed as a tutor in the Postgraduate Department at Cliff College, being involved in an International Seminar on evangelism. Revd Richard Jackson, and his wife Dr Carole, former missionaries in Sierra Leone, (1969-79) received an unexpected invitation to return in May 2001 to the Conference of the Methodist Church Sierra Leone (MCSL), a church and country ravaged by ten years of bloody conflict. This return visit inspired a vision of how an International Learning Centre, based on Cliff College, but working in partnership with the churches in Sierra Leone, might contribute to the renewal of their church ministry and mission. The media publicity given to the destruction caused, helped to prepare the way for a positive response that generated both finance and resources for a pilot training programme to be undertaken in partnership with the Christian Council Sierra Leone (CCSL).

By January 2002 we had received sufficient encouragement from The Christian Council of Sierra Leone, The Methodist Church in Britain and MMS (Ireland), Cliff College and a number of national and local sponsors to launch a CCILC pilot programme in Sierra Leone. Introductory guidelines and early documentation were presented for information and approval by those likely to be involved in any way. The positive response from organisations and individuals who cared and shared, made it possible to put in place everything that was needed to begin a two-year pilot programme in July 2002.

From the outset, the Coordinator of the two-year pilot programme added the work associated with the launch of the CCILC to his responsibilities as postgraduate tutor at Cliff College. We utilised documentation and patterns already being used for 'Diploma' courses and 'Distance Learning' postgraduate programmes. It quickly became clear that much more administration and participation would be required at Cliff College if the required standards were to be met in Sierra Leone. Whilst the two-year pilot programme continued, an early evaluation was undertaken in April, 2003 with the intention of reviewing the process and working towards a half-time appointment for the Coordinator to develop this programme. ...... 54

As early as 1995 former mission partners in Sierra Leone began to meet together at the invitation of Dr Mary Groves and through the late Revd Frank Himsworth and his wife Sheila began to raise funds and support for that troubled country. Frank & Sheila's, Sierra Leone Methodist Church News published a couple of times a year from 2002, backed up by organised get-togethers proved to be inspired. The newsletter, informed by 'official' information and visitors from Sierra Leone to the reunions served to maintain the momentum of sharing and caring with many of the friends of Sierra Leone who have supported the church there in a number of ways. The letter below from 2003, (and a 2007/5 newsletter 13) provide an insight into the personal but positive nature of these communications which have helped maintain relationships and raised many thousands of pounds for rebuilding work in Sierra Leone. ...... 79

# CHAPTER 4 2004: REVIEWING & RENEWING ...... 82

Dedicated work by the MCSL appointed National Coordinator, alongside that of the International Coordinator and a small but enthusiastic team of people willing to work with the programme brought the two-year pilot programme to a successful conclusion. Out of ninety-nine students who began the course in July 2002, 73 graduated with an 'International Diploma In Applied Ministry And Mission (IDIAMM)' in July and a further 18 in December 2004. Despite the difficulties of working, studying, travelling in a post-conflict situation a total of 91 students completed the course out of the 99 who began the pilot programme. ...... 82

# CHAPTER 5 2005: SL, NIGERIA & CUBA ................................ 95

During 2005, we began to cope with the spontaneous expansion of the work associated with what was seen as a very successful pilot project. A new two-year programme undertaken for much smaller numbers could not be justified in Sierra Leone, but an associated programme of further vocational training with Local Preachers, Lay leaders and Women Workers was undertaken by Revd & Mrs Gilbert Hall. In addition, CCILC responded to a request for: further training in 'Administration' for ministers of the Methodist Church in Sierra Leone by seeking funding for a programme planned to begin in 2006. In October the International Coordinator visited Nigeria at the invitation of the Methodist Church there, to explore with them how the two-year programme might be adapted to give further training to their evangelists and ministers as their church began to re-orientate in relation to evangelism and mission. This was followed in November by some Pastor related training undertaken with the Cuban Methodist Church. There was strong encouragement to contribute an article, but little response received from a report published in the South African Baptist Journal of Theology (pp262-9: Vol. 14 2005) outlining the successful pilot programme in Sierra Leone.

# CHAPTER 6 2006: SIERRA LEONE PLUS NIGERIA .............. 108

During 2006, the CCILC continued with further training in Administration, alongside the lay leadership training, being given in Sierra Leone. In addition after preparatory conversations undertaken in October 2005, we began a new revised two-year IDIAMM training programme with the Methodist Church in Nigeria. In July, 82 students were enrolled at Umuahia MTI and 57 at Sagamu MTI in Nigeria, 139 students in all.

# CHAPTER 7 2007: CONTINUING IN NIGERIA & SL............. 124

By February 2007, the Sierra Leone training in 'Administration' and the associated 'Lay Leadership' training was completed. Contact with the church there was maintained, but the main focus for the work of CCITC moved in the direction of a training partnership with the Methodist Church Nigeria, a much larger country. The Methodist Church has more than 2,000 workers active in ministry (ordained & lay) linked to the Methodist Conference through a hierarchical/episcopal organisation of Dioceses and Arch-Dioceses; Bishops and Archbishops; with the 'Prelate' as leader overall. As earlier in Sierra Leone, being engaged in the work related to the IDIAMM course meant that visiting lecturers, friends and sponsors generated funding also for improved student accommodation and water supplies, at Umuahia and Sagamu Methodist Training Institutions (MTI's). Support was given also to the pioneering college of Zonkwa, set in the strongly Muslim northern part of Nigeria. ............. 124

# CHAPTER 8 2008: REVIEW NIGERIAN LINKS..................... 159

Early in 2008, it became clear that the leadership of MCN was so impressed with the impact of the CCITC, that a 'rolling programme' beyond 2006-8 was expected. The innovative 'Spouses Weekend', introduced as part of the programme in January was appreciated. Graduates in July 2008 numbered 108 students and about 100 new students (with more promised) were enrolled for the 2010-12 programme. Ceremonies in Abeokuta, linked with the 19th Century death there of Mary Archer, the first wife of Revd Thomas Champness, the forefather founder of Cliff College, served to strengthen the historic 'ties that bind' us as partners in mission today. ...................................... 159

In April, we responded to a request from the MCN leadership to provide for their Episcopal Leadership (as a follow-up to the 2009 Episcopal event in Lagos-see 2009/5): a Study Course at Cliff College; followed by two by two fellowship visits to most Districts of the British Methodist Church; and an associated Methodist Heritage tour of the UK. In August, we said farewell to the retiring Prelate, Sunday Ola Makinde and welcomed the newly elected Prelate, Samuel Uche who had been in the UK with us for the Heritage Tour earlier in the year.  Later in the year we launched Part 1 of our first Training programme in both Sierra Leone and Nigeria intentionally focused on lay leaders at local, diocesan and national levels of the church.

CHAPTER 14 2014: SPONTANEOUS EXPANSION

2014 heralded the completion of the first lay training programme in Nigeria with 83 leaders graduating from the course at the two centres of Umuahia MTI and Sagamu MTI. Part 2 of the Management & Administration course was postponed in an Ebola threatened Sierra Leone. We organised a June UK study/heritage tour for MCN lay leaders and in July/August a new training (ad)venture was pioneered in Uganda. The CCITC Coordinator was welcomed as both a friend and the Delegate from the British Conference at the MCN Conference held in Port Harcourt during August.

CHAPTER 15 2015: THE END OF THE BEGINNING

APPENDICEES (1-12): TRAINERS WORKSHOP

12

# THE PREFACE

I believe that the Cliff College International Training Centre (CCITC) is one of the most exciting, innovative, adaptable programmes of 'partnership in training' that has been gifted to the church of the 21st Century.

Some friends might say quite reasonably, "But you would say that wouldn't you!" They are well aware that 'The Vision' for the programme can still be found in the jottings that I made on an aeroplane sick-bag in 2001 when returning from a post-conflict Church Conference in Sierra Leone. I will not try to justify my firm belief that those jottings were a vision from God that had as much to do with my earlier experience and friendships as with me making a personal response to the situation in Sierra Leone at that time. I will leave the reader to look through what is written here and see what has taken place since 2001 before they come to their own conclusion. My hope is that as we explore together the history of the CCITC, others will recognise what opportunities can be made available to the church if we take to heart and invest our money in 'From Everywhere to Everywhere' short-term partnership training programmes that 'In Everything' so clearly benefits all parties and individuals involved.

Close friends of the programme and colleagues know that during the past few months and even years, I have been toying with ideas as to how to publicise the history and work of the CCITC to a wider audience. Should the presentation become an academic thesis leading to an MPhil or even a PhD, which would take several years and likely be read by very few interested scholars? Might I produce a book within which themes that have arisen could be thought through and observations added to the many books that already major on training and mission? The reader will soon discover that I have decided to produce a history that has running down its year-by-year spine the reports, reflections, some correspondence and even notes for meetings as they happened. There has been little attempt made to tidy up reports, other than to correct obvious mistakes in punctuation or grammar and to omit closing courtesies.

Except where otherwise indicated I wrote the original reports, usually within days of returning from an overseas visit. As the author of this history I must take responsibility for any errors of fact or inadvertent infringement of copyright or privacy that may be discovered in both my reports and those edited reports originally produced by named colleagues and friends. Many of the original reports were illustrated by coloured photographs taken at the time, some of which it may not be possible to reproduce in whatever form this publication takes.

My hope is that what is gained through the immediacy and historic veracity of this 'documented history as it happened', will more than make up for what is lost in omissions or dulled by unavoidable repetition from countless files filled with reports and correspondence relating to the development of the CCITC. Readers who are simply interested in the 'story' of the CCITC will feel free to skip the detailed work, much of which I have included in the 'Appendices (1-12): Trainers Workshop' that will be of interest to practitioners.

Most of my friends, close colleagues, supporters, and official contacts have given up any hope of preserving anonymity, but I have tried to preserve the confidentiality of students/trainees. Please forgive any lapses here. Careful readers will note that the name Cliff College International Learning Centre-CCILC (with references to students) was changed to Training Centre-CCITC (with references to Trainees) in 2009 with the intention of broadening the scope of the programme and linking it with developing 'in-service training' for adults at work.

It would not be appropriate to name here, as in many an 'Oscars' acceptance speech, all the people to whom tribute might be paid for the successful outworking of this programme and the production of this history. Many of them are mentioned by name in the 'history' that follows. Nevertheless it would be remiss of me not to acknowledge the vital and unwavering support of successive Principals at Cliff College: (Revd Drs all!) Howard Mellor; Martyn Atkins (also first Director of CCILC); Chris Blake; and our current director of CCITC, Stephen Skuce. They, the staff at Cliff College, our Core Team, Revd Dr Malcolm & Mrs Janet McCall with the Course Administrator (unpaid) Keith Phillips and more than 60 lecturers, many of them involved in more than one programme of training, have

14

given CCITC a voice in talking up the programme and a functioning, prayerful body to action it.

Former Team Leader at the World Church Office in London (and ex-mission partner in Sierra Leone) Mike King, with his colleagues, responded early, positively and practically to the vision. Our friends associated with the 'mission oriented', MMS (Ireland) led by Revd Ken Todd and Tim Dunwoody have given constant encouragement and extra funding as required by the programme.

This history is largely associated with our work in Sierra Leone and Nigeria, with brief excursions (incursions) in Cuba and very recently Uganda. To the leadership, our partner lecturers and friends in all of these churches we pay our final tribute. They have quite literally embraced us like the warmth of the African sunshine and allowed us to be one with them in the leadership of this partnership programme, as together we have helped determine the future of their patterns of training and development.

Our training and resources and the expertise available at Cliff College relating to 'Ministry and Mission' have dovetailed into their church requirements for further training. My belief is that using the lessons learned here, 'Partnership in Training' in every aspect of the church's life could and should become much more widespread. Personally motivated, Church, Circuit, District, and even Conference programmes that presently build buildings and focus on one-off 'fraternal conference' visits might be utilised in a variety of ways to provide a 'Partnership in Training' model that gives focussed training for more people to be prepared for their mission in God's world.

After all, in this work as in all that we do in relation to development and mission, 'PEOPLE' (in their Going and Growing Together) 'MATTER MORE THAN THINGS!'

Richard Jackson (Revd)
International Coordinator,
Cliff College International Training Centre (CCITC)
November 2014

# CHAPTER 1 2001: BACKGROUND TO THE VISION

*The year 2001 began with the author, employed as a tutor in the Postgraduate Department at Cliff College, being involved in an International Seminar on evangelism. Revd Richard Jackson, and his wife Dr Carole, former missionaries in Sierra Leone, (1969-79) received an unexpected invitation to return in May 2001 to the Conference of the Methodist Church Sierra Leone (MCSL), a church and country ravaged by ten years of bloody conflict. This return visit inspired a vision of how an International Learning Centre, based on Cliff College, but working in partnership with the churches in Sierra Leone, might contribute to the renewal of their church ministry and mission. The media publicity given to the destruction caused, helped to prepare the way for a positive response that generated both finance and resources for a pilot training programme to be undertaken in partnership with the Christian Council Sierra Leone (CCSL).*

## 2001/1 JAN 4-12: WORLD METHODISM AT CLIFF

In January 2001 Cliff College hosted the 7th International Seminar of the World Methodism Evangelism (WME) Institute with the theme, "The Timeless Gospel for the New Millennium". Those present from many parts of the world were challenged as we listened to lectures and heard fresh thinking shared in seminars on the sub-themes of:

1.  "Confronting the Timeless Gospel"
2.  "Understanding the Timeless Gospel"
3.  "Proclaiming the Timeless Gospel"
4.  "Addressing the Culture with the Timeless Gospel"
5.  "Engaging Specific Cultures with the Timeless Gospel"

**"THE TIMELESS GOSPEL FOR THE NEW MILLENNIUM"**

We were encouraged throughout the Seminar to take time:
To reflect more deeply and realistically on our own experience of mission in the rapidly-changing world of the 20th Century;
To renew our personal commitment to mission and evangelism;
But perhaps more importantly early in the new millennium,
To be challenged as to how we might do things differently;

And do different things in mission;
Whilst remaining true to the "Timeless Gospel" in the 21$^{st}$ Century.

How much the impact of this conference and how much the writer's own experience has contributed to the concept that became the Cliff College International Learning Centre, we will leave the reader to judge. What we can say thirteen years on from that Seminar, is that the Cliff College International Training Centre (CCITC) has pioneered this innovative partnership in training as a 'Fresh Expression' of Christ's mission in the world and has demonstrated that it works. We are now eager to disseminate the vision throughout the global Methodist family and to other churches that have the resources and will to utilise the concept and develop similar partnerships to the glory of God.

**CCILC: A PROVEN PARTNERSHIP IN SPREAD OF THE 'TIMELESS GOSPEL'.**

We believe the concept that undergirds the vision, of building the church by "Doing training there in partnership" illustrated in this history, should be high on the World Church agenda for the following practical reasons:

1) Throughout the whole process – from invitation to graduation – spiritual authority and decision-making remains with the national church in the particular country where the course is undertaken. Thus, hosts and guests are equal partners together under a recognised, but indigenous Church authority.

2) Because the training is done in the country it can relate directly to the local culture and church situation. The church leaders being trained are not taken out of their on-going ministry, and the teaching received can be applied immediately in ministry, both ordained and lay.

3) The way of doing this is extremely efficient and "economical" in both time and finance for all involved with the course. Generally, the 'Sending' church provides the costs of international travel and of resourcing the course: the 'Receiving' church provides the training centre facilities; the cost of local travel, feeding and accommodation for the visiting lecturers. With 'Everywhere to Everywhere' ministries, the 'Senders and Receivers' increasingly are inter-changeable.

4) One "spin-off" from regular training visits with a core team plus 'casuals' and colleagues from partner churches is that it generates a unique depth of healthy cross-fertilization between the participating churches and trainers associated with the programme.

5) A real cross-cultural experience is enjoyed within the programmed 'Residentials,' as the visitors appreciate to a much greater degree "the way we do things here now" as an actual, practical expression of their church and culture.

6) All trainees and lecturers involved in and leaders associated with the programme become more aware that in the growing the church, 'People matter more than things.'

7) The 'added value' to all parties engaged in this kind of training will become clearer as we trace the history and development not only of the formal programme, but also as we note many of the value added benefits generated through regular face-to-face sharing which restores relationships and encourages fresh initiatives.

**As one enthusiastic member of our core team has noted:**

'Although words like "innovative," "ground-breaking," and "pioneering" have been rightly used about this new global initiative, yet it is important to recognise how strongly it also reflects New Testament patterns. The concept would surely not have sounded strange to the ears of the Apostle Paul – nor, for that matter, to John Wesley. "Doing-it-there" is a "makeover" of scriptural global mission patterns, reconfigured for a 21$^{st}$ Century world – in order to present Jesus as our International Saviour and LORD, for the extension of His Kingdom and "the healing of the nations." In fact it is a practical demonstration of an exciting initiative that will help spread "The Timeless Gospel for the New Millennium".'

# 2001/2 REFLECTIONS ON RETURNING TO SL
RETURNING TO SIERRA LEONE AFTER 22 YEARS

Early in May 2001 at the invitation of the Methodist Church Sierra Leone (MCSL), my wife and I had flown out as representatives of the British Methodist Church with Sierra National Airlines from London Gatwick Airport via Las Palmas to Lungi Airport, Sierra Leone. For the short trip from Lungi Airport to the capital Freetown we felt like novice paratroopers as we were crammed into the seats around an ancient Russian armed forces helicopter with everyone's baggage dumped precariously in the centre. Rumours were already circulating that the Sierra Leone National Airlines partnership with Gulf Air was having problems. Returning Monday passengers were delayed till Friday. In the event we flew back to London with a Russian crew after two weeks in Sierra Leone just one day late!

Carole and I travelled out to a war-ravaged Sierra Leone with minds full of memories from our ten years of missionary service with the Methodist Church in Sierra Leone from 1969 to 1979. The late invitation to attend the MCSL Annual Conference in 2001 allowed us little time to gather our thoughts. During the brief preparation period a kaleidoscope of memories had been revived and coloured our preparation for returning to the country where our first child Heather grew up and our second child, Peter was born. The reported ravages of the ten year 'rebel war' judged to be coming to an end faded as we anticipated being again amongst those friends who had been so supportive of our family in the formative years of our ministry in the Methodist Church.

**REMEMBERING OUR PAST EXPERIENCE (1969 to 1979)**

Beginning in 1969 as young and sometimes foolish missionaries, the writer as a 'probationer' Methodist Minister and his recently qualified medical doctor wife, Carole, experienced the warm hospitality and friendship of the people of Sierra Leone.

**WHEN WE WERE YOUNG(ER)**

Starting out with brief orientation stays in the eastern towns of Segbwema and Kenema we moved around the eastern part of the country on a circular tour to longer term appointments punctuated by furloughs in the UK every two years until 1979. We served first in rural circuits with 60 plus village churches, remote clinics and in areas where we managed many Methodist Schools in the rural circuits of Sandaru, Bunumbu and Bandajuma Yawei.

**BAPTISING BY IMMERSION IN THE MOA RIVER**

19

Later we were stationed in the Sierra Leone urban settings of Bo and finally again in Kenema as Chairman of the Bo/Kenema District responsible for overseeing Church, Agriculture, Youth, Educational and Literacy Projects touching the lives of ordinary people in many areas of Sierra Leone. Our time in the Methodist Church Sierra Leone (MCSL) came towards the end of an era peopled by 'life-time or longer-term missionaries' serving overseas but when significant numbers of missionaries, ordained and lay were still involved in every aspect of the fledgling church's development.

Since our ten years of sharing in the work there, the Methodist Church in Britain & Ireland has continued its partnership with the MCSL sending fewer 'mission partner personnel', but backing up that support with 'block', emergency, and scholarship grants that have helped the church to continue its work. Obviously, we had stayed in touch with friends in Sierra Leone whilst serving for the following twenty years in English circuits of the British Methodist Church. As we travelled back to Sierra Leone we tried to keep in mind that we were returning after more than two decades to a very different country and church from that which we had left, but it proved difficult to shake off those personal memories of people and places as we had known them.

We had known something of the destructive capacity of politically motivated coups and counter-coups during our ten years in Sierra Leone from 1969 to 1979. During the 'Palm Sunday weekend nominations' for the 1977 elections, some members of the opposition 'Sierra Leone People's Party (SLPP), with its palm branch symbol, reacted with violence to the perceived abuse of the constitution by the governing 'All People's Congress' (APC) of this democratic country. The violence then in Kenema climaxed with the burning down of its major employer 'Forest Industries' and abated only as we visited and prayed with the injured in hospital, viewed the dead and met with their grieving families in the morgue at the government hospital.

**SIERRA LEONE IN 2001: REVIEWING 'THE TROUBLES'!**

By the time we returned in 2001, Sierra Leone, a small country on the coast of West Africa had for ten years experienced violence on an entirely different scale as the setting for one of the world's cruellest and most destructive of conflicts. This fertile country rich in agricultural and mineral (iron and diamonds) resources has plummeted to the bottom of the UN economic scale indicators. The complex history of the conflict cannot be written up here. Suffice to say that external factors linked with neighbouring Liberia's own troubles (and rebel leader Charles Taylor, later found guilty of crimes against humanity at the Hague); the diamonds of Sierra Leone; youth unemployment and internal disaffected elements contributed to the tragedy that beset the friendly people, many of them Methodists, of this former British colony.

We had seen the images of boy soldiers on our TV screens in Britain, read the reports of the atrocities committed and heard eye-witness accounts. Nothing prepared us for what we witnessed of the seemingly mindless and random destruction of property, including homes, schools, clinics, churches and mosques particularly in the Eastern Province of Sierra Leone where much of our time was spent during our ten years as missionaries. It was difficult to imagine what the people there had gone through as they lost their rice harvests and small plantations of cash crops like coffee and cocoa to marauding bands of rebels and were driven from their homes by disaffected groups who took advantage of the chaos for their own ends.

### LISTENING TO THEIR STORIES OF FAITH AND SACRIFICE

Our return to Sierra Leone as former missionaries representing the British Methodist Conference at the MCSL Conference being held in the provincial centre of Bo proved to be both a heart-breaking and uplifting experience. As I led prayers in the Ministerial Session of the Conference, we were reminded of the troubles in church and state that had been survived in the past. We were encouraged by MCSL's positive response to suffering endured; a testimony to faith underwritten by God for the still uncertain future. The Conference and the associated trek around the accessible parts of the country in the two weeks that we were there brought home to us as correspondence and conversation couldn't the wanton destruction by the rebel forces (with their drugged and dragooned boy soldiers) of whole communities. The destruction of property, painful as it was to view, was as nothing

21

compared to the cruel torture evidenced in the amputee camp in Freetown, where the sufferers told us their stories of arms and other limbs being hacked off by drug-crazed rebels determined to instil fear and submission among the general population.

**THE GRAVE OF HON BRIMA S MASSAQUOI**

And again as we stood at the graveside of a much-loved leader of his church and community and remembered a dear friend in Kenema, Brima S Massaquoi, who, having refused to leave his own people to their fate had been brutally tortured before being murdered by the retreating rebels.

The largely Christian company that we kept in the MCSL refused to allow us to dwell too long upon the heart-break as the voices of sanity and hope spoke of the future. Countless voices from high-ranking officials down to the suffering villagers who have lost so much told us that the turning point for Sierra Leone was the coming of the British forces, more than matching the firepower of the rebel forces as they helped train and equip the Sierra Leonean Army to defend their own country. Clare Short, the British Minister for Overseas Development, was viewed as a candidate for canonisation because she sat alongside the people there, listened and then used her influence to get things done with the governments heavily involved in resolving the conflict and helping to rebuild the country.

Even in the long-standing Refugee Camps, where the Christians built mud-stick churches with thatched roofs and bamboo benches; where teachers had faithfully continued their work in makeshift schools with hundreds of children and few resources; the people saw the conflict coming to an end. The talk was of returning home to their villages to rebuild communities, schools, churches and mosques that had been destroyed. In a refugee camp near Freetown, we tracked down a former teacher who later became a Methodist Minister. As we marvelled with this old man, recently returned from a refugee camp in neighbouring Guinea at the route he had taken and the distances that he had walked to escape the rebels, he responded with a smile on his face, 'It's amazing how far and how fast you can walk when there are guns behind you!'

THE CHURCH AS A KINGDOM PRESENCE: HOPE FOR THE FUTURE

The smile on the faces and the hope in the hearts of the people are the abiding memory of our return to Sierra Leone 2001. We found many of our now much older friends and the MCSL, under the able leadership of its (then) President, Right Revd Francis Nabieu, in good heart. The theme of the Methodist Conference in Bo was 'The Church as the Kingdom Presence'. Then, as now, there is much still to be done in re-building this shattered nation and re-establishing much of the church work providing medical, psychological, educational and agricultural support in re-resettling shattered and scattered communities. The testimony to the devoted and faithful work of their church 'as the Kingdom Presence' in fighting for justice and alleviating the suffering of people from all religions during the past ten years could be found in growing churches as people returned to their towns and villages to rebuild their homes and lives.

On the 22$^{nd}$ May 2001 my wife, Dr Carole Jackson and I flew back from Lungi Airport, Freetown, Sierra Leone to Gatwick Airport, London. Despite our commitment to the Methodist Church and Sierra Leone, we gave little thought on that day in May 2001 to the experience that changed the lives of the Wesley brothers in 1738 as Charles on the 21$^{st}$ May and John three days later on the 24$^{th}$ May, were touched by God in a way that transformed their ministry. Neither Carole nor I realised what a difference that visit would make to our lives as we moved towards our so-called retirement age!

# 2001/3 REPORTING BACK AS EYE-WITNESSES

On our return from the visit (7$^{th}$ to 22$^{nd}$ May 2001) to Sierra Leone, we reported back to both church and political leaders, including the then Prime Minister, Tony Blair, and other party leaders. We shared widely in the UK and in Sierra Leone some of the following reflections *(re-phrased slightly with sub-headings added here and throughout this history for the convenience of readers)*, according to the addressee and our purpose in writing to those with a concern for Sierra Leone.

Conversations with sources close to government, religious leaders of all denominations and ordinary people suggest that the 'war' of the past ten years is coming to an end. There is recognition that there are problems to be overcome in the peace process, but the widespread violence is no longer in evidence. Most people attribute the changed political situation to the direct action of the British troops in confronting the rebels known as the 'West Side Boys' and note the training and equipping of the Sierra Leone Army as a significant factor in the continuing process. The imprisonment of Foday Sankoh and other rebel leaders has contributed to the process. Though rebel 'warlords' still control parts of the Eastern Province beyond Kenema and north of Makeni towards the diamond rich areas of Kono, 'boy soldiers' are being released and peace initiatives/talks continue. The general impression given is that all sides are weary of the war and looking to find a pathway to peace. That way will not be easy in the current climate where it is clear that even the church is pressing for signs of repentance from the rebels and appropriate justice as a prerequisite for reconciliation and peace.

## AID AND DEVELOPMENT

The immediate impression received in the chaotically expanded communities of Freetown, Bo and Kenema to which villagers fled for safety is that the 'Aid Industry' is hard at work. The huge numbers of vehicles linked to the United Nations in Sierra Leone are more than matched by the large number of vehicles associated with a variety of 'caring' organisations involved in relief, reconciliation or redevelopment. The Sierra Leone government is trying to address one of our concerns by insisting on the annual registration of these Non-Government Organisations (NGO'S) which number well over 400. At this point in time fewer than two hundred (including MCSL) have been registered. The danger is that unless the relief efforts are controlled, co-ordinated, prioritised, and given direction, major resources will be dissipated as well labelled vehicles trundle around the main towns without making a difference to the places of real need. The complaint of one young soldier suggesting that NGO's actually doing something were a rare sighting up-country rang true for me. The displaced persons camp leadership's complaint that an aid sponsored water delivery was being diverted from the camp for use by builders of private houses points up the dangers of inadequate supervision. This 'Aid Industry' costing millions, unless channelled, could quickly drain away into the ground like the 200 inches of rainfall in the rainy season without making too much difference to the communities in need.

## THE CHURCH AND DEVELOPMENT

The church has led the way in the relief, re-settlement and re-development process. It faces the same dangers as the 'Aid Industry'. Fortunately, the accountability structures already in place at the different levels of the church structures have helped to avoid the more obvious excesses of those organisations, which have had to start from scratch. We were impressed by the way in which the church has been involved in ensuring that aid, whether relief or development, reached ordinary people in the camps or re-settled communities. Nevertheless, the Methodist Church, and its sister churches in the Christian Council of Sierra Leone must be wary lest the process become institutionalised in 'Programmes', 'Desks', 'Offices' and vehicles and they lose the motivation that has taken people out of their offices to the places where the help given has made a difference. Many of the church 'Institutions': like the Segbwema Hospital, some Secondary Schools and the Lay Training Centre at Njaluahun have been badly damaged or destroyed. The work of others like the Tikonko Agricultural Extension Centre and the Literature Bureau at Bo have come to a standstill during these troubled times. Some as with Segbwema Hospital will be strongly backed by government in its rebuilding programme; others will have to make their own way with minimal support. Whilst it is important for the church to seek funding for re-building and renewal, it is perhaps even more important that the Boards of these diverse institutions should be seeking a fresh and sustainable vision for the future. The visionaries are there in the Methodist Church Sierra Leone and in the Institutions. Now is the time for the thinking to be written down and programmed into what is being planned in practical terms so that funding and support that is being sought may be dovetailed into realistic business plans and mission statements.

## THE METHODIST CONFERENCE

We arrived in SL on Tuesday 8th May, 2001, made contact with the Conference Office and some old friends in Freetown before travelling east on the five-hour journey to Bo on the 9th. Camps and casualties of the conflict were seen 'en route'. There was little time to acclimatise, physically, mentally or emotionally. On our first day in the much-enlarged second town of Sierra Leone, Bo, we managed some sightseeing and visits to Bunumbu Press, Tikonko Agricultural Extension Centre (TAEC), and to Bob Moran, former TAEC Director, now working for Catholic Relief Services. Later in the day the Methodist Church's President of Conference, Right Revd Francis Nabieu took us to Tikonko to see the damage done to manses, churches and schools by repeated rebel attacks. On Friday, the ministerial session of Conference gathered with double the number of ministers that we had left behind in 1979, but some of them were recognisable as the young men grown older from our time in SL. That same day, Nancye the matron, (daughter of lay leader Kpanga Edwards), gave Carole a guided tour of Bo hospital. Both Carole and I were impressed by the dedication of the staff working with few resources in dilapidated buildings with little equipment in all the medical and educational facilities visited in Bo, Kenema and the Displaced Persons Camps.

**BRIEFLY: THE BUSINESS OF THE METHODIST CHURCH CONFERENCE**

A detailed diary of the Conference would not be appropriate for this report. Highlights were associated with support for the Revised Constitution, allowing up to ten years in office for the President of Conference and, five years for the Vice-President and agreement to a Biennial Conference. The President's address at the packed Sunday Conference Service on the theme of 'The Church as the Kingdom Presence' was comprehensive and thought provoking whilst the service that combined the ordination of three ministers with the reception of six new probationers was an inspiration to those present. The church through its Finance and Investment Committees has taken a fresh look at many aspects of funding and was rewarded by a positive response from Conference to its radical proposals for fund raising and proposed Assessment Rates for Circuits.

Many reports evidenced the impact of the armed conflict upon the work of the church, but the Development and Rehabilitation Report brought together in helpful ways aspects of the church's response. It was good to see the Trustees of the Methodist Church (many from Freetown) taking the opportunity to make on-site visits to Sumbuya, Tikonko, and Kenema as well as to the Institutions in Bo to assess needs. They returned to the Conference with first-hand knowledge and a determination to get things done on their return to Freetown. Overall, the impression received is of a church maturing under gifted and competent leadership that has coped well and grown through difficult circumstances. As peace comes to the former strongholds of Methodism in the Eastern Province and Kono where so many schools, clinics, manses and churches have been destroyed, bilateral relationships with, and increased commitment to the MCSL is vital if the opportunities for developmental and church growth are to be realised.

## THE METHODIST CHURCH SIERRA LEONE (MCSL)

Our own visits to people and places outside the Conference itself reinforced for us the view that the Methodist Church Sierra Leone has grown stronger through the trials and tribulations of the past ten years. Inevitably, there have been blips and blemishes in the work that it has undertaken, but this under-resourced church has coped magnificently with the needs of displaced persons camps and embattled communities in Sierra Leone and beyond its borders. The MCSL has given relief to, and cared for, people of all religions, tribes and tongues. Above all the church, its ministry and its members have remained faithful to their calling. Church leaders have been killed and old age has sapped the strength of some faithful servants but we were impressed by others who have grown in stature and begun to take their fruitful place in the councils of the church.

## WE LIVE ON IN THE LIVES OF OTHERS!

As a former missionary I couldn't help but wonder if the MCSL would have coped so well and grown so strong if we had continued to be there in such large numbers. With this reflection I will leave the last word to the President of Conference, the Right Revd Francis Nabieu. (The 'very' for him as leader of the church was agreed at the Conference!) Between us we confused an interviewer on Sierra Leone's national radio. I had responded to a question from the radio interviewer by saying, "We left Sierra Leone twenty-two years ago". Following on, the President then told the bemused interviewer that the Jacksons had never left Sierra Leone. Francis Nabieu went on to say that the Jacksons had carried on their work in and through the lives of those who had been influenced by their ministry. A tribute indeed, not just to the Jacksons, but to all who have served overseas in any capacity and wondered about the long term value of their service.

# 2001/4 POLITICAL LEADERS AND RESPONSES

THE PRIME MINISTER,

10, Downing Street,
London SW1A 2AA

Tuesday, 12 June 2001

Dear Mr Blair,

Congratulations to you and the party on being returned to power through the recent election. I wonder why it is that a low turnout at shareholders' meetings is seen as an indicator that most people are happy with things as they are, but when it comes to the polls it indicates dissatisfaction? Ah well, let's get on with the real reason for this letter.

For ten years from 1969-79 my wife Carole, who is a doctor, and I worked with the Methodist Church largely in the Eastern Province of Sierra Leone. At different times during those ten years we were associated through the church with educational, agricultural, medical, youth and community development projects. Since leaving Sierra Leone we have maintained personal contact with some people there and have been saddened as we have monitored the tragic events which have caused so much distress to that small nation over the past ten years.

### OUR RETURN VISIT TO SIERRA LEONE

Recently (7th to 22nd May 2001) we were able to return to Sierra Leone for the first time in 22 years at the invitation of the church there. The primary purpose of our visit was to attend the Methodist Conference taking place in the provincial town of Bo. At the Conference we received first-hand information from the people who travelled to be there and who have suffered so much in the on-going conflict. Outside the Conference we were able to travel widely and went as far as Kenema in the Eastern Province. Our informants who shared their experiences ranged from ordinary people living in displaced persons or amputee camps through to political and religious leaders, some of whom were friends and colleagues from our time in

Sierra Leone. A briefing report prepared primarily for church consumption is enclosed for information.

**POSITIVE RESPONSE IN SIERRA LEONE**

The reason for writing to you in this way is say that almost without exception those people to whom we spoke paid tribute to the British forces for their role in as they put it 'sorting out the rebels'. Whilst acknowledging the peace-keeping role of UNAMSIL they saw the British initiatives in helping the government forces to fight back and in equipping and training the Sierra Leonean army to defend its own country as crucial. Obviously, there is much more to be done by Britain, the UN and other organisations if this hard-won respite is to become a lasting peace, but the people of this former British colony have put their faith in the British commitment to that cause and would feel betrayed yet again, if political or financial pressures in the UK should lead to an early and ill-timed withdrawal.

It was made very clear to us that the investment of our government, alongside the training of key personnel in the army and other forces of law and order, is making a major contribution to the stability of Sierra Leone and is valued by the people there. It would be a tragedy if financial and other pressures here caused us to reduce our commitment to the cause of peace there. Those in the media who bleat about third world conditions in the health and education provision for this country need to look again at how devoted people who are paid a pittance do so much with so little in the schools, clinics and hospitals of Sierra Leone.

**POLITICAL APPRECIATION**

As I write this letter your 're-shuffle' is taking place. Personally, I am pleased that you have not chosen to 'promote' Clare Short from her position as International Development Secretary. She is doing a great job where she is! Her ability to listen, learn and then get things done was remarked upon by both political and religious leaders up-country as well as in the capital Freetown where so many 'politicians' have focussed their attention in the past. Clearly, she has made an excellent impression on people in Sierra Leone as being willing and able to make a difference to the cause of peace and the redevelopment process.

I planned to write to you and other party leaders immediately upon my return from Sierra Leone, but realised that I might be accused of political point scoring in an election climate. Sierra Leone has suffered too much at the hands of political expediency for me to risk that. In this post-election atmosphere I trust that both the government and the opposition will be united in supporting the continuation of those policies in relation to Sierra Leone that have begun to bring peace and restore our good name in this former British colony.

During the de-briefing (I'm not sure I should mention 'briefs' in a political context) by our Methodist World Church Office in London it was suggested that there might be those in the Foreign & Commonwealth Office or the Department for International Development who might be interested in hearing more 'informed comment' on Sierra Leone from a different perspective. Please feel free to copy any part of this letter and report to others who may be interested. Certainly, my wife and I would be willing to share further in conversation with any interested parties.

Yours sincerely,

Richard Jackson (Revd)

Copies to: The Leader of the Conservative Party, William Hague
The Leader of the Liberal Democrat Party, Charles Kennedy

**OFFICIAL ACKNOWLEDGMENTS RECEIVED**

Official acknowledgements were received on behalf of Mr Hague and Mr Blair with indications that the communication had been passed on to others. Following on from this a very full and positive response was received from Rosie Tapper (see below) at the Foreign & Commonwealth Office and there were confidential indications that others, including the International Development Secretary, Clare Short, appreciated what had been shared about our visit.

23 July 2001
**King Charles Street**
**London SW1A 2AH**
Tel: **020 7270 2515**
Fax: **020 7270 2325**

'Oak End'
42 Drummond Way
Macclesfield
Cheshire
SK10 4XJ

Dear Revd Richard and Dr Carole Jackson

Thank you for your letter of 12 June to the Prime Minister. As Desk Officer in Sierra Leone Section I have been asked to reply. The UK is working with the Government of Sierra Leone, the UN and the international community to bring sustainable peace to Sierra Leone and the sub-region. To this end we have are investing over £100 million to repel the rebels, restore the peace and rebuild Sierra Leone. There are good reasons to think that our strategy is working and that after ten years of conflict stability will return.

### MILITARY INVOLVEMENT

As you recognise, the recent positive progress made in Sierra Leone is in part due to our military involvement. We have invested heavily in training and equipping Sierra Leone's armed forces because we believe a well-trained and accountable army is essential to long term regional security. The UK is running a series of six week exercises to train and equip new recruits. These started in June 2000 and on present planning will continue to September 2001. An international team, including the UK, will then take over responsibility for longer term training. We are also providing advice and support to Sierra Leone's Defence Headquarters. But we recognise we cannot work alone so our work is complementary to that of the UN, which has its largest peace keeping operation in Sierra Leone. We have contributed fifteen United Nations Military Observers, technical advice and logistical support to the UN's mission in Sierra Leone, and Headquarters staff, including the Chief of Staff.

Our military assistance is intended to help the Government of Sierra Leone regain control of the entire country, including the diamond fields in the east. Much of the country continues to be held by Revolutionary United Front (RUF) rebels backed by President Taylor of Liberia. Long term stability is dependent on a successful demobilisation, disarmament and reintegration (DDR) programme designed to end rebel activities and give the rebels the opportunity to start normal lives. We are working with the Department for International Development (DFID) and the international community to make DDR a success. We are encouraged that over 21,000 former combatants have entered DDR, and that many are receiving training to equip them for civil life. The DDR process began in Kambia district in May and disarmament has now extended eastwards to Kono district, where two disarmament camps opened on 2 July. After disarming the former rebels are taking up a range of opportunities intended to facilitate their reintegration into society and rebuild Sierra Leone. Some will meet stringent criteria for entry into the army while others are involved in training, including forestry clearance and replanting programmes intended to re-establish the Forestry Department. Many will be involved in initiatives such as road building to restore Sierra Leone's infrastructure. We are optimistic that the positive momentum will continue. This is why DFID have this financial year committed £35 million to Sierra Leone.

### SL GOVERNMENT: SPECIAL COURT, TRUTH & RECONCILIATION COMMISSION

Besides regaining control of its territory and enabling the former combatants to contribute positively to society, the Government of Sierra Leone is taking a number of measures to build a strong democratic society. These include steps to promote good governance, preparations for democratic elections, establishing a Special Court to try those responsible for atrocities committed during the war and setting up a Truth and Reconciliation Commission. Under its governance programme, DFID is supporting the Anti-Corruption Commission and local government through the restoration of the Paramount Chiefs. It is also building an effective police force, assisting with law reform and helping with equipment and training for media development. Alongside the EU and the World Bank, it is providing technical assistance to the Ministry of Finance. Elections will be held as soon as Sierra Leone is secure, those who took refuge in Guinea and Cote d'lvoire have returned home and the logistics are taken care of. Preparations are already underway. The National Election Commission set up in April 2000 published its election strategy in March 2001. By providing advice on good governance and democracy we are working with the Government of Sierra Leone to achieve its aim that the elections bring stability and accountability.

Sierra Leone has witnessed horrific human rights abuses and it will take time to recover. The Special Court and Truth and Reconciliation Commission are intended to initiate the healing process. Requested by the Government of Sierra Leone, and supported by international donors, the Special Court will try those suspected of instigating and committing the worst atrocities. The Truth and Reconciliation, based on the South African model, will allow those who have suffered in the war to share their experiences and feelings so that they can begin to forgive or be forgiven, and begin the gradual return to harmony.

We are proud of what we have achieved so far and are watching keenly events on the ground. Indeed Ms Short visited Bo on 18 April, shortly before yourselves. But there is a long way to go and we remain committed to restoring durable stability in the region and to rebuilding Sierra Leone. To find out more about our commitment to Sierra Leone, and to see how we are progressing, you might like to visit our website at www.fco.gov.uk.

Rosie Tapper
Africa Department (Equatorial)

**RESPONSE TO FOREIGN & COMMONWEALTH OFFICE**

Subj:   Ref Sierra Leone
Date:   7/27/01

Dear Rosie,

Thank you for your very full reply and update received yesterday on the Sierra Leonean situation. It is good to see a careful and worked through strategy beginning to bear some fruit. I presume that I am free to circulate this information to interested friends.

Some of those interested friends (about 60 in all) who have lived and worked in Sierra Leone met together last Saturday, 21st July at St Albans. People like Right Revd Francis Nabieu, the President of the Methodist Church Sierra Leone (MCSL), here for the World Methodist Conference in Brighton, and Ron & Liz Fennell, (presumably known to you) recently returned from SL were able to update people on the current situation and various initiatives were discussed.

**PERSONAL INITIATIVES**

One of those initiatives being encouraged at all levels of the church came out of discussions and observations made during our visit there. My jottings on a 'sick bag' in the plane on the way home provided an inauspicious beginning, but you may be interested in what is now being organised, which in church terms fits into your own strategy.

For many years now at great expense church ministers from overseas have been brought out in one's and two's for further training/education in Europe and the USA. Some never returned home! In many countries like Sierra Leone basic training for ministry is done ecumenically in places like The Theological Hall in Freetown. We recognised the need for further training/refresher courses for those in ministry. (Some, like the general population, lost everything including study books, are traumatised, and have been living and working in displaced person's camps inside and outside Sierra Leone.) We agreed that the best way to provide that training was to do it for larger numbers of ministers of all denominations through short courses undertaken within SL. This idea is being strongly supported by the Christian Council in SL.

The detailed planning is still being worked out, but the broad intention is that Cliff College where I am an Associate Tutor, (Methodist sponsored, but supported ecumenically), will set up an International Learning Centre, twinned with its existing Open Learning Centre and provide a Diploma Course over two years in Sierra Leone, which will focus around a two week concentrated course beginning 6th August next year. This Course will be delivered in the Theological Hall premises by a team of visiting resource people in partnership with a team of locally designated people. Francis Nabieu, Ron Fennell and I are particularly keen to see the issues of Justice, Truth, Reconciliation and forgiveness that you referred to addressed during this Course. You may have access to resources/facilitators in this field that might be useful. Certainly, I found the SL edition of 'Accord' supplied by Ron Fennell extremely helpful. We may have to commission someone with the appropriate background and training to produce for us a 'Distance Learning' study guide that will help our ministers grapple with these issues. Would any general funding, resources be made available for this kind of initiative?

### SIERRA LEONE & INFLUENCE WITHIN COMMUNITIES

I note the work being done to restore local government through the Paramount Chiefs and the Courts. I am sure that it will not have escaped your notice that due to an early comity agreement between the churches working in Sierra Leone each major denomination has a strong sphere of influence in different regions of the country. Though that has broken down to some extent with all denominations and many smaller 'Pentecostal' groupings at work in the major towns the 'spheres of influence' can be clearly identified in the villages of the provinces. So in the villages of the Eastern Province beyond Kenema and towards Kailahun, (seemingly the worst hit area) the British influenced, Methodist Church Sierra Leone is historically the strongest influence amongst the churches.

You may or may not be aware of all that, but it does provide a basis for the point that I do want to make. Religious Leaders, whether Traditional Religion, Islamic or Church pastors will be key people in the restoration of right relationships within communities as people return to their village homes.

All of these community leaders are accessible for Seminars, etc. through the Religious Council of Sierra Leone and bodies, like the Christian Council of Sierra Leone. Time and money invested in restoration and training with them will be money well spent. It seems to me farcical when 'Aid Agencies' offer material help to rebuild houses in communities, but refuse to offer the same assistance to religious houses whether that is Manses or Mosques that will help re-create 'Community'.

### THE AID INDUSTRY & NON-GOVERNMENTAL ORGANISATIONS (NGO'S)

One final concern to bring to your attention is becoming a major problem, not easy to resolve. Recently, our MCSL accountant in Freetown joined the stream of those leaving well established church and charitable organisations in Sierra Leone for a better paid job with a Non-Government Organisation. The 'Aid' industry developing in Sierra Leone is offering much higher levels of pay and conditions of service than is possible to other organisations and many trained teachers and the like are being lost to the work at the grassroots level upcountry.

Our Government, Ms Clare Short, the Foreign and Commonwealth Office and your department have good reason to be "proud of what we have achieved so far". As a UK citizen who worked for so many years in Sierra Leone and has never lost interest in that country and its people, I am proud too. I look forward to some continuing communication that may be beneficial to both parties in the longer term.

Thanks again for taking the time to respond so fully to my letter. All of us with a concern for the future stability of Sierra Leone would want to encourage you in the work that you are doing.

Richard Jackson (Revd)

### NO GOVERNMENT FUNDING FOR FAITH ORGANISATIONS

N.B. Subsequent political contacts made through friends at the British Council both in Britain and in Sierra Leone prompted positive comments, but no practical or financial support for what we were doing as a church. The leaders of 'faith organisations' are acknowledged leaders of the community in villages, towns and cities, but rarely (even now) is government funding released to them for training and community development purposes.

# 2001/5 THE NEW VISION & RESPONSES TO IT

It was no doubt the immediate experience, several conversations and at the time random insights such as these that challenged me on our return flight from Sierra Leone. Somehow my thoughts of bringing a few of the MCSL ministers back to Cliff College, (where I was working as a tutor in the Postgraduate Department) for encouragement and a refresher course seemed an inadequate response. Instead the jottings that I was then inspired to make on an aeroplane sick-bag became the vision that gave direction to the setting up of the Cliff College International Learning Centre.

Personally, however prompted, I have never doubted that God's direction was given to me as I returned from the 2001 Conference in conflict-devastated Sierra Leone and jotted down on that 'sick-bag' the outline of what has grown into the Cliff College International Learning (changed in 2009 to Training) Centre. Nor can I doubt the direction given to countless people, named and un-named, who have helped us in so many ways to realise this vision and become a blessing to everyone involved both in the UK and in the countries where we have shared with partners overseas in training leaders.

**THE NEW VISION**

The 'sick bag' jottings pictured as written down spontaneously on that flight of the 22nd May 2001 read as follows:

CLIFF COLLEGE INSTITUTE: MINISTRY, MISSION & EVANGELISM

One month-July /August 2002 in Theological Hall premises, Freetown
For those Active in ministry
" " Attending Theological Hall
" " Attending Bible Colleges

SPONSORS
Cliff College
Methodist Church Sierra Leone (MCSL)
Christian Council of Sierra Leone (CCSL)
Methodist Church Overseas Division (MCOD)
SPCK/TEF Books

DELIVERY OF COURSES BY
Cliff College Staff & Associates
Sierra Leonean based lecturers
Lecturers/Minister with overseas experience.

FUNDING
MCOD – Lecturers flights
Irish Conference
Books – TEF (SPCK)
Materials/Study Notes-Cliff College from fees (at cost)
MCSL (CCSL Accommodation
Fees £10 per week-£40 per course

### THE FIRST STEPS IN RESPONDING TO THE VISION

Night-time musings, whether simply in the mind or thoughts put down on paper often fade with the dawn. The vision was kept alive on my return to Cliff College by the Principal, Howard Mellor's offer of practical support: "If it is not going to cost the college financially" and a cautious, but positive response from Mike King, Team Leader of the World Church Office (WCO) of the Methodist Church in London. This held out the possibility of some funding if I, with the expertise available at Cliff College, would be willing to bear the administrative and logistical burden of setting up a pilot project to test out the vision.

The Cliff College International Learning Centre (CCILC) was set up and a draft 'Rationale' inspired by the 'sick bag jottings' gave direction for a programme leading into what was to become the International Diploma in Applied Ministry & Mission (IDIAMM). The fundamentals of the vision for 'Doing Training There in a Partnership' are little changed since its inception. As might be expected the associated documentation went through several revisions at the hands of sponsors and interested parties both in Sierra Leone and the UK whilst the proposal to undertake in 2002-4 a Pilot Programme in Sierra Leone was being presented to anyone who would listen. Those who listened at that time have played their part in the success and the continuing development of this innovative and pioneering programme which has grown into the Cliff College International Training Centre (CCITC).

## 2001/6 PERSONAL CONTACTS MADE IN 2001

In 2001, child soldiers in Africa and Sierra Leone in particular were of interest to the media. Consequently, the hackneyed, but largely true adage that 'there is no such thing as bad publicity' applied as individuals and organisations responded to our appeal for support for this 'Vision'. As we began to put together a pioneering programme of relief through in-country as well as in-service training in partnership with the churches in Sierra Leone there was a willingness to respond internationally in ways that went beyond our expectations.

Obviously, the churches in Sierra Leone through the Christians Council were keen to support such a development. Older friends who had served the church in Sierra Leone, now leaders of the church in Britain and Ireland, provided encouragement and in many cases practical help. News of this new initiative began to ripple out from the 'whirl'-pool of Cliff College activities, through the World Church Office of the British Methodist Church and MMS (Ireland) and one friendly contact led to another in ways that established financial and logistical support for many aspects of the developing programme.

### TAPPING THE RESERVOIR OF GOOD-WILL

What quickly became clear was that there existed a reservoir of good-will waiting to be drawn upon in Sierra Leone and elsewhere which helped the original vision to transition into a pilot scheme being undertaken within fifteen months of our return from Sierra Leone. In Sierra Leone the inter-religious council and a war-weary people supported the protracted and complex negotiations required to bring an end to the brutal conflict; refugees returned from larger towns and displaced persons camps to begin the heart-breaking task of rebuilding devastated communities. Whilst our original vision backed by prayer provided the inspiration, in these chapter by chapter (year following year) reflections we will return again to our theme that in both practical coordination and implementation we learned afresh that: 'People Matter More Than Things'. Friends associated with our past now appointed to leading roles in state and church; people involved with us through the years and in our present ministry; and supporters who have cared enough to become involved have contributed in a variety of ways to the documented success of this programme and the added-value generated by personally sponsored projects and renewed relationships.

It would be invidious to name individuals here, (many will be acknowledged in the text of what follows), but I must make mention of a few key early groups who encouraged us and gave invaluable practical support in the launching of the programme:

Experienced staff at Cliff College provided the academic back-up and expertise lacking in the author for the birthing of CCILC;

The Methodist Church in Britain and MMS (Ireland) with their world church interests responded positively and generated the pump-priming funding;

Through these contacts SPCK; the Langham Trust; Feed The Minds; and other organisations agreed to supply books and resources at much discounted prices;

The container ministry of MMS (Ireland) in Lurgan helped ferry the books, office equipment and other materials to their destination in Sierra Leone free of charge.

### MISSIONS OF MERCY

The theme of the 2001 Methodist Church Sierra Leone Conference which we attended in Bo, 'The Church as the Kingdom Presence' was inspired by the churches response to the troubles of the previous ten years later dramatized by Hollywood in the 2006 Leonardo Di Caprio film, 'Blood Diamond'. The 'Kingdom Presence' of people here as elsewhere became much more valuable than diamonds as the churches and other organisations at the heart of the communities began the slow process of helping in the rebuilding schools, hospitals, clinics and associated staff accommodation in Sierra Leone. Every village re-settled and building replaced was an unspoken tribute to those community leaders who had suffered and died in the so-called 'Rebel War', often quietly understated as 'The Troubles'.

An April warning about Malaria and an outbreak of Lassa Fever *(c.f. Ebola in 2014)* among peace-keepers and sporadic outbreaks of violence kept Sierra Leone in the news-headlines. Even more importantly voluntary agencies, trainers, peace-keepers of the UN and the British armed forces through 'home' contacts generated their own caring response to what they saw as immediate needs for the traumatised of all generations in Sierra Leone. The Darlington based

Northern Echo newspaper tribute of Friday, September 7th 2001 and associated fund-raising for what their editorial comment describes as a 'Mission of Mercy', by members of the Second Battalion, Durham Light Infantry, must suffice here as a tribute to countless other individuals and groups. Through their 'Liberation Ministry' response of compassion, which went way beyond duty, they, and many other groups, have earned the 'incalculable gratitude' of the people of Sierra Leone, 'for a humanitarian mission, which has established some sort of peace and normality in a country ravaged by civil war'.

A positive response to personal contact made with the United Methodist Church and the head of the United Methodist Committee on Relief (UMCOR) in the United States was soon overtaken by the tragic events of the 9:11 destruction of the twin towers in New York. But those early contacts provided a later longer-lasting legacy of support for the proposed programme from the United Methodist Church in Germany.

In the light of all of this outpouring of sacrificial good-will, there is little wonder that I reacted strongly to a throw-away London Committee comment implying that supporting the CCILC might be encouraging retired missionaries to return to Sierra Leone on a 'Jolly'!!!

# CHAPTER 2 2002: LAUNCH OF PROGRAMME

*By January 2002 we had received sufficient encouragement from The Christian Council of Sierra Leone, The Methodist Church in Britain and MMS (Ireland), Cliff College and a number of national and local sponsors to launch a CCILC pilot programme in Sierra Leone. Introductory guidelines and early documentation were presented for information and approval by those likely to be involved in any way. The positive response from organisations and individuals who cared and shared, made it possible to put in place everything that was needed to begin a two-year pilot programme in July 2002.*

## 2002/1 JAN: CCILC 'RATIONALE' SL PILOT

After ten years of fighting, UN economic indicators show Sierra Leone as one of the poorest countries with the lowest life expectancy in the world. At last, the signs are hopeful that peace and re-settlement are becoming a real possibility. As far as the churches of Sierra Leone are concerned, reorientation and further training for those in full-time ministries is now a priority. (Deep questions relating to justice, forgiveness & reconciliation; ethics and politics; tradition and transformation in society & church; and the endemic problem of Aids will need to be addressed by those in ministry.)

Many of these ministers and other church workers have lost their homes and books in 'The Troubles'; some have been living in displaced persons camps. It is not feasible for both practical and financial reasons to contemplate providing further extended training outside the country for such a large number of ministers, most of whom received their foundation training for ministry at the Theological Hall in Freetown. What has become clear through consultation is that the churches would value intensive courses of in-service training, being delivered at the Theological Hall during the long vacation July/August (Rainy Season!).

This immediate and practical need has prompted deep and detailed discussion with concerned partners in Sierra Leone. As a response to these discussions we have set up the:

**CLIFF COLLEGE INTERNATIONAL LEARNING CENTRE (CCILC).**

Its objectives were outlined under the following headings:

**AIM-IN PARTNERSHIP WITH THE WORLD CHURCH WE PLAN TO:**

Go to partner churches and share in the delivery of courses related to ministry and mission.

Go together with our ecumenical partners and associated partners in the world church.

Go at the invitation of the local Council of Churches and their local Training Centre.

Go expecting local involvement in providing course/team/facilities, but not funding.

**PIONEERING CONCEPT-IS FOR CLIFF COLLEGE WITH THE SUPPORT OF SPONSORING BODIES TO:**

Enter into partnership with National Church Councils world-wide and make available free to Church designated students two-year courses & materials/books etc. delivered in a local context. (This shares with the World Church, experience gained at Cliff College of reflection linked with praxis that have become the hallmark of our popular distance learning courses. These courses are based on part taught (during residential weeks), part self-study (reading and assignments) and researched (research dissertations) over two-years from Diploma through to MA level.

E-mail contact allows for overseas team contact and some marking/moderating in the UK.

**RATIONALE-THIS IS A PRACTICAL RESPONSE TO THE EXPRESSED NEED OF MANY PARTNER CHURCHES:**

It costs less to teach/train large numbers at home than to provide for small numbers elsewhere.

We make more productive use of mission/scholarship monies available in Europe and the USA.

Tailored courses in local ministry can explore contextual theology and deal with social issues.

Further in-service training and praxis can be done and assessed in the local context and culture.

**RESOURCING-CLIFF COLLEGE FOR ONE RESIDENTIAL MONTH PER YEAR FOR EACH COURSE CAN MAKE USE OF:**

The short-term availability of academically qualified teacher/trainers in many fields.

The short-term availability of culturally sensitive staff. (Experienced in different cultures.)

The short-term availability of ecumenically staff and released for this purpose.

Books/distance learning material funded from here and adapted for use in partner churches

**RESULTS-LARGE NUMBERS OF REFRESHED CHURCH WORKERS BETTER EQUIPPED FOR LOCAL MINISTRY.**

'Students' who would benefit the local church most can be targeted for further training.

The joint staff team, local and visiting, working together will be mutually enriched.

Working ecumenically with local Council of Churches will encourage everyone involved.

Will provide a more fruitful and regular two-way contact in the post-missionary era.

# 2002/2 JUL 14-AUG 13: CCSL FIRST RESIDENTIAL

**(IDIAMM 2002-04 PROGRAMME)**

## LAUNCH OF PILOT PROGRAMME IN SIERRA LEONE

**WHY ARE WE THERE?**

Everybody in Sierra Leone has a story to tell of the ten years of brutal civil war that has devastated the country. Like someone waking slowly from a nightmare they try to put into words the horror of a whole decade of suffering which came to an end with the new millennium as UN and British soldiers 'sorted out' the rebels, trained and equipped the Sierra Leonean army. This response paved the way for democratic elections that took place peacefully earlier this year.

**THEIR GIFT TO US**

Everybody will tell you of how a member of their family, friend or neighbour was killed. They will talk to you of their homes, schools and churches being plundered and destroyed. Some will describe for you in vivid eye-witness detail the torture and callous execution by the rebels of a much loved church leader and former Member of Parliament, Brima Sandy Massaquoi in Kenema. Others, like the President of the Methodist Conference, Right Revd Francis Nabieu tell of how friends misled the rebels by saying that he was just a cook so that he and his family could escape. Doctors and nurses from Nixon Memorial, our Methodist Hospital in Segbwema, share how they fled the rebel onslaught at Christmas and found safety after hiding and walking for many miles in the bush. There are countless stories of courage and sacrifice with scars and maimed bodies being used to illustrate the vindictive cruelty of the aggressors.

Inevitably among the ever-positive Sierra Leoneans there is humour too. Francis Makiu, a blind church member who finds his way effortlessly around the rutted streets of Kenema, pictured the moment when he hid trembling in a toilet until the danger had passed. Others, with smiles of relief and a lingering feeling of guilt, give their own

45

testimony as to how they escaped when so many others were killed or maimed.

Sierra Leoneans tell the stories of what has happened in the midst of one of the cruellest conflicts that an Africa inured to suffering has ever seen, but they look now with hope to the future.

### COME OVER AND HELP US

Last year representing the British Conference in Sierra Leone, (where my wife and I spent ten years 1969-79), I heard their call clearly, 'Come over to Sierra Leone and help us', but how? In the fifteen months since that call, and the germ of an idea that became jottings on a sick bag on the Russian jet that brought us back from Sierra Leone last year, a vision has become a reality.

### NOT QUITE A DAD'S ARMY-YET!

Now a question to make you think! What do a retired University Professor from Scotland, the Head of the United Methodist Church in Germany, a Principal of a Theological College in Belfast, a Methodist Circuit Superintendent in Bishop Auckland and Cliff College lecturers have in common? No, it is not one of those jokes! This July we took a team of visiting lecturers which included Prof Andrew Walls, Revd Dr Walter Klaiber, Revd Dr Dennis Cooke, Revd Dr Michael Thompson and Susanne Garnett from Cliff College, to Sierra Leone. There they joined with designated Sierra Leonean counterparts, in launching what is now established as the Cliff College International Learning Centre, or as the students themselves put it now, the 'Sierra Leone Branch of Cliff College.'

### THE VISION BECOMES A REALITY

The vision has become a reality through a pioneering pilot project initiated in response to an invitation from the Christian Council of Sierra Leone (CCSL) and it is being implemented in partnership with the churches of Sierra Leone (SL) and the Principal and Staff of the churches' own Theological Hall (TH) in Freetown.

Sierra Leone is now listed at or near the bottom of all UN economy and life expectancy indicators. Many church pastors and lay leaders too have lost family, homes, and resources for ministry. Some have been living in displaced persons camps inside and outside of the country. They, with their people, are having to come to terms with the consequences of a particularly cruel and bitter conflict in the context of economic poverty and social deprivation.

A stated aim of the Cliff College International Learning Centre is to provide these church pastors and community leaders in Sierra Leone with a practical and culturally oriented part-time two year, level-two further training (refresher) course leading to an International Diploma In Applied Ministry and Mission (IDIAMM). Utilising experience gained at Cliff College of providing part taught (during residential weeks), part self-study (reading, assignments, portfolios) and part researched (dissertation) courses, we are sponsoring a practical course in ministry and mission that is relevant to the local context.

**PARTNERS TOGETHER IN TRAINING LEADERS**

**REVD DR DENNIS COOKE: RECONCILING**

Our two-year programme is made up of ten modules linked with biblical studies, ministry and mission. The above ecumenical team of five visiting lecturers recruited for the July 2002 'Residential' at the Theological Hall in Freetown will be followed by a different group who will be going in 2003. Expenses for the tutors are met, but no charge is made to the ILC for their services. The visiting lecturers partnered local tutors of different denominations in providing ten sessions on each of the first five themes:

Revd Dr Michael Thompson & Revd Dr Leopold Foullah: Religion & Mission Theology – Old Testament
Revd Dr Walter Klaiber & Revd Vidal Kamara-Cole, MA: Church & Mission Theology – New Testament

Prof. Andrew Walls & Revd David Cole, MA: Church History and Mission in Africa, with special reference to Sierra Leone
Mrs Susanne Garnett, MA, MEd & Mr Samuel Forde, MA, MEd: Spirituality in Ministry
Revd Dr Dennis Cooke & Revd Canon Emerson Thomas, MA: Reconciliation following conflict

Included in the timetable were lectures on Study Skills (and for next year, Communication & Adults Learning) with Revd Richard Jackson. Students led worship and shared personal experiences. Locally invited speakers e.g. Truth & Reconciliation Commission conducted seminars. The local co-ordinator Revd Vidal Kamara-Cole was ably assisted in the office by Keith Phillips, an Anglican and former VSO in SL who served as the course administrator.

### OUTLINING THE PILOT PROJECT

The Pilot Project will run for at least two years (2002-2004) during which students will attend two 'Residentials' of two weeks in July (SL rainy season) each year. At roughly two month intervals students will submit work (assignments, portfolios of practical work undertaken, journals-see the Course Booklet for details) to be marked locally. In the January following the 'Residentials', the Co-ordinators will meet with the students in 'Regional Groups' at which progress can be assessed and further guidance given particularly in relation to the required ministry-related 'Research Project'. At the end of two years, successful students will receive an International Diploma In Applied Ministry and Mission. Further consideration will be given by the churches to their continuing training in ministry. The developing relationship between the ILC of Cliff College and the Theological Hall of the CCSL in Sierra Leone is prompting thoughts of a longer term 'formation in ministry' programme.

### THE STUDENTS REGISTERED FOR CLIFF COLLEGE IN SIERRA LEONE

**There are 99 students enrolled on the Course.** Only applicants supported by their own church were accepted and all have completed their first two residential weeks. (July

48

2002) Of students registered: 52 students are recorded as belonging to the Methodist Church Sierra Leone; 14 United Methodists; 10 West African Methodists; 9 Anglicans; 6 Lutherans; and 8 others including members of the: Baptist; Deeper Life; Pentecostal and Roman Catholic Churches. There are 77 male students and 22 females of whom 68 are ordained and 31 are church and community leaders. 69 students reside in the capital Freetown and surrounding districts; 30 students live in the provincial districts of SL.

### MODEST AIMS TO: ENCOURAGE; RESOURCE; REFRESH

We began the course with modest aims in the context of Sierra Leone's need:

**To encourage -** With 95 evaluation forms returned from the 99 students who attended the first 'residential' making very positive comments this is clearly being achieved. One brief quote is used to sum up the general response, 'Rich, motivating and inspiring'.

### BOOKS: SOURCED, CARRIED & SORTED

**To resource -** This initiative undertaken with a £20,000 a year grant out of your giving through the World Church Office of the British Methodist Church has attracted funding from Feed The Minds and other organisations. Christian Publishers provided new books at such reduced prices that we were able to supply free to every student (and SL staff partners) the same 24 books for the course retailing at approximately £300. These included a number of SPCK International Study Guides, four larger Commentaries and Theological, Bible Dictionaries resourced through the Evangelical Literature Trust. Writing and other materials were supplied free by the Irish Methodist Church (MMS) who organised and paid for the 'Course Container' with everything from pens to filing cabinets to be shipped to SL.

A presentation was made to the Theological Hall Library in Freetown of course books, new books donated by SCM, and large numbers of other second hand Biblical/ Theological books.

**To refresh:** The excitement and enthusiasm generated by visiting lecturers and their Sierra Leonean counterparts in two weeks of concentrated lecturing, sharing and worshipping together impacted not only on those present, but also on the churches and others who heard about the course through local radio. Many people made it clear that they wished they had been involved and a new waiting list will help gauge the demand for a 'rolling programme' or alternatives.

A GOOD BEGINNING

The visiting team, four of whom, were able to stay on to 'tour' the provinces and conduct two seminars in Kenema and Bo have each testified to the positive impact that participation in the project has made upon them personally. There is much more to be done and all of us will be encouraging you to play your part in the rebuilding of Methodist manses, schools, churches and the hospital destroyed in the conflict. Perhaps your church project for this 2002/3 might be to identify a project with the Methodist Church in Sierra Leone and raise the funds about £1,000 for one building to help in the work of reconstruction.

As the UK initiator and co-ordinator of this pilot project (which with funding is repeatable elsewhere), I am wary of claiming too much for it in these early stages, but there is much that happened in a largely trouble free initiative for which we can give thanks. The mutual enrichment and encouragement can be taken as read.

REVD DR WALTER KLAIBER: NEW TESTAMENT

Various sponsors and readers of earlier information relating to the planning of the project will recognise hopes fulfilled in this report. (Reports, a team SL diary, digital photographs, and accounts, can be made available if requested.) Whilst we are pleased that such a positive start has been made and some objectives have been achieved, we must await the presentation of good quality work on the deadline dates by the majority of the students enrolled, before we can claim an unqualified success!

Nevertheless, there is sufficient in this report for those responsible, as sponsors, donors and supporters, to feel that effort, money and resources have gone into a worthwhile and innovative project. As a former missionary of an earlier generation, it feels good to be told, 'This is your second period of missionary service!' Certainly, with a budget that would hardly support one 'missionary couple' overseas, or here, we are convinced that we have established a programme that will encourage, resource and refresh in such a way as to have a significant impact upon the ministry and mission of the churches in Sierra Leone.

## 2002/3 RENEWAL OF RELATIONSHIPS

The United Methodist Church reflection from Germany *(See Appendix 6)* draws attention to how this project allows us to renew and maintain relationships with partner churches and institutions in fresh ways, even in difficult and changing environments.

### RELATIONSHIPS RENEWED BY SHARING IN THE PROGRAMME

Regular visits by a known core team have proved invaluable in sharing concerns about ministry and mission between partner churches. Whilst the primary training focus of the visit is acknowledged by both parties there are countless spin-off benefits of regular meetings that generate mutual respect and growing confidence in each other. Obviously, the

author's earlier service with the Methodist Church in Sierra Leone (1969-79) provided a foundation on which to build, but the platform provided for all associated with the CCITC has proved beneficial in so many ways that can only be highlighted briefly here, but will be picked up again later.

MEETING FRIENDS AT MCSL HQ

Busy people within organisations throughout the world can more readily use a non-structured forum (rather than an organised conference) to interact and find common ground about politics, policies and private interpretations. Relationships develop and people grow as we enthuse about new projects and stimulate personal involvement; share about worship and witness in terms that that are the fruit of personal experience and questioning rather than 'parrot a party-line' justifying the maintenance of the status-quo.

Visiting a New Generation/Pentecostal Church in Freetown for a London sponsored graduation with long-standing Methodist friends in Sierra Leone may have planted a seed that germinated in jottings on a sick-bag! Certainly a number of personal and church donations to a variety of projects have been generated through visiting team members as they have renewed relationships or made new friends in the coming and going linked with CCILC. Sharing with Principals, lecturers, students and others associated with colleges overseas has been a mutually enriching experience, particularly as travel between countries, rather than in one direction has allowed many of us to return some of the hospitality received overseas in our own homes.

### REVIEWING PROGRESS THROUGH REGULAR REPORTING

The regular reports which are a key component of this presentation overall are sufficient testimony to the interest generated when stereotypes are challenged by the meeting together. Minds are re-focussed on mission, but the motivation for mission is revived in ways that stimulate as much a concern for Wesley's world as seen in Britain today, as for that 'World Parish' to which Methodism has been drawn.

### NETWORKING OF RELATIONSHIPS WITH AND THROUGH SPONSORS

Whilst there have been many 'dead ends' as we have sought sponsorship, it is as contact has been made with one organisation that we have been pointed in the direction of others where a more profitable partnership has developed. So the United Methodist Church in the USA helped us enlist support from their European partners in Germany. Networking through SPCK, Scripture Union and Feed the Minds led us into a fruitful relationship with the Langham Partnership and receive the support of the John Stott trustees. Personal involvement with the, 'British Church Growth Association' and 'Administry' helped release very valuable training materials and books at give-away prices to be used in the programme.

As noted elsewhere the, 'Friends of Sierra Leone' linking former mission partners in Sierra Leone and personal friends have been at the

heart of the practical support given through the 'Container Ministry' and funding received from MMS (Ireland). Local churches associated with partner lecturers who have travelled to Sierra Leone have helped with church, schools and manse re-building projects.

**"HAVE YOU GOT HOLD OF IT AT YOUR END?"**

Obviously, the support and expertise available through Cliff College has been invaluable, but articles published in Cliff Today (Autumn 2002 edition) and the Methodist Recorder (10th October 2002) have reached a much wider interest group, many of whom have responded with personal encouragement and smaller donations. Strangely enough, it is the most unlikely people who have recognised the value of this innovative and pioneering programme and acknowledged the positives of 'Doing Training there in a Partnership with them'.

# CHAPTER 3 2003: PILOT PROGRAMME REVIEWED

*From the outset, the Coordinator of the two-year pilot programme added the work associated with the launch of the CCILC to his responsibilities as postgraduate tutor at Cliff College. We utilised documentation and patterns already being used for 'Diploma' courses and 'Distance Learning' postgraduate programmes. It quickly became clear that much more administration and participation would be required at Cliff College if the required standards were to be met in Sierra Leone. Whilst the two-year pilot programme continued, an early evaluation was undertaken in April, 2003 with the intention of reviewing the process and working towards a half-time appointment for the Coordinator to develop this programme.*

## 2003/1 JAN 20-FEB 4: CCSL SECOND RESIDENTIAL

**(IDIAMM 2002-04 PROGRAMME)**

ARRANGEMENTS MADE DURING FOLLOW UP: REGIONAL GROUP RESIDENTIALS

Preliminary enquiries about the possibility of a second programme beginning July 2003 was sent to CCSL and Church Leaders by the National Coordinator, Revd Vidal S. A. F. Kamara-Cole. The only response came from Anglican Bo Diocese; Suggesting

8 names (29/01/03). No further action to be taken on a new ecumenical programme in SL.

Regional Groups were organised in preparation for the visit: Primarily for discussion about pre-preparation of Research Projects for current course and follow-up with partner lecturers.

AT THE THEOLOGICAL HALL AGAIN

**Freetown Area at Theological Hall**
on Thursday/Friday 23/24th January 2003
(Thurs-52 students present; 15 Absent: Fri-50 Present; 17 Absent:)

Regional Group Day opened with Prayers led by Revd Vidal Kamara-Cole (Thurs) Revd Canon Emerson-Thomas (Fri). Sessions led by Revd Dr Leo Foullah on Social Concerns relating to re-building of Sierra Leone;

## Provincial Districts at Bo Methodist Community Centre

on Tuesday, 28<sup>th</sup> Jan 2003 (Tues-33 students present)

(88 out of 99 from 67 ministers & 32 Lay students attended the regional groups-They and tutors received the 110 copies of Research Booklet taken for distribution at Regional Groups)

**DR JENNY GIBSON PUNCHES MESSAGE HOME**

Dr Jenny Gibson gave some supplementary HIV/Aids Training in Bo

Duplicate copies of all application forms completed for Cliff College students, prepared at both centres.

Distribution of additional books and materials at both centres.

Introduction to Research Booklet-Revd Richard Jackson gives guidance in preparation of proposal form for dissertation at both centres.

**Friday 30<sup>th</sup> Jan in Freetown:** Review meeting with partner lecturers and related staff reviewing progress, with marking, supervision so far. Planning for the July Residentials and all aspects of the programme. Letter to be sent to all students about use of Zion Methodist Church in Wesley Street for July lectures etc. British Council to be booked and used for Graduations.

**ANOTHER YEAR YOUNGER IN HEART**

Saturday 31<sup>st</sup> January:
Revd Vidal Kamara-Cole, MCSL Coordinator's wife:
**Melinda Kamara-Cole 48<sup>th</sup> Birthday Party shared at 4, Guy Street. Freetown.**

55

## 2003/2 APR: MID-COURSE EVALUATION

The chosen method of evaluation is to examine the original documented aims and objectives outlined in 2002/1 and to critically assess mid-course the progress of the project. *(Note: more detailed information linked with evaluation can be found in Appendix 7)*

### SPONSORSHIP AND SUPPORT

The strongest encouragement for, and the largest financial contribution to the project, has been made through the World Church Office of the Methodist Church (UK). An initial block grant of £20,000 a year for 2001/2 & 2002/3 has in the current year been augmented by a grant of £12,000 to Cliff College in support of a half-time co-ordinator **(See Appendix 7A-Draft job description 19/10/02)** for the pilot project in Sierra Leone and its possible development elsewhere.

£5,000 a year for the same two years has been given through the Methodist Missionary Society in Ireland. In addition they have provided logistical help with their 'Container ministry'. Course books, office equipment and student materials were provided and transported at no cost to the project. The container arrived on time in Freetown.

Early contacts with the United Methodist Church in the USA seeking funding and personnel proved unfruitful, but the UMC became involved with a very positive response from Germany. Their Presiding Bishop, Walter Klaiber, (and his wife Dr Annegret) joined the team of visiting lecturers for July 2002 and Prof Achim Härtner from Reutlingen University is designated for 2003. The UMC, Germany paid travel expenses in 2002 through a grant to the project of £1,896 (2,000 Euros). Its Secretary, Thomas Kemper has positively publicised the Project. Dr Engel of the EMW Theological Desk enthusiastically wrote up the project as 'An Alternative Experiment in Sierra Leone' in the EMW 2002 Yearbook. *(See 2002/4)* Now the EMW have approved a grant to the Project of 10,000 Euros for 2003 and 7,500 Euros for 2004. Personal donations to the project have not been solicited though small amounts have been received. Larger 'Response' donations have been channelled through the World Church Office in consultation with the President of the MCSL to specific rebuilding projects.

The Christian Council of SL (CCSL) has hosted the project through the Theological Hall and the Methodist Church Sierra Leone has provided transport and office support for the visiting team and co-ordinator. MCSL have seconded Revd Vidal Kamara-Cole, part-time lecturer at the Theological Hall as local co-ordinator for the project.

Many publishers of books contacted have welcomed the 'visionary' project. Some have given books for the course and for the re-stocking of the Theological Hall Library in Freetown. A notable contribution has been made through SPCK, who supplied at what is roughly one third of the retail price 110 copies of each of the International Study Guides that were chosen to be used as the basic books for teaching the course. Feed the Minds made a grant for books and materials of £2,500 for 2001/2 and increased that to £7,500 for the current year. The Evangelical Literature Trust subsidised the purchase of 110 copies of four larger commentaries and dictionaries at about one quarter of the cost. The combined subsidies/grants mean that out of a literature budget of less than £9,000 in Year One each student and local partner lecturers received about £300 worth of new books. The remaining books were added to the Theological Hall library.

Inevitably, this initiative, co-ordinated through Cliff College, WCO of the Methodist Church and MCSL has a Methodist feel about it. Staffing, (though ecumenical) and funding (though diverse) relies on personal contacts made through Methodist channels, but the support team is thoroughly ecumenical. Efforts have been made to publicise the project in Ecumenical forums and direct contact seeking support was made with the Church Missionary Society (CMS) through a designated Anglican visiting lecturer for 2003, Margaret Baxter, who served overseas with the CMS, but the response was negative. Any development of the concept might be slowed down by a stronger link with other western missionary societies, but a loose affiliation or forum of interested parties could both strengthen the financial base and enrich the association with churches both here and in different world church settings.

Regular reports, with photographs where appropriate, have been provided for our sponsors. These have been circulated widely and used for publicity purposes.

We continue to work out what partnership in training for ministry and mission can mean in practice. The ILC initiative developed out of a long established relationship and conversations in 2001 between the President of the MCSL, Right Revd Francis Nabieu and a former missionary in SL and current UK Co-ordinator Revd Richard Jackson. The contribution that this and other personal relationships have made to the successful launch of the Project needs to be acknowledged and recognised as a major factor in any expansion of the programme.

Partnership with the CCSL has been limited to warm hospitality, shared greetings and encouragement, but there has been little direct involvement on the part of key personnel including the Heads of Churches other than through the President of the MCSL. Whilst we recognise that local church resources are stretched in the aftermath of the war the relationship with the other churches of the CCSL must to be nurtured if there is to be the intended ecumenical involvement of the partner churches.

Bishop A. F. Kulah, the UMC Principal of the Theological Hall, has been supportive, always personally available and willing to offer both facilities and practical help in running the Teaching Blocks for the course at the Theological Hall. In turn we are helping to build up the Theological Hall library and we are being used to promote the Hall's own image and development as it seeks University validation *(since received)* for its own courses. To quote from the Principal, Bishop A. F. Kulah's Graduation Ceremony Report, 'The success of this programme will also enhance the College's status and facilitate progress towards an accredited Theological College.'

Every visiting lecturer is 'partnered' by an academically qualified Sierra Leonean who has shared in the lectures and the lecturing. Most of the team (visiting and local) met to prepare together before the teaching block and afterwards to conduct a review. The local team and co-ordinator work together at the Theological Hall (TH) and they met again with the visiting co-ordinator for a review and planning meeting in January 2003. It was agreed that Vidal Kamara-Cole should be the supervisor for students outside Freetown and that the Freetown students would be allocated tutors for supervision according to dissertation topics. The students will have group tutorials with their supervisors (and visiting partner lecturers) at the July 'Teaching Block'.

The local lecturers testify to the refreshing that they are enjoying as they help with the course. They contribute in both a personal and academic way to what is being delivered in the teaching blocks, but it is their view that the visiting lecturers from different church traditions and backgrounds should be utilised to the full whilst they are in Sierra Leone. The local partners, in turn, have been diligent in marking up to 98 scripts of completed work which are being received on average every two months.

This partnership with the Theological Hall is fruitful, and might become more so, if funding can be found for developing the relationship in the direction of short-term exchanges. This would help freshen up the staff of the Theological Hall, bring a World Church dimension to more of our colleges, and promote a wider understanding among the 'lecturers' who can spend 'exchange time' in a different culture and environment.

The anticipated practical and local contribution to the project 'in providing course/team facilities, but not funding' has been forthcoming, with a dedicated office and store being provided for the Project at the Theological Hall. Students or their sponsoring churches pay a registration fee of £50 per year towards the cost of the course, but we remain sensitively aware that what seems so little can be very costly in real terms in a country where £1=Le2 in 1979=Le2,300 in July 2002 and Le3,000+ in January 2003.

### PIONEERING CONCEPT & ADAPTATION OF CLIFF COLLEGE PRACTICE

The basic model of part taught (during residential weeks), part self-study (reading, assignments, portfolios & journals), examinations and researched dissertations is that utilised at Cliff College for distance learning courses from Diploma through to Master's level. The content of this course pitched at level 2 was intended as a refresher in basic biblical studies, theology and mission leading to a fresh understanding of roles and models of ministry and mission. The expertise, encouragement and support of Cliff College Staff was invaluable in the process of preparing, documenting and producing a Diploma Level

Course that has become the International Diploma In Applied Ministry And Mission (IDIAMM). Alongside the core subjects, seminars and supplementary teaching are being provided seeking to equip those in ministry and leadership to respond to the practical challenge being presented by post war issues of justice/reconciliation and the epidemic of HIV/AIDS. Overall, the primary focus has been to provide a course on contemporary ministry and mission in a local context. Obviously, much of the direct involvement with the students is associated with the two week teaching block undertaken in the July rainy season in SL and when they attend the January/February Seminars.

STAFFING

The visiting lecturers have been chosen for their qualifications (Academic CV's are on file) and expertise in particular subjects, their denominational spread, and their sensitivity to (and in most cases) experience of other cultures. A sense of humour and ability to adapt to changing circumstances is taken as read. An ecumenical team of five visiting lecturers was recruited for the July 2002 'Residential' at the Theological Hall in Freetown and others will be going in 2003. Expenses are met, but no charge is made to the ILC for their services. The visiting lecturers partnered local tutors of different denominations in providing ten sessions on each of the first five themes as follows:

Revd Dr Michael Thompson & Revd Dr Leopold Foullah:
Religion & Mission Theology - OT
Revd Dr Walter Klaiber & Revd Vidal Kamara-Cole, MA:
Church & Mission Theology - NT
Prof. Andrew Walls & Revd David Cole, MA:
Church History and mission in Africa/SL
Mrs Susanne Garnett, MA, MEd & Mr Samuel Forde, MA, MEd:
Spirituality in Ministry
Revd Dr Dennis Cooke & Revd Canon Emerson Thomas, MA:
Reconciliation following conflict

Included in the timetable were inter-active lectures on Study Skills led by Revd Richard Jackson. Opportunity was given for students to lead worship and share deeply moving personal experiences of the past ten years. Attendance by organised groups of students at Sunday worship in local churches and reflection upon the experience will be included in their worship portfolios. Locally invited speakers e.g. Truth & Reconciliation Commission conducted seminars. The local co-ordinator Revd Vidal Kamara-Cole was ably assisted in the office by Keith Phillips, a former VSO in SL who served as the course administrator.

**Visiting team (14th July to 8th August 2003) will be made up of:**

Revd Dr Martyn Atkins, who leads the Postgraduate Department at Cliff College lecturing on Evangelism. Accompanied by:
son James doing video/publicity project for course.
Margaret Baxter, Anglican will be working with the students in sessions on Adult Learning.
Revd. Dr John Cree, Anglican Rector , Chorley, Lancashire,
tackling the Contextualisation Module;
Revd. Prof Achim Härtner a United Methodist Seminary in Reutlingen will be teaching Worship & Preaching.
Accompanied by his 11 year old son Lukas. (via Brussels 17/7 to 4/8)
Revd. Dr Sahr Yambasu, SL Methodist from Ireland:
is looking at, Joining the Church: A History;
Prof. Andrew Walls, Keith Phillips and Richard Jackson as returnees will, with the local tutors, provide some continuity over the two years of the course.

Partner tutors for 2003 have been linked up as follows: Atkins with Foullah; Baxter with Kamara-Cole; Cree with Forde; Härtner with Thomas; Walls with Cole; Jackson with Yambasu.

Every visiting lecturer becomes responsible for producing 10 lectures (providing student notes-indispensable with English as a second language and where access to books/library is minimal) supported by the chosen books provided for every student on the course. Each lecture in 2002 (because of limited size and lack of ventilation in classrooms) was delivered twice to roughly half of the students. Time-tabling was adjusted during the teaching block to cope with some visiting lecturers arriving a couple of days late in SL and to provide the lecturers with more concentrated days of teaching followed by a lighter day with time off. The positive evaluation forms completed by 95 out of 99 students at the end of the two week teaching block in July 2002 indicate that the lecturers' contributions were appreciated **(See Appendix 7B-Resume of Evaluation Sheets)**. A late addition to the timetable of a day given over to group tutorials with two tutors present was clearly welcomed as an opportunity to share in a more personal way.

A number of students found the accents of some lecturers difficult to cope with, but such problems seem to be linked with the poor acoustics of one of the two lecturing venues. A church adjacent to the Theological Hall which has an amplification system is to be used for key lectures in 2003. Local churches were to arrange accommodation for students from outside Freetown and provide one meal per day at lunchtime for each of the students. Accommodation arrangements were patchy and the lunchtime meal was not provided. This failure, associated with long days of required attendance became an issue that was diplomatically dealt with, but concerns were reflected on the evaluation forms. For the Freetown and Bo Regional Days in January (3 days in all) we tested out arrangements by which the Project funded the cost of meals provided locally at an approximate cost of 50p per person per day. This worked well and will be implemented for the 2003 teaching block at an additional cost of £800 to be found from the existing budget or through additional local funding.

**RATIONALE, RESOURCING AND BENEFITS (INTER-RELATED SECTIONS EVALUATED TOGETHER.)**

Completed applications for the Course were received through sponsoring bodies from 99 students. These were processed by the local co-ordinator. Only applicants supported by their own church were accepted and all completed their first two residential weeks in July 2002. Of students registered: 52 students are recorded as MCSL; 14 UMC; 10 WAMC; 9 Anglican; 6 Lutheran; 8 others included members of the AME; Baptist; Deeper Life; Pentecostal and Roman Catholic Churches. There are 77 male students and 22 females of whom 68 are ordained and 31 are church and community leaders. 69 students reside in the capital Freetown and surrounding districts; 30 students live in the provincial districts of SL. It should be noted that most of the qualifying MCSL ministers are enrolled already on the course. Any repetition/continuation of this level 2 course would be dependent upon recruitment from other denominations or the laity. This would not preclude the development of a higher level course, in association with the Theological Hall, but utilising the same pattern of distance learning.

The January 2003 review **(See Appendix 7C-List of students with initial marks and dissertation themes)** shows that of the required work to be submitted by September and November deadlines only one student has failed to submit any work for marking by our local partners. Outstanding is one other OT assignment and nine NT assignments. Four NT assignments did not meet the standards required and have been returned for resubmission. Recognising the difficulties and constraints that all are working under we decided to be as generous as we could be and live (as we do at Cliff College) by grace in relation to deadlines. We kept in mind (without communicating this directly to every student) a cut-off point (unless a delay was sanctioned for medical or other serious reasons) that expected the two pieces of work due to be submitted by the 30th November to be in and marked so that they scripts can be moderated during our Regional Groups in January. Similarly, the Jan, Mar and May pieces of work should be in and marked before the July 2003 Residential and so on throughout the course. Any student who has not submitted all of the work required for the first year by the 31st May 2003 (without a delay being officially sanctioned) will not be allowed to proceed to the second year of the Course.

All but 16 students have submitted a proposal form that outlines their planned dissertation **(See Appendix 7C)**. Many of these will be adjusted in the light of our discussions about dissertations at the January 2003 meetings, but the concentration on local and contextualised concerns is clear. Research for the course is limited to 8,000-8,500 words, but students tackling larger topics, e.g. the history of a church, are being encouraged both to focus on issues or a limited time-scale for the requirements of the course and also to continue with a serious and substantial piece of research and documentation as a resource for their church. The intention is for the completed dissertations to be submitted for review by the local supervisors before 31st December 2003 and to be finalised with binding by 31st May 2004.

Administratively, the local co-ordinator Vidal Kamara-Cole has done excellent work, despite telephone breakdowns and intermittent internet services (using an Internet Café). We are exploring the possibility and cost of providing direct telephone/email access to the dedicated office allocated for us in the Theological Hall.

Questions have been asked about the increase from the Guesstimate Budget submitted with applications for funding in the summer of 2001. The current account and anticipated budget position for the current year is set out clearly. **(See Appendix 7D-Cliff College ILC Accounts & Budget)**.

What follows by way of an updating commentary on these accounts and this budget is in essence the response made to specific questions asked by the EMW in November 2002 before they agreed to make a grant to the project. So we replied as follows:

"The growth in the budget was almost inevitable and is an indicator of the success of the project. You will receive a clearer picture from the attached summary of Budget, (not quite the original from the booklet which was termed a 'Guesstimate Budget'); Actual figures to 31st August 2002; and Proposed Budget for this current year. As we are looking now at £50,000 per annum (including the hoped for £7,000 from EMW) some background and further explanation will be helpful as you seek to interpret and present the figures to others.

I'm not sure whether you have an equivalent in German to 'Flying by the seat of your pants', but that is what I have been doing since this pioneering and innovative project was conceived last year. We had nowhere else to look for guidance as to what this kind of project was going to cost and the principles that to some extent have determined the budget have been developed as we have gone along.

Cliff College said that I could co-ordinate the project and utilise college staff, expertise, office and administration facilities providing that it would not cost the College (which is running a budget deficit already) financially. Our Methodist World Church Office sanctioned initially a budget of £20,000 per annum and other sponsors like your own church came in with some smaller sums of money which we have accounted for. The major plus factor that we do not see in terms of benefit in the budget is that the project attracted in terms of new books, study and writing materials alone well over £300 each for all of the 99 students and our partner lecturers in Sierra Leone.

This benefit has been acknowledged by an increased grant from Feed the Minds, which has been received already, along with the recognition that if we are to dovetail practical teaching on issues like HIV/Aids into the Course, we will need more materials and may have to commission at cost Distance Learning modules/consultations related to these topics.

The work involving me but related to the project has simply snowballed as I have become a conduit for many things related to SL. There is recognition in most quarters that I need to be set aside, at least half-time with funding provided for a half-time co-ordinator for maintaining this project and exploring the possibilities of developing similar initiatives in other parts of the world. The £12,000 per annum for this included in the budget has been applied for (since approved) as an additional grant from WCO.

With regard to staffing and the related costs, we began with the intention of carrying the course with just 3 lecturers plus the co-ordinator being involved and the original budget envisaged their travel, accommodation and food being paid for. It quickly became clear that if we wanted to do the job properly and maintain an ecumenical visiting team as well as the ecumenical dimension in SL we would need to increase numbers. In the event we took with us five subject lecturers, plus myself as co-ordinator and Study Skills lecturer with Annegret accompanying Walter and Keith Phillips (a former VSO in SL) coming to help look after the logistical arrangements, including getting the course container off the docks and organising the distribution of masses of books, materials, etc. It might have been possible, but would have not been advisable to do the SL end of things with fewer people.

The original team of four were nominated on the basis of their experience, ecumenicity, and expertise in particular subjects and we had promised that all their expenses would be met. In the event, others were added for whom a variety of arrangements were made. As you know, the UMC grant of £1,895 covered the travel costs for Walter & Annegret, but not much more. Accommodation and feeding for both was paid for from the budget. The Irish Conference gave us £5,000 per annum for two years (spent in advance), but that donation was in part-payment for the costs of sending one tutor from Ireland for each of the two years. Prof. Andrew Walls and Keith Phillips paid for their own flights, but we met their other costs.

**PERSONAL FUNDING BY PERSONNEL**

As long as we are looking for and choosing people with particular expertise and gifting, it seems important to me that we maintain the principle of agreeing to pay expenses, where necessary, but remain open to ad-hoc arrangements as indicated above for individuals and sending organisations to support them in some way. Even where that does not happen, the spin-offs for the home churches from those who have been involved can be quite considerable. One of the returning tutors, Michael Thompson, has raised already nearly £3,000 for a specific project in SL. I am out most Sundays now publicising Sierra Leone in general and the Project in particular and churches are responding with offers of help to rebuild churches, manses and schools. I am sure that Walter and Annegret Klaiberg, like the rest of us, are speaking to the churches as more informed returnees.

Undoubtedly, the costs relating to staffing are a major part of our expenditure. As you know accommodation cost us much more than anticipated with the influx of aid agencies prepared to pay 'London' rates for accommodation.. The planned-for RC Retreat Centre became unavailable at the last minute and would not have catered anyway for the longer stay. We were well looked after at 'Elly's', but as you will see from the Accounts if you add the £6,724 to the £5,157 under the MCSL account, the £11,881 was still within our £12,000 budget figure. To keep the whole thing in perspective, we do need to note that to bring just one student to Europe for a one year course would cost the church here more than the £12,000. Going there with the course, means that we provide for much greater numbers of people in their own culture and context, with no fall-out from 'westernised students' and problems about returning. Certainly, it will be good to see what the students produce in terms of dissertations/projects relating to their own country and church in Sierra Leone."

**CONCLUDING COMMENTS (with one eye on the future)**

The likelihood is that the two-year IDIAMM Course (which spans three budget years) with no continuing programme will cost in the region of £100,000. At a cost of roughly £500 per student per annum 99 ministers and lay leaders already working in the churches of SL will have been refreshed and resourced (having received already £300 worth of books each) and most will complete a two-year practical training in ministry and mission package adapted to their own culture and current needs. Even if there is a significant and unanticipated drop-out of students in the second year the benefits anticipated at the outset will have been realised. Clearly, there is an issue to be addressed as to how money spent on this project relates to the larger 'scholarship programmes' of funding churches, but a similarly constructed programme at Masters level (with University validation in the UK or through a local institution) could be both contextualised and cost-effective.

## STAFFING

The UK co-ordinator's established relationships with key people in Sierra Leone, interested parties in the UK who have provided contact with others further afield and Cliff College have been crucial. If similar programmes are to be undertaken elsewhere, an administrative template has been produced and a programme tested out. The recruitment of appropriate (sub)co-ordinators with the time, inclination and prior relationships/knowledge should not prove impossible, but would need to be handled sensitively in consultation with partner churches.

Recruitment of suitable lecturers for this pilot project through the 'grapevine' both here and in Sierra Leone has not proved difficult. (Turning down some who hoped to be involved was more difficult!) The knock-on effect of the project has been to revive the interest of many people in the UK and beyond who have been associated with SL in the past and in association with the circulation of the 'Himsworth – SL Methodist Church News' *(details elsewhere)* has engendered fresh enthusiasm and support for the rebuilding work that needs to be done there. Obviously, the traumatic events in SL over the past ten years have elicited a particularly positive response, but such events and consequent needs are not peculiar to SL. Care needs to be taken in using 'retired missionaries', but a balance has been kept. Future developments might include more people, like Revd Dr Sahr Yambasu, serving in partner churches 'returning' or suitable international lecturers from Africa and beyond being recruited to service these short-term courses.

PARTNERSHIP

An evaluation that takes full account of responses from partner churches is for the longer term, but sufficient by way of response has been included in this evaluation to suggest that the project has made a positive impact on students, churches and the Theological Hall in particular. Whatever the future of the ILC, it seems clear that there will be an ongoing relationship through Cliff College with the Theological Hall. An exploration of the possibility of 'twinning' theological/bible colleges across international boundaries could benefit both parties.

EVALUATION CONCLUSION

In its own terms this pioneering pilot project is achieving what it set out to do. That the problems have been so few is a tribute to everyone who has caught the vision, responded positively and been willing to adapt quickly to changing circumstances and needs.

This pilot project would not have happened if Cliff College and all the sponsors, especially those at the Methodist World Church Office had not said 'yes' when it would have been much less of a hassle to say 'no'.

With a sense of adventure and growing support, I am convinced that these jottings on an aeroplane sick bag from two years ago that have become a project used so effectively in the SL setting, can be adapted to the needs of a particular context. This programme is repeatable elsewhere. It is for those who sponsor us, most of whom have demonstrated by increased funding that they are likely to stay 'on board' for the foreseeable future, to decide what commitment they are prepared to make and what guidance they want to give in the continuation and development of the ILC programme.

Richard Jackson (Revd.) Co-ordinator,
Cliff College International Learning Centre 11th April 2003

# 2003/3 MAY: REVIEW IN LIGHT OF EVALUATION
## PERSONAL REFLECTION (WITH A LITTLE REVISION): SEEKING MORE SPONSORS

Two years ago almost to the day (23rd May) my wife Carole and I were sitting on a Russian aeroplane, lifting off from Freetown in Sierra Leone and trying to make Christian sense of all that we had seen and heard over the previous two weeks. In 2001, more than 20 years after our 10 years of service in that country we had gone back as the official representatives of our own British Conference. The Sierra Leone that we found was very different from the one that we had left. Ten years of brutal civil war had made sure of that.

Freetown, poverty, open sewers, buildings destroyed, 2,600 Leones to the £. In the Amputees Camp we talked with those who had limbs chopped off simply to frighten others into obedience. The boy soldiers that are news for TV and newspaper reporters were a terrifying reality in SL as drug crazed youngsters were armed with guns and let loose by the rebels to destroy community and create a climate of fear. A contrast might be seen with the Aid agencies at work but comments made by one observer in relation to a planned-for book on the 'White Land-Rover' raised questions about how the 'Aid' provided was being used.

On the long time, (but not distance) road to Bo we saw some of the devastation and rebel ambush areas. There were UN peace-keepers, living up to their brief as 'peace-keepers but according to the indigenous population it was the British soldiers who went in and 'sorted them out'. The prevailing message to the much-appreciated Clare Short was, 'Do not withdraw them.' During a Bo and Tikonko tour-we saw the remains of manses, schools, and churches where I had preached, and whole villages destroyed by the rebels.

### MINISTERIAL SESSION OF CONFERENCE

We heard something from old friends of what the ministers had gone through and what they were doing now. Most had lost their books, homes, members of their families, but they had continued in ministry even when they found themselves in displaced persons' camps in neighbouring Guinea or foreign parts of Sierra Leone.

My wife, Carole, a medical doctor toured the Governments Hospital with a Methodist Sister and was appalled. Later, I visited the Methodist Hospital in Segbwema, where our son Peter was born, and found a derelict shell, but even there devoted Methodists had begun to re-establish the work with a small clinic serving the needs of the people. Representative Session of Conference confirmed initial impressions that in the face of danger, awful conditions, and some persecution the church had matured and was in good heart.

Kenema was the town where we had worked longest whilst in SL. Refugees from the villages had flocked to the security of the town. Schools built for a couple of hundred children were coping with 2,000 in two shifts. Teachers there and in the displaced persons camps continued to fulfil their vocation even when salaries were not forthcoming and equipment was almost nil.

**OVERCROWDED SCHOOLS**

Please don't talk to me about third world schools or hospitals in this country-Have these reporters ever been to the third world? Re-built shanty churches are coping with thousands of additional people impressed by the work of the church during the struggles. Yes, there will be rice Christians among them looking for food and housing, but isn't that part of what the church should be offering in these circumstances?

Perhaps the most moving time on our visit was at the graveside of a Methodist Church leader, B. S. Massaquoi. Memories came flooding back of him as I talked with him in 1977 and heard him say, 'How can I sit in comfort, whilst my people all around me are suffering'. His decision then to return to politics led ultimately to his death at the hands of the rebels. We were on another veranda in 2001 as a friend told us the story of his courage.

Yes, as I sat on that Russian aeroplane, assaulted by a kaleidoscope of sounds and images, I questioned, 'What can I do for this country and these people who have moulded my own life and ministry?' As shared earlier, I turned to the sick bag (as you do!) and

70

began to jot down a few thoughts, that seemed to me to come as a vision from God. The obvious thing would have been to say that we would bring some ministers from Sierra Leone to Cliff College for a refresher course. What follows are personal notes about what followed when I began with others to pursue the vision. Thanks to the adventurous and committed support of a large number of 'boring' church people, the last two years have seen this original vision expanded and fulfilled in ways that I could not have dreamed possible.

College reaction: Colleagues: Principal Howard Mellor-great idea, but cautious about the money required. Pete Phillips-great idea, he didn't know then that he would have to do half the work of keeping me right in relation to academic requirements. Paul Ashby, OT with overseas experience, great idea-anything I can do. Phil Clarke (Cliff & Conference Evangelism), great idea, checking drafts for me. Susanne Garnett-great idea, one of first group of lecturers to travel-changed course of her life. Ian White-great idea, encouragement out of what he was already doing with 'Highway' in Palestine. Martyn Atkins-great idea, go for it-and now he is going for it as a lecturer going this year to SL.

### REFLECTION ON FINANCE AND RESOURCES
#### FINANCE

Methodist Church Overseas Division (MCOD);
Methodist Missionary Society {MMS (Ireland)};
Hoped for United Methodist Church (UMC) in the USA
became the UMC from Germany.
Feed the Minds (FTM)
     All had one thing in common, they were prepared to cut the red tape and in some cases by-pass committees to make the funding available when it was needed.

#### PLANNING THE PROGRAMME

(Booklet-International Diploma in Applied Mission and Ministry) Cliff College experience of teaching through extension studies translated into a different context.

#### RESOURCES

     Key resource needed were books-with an anticipated student intake of 100 students, plus our partner lecturers in SL. Where were we going to find the money for 110 copies of every book that we planned to use? In the end we had to find money, but nowhere near as much as we thought. My friend and postgraduate administrator, Theresa Phillips, who keeps the postgraduate department functioning, made contact with a large number of Christian Book publishers. We had already decided to use as our basic books the SPCK International Study Guides, which were produced with people for whom English is a second language in mind. SPCK let us have them at roughly one third of the basic cost. A network developed as interest grew and other publishers provided books free of charge or with a similar discounts. The Evangelical Literature Trust provided larger Biblical and Theological Dictionaries at a quarter of the cost and our good friends at Feed the Minds gave us an emergency grant last year of £2,500, which increased to £7,500 this year to help defray the cost of literature.

In the event last summer we were able to provide all of our 99 students and staff with about £300 worth of books each and will be doing the same again this year.

**TRANSPORT OF MATERIALS**

Count on the Irish Methodist Church and their Aladdin in Lurgan, William Carson. William has a cave (warehouse) at the Lurgan Methodist Church, which not only sends containers to different parts of the world, but also helps to fill them. You need biros, here's a few hundred of them, pads of paper-no problem; filing cabinets, a desk-I began to have visions of an unmanageable container, but all arrived safely and on time in SL.

**STAFFING**

The German Methodist Church said: we will give you our best and sent their President and well-published theologian Revd Dr Walter Klaiber to deliver New Testament lectures. The Irish Methodist Church gave us Revd Dr Dennis Cooke, the Principal of their Methodist Training College in Belfast to lead thinking about reconciliation and reconstruction. As shared in the reports, others were recruited to partner lecturers already based in Freetown.

# 2003/4 JUL 14-AUG 4: CCSL THIRD RESIDENTIAL

(IDIAMM 2002-04 PROGRAMME)

REPORT ON PROGRESS PRESENTED TO SPONSORS *(SOME NEW)* IN THIS OCTOBER 2003 SUMMARY

During the past two years Cliff College through its International Learning Centre has been involved in giving further training to large numbers of ministers and lay-people in Sierra Leone at cost of just £500 per student per annum. We are seeking further financial support and additional sponsors for this programme.

## PIONEERING PROJECT

This exciting and innovative pioneering project was initiated in response to an invitation from the Christian Council of Sierra Leone (CCSL) and is being implemented in partnership with the churches of Sierra Leone and the Principal and Staff of the churches' own Theological College in Freetown. The well-documented tragedy and brutality of the ten-year civil war in Sierra Leone devastated the church as well as the country. A stated aim of this project was to provide church pastors and community leaders of all denominations in Sierra Leone with a practical and culturally oriented part-time two year, level-two, further training (refresher) course leading to an International Diploma In Applied Ministry and Mission (IDIAMM). Utilising experience gained at Cliff College of providing part taught (during residential weeks); part self-study (reading, assignments, portfolios); and part researched (dissertation); courses, we have undertaken a practical course in ministry and mission that is relevant to the local context.

## PROGRAMME AND STAFFING IN SIERRA LEONE

Our two-year programme is made up of ten modules linked with biblical studies, ministry and mission. Ecumenical teams of five academically qualified visiting lecturers were recruited for the July 2002 & 2003 'Two Week Residentials' based at the churches' Theological College in Freetown. Expenses were met, but no charge was made to the ILC for their services. The visiting lecturers partnered qualified local tutors of different denominations in providing ten sessions with study notes on each of five themes covering ten modules in all:

Revd Dr Dennis Cooke & Revd Canon Emerson Thomas, MA:
Reconciliation following Conflict
Mrs Susanne Garnett, MA, MEd & Mr Samuel Forde, MA, MEd:
Spirituality in Ministry
Revd Dr Walter Klaiber & Revd Vidal Kamara-Cole, MA:
Church & Mission Theology - NT
Revd Dr Michael Thompson & Revd Dr Leopold Foullah:
Religion & Mission Theology - OT
Prof. Andrew Walls & Revd David Cole, MA:
Church History and Mission in Africa/SL
Revd Richard Jackson, BD, MA, Cliff College Co-ordinator:
Study Skills

WITH HON DR SAMA S BANYA METHODIST LOCAL PREACHER

JULY-2003

Revd Dr Martyn Atkins, Cliff College Course Director (& Foullah): Being the Church: Evangelism.
Mrs Margaret Baxter, BA(Hons), PGCE and author (& Kamara-Cole): Adult Learning.
Revd Dr John Cree, Anglican Rector (& Forde):
Being the Church in the World: Contextualisation.
Revd. Achim Härtner, MA United Methodist, E. Stanley Jones Professor of Evangelism at Reutlingen Seminary (& Thomas):
Being the Church: Worship & Preaching.
Revd Richard Jackson, BD, MA, Cliff College Co-ordinator:
Being the Church: Ministry
Revd Dr Sahr Yambasu, Sierra Leonean Methodist from Ireland:
Joining the Church: A History.

Students have led worship and in groups shared personal experiences of traumatic times when many lost members of their family, their homes and belongings (including books) and some spent years living in displaced persons camps. Locally invited speakers, e.g. Truth & Reconciliation Commission and the Special Court have conducted seminars. The local co-ordinator Revd Vidal Kamara-Cole is assisted in the office by Keith Phillips, CQSW, Cert Ed., a former VSO in SL, who serves as the Residential Course Administrator.

The current Two Year Pilot Project (2002-2004) will conclude with a July 2004 Graduation. Students have attended two 'Residentials' of two weeks in July (SL rainy season) each year. At roughly two month intervals students have submitted work (assignments, portfolios of practical work undertaken, journals-see the Course Booklet for details) which are marked by the local tutors. In the Jan/Feb following the 'Residentials', the Co-ordinators meet with students in 'Regional Groups' where Aids awareness Courses have been conducted and at which progress has been assessed and further guidance given particularly in relation to the required ministry-related dissertation.

During the Jan/Feb and July visits marking already done is moderated by the visiting co-ordinator from Cliff College. At the end of two years, successful students will receive an International Diploma In Applied Ministry and Mission. Further consideration is being given by the churches to some students becoming local trainers for specific ministries. The developing relationship between the ILC of Cliff College and a strengthened Theological College of the CCSL in Sierra Leone is prompting thoughts of a longer term 'formation in ministry' programme.

In July 2002, 99 students were enrolled on the Course. Only applicants supported by their own church were accepted and 90 have now completed both residential weeks. (July 2002 & 3) Of students registered: 52 students were recorded as MCSL; 14 UMC; 10 WAMC; 9 Anglican; 6 Lutheran; 8 others included members of the African Methodist Episcopal; Baptist; Deeper Life; Pentecostal and Roman Catholic Churches. There were 77 male students and 22 females of whom 68 are ordained and 31 are church and community leaders. 69 students lived in the capital Freetown and surrounding districts; 30 students lived in the provincial districts. 90 students completed the required work and continued into the second year.

**AIMS** *(Largely a repetition of what was shared under 2002/3, but note-now 'achieved')*

## We began with modest aims in the context of Sierra Leone's need:

TO ENCOURAGE

With 95 very positive evaluation forms (on file) being returned from the 99 students who attended the first 'residential' and 80 out of 90 returned from this year's residential this is clearly being achieved. One brief comment sums up the general response, 'Rich, motivating and inspiring'.

TO RESOURCE

This initiative undertaken with a pump-priming £20,000 a year grant from the World Church Office of the British Methodist Church has attracted increasing funding from Feed the Minds and other organisations as its value has been recognised. Students or their sponsoring churches pay a nominal enrolment fee of £50 per annum. Publishers provided new books at such reduced prices that in return we have been able to supply free to every student (and SL staff partners) more than 40 new books for the course retailing at approximately £700. These include a number of SPCK International Study Guides and several larger Commentaries and Theological/Bible Dictionaries resourced through the Evangelical Literature Trust. Writing and other materials were supplied free by the Irish Methodist Church (MMS), who organised and paid for the 'Course Container', filled with everything from pens to filing cabinets, to be shipped to SL. Presentations have been made of course books, new books donated by SCM, and large numbers of second hand books to the libraries of the Theological College and Fourah Bay University in Freetown.

TO REFRESH

The excitement and enthusiasm generated by visiting lecturers and their Sierra Leonean counterparts in two weeks of concentrated lecturing, sharing and worshipping together impacted not only on those present, but also on the churches and others who heard about the course through local radio. A waiting list in Sierra Leone largely made up of UMC and Anglican applicants who 'missed out' is indicative of a demand for a 'rolling programme' beyond the first two years and/or for some alternative training.

In the setting up of this 'level two course' and its delivery, we have borne in mind both academic requirements and the potential practical benefits to those (lay and ordained) working in ministry. Already, the indications are that on my visit in February, 2004, I shall find that most of the students have completed the required written work including their first draft of Sierra Leone oriented dissertations (8,000-8,500 words) on a variety of subjects but with many linked to understanding traditional beliefs and post-conflict reconciliation and reconstruction. We anticipate that at least three-quarters of the students who began the course will complete. Even those who do not complete will have been resourced in ways that would have not been possible for the local churches to do alone. The unit cost for the whole course (including the books and course materials provided free to students) works out at roughly £500 per student per annum.

As initiator and co-ordinator of this pilot project based at Cliff College in the UK, I am wary of claiming too much for it, but there is much that has happened in a largely trouble free initiative for which we can give thanks. The mutual enrichment and encouragement of staff and of everyone associated with the project can be taken as read. The local and international partnership has worked well, giving the project a 'From Everywhere To Everywhere' dimension. On being asked to sum up what is different about this approach, I responded almost without thinking, 'Doing it there!' With the primary funding being provided by the Methodist Church, we have 'done it there' in Sierra Leone for students of all denominations. Any continuation of the project in SL, or indeed development elsewhere, will depend on there being a positive response by church 'mission' agencies (and others) to the vision behind this highly successful pilot project.

Utilising the untapped resources of short-term (wo)manpower available for general and specialist courses, we can help train large numbers of people by 'doing it there' in partnership with local churches for large numbers of people. This costs much less than if one or two students receive scholarships to do less focussed training in a culture that is not their own (with all the consequent casualties). Our hope is that this developing programme will now attract further sponsors including you. This brief paper has been produced for personal and committee use but an April 2003 evaluation and further information, including digital photographs and audited accounts are available for interested parties.

# 2003/5 STUDENTS COMMENT ON BOOKS RECEIVED

STUDENT COMMENTS ON COURSE BOOKS RECEIVED IN SIERRA LEONE

On receiving books partly funded from grants provided by:

FEED THE MINDS and MMS(IRELAND)

**SOME COMMENTS FROM 2002**-*(The English has not been corrected, but we are reminded regularly that our students' capability in English is far better than our own foreign language ability!!)*

'The books which are given to us will never be in our hands if it was not for this course, because they are very costly outside in the market.'
'They help to enrich our personal libraries.'
'I hope we as students will make good use of these in our mission and theology.'
'They are really a source of inspiration for the course as they are current and provide the necessary materials needed.'
'However the books supplied to us are excellent because they are not to be returned but are our personal property.'

'The books are well laid out, the explanations are to the point and hence very easy to read and understand.'
'The books supplied to us are considered to be a gift from God.'
'With these books I will start my own little library which every minister should have.'
'It's been wonderful having such a collection of books provided by Cliff College. It will definitely go for a life time. Very much appreciated. It's worth a million more than its price.'
'This has helped us regain most of our books stolen or burnt during the rebel crisis.'

'The books were a real God sent especially for us whose whole collection were destroyed when our houses were burnt down by rebels.'
'The things that have been hidden from us as blind man, our eyes have opened for us through these books.'
'Most of these books are not available in this country.'
'These books are a treasure not only for this course, but also for future use to us as preachers of God's word.'
'It came to us like manner from above.'
'The book materials provided to students, is first of its kind in our history.'

**FEWER COMMENTS FROM 2003** where we provided a tick box (Excellent; Very Good; Good; Satisfactory; Poor;) for appreciation of books received. Most students ticked Excellent and a few made comments

'As students we can boast of a very good library through the support of the college.'
'A good library has been created for those living in rural areas to study hard and be well equipped.'
'With the help of Cliff College we now have a semblance of a library.'
'Where else would we have got so much relevant material.'
'We thank the donors.'
'Hope we shall find time to make best use of them all.'
'I now have a quality library that I am proud of. Thank you, God Bless You.'
'The books made available to us are prizeless.'
'They are my life treasure.'
'This would help me very much not only in my studies, but in the preparation of sermons as they cover every topic.'

This information is taken from Evaluation Sheets completed by students anonymously at the end of the 'Residential Fortnight at which they had received their books.

*Extracted by International Co-ordinator, Revd Richard Jackson, 12<sup>th</sup> August 2004*

## 2003/6 FEB: FRIENDS OF MCSL (2001-14)

*As early as 1995 former mission partners in Sierra Leone began to meet together at the invitation of Dr Mary Groves and through the late Revd Frank Himsworth and his wife Sheila began to raise funds and support for that troubled country. Frank & Sheila's, Sierra Leone Methodist Church News published a couple of times a year from 2002, backed up by organised get-togethers proved to be inspired. The newsletter, informed by 'official' information and visitors from Sierra Leone to the reunions served to maintain the momentum of sharing and caring with many of the friends of Sierra Leone who have supported the church there in a number of ways. The letter below from 2003, (and a 2007/5 newsletter 13) provide an insight into the personal but positive nature of these communications which have helped maintain relationships and raised many thousands of pounds for rebuilding work in Sierra Leone.*

## EXAMPLE OF SIERRA LEONE MAILINGS & RE-UNIONS
*(See also 2007/5)*

Dear Friend,

Please book the date of 6 & 7 September 2003 for a re-union. This has been requested by Revd Francis Nabieu in several conversations and letters. Some of us had raised the idea of a residential meeting so this has been arranged from morning coffee on 6 Sep to lunch on 7 Sep at Cliff College, Derbyshire. The cost including all meals is £40 per person. Cliff can accommodate 65 people, nearly all single rooms, and 1 invite you to return the form at the bottom of this page to me asap to state your interest and 1 hope, your commitment to be there.

Francis will be in the UK from near the end of August until mid Sept. and in May those attending the Conference in Sierra Leone include Leslie Wallace, Ken Todd, Michael. and Isabella King. In July Richard Jackson, Sahr Yambasu and others from Cliff will be going to Freetown for the second summer school for Ministers. It is hoped that most of them will be at Cliff with Francis to tell us the news. An overnight stay will give much more time as well for an exchange of personal news.

In January Richard was in Freetown and Bo for the first follow up for Ministers' studies, and is pleased to report that only 1 out of 99 starters has dropped out. He also got to Daru for the District Synod. He found travelling easy and all of them in good heart. Jenny Gibson has taken herself to SL and is working with Dr Missa in Kenema. As one doctor's house is now ready and two staff houses almost ready the work should by now be in Segbwema. Mr John Cooper-Poole is going to Segbwema shortly to take charge of administration as the hospital extends the work from the small base now possible.

The Trustees of the Methodist Church, Sierra Leone, have been doing a tour of the properties in the Provinces. They were meeting in Bo to assess priorities and the amount of local input available for rebuilding of local churches, schools etc. Once work starts they hope to send photographs of the various phases of the work. As the work begins they will draw on the funds donated by people here and at present held in the World Church Fund in London. They have got some funding for Kailahun Secondary School but Wesley School, Segbwema, still needs funds to re-roof the upper floor. It is estimated that '25 bundles of zinc' are needed at about £40 a bundle, but they do not have it. I have written to Francis saying that some of the money in London has been donated for Wesley School, but more is needed.

In the country elections have been taking place for new Paramount Chiefs and this has been going peacefully, and the country's President Kabbah has been on tour for their 'installation'. Richard reported that there was some concern in our Church in Sierra Leone about 'personal funding' to projects, which may overlap with central funding. If funds are sent we ought to tell the central office, but better still would be for funds to be channelled through a Redevelopment Fund to give a more accurate overview. About £11,000 has been sent to me since July 2001, much of it has been gift aided and quite a lot ear-marked for particular projects.
Perhaps we can continue that!

Frank Himsworth
28 Feb. 2003

**SIERRA LEONE RE-UNION Cliff College, 6 to 7 September 2003**

1/We will be very interested and hope to attend.

Name ...............................................................

Address

...............................................................................................

.......................

...............................................................................................

Tel No.                                                    email

81

# CHAPTER 4 2004: REVIEWING & RENEWING

*Dedicated work by the MCSL appointed National Coordinator, alongside that of the International Coordinator and a small but enthusiastic team of people willing to work with the programme brought the two-year pilot programme to a successful conclusion. Out of ninety-nine students who began the course in July 2002, 73 graduated with an 'International Diploma In Applied Ministry And Mission (IDIAMM)' in July and a further 18 in December 2004. Despite the difficulties of working, studying, travelling in a post-conflict situation a total of 91 students completed the course out of the 99 who began the pilot programme.*

## 2004/1 FEB 13-MAR 1: CCSL FOURTH RESIDENTIAL

### (IDIAMM 2002-04 PROGRAMME)

#### GROUP RESIDENTIALS & PREPARATION FOR GRADUATIONS

In February 2004, the co-ordinator, Revd Richard Jackson and the administrator, Keith Phillips embarked on a further two-week visit to Sierra Leone. Apart from spending time with Heads of Churches, members of the Christian Council of Sierra Leone and the Principal of the Theological College, we met with the local staff, led by the National Coordinator, Revd Vidal Kamara-Cole who had been marking assignments and supervising the research work undertaken by students as part of their course. In addition we met with groups of students both in the Provinces and Freetown for further training/teaching sessions with a particular emphasis on progress being made towards finalising dissertations in good time for marking prior to the Graduation Ceremony in July. Logistical arrangements for the Graduation, which included everything from hiring a venue through to having preaching scarves for the presentation made locally were also initiated. In the event it became clear that the CCILC administrator would need to return to Sierra Leone in advance of the visiting graduation party to join the local co-ordinator, Revd Vidal Kamara-Cole in finalising results and making sure that documentation and practical arrangements were in place for the event.

# 2004/2 FEB: MCSL LAY TRAINING (G & S HALL)
COOPERATION WITH LAY TRAINING FOR LOCAL PREACHERS AND WOMEN'S WORK

Independently of CCILC, but by 2005 to be harnessed to it: Revd Gilbert Hall and his wife Sylvia conducted some Local Preachers' and Women Worker Workshops for Lay Leaders in the three Districts of MCSL in February 2004.

The programme of Workshops for the Local Preachers and Women was arranged by the President, Rt. Revd Francis Nabieu, together with the Revd Gilbert and Mrs. Sylvia Hall, who had previously served in Sierra Leone 1971 - 1975. During that time, Revd Hall was the Superintendent of the Kenema Circuit and then Chairman of the Bo/Kenema District.

## THE LAY TRAINING WORKSHOPS

Following a Reunion of ex-Sierra Leonean missionaries in September 2003 which the President Rt. Revd Francis Nabieu attended, *(See 2003/6)* Sylvia and I (in retirement!) expressed our desire to encourage our brothers and sisters in the Methodist Church S.L. to get back on their feet following the war years that had played havoc with their lives. As Cliff College, under the leadership of the Revd Richard Jackson had devised a retraining programme for the ministers, we suggested a series of meetings to support and encourage the Local Preachers and Women in the Church through the three Districts of the Methodist Church in Sierra Leone.

On receiving an invitation from the Rt. Revd Francis Nabieu to visit S.L. and organize these Workshops we presented the scheme to the U.K. Methodist World Church Office asking them to consider supporting the venture. They generously agreed to cover our travel and accommodation for the period February 6th to March 1st so making the visit possible. As a result the three day workshop for each of the Districts was born.

Over the three days of the Workshop, Biblical and Theological studies and general training about Methodism was backed up by more specific training done in groups with women and Local Preachers.

Attendance at each Centre
Freetown - average    - 28   ( 8  L.P. and 20 women )

| Kenema - | " | - 26 | ( 18 L.P. and 8 women ) |
| Bo (one day ) | | -24 | ( 13 L.P. and 11 women ) |
| Segbwema | " | -47 | ( 36 L.P. and 12 women ) |

**FEEDBACK FROM PARTICIPANTS IN THE PROGRAMME**

There was general agreement about the value of this and other training programmes. Planning and publicity need to be done well in advance and dates/timing adhered to other than in exceptional circumstances.
Those lay leaders with specific responsibilities: Local Preachers; Women Workers; Youth Facilitators; etc. need regular training programmes and provision of appropriate resources.

We asked the question, 'What is the vision of the church that could inspire and facilitate each church to meet the needs of their non-members?'

Each Workshop identified the needs of their non-members and categorised them as follows:-

a.      Social Concerns:-Humanitarian needs;- Food, clothes, water, shelter, homes, security of land, the eradication of corruption

b.      Evangelism:- Explore methods to win others for Christ

c.      Worship:- Explore styles of worship to suit local people.  Use of bands. Hymn books, bibles needed

d.      Training:- Continual training of the Local Preachers and women; Discipleship of the membership; 'Love one another ' programme; Provision of materials for each.

e.      Property and Finance:- Buildings needed or repaired :- Church, Manse, Schools, Hospital Clinics - Transport for Minister, Local Preacher ( to attend Church Worship in another village or town )

*Extracted from a full and detailed report (March 2004) by Revd Gilbert and Mrs Sylvia Hall which was circulated to interested parties in MCSL and the UK.*

# 2004/3 FEB: ECUMENICAL CONTACTS UK & MCSL

COOPERATION ECUMENICAL: CHURCH MISSIONARY SOCIETY & OTHERS

Revd Canon Tim Dakin,
General Secretary,
Church Mission Society,
Partnership House,
157 Waterloo Road,
LONDON SE1 8UU

Thursday, February 05, 2004

Dear Tim,

The Principal of Cliff College, Revd Howard Mellor and I met with the Archbishop of Canterbury on Tuesday this week to discuss aspects of the successor to the Springboard Project.

During our conversation Dr Williams made it clear that he was well briefed on the work that Cliff College has been doing through its International Learning Centre with churches of all denominations in Sierra Leone. He expressed a view that this exciting project provided a very positive way forward in theological education/training and he invited me to be in touch with you about CMS cooperation in developing and expanding the programme.

You may (or may not) be aware of the informal contacts that have been made already with both CMS and USPG seeking co-operation with the further development of the ILC that would particularly benefit Sierra Leone Church clergy. Certainly, Bishop Lynch from Sierra Leone has written a very positive letter in support of the project to CMS and copied our ILC Co-ordinator, Revd Richard Jackson. The enclosed report gives a fair summary of what has been achieved so far with the very limited means at our disposal.

Our hope is that with a very successful pilot project in SL behind us it will be possible to move forward ecumenically in ways and situations that reinforce our partnership with the world church. By doing in service training there in their own environment at a cost of roughly £500 per student per annum we can make much better use of the limited funds available to our churches. The spin-offs with such an approach are highlighted in the report enclosed.

It would be helpful to me as Principal Designate of Cliff College, if the Co-ordinator and I could arrange a meeting with you to explore options for the future which might reinforce the already strong links in equipping for mission that we at Cliff College have with the Anglican Church.

The co-ordinator will be returning to SL for two weeks from the 13th February. It would be good if we could meet together sometime on his return. I look forward to your reply.

Every blessing,

Yours sincerely,

Martyn Atkins (Revd Dr)
Enc.

**N.B**. Sadly, despite follow up letters and positive conversations for some months with CMS and USPG representatives, there was little practical response that might have encouraged us to continue to develop the CCILC programmes ecumenically.

# 2004/4 JUL 5-13: CCSL GRADUATIONS-GROUP 1

### (IDIAMM 2002-4 PROGRAMME)

A team which included the Cliff College Principal, Howard Mellor, the immediate Past President of the Methodist Conference (UK), Revd Dr Neil Richardson with his wife Rhiannon and the co-ordinator, Revd Richard Jackson, arrived 6 hours late in Freetown, Sierra Leone in the early hours of Tuesday morning, 6th July. Despite the late arrival we were welcomed by the President of Conference of the Methodist Church Sierra Leone, the Right Revd Francis Nabieu, the local co-ordinator, Revd Vidal Kamara-Cole, the course administrator Mr Keith Phillips and representatives of Network, the Women's Fellowship.

A full programme of public lectures and courtesy meetings with the Christian Council of Sierra Leone and other groups was adhered to over the following days. The highlight of these events was our meeting on Friday, with the President of Sierra Leone, His Excellency Alhaji Dr Tejan Kabbah at State House.

**CCITC WELCOMED BY LEADERS OF CHURCH AND STATE**

**CCSL GRADUATIONS FOR COMPLETED (2002-4) PROGRAMME**

However, the whole programme was geared into the focus of our visit which was to be the graduation of a number of students who had completed successfully the two-year diploma course which they began in 2002. Late submissions, re-submissions, marking and moderation meant that the final list of successful students was not completed until the day before the graduation.

## SATURDAY 10th JULY 2004 AT THE BRITISH COUNCIL HALL, FREETOWN, SIERRA LEONE

The day itself dawned damp, not unusual in 'rainy season' Sierra Leone, but it brightened up as the 55 students to graduate, their families and friends gathered at the British Council Hall in time for the afternoon ceremony. Apart from the visiting group, Christian Council and Methodist leaders and local tutors, special guests included the Minister of Education, the Vice Chancellor of the University, the Principal of the Theological College and Methodist Local Preacher, Dr Sama S Banya, who is a senior politician and special advisor to the President of State.

The ceremony itself followed the traditional format with a welcome, worship and introductions leading into Principal Howard Mellor's address to the students, their families and friends. As names

87

were called by the local co-ordinator, Revd Vidal Kamara-Cole, Principal Mellor presented the certificates; co-ordinator, Revd Richard Jackson draped each student with a locally made scarf in the Cliff College colours of blue and gold; Principal Kulah congratulated students individually and Keith Phillips presented them with the English translation of Achim Härtner and Holger Eschmann's book on preaching. This final book was symbolic of the £700 worth of books which thanks to 'Feed the Minds' and other donors each student had received over the two years of the course.

**THE CLIFF COLLEGE PREACHING SCARF AND MOTTOS**

The Preaching Scarf, produced in Sierra Leone for CCILC with a Cliff College badge on one side and the Sierra Leone coat of arms on the other with their respective mottos 'Christ for All: All for Christ' and 'Unity, Freedom and Justice' summed up for me the dual purpose of the course in the context of a Sierra Leone recovering from a devastating conflict. The Minister of Education, Dr Wurie paid tribute to the vision and its fulfilment. Mrs Selina Ade-Williams who gained a distinction responded on behalf of the students before the Dean of the Cathedral closed with an encouraging word followed by prayer. Refreshments were provided as countless photographs were taken of groups and individuals associated with the course.

On Sunday afternoon at a well-attended thanksgiving service in Buxton Methodist Church, Freetown, students gave testimonies and paid tribute to everyone who had been involved in the course before making presentations to the team of visiting and local lecturers.

Whilst a more complete report of the visit will appear in the Methodist Recorder under the name of Revd Dr Neil Richardson, this is a brief, but immediate response to what was for me a moving climax of three years of hard work on the part of everyone involved with the CCILC, co-ordinators, tutors, staff and students. A further 20 students with re-submissions or dissertations to complete by the 31$^{st}$ August are likely to graduate at the Theological College ceremony which I hope to attend on the 4$^{th}$ December.

A full evaluation of this successful programme and prospects for the future development of ILC will be prepared at a later date, but I hope that this report, with a couple of pictures will be received as a thank you to all of you who have in some way helped bring this programme to fruition, and also as a prompt to those who are linked with its future.

Richard Jackson (Revd)
Co-ordinator, CCILC

## 2004/5 OCT: CCILC LOGISTICS (KEITH PHILLIPS)

### WITH CCILC IN SIERRA LEONE-MR KEITH PHILLIPS-COURSE ADMINISTRATOR EXTRAORDINAIRE:-

At the request of Richard Jackson, I have made the following notes of my recent involvement with and in Sierra Leone.

**ANTECEDENTS:**

Between 1975 and 1977, I was working as a teacher at the Holy Trinity Secondary School in Kenema, Sierra Leone with the Voluntary Service Overseas programme. During this time I met both Richard Jackson, then Circuit Superintendent from the Methodist Church in Sierra Leone, and a young man (now President of the Methodist Conference), Francis Nabieu. I also enjoyed the hospitality of the Nixon Memorial Methodist Hospital in Segbwema.

**2001** A Christmas letter from Richard Jackson mentioned that he had been to S.L. and was setting up the International Learning Centre to deliver a training course for ministers and church leaders in Freetown.. We very quickly agreed that I should join the group travelling in July 2002 although the role was somewhat fluid.

**2002 FIRST VISIT:**

As I had joined the team late and with no clearly defined role, I travelled at my own expense, although in-country expenses were met by the ILC budget. My role rapidly developed to include assisting new-comers (to S.L.) to cope with the Sierra Leonean way of doing things, language, administrating the day-to-day running of the non-academic matters (changing money, sorting temporary residence permits) and assisting the in-country Co-ordinator, Revd V. Kamara-Cole, to enrol the students, to record their personal details and generally setting up the office practices. Establishing a friendly working relationship with Vidal has been most important throughout.

Problems with clearing our container, which held all of the books to be supplied to the students, tutors, etc., led to me being asked by both Richard and Rt. Revd F. Nabieu, President of the Methodist Church in Sierra Leone, to see what I could do. I was able to navigate the nightmare of bureaucracy involved and extract the container with all its contents intact, getting the very large supply of books to the Theological Hall (now College) safely and in time. This part of the work is now automatically delegated to me. I also travelled up-country with the group as far as Kailahun, taking a special interest in the Nixon Hospital. Throughout I contributed to the photographic recording of the trip with my own camera and those of others when they were in the middle of the action.

**2003 SECOND VISIT:** My role now firmly established, I again accompanied the group of lecturers, this time fully "on the strength" of the ILC. From the outset, the container (and it's two accompanying pallets) were my special responsibility, complicated by an inefficient shipping agent, a lack of papers (Bill of Lading etc. arrived late) and confusion over the two pallets which got lost on the dock. This involved resolving the problem of two National Library Board pallets, released to my Sierra Leonean counterpart in error. I also took charge of the office, local administration and logistics. This included collating and tabulating the marks for the various assignments and exams, supervising the re-registering of those students who were still on the course, calming down some local antipathies. Again, I contributed photographically. The biggest single issue was getting the course books from the docks and ready for distribution to the students.

**2004 THIRD VISIT: FEB. 2 WEEKS:**

With Richard Jackson, I travelled to and within Sierra Leone to check on progress and to prepare for the Graduation in August. We were chasing and collating marks, nagging individual tutors, and encouraging students. Preparations for the Graduation included arranging for the local production of the Preaching Scarves, the venue for the ceremony, trying to fathom the finances, etc. During the trip up-country, I was able to visit the Nixon Hospital to assess progress with rebuilding. Another reason for this visit was to investigate whether a longer stay in June/July/August would be useful or possible.

Belfast: May 36 hours: In order to make the container business more easily handled, particularly at the Sierra Leone end, I visited William Carson, of the Methodist Missionary Society (Ireland) in Lurgan, Northern Ireland and we discussed the logistics, paperwork etc.. Thanks to cheap flights, I was able to do this at my own expense.

2004 FOURTH VISIT: JUNE/JULY/AUGUST 8 WEEKS: I travelled 2 weeks in advance of the main group to press on with preparations for the graduation. As feared, there was much to do. Marking was seriously behind and local personality clashes were not helping. By being a neutral, I was able to move most things forward. With Revd Vidal Kamara-Cole, the national coordinator, I got an invitation list sorted, invitations printed and distributed, and confirmed accommodation for the rest of the group. Holding every ones' concentration on the main issues regarding the course and graduation occupied quite a lot of time, and the non-arrival of the promised container was a blessing, although trying to establish what was going on with it took some time.

I met the main group at the Hoverport. I again assisted in helping the less experienced (in terms of West Africa) members to avoid malaria, pick-pockets, paying excessively inflated prices, dealing with money-changes for them, sorting mobile phones and generally to help them get the best out of their visit. An important part of the preparation for Graduation involved working closely with Vidal to get information and with Principal, Howard Mellor to collate this, preparing lists of Graduands, grades, marks, and letters to those who had not completed all the work on time. With the immediate past President of the Methodist Church, U.K., Revd Neil Richardson included in the party, the photographic role was particularly important. Again, I travelled up-country with the group. With two Church Presidents in the party, the trip took on the aspect almost of a royal progress, which was great fun, but, due to the enthusiasm of the Sierra Leoneans, the programme was very intense and some events had to be curtailed or cancelled. Some informal diplomacy was called for. During this trip, I was able to see progress at the Nixon Hospital and identify at least one major project for the second part of my visit, after the ILC group had left.

The second month of my visit was working with the MCSL, rather than CCILC although some further interaction with Vidal occurred continuing to collect marks and looking forward to the later graduation in December 2004, including planning for the production of additional Preaching Scarves. My container ministry was continued with sorting a container that had been abandoned in Kenema the previous March en route for the Nixon Hospital. As usual, my mixture of local knowledge, diplomacy and tenacity saw the contents safely delivered, although the container remained (and still does–Oct. '04) in Kenema. I also arranged two other lorry-loads from Freetown to the hospital.

**2004 FIFTH VISIT: SEPT/OCT. 2 WEEKS:** At the instigation and on the budget of the Methodist Missionary Society (Ireland), I flew over again to sort the container that should have arrived during July/August but didn't leave Ireland until the end of August. Particularly I was to ensure the safe delivery of medical supplies to the Nixon Hospital. I also spent a little time with Vidal Kamara-Cole recording marks and planning for the December graduation. This included delivering and unpacking (but not setting up – no power until the generator I also delivered is installed) a computer system for the ILC office in Freetown. I collected some information on the ILC finances but ran out of time so was not able to take things further.

**U.K. INVOLVEMENTS:**

I have used my time and skills to share the administrative responsibilities related to the programme *(See Appendix 7A)*.

*And next I am going to ............?......................*

Keith Phillips          20th Oct. 2004

*Coordinator's Note: Every programme needs a Keith Phillips, as part of the 'Core Team'. He oils the wheels of the organisation in so many practical ways, that it would embarrass him to list them here.*

## 2004/6 DEC 4: CCSL GRADUATIONS-GROUP 2

(IDIAMM 2002-04 PROGRAMME)

On the 4th December, Revd Richard Jackson, his wife Carole and Prof Andrew Walls (on a private university visit) were the special guests at the Theological College Annual Graduation ceremony in Freetown when a further 18 of our ILC students with re-submissions or dissertations which they had completed by the 31st August graduated. For me this second ILC occasion shared with the local college students was a moving climax and the fulfilment of a vision received in 2001 for doing a training programme for large numbers of ministers and church leaders in post war Sierra Leone. 73 of the 99 students who began the course completed successfully. They and even those students who did not complete were each resourced with books and teaching that will continue to enrich their ministry in the years that lie ahead.

This December event was the culmination of three years of hard work on the part of everyone involved with the Cliff College International Learning Centre: co-ordinators; tutors; staff and students. We are grateful to our sponsors in the UK, MMS Ireland and both the Methodist Church and EMW Germany whose funding helped bring this pioneering pilot project to a successful completion. This project has proved that 'doing it there' is practically possible and financially viable. It has prepared the way for new partnerships in mission training that should prompt donor churches/organisations to look first at funding the training of people 'there' in their own culture and context with all the attendant benefits described in earlier reports and evaluations. It is my view that only where it is impossible to provide the level of training required locally or on the same continent should scholarships be provided for further education/training to be provided in the west with our inflated costs and attendant problems for students and their churches.

A full evaluation of this successful pilot programme would need to be researched on the ground in Sierra Leone to determine the local impact of the training given. In the meantime we take heart from the comments of many observers in Sierra Leone about the improvement in the standards of preaching and changing attitudes towards leadership in both community and church. Enquiries are being received from other countries/churches as to how the principles tested out in this programme can be adopted and adapted for training schemes to be undertaken elsewhere. I hope that this report will encourage all of us who share in partnerships with a world church to look again at how best we become involved with our brothers and sisters in doing as much training as possible alongside them in their own culture and context.

EXODUS 9:12-17 A COVENANT PROMISE THAT WILL BE KEPT

**Richard Jackson (Revd):**
**18<sup>th</sup> January 2005**

# CHAPTER 5 2005: SL, NIGERIA & CUBA

*During 2005, we began to cope with the spontaneous expansion of the work associated with what was seen as a very successful pilot project. A new two-year programme undertaken for much smaller numbers could not be justified in Sierra Leone, but an associated programme of further vocational training with Local Preachers, Lay leaders and Women Workers was undertaken by Revd & Mrs Gilbert Hall. In addition, CCILC responded to a request for: further training in 'Administration' for ministers of the Methodist Church in Sierra Leone by seeking funding for a programme planned to begin in 2006. In October the International Coordinator visited Nigeria at the invitation of the Methodist Church there, to explore with them how the two-year programme might be adapted to give further training to their evangelists and ministers as their church began to re-orientate in relation to evangelism and mission. This was followed in November by some Pastor related training undertaken with the Cuban Methodist Church. There was strong encouragement to contribute an article, but little response received from a report published in the South African Baptist Journal of Theology (pp262-9: Vol. 14 2005) outlining the successful pilot programme in Sierra Leone.*

## 2005/1 OCT: METHODIST CHURCH NIGERIA (MCN)

At the invitation of His Eminence Sunday Mbang and the Methodist Church Nigeria (MCN) the CCILC co-ordinator visited

HIS EMINENCE SUNDAY MBANG AND LEADERS
AT TINUBU METHODIST CHURCH, LAGOS

Nigeria and two Methodist colleges at Sagamu, near Lagos and Umuahia in the east for exploratory talks from the 3$^{rd}$ to 10$^{th}$ October 2005. The Very Revd Okon Ekerendu, the local organiser was hospitality personified.

Archbishop Ayo Ladigbolu and the Rectors (Principals) of the two colleges led us in meetings that discussed the focus and means by which we might implement a training course to be developed in Nigeria.

These discussions held with church and college authorities shaped our thinking about a proposed course basically on the lines of the course in Sierra Leone, but with a special emphasis on training 'evangelism trainers' as the church re-positions itself with a fresh focus on mission.

### 2006-08 PILOT NIGERIA

Subject to funding being made available, it was agreed that we would begin a rolling programme of training beginning with residentials for up to 100 students at each of the two centres:

for Year 1 from the 5-20 July 2006 and 8-12 January 2007
with Year 2 from July 4-19 2007 and January 7-11 2008.

At this early stage the suggested programme includes modules on:

Year 1
Study & Research Skills;
Adult Learning and Training Evangelists;
Mission in the Old Testament;
Evangelism in the New Testament;
Encounter with other Religions

Year 2
Applied Ministry (incl. Pastoral);
Worship & Preaching;
Christian Spirituality;
Church Growth in Church History (including Methodism);
Applied Evangelism.

It was agreed that we should incorporate in the IDIAMM programme of training a requirement upon the students (mainly ministers) that they should be training evangelists in their local situation throughout the two year course. Their success (or otherwise)

96

with this will be assessed along with a research project as part of the overall course.

The Nigerian Methodist Church have promised to fund the accommodation and feeding of visiting lecturers. Local lecturers (as with Sierra Leone) in each centre will partner the visiting team and provide student supervision/support between the 'residentials'.

**A draft budget based on previous experience includes x 2 for the two years:**

Travel & expenses for a team of six people running the residentials in July 2005 & 2006                      £6,000 x 2= £12,000
Travel & expenses for co-ordinator plus one running short residentials in Jan 2007 & 2008                      £2,000 x 2= £  4,000
Course Books and materials (for 200 students-hopeful of Feed the Minds grant etc.)                      £8,000 x 2= £16,000
Cliff College Administration and member(s) of staff
                      £4,000 x 2= £  8,000
Contingencies & Local Costs (incl. honorariums for local staff markers/supervisors)                      £5,000 x 2= £10,000
**Total cost for two year course for two hundred students in two centres                      £25,000 x 2= £50,000**

Primary funding of £20,000 per annum has been approved through the Scholarship And Leadership Training (SALT) Committee of the World Church Office of the Methodist Church in Britain.

LOOKING TO THE FUTURE (DOING TRAINING THERE IN PARTNERSHIP WITH THEM)

The CCILC concept of 'Doing training there' in partnership with the local church(es) is proving itself economically viable, practically possible and adaptable to differing situations and circumstances. The concept has limitations, but mainly these are associated with administrative and logistical support; finance and resources.

Whilst this programme has been developed through Cliff College with the larger part of the funding being provided by the Methodist Church, our hope is that at a time when funding/resources support through the 'western church' is diminishing, there will be a general recognition on the part of all churches (and former missionary societies) that 'Doing it there' in partnership, with all of its associated benefits for all parties concerned, is a worthwhile investment for the future of the church worldwide.

As more of our partner churches in different parts of the world express an interest in our programme(s) we shall be pleased to share whatever expertise we have gained with others who have developed or are developing similar programmes.

At the same time, we want to say thank you to those sponsors who have been supportive of the original vision, even when the outcome was uncertain. That early vision has matured into a fully-fledged programme. We would welcome further donations from individuals or organisations who wish to support the kind of work that we are doing through the Cliff College International Learning Centre.

With some adaptation influenced by needs, country, context and sponsors the draft principles outlined earlier that guided us from the outset with our pilot programme in Sierra Leone will continue to provide guidelines for the work of the Centre, as we seek under the direction of the Holy Spirit, to respond to requests to establish similar programmes in different parts of the world.

**THE PROPOSED TRAINING CENTRES FOR MCN 'RESIDENTIALS'**

**IN THE WEST: SAGAMU MTI**          **IN THE EAST: UMUAHIA MTI**

# 2005/2 NOV 6-17: CUBAN METHODIST HIGHLIGHTS

LEARNING WITH CUBAN METHODISM: TRAINING IN CUBA WITH (EDITED) OBSERVATIONS SHARED BY DOUGLAS PARKER (OUR ADMINISTRATION & RESOURCES PARTNER ON THIS VISIT)

Following on from the fraternal visit of the Newcastle upon Tyne District Chair to Cuba in the autumn of 2004, conversations were taking place between the leaders of the Methodist Church Cuba (MCC) and the British Methodist Church about strengthening links with what is still seen as the Mother Church of Methodism. One outcome of these conversations was that Cliff College represented by the Coordinator of the CCITC, Revd Richard Jackson and its Director, Revd Dr Martyn Atkins were invited to visit Cuba and to contribute from a British Methodism perspective to the, FACULTAD LATINO AMERICANA DE ESTUDIOS TEOLOGICOS (Florida based-FLET) training programme for pastors of the Cuban Methodist Church.

Some information was gleaned through correspondence, which helped us to prepare for a church, traditionally Methodist, in its opposition to such frivolous activities as dancing, (even Cuban style); drinking alcohol, (especially rum); and smoking (of world-famous cigars), but which is growing in numbers and in maturity of mission activity. In advance of the visit we were pleased to learn more of the history of the Methodist Church in Cuba from their (2005) web-site *(see Appendix 9)* and from those whose reports of visits challenged our own thinking about the (USA influenced view of Cuban society) and the Methodist Church there. Pump-priming funding of £7,000 provided through the SALT Committee of the Methodist Church (Britain) allowed a response to be made to a request from Bishop Ricardo Pereira and the 'Iglesia Metodista en Cuba' for us to share in their November 2005 training programme for pastors and to explore with them possibilities for future co-operation.

**IGLESIA METODISTA EN CUBA HQ**

The Principal of Cliff College, Revd Dr Martyn Atkins, the International Coordinator, Revd Richard Jackson and Mr Douglas Parker, IT, Administration &

99

Resources, followed a planned itinerary in Cuba from Nov 6-17 2005. At the Pastors' training programme in Camp Canaan, near Santa Clara, the Principal delivered lectures on homiletics, the co-ordinator tackled issues relating to ministry and seminars on the use of computers and Methodism were made available. An albeit brief contact with Bob Simons, the Interim Academic Dean of the Facultad Latinoamericana De Estudios Teologicos (FLET), who is doing PhD work on the New Testament at Bristol University provided an introduction to their training programme into which our teaching was being incorporated and hinted at possible areas for future co-operation between Cliff College and FLET. Excellent hospitality was provided throughout the visit and opportunity was given for us to have an overview of the variety of work, and to share in the worship and training being offered by this charismatic and growing church.

**GRACE IN WORSHIP DANCE**

Growth of 10% per annum is expected; young enthusiastic prospective pastors prove their calling (before undergoing largely in-service training) by planting missions/house churches; evangelists work alongside pastors, creating in every church/community an orientation towards evangelism with an expectation of conversions; and worship with Cuban music and songs, dance, drama and puppets involves the whole congregation of every age-group. With dedicated leadership at all levels, vibrant younger people providing the larger proportion of most congregations and a clear expectation that the Holy Spirit will continue to work powerfully the present church is stimulating and future prospects with large numbers of pastors to be trained exciting.

Discussions took place with the Bishop, national & local church leaders, professors (lecturers) linked with the Matanzas Theological Seminary (Ecumenical) as well as with those people responsible for training at all levels in the Methodist Church of Cuba. At the request of Bishop Ricardo we will be looking into possible ways of sharing in partnership with others for the future training programme of the church in Cuba. In the meantime the visits by the Revd Tom Quenet, WCO Area Secretary in December and Revd Tom

Stuckey, President of the Methodist Conference in Britain during January 2006 will serve to build upon the developing relationship between the British and Cuban Methodist churches. A further training visit by the CCILC planned for 2006 was postponed in the light of local developments with training programmes. With continuing contact it is anticipated that all parties will be in a position to co-operate together in planning a programme that will help meet the current needs of the Methodist Church in Cuba in a way that takes into account its 'cultural' context.

**BISHOP RICARDO PERIERA ACCEPTING**
**'CLIFF IS MORE THAN A COLLEGE'**

Being welcomed on arrival at the airport as friends and VIP's set the tone for the whole of our visit. At a Monday morning meeting with the leader of the church Methodist Bishop, Ricardo Pereira, courtesies were exchanged. The Bishop introduced us in a more personal way to the (his)-story of the Methodist in Cuba and we talked together about their vision for mission and the current training programmes. In the 1960's, following the Revolution, 80% of the traditional leadership of the Methodist Church left the country. In 1962-3 there were only two ordained ministers. Too little significance is generally attached to this exodus of the respected, but conservative middle-class leadership as paving the way for renewal and growth. The 'Thinking outside the box' promoted by Edward De Bono encourages us to do more than switch off the TV and think our own fresh and exciting thoughts! The Cuban Exodus allowed the new and non-traditional leadership of the church to think outside the traditional box and re-define the church's approach to ministry and worship in ways that have led to a re-discovery of the priority of the 'Mission Dei'. Release from patterns of the past has paved the way to renewal in the Cuban Methodist Church.

In the best of Methodist traditions pioneered by John Wesley, the church is a pragmatic movement, making the most of its opportunities. Whilst they recognise the need for seminary trained theologians their priorities are determined by the need to train good pastors with a heart for mission in and through the local church.

Their policy, following lessons learned from growing churches elsewhere is to encourage those who feel called to the ministry to plant a Church before training is given. Much of the training then given is at residentials (shared with spouses) two or three times a year backed up by distance learning. There are planned timescales for longer-term development through the ecumenical seminary at Matanzas, but numbers trained there are limited by affordability. The church has taken the Seminary curriculum and adapted it for Lay Preachers.

**(1958) RECENTLY RESTORED:CHRIST OF HAVANA**

The system in a Castro-led Cuba is not the same as that in China, but there are sensitivities to be observed by both church and state. Those sensitivities can lead to misunderstandings on both sides and local or national clampdowns or legislation may follow. Much of the growth in membership takes place where the church has no official church building and door to door missions are encouraged in association with business meetings at all levels (including the national!) of the church.

## JOURNEYING IN CUBA

It was noticeable as we travelled that hitchhikers were part of the 'socialist scenery', some waving money indicating that they were prepared to pay, but even without the money there was an expectation that transport would be shared. The journey to Santa Clara and the nearby training centre of Camp Canaan took three and a half hours for 150-200 miles.

## MONDAY NOVEMBER 7 TO 11: CAMP CANAAN TRAINING CENTRE

The hotel in which we were hosted at Santa Clara (where the Cuban Methodist Camp Canaan Training Centre is located) was tourist standard with a swimming pool and self-contained thatched huts as accommodation.

Regular meals were eaten together with the 100 plus pastors in training at Camp Canaan. Worship was lively! Long prayers, said individually during which the congregation were interjecting their affirmation would get faster and faster, and louder and louder. The musicians look and sound like professionals. The sermon was performed, yes performed, without a single note! A visit to the Che Guevara monument was a reminder of the turbulent history of Cuba, much of it associated with the Revolution. We led lectures, seminars and worship throughout the day from Tuesday to Thursday before our Friday return to Havana and being housed by the Cuban Church on the executive floor of 'The Riviera', a five star hotel.

### CUBAN CHURCH VISITS (FLEXIBILITY WITH LESSONS ABOUT MISSION)

We were taken to visit house churches on several days: the first at Mayorkin, which consisted of a number of what looked like wooden huts and the odd breezeblock building. The first church blew down in Hurricane Charlie, so they built a new, slightly bigger one. Polystyrene partitions are placed in the church. It appears that all new buildings need to be registered in the name of an individual because the church cannot hold public property. Therefore, the re-built slightly larger building is registered in the name of the Pastor. The large polystyrene partitions serve to divide the larger meeting room for the church up into the "rooms" of a normal home. Despite the pretty basic conditions and obviously poor congregation, there was a lovely front garden at this house church.

Everywhere, even in the very small rooms of house churches there are large PA systems and microphones. When asked why, they reminded us, **"We are Cubans, and we like loud music".**

**LOUD MUSIC AND LIVELY WORSHIP**

The Mariel House Church is led by Pastor Enrique, who was at Camp Canaan. A simple little church with a newly laid path, and a brand new "cafeteria", put up in a week in order to serve drinks at the end of service. Again, as in other cases, the land had been donated by people who then lived behind the church building. As elsewhere, there was a faith band and a PA system. The band had a bongo player and worship was supported by a choir. The worship leader, a lady in a bright blue dress took the microphone and livened up the congregational singing.

### LA EURPA

Again, the Pastor here was another attendee from Camp Canaan. This church has three associated missions – meaning that they are church plants outside the township limits. It also had five "house churches" with groups meeting in houses of the members of the congregation in the immediate vicinity. It appears that these additional groups occur both by accident and by design. We were taken through a building under construction before meeting for worship on a covered veranda which had pews. This time there was no music group as such but a tape player linked with a PA system maintained the accustomed sound levels. As to be expected, the choir fired up.

### PASTOR LOURDES CHURCH

This was a large old Church (Chandler College) led by Pastor Lourdes. A membership of 40 people has increased to 300 in the past four years. Again the band was of professional standard with drums, bass, lead guitars and a keyboard player. Four or five the worship leaders functioned as a choir. At the end of the service the church provided Sunday school for all age-groups. Their procedure for dealing with newcomers: they are visited the next day following the service; first 3 months in a new convert Sunday school class; 3 months 2nd stage-membership preparation + baptism, in the pool outside, by total immersion.

NO 'NEW' CHURCH BUILDINGS BUT..

104

We were greeted by Antonio Gonzales who was the Superintendent and pastor for the church. He had 17 missions and 3 new churches with 3 full time Pastors. The Church was on a building site. It was explained quite matter-of-factly that the original church was over 100 years old and it was decided they needed a new building, so they moved and 5 months later the old building fell down in a hurricane.

Whilst we had been invited to share in developing relations with the Methodist Church in Cuba, none of us could have imagined the impact that their sharing with us might make upon our own ministry and subsequently upon the development of the CCITC concept.

**"IT HAS BEEN GOOD TO BE WITH YOU AND TO LEARN FROM YOU."**

Space and personal/political sensitivities limit what can be shared through these edited highlights of our visit. Despite the limited progress since made in this particular partnership, it will become clear that our view of so much of what the Methodist Church in Cuba has achieved is a positive contribution to a world-wide 'missionary Methodism' for the 21st Century and has stimulated our own presentations as to the possibilities open to the churches of West Africa. For that we can only express our appreciation for the hospitality received and the lessons learned.

# 2005/3 NOV: CCSL PILOT POSTSCRIPT

## PLANS FOR PROGRESS IN THE FUTURE (NOV 2005)

Cliff College is a Methodist institution with an evangelical and mission ethos. It has a proud history of giving training to Christian lay-people of all denominations from many parts of the world for over 100 years. More recently it has become a chosen centre for the further training of both ministers and lay people through its pioneering and popular distance learning courses validated by Manchester University and offered from Diploma through to Masters Level. Learning and reflection linked with praxis has become the hallmark of these part taught (during residential weeks), part self-study (reading and assignments) and part research (mission oriented dissertations) courses which are usually completed over two-years.

The College made good use of its historic tradition, academic expertise and practical experience in training for mission when in response to the post-conflict needs of the churches in Sierra Leone we established the CCILC in 2001. At the invitation of, and in partnership with, the Christian Council of Sierra Leone (CCSL) the College ran a very successful pilot programme at the ecumenical Theological College in Freetown. This resulted in 73 of the 99 students who began the course in 2002 completing and being awarded by Cliff College an International Diploma in Applied Ministry and Mission (IDIAMM) in 2004.

Major funding for the course (approximating to the cost of providing two scholarships for students to study in Britain for each year) was provided from the general Fund for World Mission (FWM) by the World Church Office of the Methodist Church in Britain but the project also attracted additional support from a variety of sponsors. This meant that over the two years of the course in Sierra Leone all of the students, including those who were not successful, were resourced with books (retailing at £700 for each student) and received contextual teaching (from a partnership of local and international lecturers) that will continue to enrich their ministry in the years that lie ahead.

### PILOT PROJECT AND EXPANSION

A positive evaluation of the two-year pilot project in Sierra Leone and circulated reports has prompted further requests for similar programmes elsewhere and this report summarises the subsequent expansion and adaptation of the CCILC programme.

### FURTHER TRAINING IN SIERRA LEONE

At the request of the Methodist Church in Sierra Leone (MCSL) the focus of a new course beginning in March 2006 will be 'Administration for Ministry'. Initially this training will be undertaken with two groups of people and will be completed with a second phase later in the year/early 2007.

The course delivered by local and visiting trainers will include one week of administrative and practical training for ministers of the church and a second week will be devoted to training personnel in the Conference Office along with administrators of church development and other programmes. In association with this new ILC programme there will be a continuation of the training programme for local preachers and women workers in Sierra Leone which has been provided for the last two years by Revd Gilbert and Mrs Sylvia Hall.

Basic funding for this training provided by the Fund for World Mission (FWM) of the Methodist Church (Britain)

# CHAPTER 6 2006: SIERRA LEONE PLUS NIGERIA

*During 2006, the CCILC continued with further training in Administration, alongside the lay leadership training, being given in Sierra Leone. In addition after preparatory conversations undertaken in October 2005, we began a new revised two-year IDIAMM training programme with the Methodist Church in Nigeria. In July, 82 students were enrolled at Umuahia MTI and 57 at Sagamu MTI in Nigeria, 139 students in all.*

## 2006/1 MAR: MCSL ADMIN COURSE PART 1
MARCH: 2006 (3rd-20th)

**Visit 1** by the core training team utilised Revd Gilbert & Mrs Sylvia Hall; Mr Keith Phillips, Administrator; and Revd Richard Jackson, Coordinator.

On the successful completion of the pioneering 'Doing it There in Partnership' programme which gave the opportunity for up to 100 ministers and lay leaders of all denominations in Sierra Leone to complete a two-year training course leading to an International Diploma In Applied Ministry and Mission (IDIAMM), we were asked to continue our work with the Methodist Church Sierra Leone (MCSL) by providing some training in Leadership and Administration.

INTRODUCTION

Once again the primary funding of £20,000 was provided through the World Church Office of the Methodist Church in the UK. In consultation with the MCSL the ILC prepared an outline programme and planned for three training visits to be undertaken in March 2006; October 2006; and February 2007. In keeping with its well-earned reputation for flexibility, experimentation and innovation, the CCILC incorporated within its programme and budget the ongoing work of training Local Preachers and Women Leaders in Sierra Leone already being done by Revd Gilbert & Mrs Sylvia Hall. The new core team agreed with the MCSL that the main focus of our new programme should be threefold: To continue the work being done with Local Preachers and Women Workers, whilst training 'trainers' to maintain the work locally.

To build on the work done through the IDIAMM course with Ministers and Lay Leaders, with a specific focus on training in Leadership and Administration.

To rationalise and improve the conditions and workings of the Conference Office and associated staff in accordance with Methodist practice; and to incorporate a burgeoning 'development department' along with the long-standing Conference Institutions into a workable and working structure.

To this end, we acknowledged the need for a general and fairly basic training course, which we based on what is taught in NVQ level 2 courses on administration. Along with this we sought to balance traditionally autocratic forms of leadership with an exploration of differing styles, but with a particular emphasis on 'Parallel Thinking' pioneered by Edward De Bono and encapsulated in what has become known as 'Six Thinking Hats', but with our permitted adaptation for the African context has become 'Six Thinking Caps'. In addition we have worked together with the President and Secretary of Conference and their staff in the Conference Office to improve both the conditions and working practice within the limitations of the current environment and local budgets.

### THE PROVINCIAL DISTRICTS IN KENEMA

Late, and as it transpired, right decisions gave an early and much needed freedom for open sharing. On arrival we agreed to deliver separate training courses for ministers in the two Provincial Districts for three days in Kenema, followed by a course in Freetown for ministers of the Western District. Due to some confusion in communication as to whether the courses were for all ministers or just Superintendent Ministers there were only six Bo/Kenema District ministers and nine Kailahun/Kono District ministers including Chairmen of Districts in attendance at Kenema. The Western District attendance (with more time to prepare) included the President and Secretary of Conference and the District Chair and numbered twenty seven ministers. The same basic training in Leadership and

Administration was delivered at both centres with interspaced devotional sessions and teaching about Methodism which concentrated on the theme of developing good relationships through better understanding.

A particularly effective session which became a model for use in our October 06 further training invited the Chairmen of Districts to share something of their personal experience in that particular role. Having contributed to the Kenema ministerial training, Revd & Mrs Hall, followed up their 2002 training of Local Preachers and Women Leaders holding two-day courses for 15 LP's and 8 WL's in Kenema; 23 LP's and 8 WL's in Segbwema; 31 LP's and 9 WL's in Freetown.

**THE WESTERN DISTRICT IN FREETOWN & CONFERENCE OFFICE**

On completion of the ministerial training programme Keith Phillips and Richard Jackson spent the next week with the Conference Office staff in Freetown giving much of the same basic training, but adapting it for staff working together much of the time, recognising that most were full-time office workers. Mornings were used largely for general lecture/seminar input and the afternoons for working one to one and with teams of office staff in their working environment. Conversations were aimed at discovering concerns and promoting better understanding through reviewing job descriptions whilst encouraging staff to take personal responsibility where possible for improving their own working conditions.

IF ONLY!

In the event, the visit went much as expected, rather than as planned! Fortunately, the visit was viewed as foundational with time given in all settings to creating and cementing relationships with individuals that would make for future cooperation as the programme developed. It was during this visit that Keith Phillips was given time to 'loiter with intent' in the Conference Office and provide the observations outlined here which provided some direction for later in the three-part programme.

# REVIEW
## MCSL ADMINISTRATION: CONFERENCE OFFICE

Issues arising from March 2006 training visit to the Conference Office of MCSL and ideas to follow-up in Parts 2 & 3

**Noise:** At both Offices, the use of very noisy generators seriously affects the effectiveness of the staff and visitors.

**Heat:** Air conditioning is available in a few offices (generally those of the senior staff). Fans (not always functional, due to power and/or repair problems) are available in some of the other offices but can disrupt work by blowing papers about. Otherwise, there is nothing; the heat is debilitating and sweaty hands do not help with paperwork and handling money.

**Safety at work** – I didn't find any evidence of any statutory requirements regarding the employer's responsibility for the safety of staff in general. Specific issues:

Fire procedures and precautions : nothing organised.
Fire evacuation procedures – nil
Fire extinguishers and their use – nil

VDU operators – no understanding of the issues
(seating position/posture, repetitive stress, eye strain etc.)

Control of access to the building; recording of visitors; rights of admission vs. security from intruders; security of personal property.

MANAGEMENT, SUPERVISION, JOB DESCRIPTIONS, DISCIPLINE

There are issues that involve all four of the above (which are closely inter-related, of course). For example, it is unfair to criticise a person's work if their manager has not provided a clear definition of the work required. This should be summarised in the Job Description, which then forms the basis of Supervision and, when appropriate, Discipline.

Such Job descriptions as were available were not universally up-to-date; the job had "moved on" but the Job Description (usually attached to the Letter of Appointment) had not. In one case, the original job no longer existed so the job description was entirely redundant and no new guidance had been given. The employee is much criticised by his peers and by management for not doing his job, but no-one seems to know what his job is, certainly not he, himself!).

The way forward must follow some path along the line, as follows:

Management needs to have a clear idea of the purpose of the organisation and the work that needs to be undertaken to achieve this purpose. This work must be divided in to "jobs", each with a job description. Now a staff structure can be agreed that will place appropriate personnel in each of these jobs, with suitable lines of responsibility.

Line managers supervise the work of individuals, using the job description as a tool/starting point. Strengths and weaknesses should be identified. The former might be indicators for promotion or of an ability to train and support other workers. Weaknesses identify potential areas for either training, discipline or redrawing job descriptions (tasks might be exchanged between staff job descriptions to maximise on strengths). Line Managers can only do this when they also have a clear idea of the employee's job, of course. Job descriptions may need up-dating as roles develop. The closure/completion of a project that figures on an employee's job description would create a void that good management would wish to address.

There should be a clear and universally understood disciplinary procedure and staff should feel confident that it is fair, effective and used (and only used) when appropriate. The first action by a manager is to ensure that the employee knows, is capable of and has the facilities to do the job, not to consider sacking that individual.

My impression of all the staff that I spoke with on a one-to-one basis (and I spoke with very nearly all) was that they were keen to do a full day's work for a full day's pay (paid on time, of course!); they

112

were engaged in the organisation and several had aspirations to advance within it. They were keen that others who they saw not working effectively should not get away with it! They didn't want to carry passengers.

Corridor Offices – some offices are only or routinely accessed through other offices. It is common practice for a manager's office to be accessed through that of his/her secretary/P.A. and there are good reasons for this. However, it is less satisfactory for other staff trying to work, sometimes in confidential discussions, in what is effectively a corridor. An example is the office shared by the Project Engineer and Project Officer which is, at the same time, the access corridor to the office of the Assistant Development Secretary.

### RECEPTION, SECURITY AND SAFETY

## Receptionist

I was interested in the role (and therefore Job Description) of the Receptionist. Firstly, there are two, one for the Conference Office and one for the development Office. If the Wesley Street Office staff move back to George Street, a decision will have to be made as to whether two receptionists are needed. If so, how their jobs descriptions are worded to make clear to them and others what their respective jobs are and how they differ; and if only one is needed, what is to be done about that! Both post-holders seem competent, keen and ambitious! Aside from that issue, it seemed to me that the role of receptionist could encompass some functions that are currently either missing or scattered, effectively or not, among other staff. These functions could include some or all of the following tasks:

## Security

In terms of security, efficiency and safety, the organisation should know and record who is in the building at any time; who is visiting and for what purpose; where staff are when out of the building and when they should return; perhaps how to contact them while they are absent. The receptionist is the obvious person to maintain these records.

Visitors should only be admitted if they have a good reason to be! This is fairly obvious but casual visitors can and do waste a lot of time. Should visitors be issued with a badge so others will know that they are legitimately in the building? If so, the receptionist, as the first contact, would seem to be the obvious person to manage this. No-one, regardless their perceived or actual importance, should enter the building without the Receptionist's knowledge and approval.

**Fire Safety**

There seem to be no Fire Regulations incumbent on offices in Sierra Leone. This does not stop (or excuse) MCSL from having its own rules. Of the staff I spoke to, only one said that, in the event of a fire, she would leave the building quickly! Obviously, evacuation of the building would ensure the safety of staff (first priority). However, there is also a need to advertise the event so that all staff realise the situation at as early a moment as possible; but then it is vital to establish that everyone is out and safe (or not, and therefore needing rescue). MCLS should develop procedures for this as a matter of urgency. Part of this would probably be the maintenance of a register of who is in the building; the most appropriate person to do this might well be the Receptionist. Part of the current role of the Receptionist is to receive and distribute mail and telephone calls. Should this extend to e-mails?

**Induction**

I asked various staff about Induction. Those that recalled their first day did not recall any organised induction process. To get the best out of new staff at as early a time as possible, they need to be helped to fit it and find their way about. Some of this induction could be given by the Receptionist (e.g. where the W.C. is; who do you ask to help when your light bulb fails, "what is that person's name – I've been told 3 times but I keep forgetting and it is embarrassing to keep asking her!"; who would have some spare staples for my office? Who do I call if I am sick and cannot get to work?

TRANSPORT AND ITS USE

I spent a little time reviewing the situation regarding heavy transport with the MCSL leadership. Obviously, expectations in the working environment of Sierra Leone and in the MCSL Conference Office differ from elsewhere, but our hope is that along with the training and equipping at the heart of this programme, those responsible will take a fresh look at this and many other aspects of conditions and working practices.

# 2006/2 JUL 3-21: MCN FIRST 'RESIDENTIAL'

(IDIAMM 2006-08 PROGRAMME)

## INVITATION

The original invitation for the CCILC to extend its work to Nigeria came from the Head of the Methodist Church Nigeria (MCN) His Eminence Sunday Mbang in a letter dated November 1 2004. The Prelate had heard about the successful programme that had been undertaken in Sierra Leone and invited us to be involved in a similar partnership programme for a country of about 140 million people which is geographically one and a half times the size of France and with churches that are some of the largest numerically in the world. The invitation was linked with the comment, "Recently our Conference approved repositioning Methodist Church Nigeria for the $21^{st}$ Century and evangelism was put as the key to achieving this dream."

The MCN appointed the Very Revd Okon Ekerendu as the National Coordinator to liaise with the International Coordinator of the CCILC, Revd Richard Jackson. Regular correspondence between all the parties involved led into a preparatory visit by Revd Jackson in October 2005. During this visit key people, including the Rectors (Principals) of the two proposed college centres, Sagamu, just north of Lagos and Umuahia in the south-east (between Enugu and Port Harcourt) contributed to what became the outline plans for a large number of students to be recruited and given training from July 2006. This training, as with the Sierra Leone programme, will lead after two years to the award of an International Diploma in Applied Ministry and Mission (IDIAMM). It was agreed that the orientation for the programme should be "Applied" and "Mission/Evangelism".

By Easter 2006, it was clear that a sufficient number of students had been enrolled to make the course viable. With the continuing support and encouragement of the World Church Office of the Methodist Church in the UK and positive soundings from earlier sponsors Feed the Minds/SPCK and the Methodist Church in Ireland, plans were put in place to launch the two-year programme with a two week residential beginning in July 2006. Lecturers (some already on stand-by!) were recruited, visas applied for and flights were booked for the visiting team to travel to Lagos with KLM via Amsterdam (where we all met up for the first time) on the 3rd July. Fortunately, the KLM luggage allowance is generous, because all of the lecturers were asked to carry their 10 lectures on their topic already printed out for up to 140 students plus local staff. Past experience has taught us that very few tropical destinations can cope with mass photocopying done to time and order in what is the rainy season there.

**THE VISITING TEAM WHO WERE PARTNERED WITH MEMBERS OF THE NIGERIAN STAFF TEAMS AT SAGAMU & UMUAHIA WAS MADE UP OF:**

Major Nicola Garnham MA BSc:- Salvation Army Officer and former lecturer at William Booth Salvation Army College in London

Mrs Audrey Hensman MA:- Methodist Local Preacher, Graduate with Distinction of the CC MA in Evangelism Studies Course and former Social Worker

Revd Richard Jackson MA BD:- International Coordinator of CCILC, Methodist Minister and former Postgraduate Tutor at Cliff College

Revd Dr Malcolm McCall MA :- Methodist Minister in the Shetland Isles, former teacher in Africa and Royal Navy Chaplain

Mrs Janet McCall BA (Hons):- Methodist Local Preacher, Former teacher in Africa with French and other language skills

Mr Keith Phillips CQSW:-Anglican, former VSO in Sierra Leone and Social Worker with Child Care expertise. CCILC Logistics and administration

*and for the first time with CCILC a, 'from Africa to Africa lecturer':*

Revd Albert Beah, MA, BA:- Secretary of Conference to the Methodist Church Sierra Leone with particular expertise in Community Development and mission.

**THE NIGERIAN STAFF PARTNERS AT SAGAMU MTI**

Very Revd J Sunday Aluko, M. Ed.          Rector
Very Revd Sanmi A Osanyingbe, B.A. Ed.   Lecturer
Very Revd Benjamin E Acham, B.A.          Registrar,
Revd Honore M Sewakpo, M.A.               Chaplain
Revd Olugbemiro O Berekiah, M.A.          Lecturer

Deaconess Nancy Kennedy Johnson, BA     Warden
Miss Eze Patience,                      Librarian

**THE NIGERIAN STAFF PARTNERS AT UMUAHIA MTI**

Very Revd Dr Chikwendu O Igwe BA (Hons), MA,     Rector:

Very Revd S O Eze, BA (Hons), Registrar, MA in New Testament (pending)
Very Revd A E Okpo, BA (Hons), Lecturer, MA in Church History (pending)
Very Revd E Oji, BA (Hons), MA,   Lecturer
Very Revd N U Chukwu, BSc,         Lecturer Management
Very Revd I K Tasie, BA (Hons),    Chaplain, MA in Christian Ethics (pending)
Revd H K Anozie, B Ed (Hons), MA Lecturer
Revd Emmanuel Akpan, B Ed, MEd Lecturer

**STUDENT ENROLMENT (AT UMUAHIA)**

The final figures for enrolment at Sagamu, near Lagos are 57 students of whom 7 are female.

At Umuahia, 82 students are enrolled of whom ten are female.

All students registered are linked with the Methodist Church. There were fewer college graduates and more practising evangelists than anticipated, but all worked studiously and enthusiastically throughout the two weeks. As planned the visiting team was divided into two with one group involved for the first week in the training at Sagamu and for the second week at Umuahia. The second group began at Umuahia and then moved on to Sagamu. We managed to compare notes briefly at Owerri airport on the mid-course changeover day. Spasmodic connections through the mobile phone network made it possible to have both groups working in tandem. Both students and staff were guided overall by the Course Booklet that was distributed to everyone, but as with the initial setting up of any course there were adjustments that needed to be made as the weeks progressed.

Apart from a full time-table of lectures and seminars students were involved in worship experiences, usually outside their own denomination, each weekend. Under the supervision of a local tutor, with associated visiting tutors, small groups visited and later discussed their experience of worship in a mixture of non-traditional, but growing church situations. Their writing up of such experiences over the two years will form a major part of their Worship and Preaching portfolio. With the support and supervision of their church authorities every student will be required to set up and begin to train a group of 'vernacular' evangelists in their own local area and they will be assessed on progress made.

As you will see from the following extract taken from the current Course Booklet there is much work for the students to complete between the July and January 'Residentials' and some deadlines to be met which will keep them fully stretched over the next two years.

**COURSE DATES OUTLINED**

DATES OF THE RESIDENTIAL TEACHING PERIODS AND SCHEDULE FOR PRESENTATION OF WORK TO TUTORS FOR MARKING/ASSESSMENT (Non-attendance or non-submission may lead to exclusion from the course)

**2006**   **4th July – 20th July** inclusive (Registration 4th July)
Oct 31  Submission of NT Assignment (1,500 words)
         Continuous study of ISG's preparing for Jan 2007 exam.
Dec 31  Submission of Dissertation Proposal for evaluation
         with tutor during January residential
**2007**   **4th Jan – 9th Jan incl. Umuahia**- includes NT examination.
         Submission/initial assessment of applied evangelism project)
**11th Jan – 16th Jan incl. Sagamu**-includes NT examination.
Submission/initial assessment of applied evangelism project)
Feb 28 Submission of Becoming the Church: History-Practice of Evangelism (Assignment-3,000 words)
May 31 Submission of Being the Church:
         Spirituality & Mission        (Reflective Journal-3,000 words)
**2007**   **3rd July– 19th July incl. Umuahia & Sagamu**
         Registration 3rd July (Prelim. assessment W & P portfolio)

118

Sep 30 Becoming the Church:

Church Growth in Church History (Assignment-3,000 words)

Nov 30 OT Assignment (1,500 words)

Continuous study of ISG's preparing for Jan 2008 exam

**2008   3ʳᵈ Jan–8ᵗʰ Jan incl. Umuahia:** includes OT examination: Submission of Draft Dissertation & Spirituality Reflective Journal

**10ᵗʰ Jan–15ᵗʰ Jan incl. Sagamu:** includes OT examination: Submission of Draft Dissertation & Spirituality Reflective Journal

Feb 28 Submission of Worship & Preaching Portfolio

Mar 31 Submission of Dissertation

Apr 30 Submission of Applied Evangelism Portfolio

**2008   1ˢᵗ July - 17ᵗʰ July incl.**

**(To include ceremony for first graduates)**

N.B.   The student is responsible for making sure that the completed work is in the hands of the college/tutor/marker by the deadline date.

STUDENT ENROLMENT (AT SAGAMU)

BOOKS AND LIBRARIES

The positives are that a good start has been made with most of the students completing strongly affirmative evaluation sheets and displaying a willingness to study and achieve what is possible academically whilst majoring on the 'Applied' aspects of the course. Certainly, the course was much easier to run with students (and local staff) being resident on the campus. The students are looking forward to receiving "promised" books that will help them towards their graduation goal. All of the students have been allocated to a local college tutor (roughly 9 to 13 students to a tutor allocated in geographical area groups based on dioceses) who will supervise their work and meet with them once in their local area in between the 'Residentials'.   Already, local leaders involved are questioning whether it would be possible to run a 'rolling programme' with students being added in 2007, who would begin with their second year

119

and do their first year in 2008. Obviously, with funding it is possible, but we recognise the need to improve the lecturing/library facilities at both centres if that is to take place.

SAGAMU LIBRARIAN 'PATIENCE'

There is an urgent need to upgrade the libraries at both centres and to work towards updating the books that are available to the regular residential students/staff as well as to our CCILC students. Lecturing to 57 students at Sagamu was made difficult because there was no lecture room of adequate size to cope with such numbers. The college has built to roof height a large lecture room/conference hall/chapel, but it will need another £20,000 to complete this project. At Umuahia they have an airy and large lecture room chapel already, but the student accommodation/facilities are limited until they can raise about £5,000 to complete the ceiling and facilities in their new student block. We will be actively seeking funding for these projects as part of the CCILC vision to build up local colleges for their continuing work. Any offers of immediate support for these priority building projects would be much appreciated. Early completion would facilitate the work that we are doing but it would also have a long-term impact on the development of these colleges.

We will keep our friends and sponsors informed as the programme develops in Nigeria, alongside the other programmes that the CCILC continues to be involved in. Experience suggests that if too much unsolicited information is sent out, it is rarely read and digested, but if there is any further information/documentation that anyone would like to see at this stage I shall be pleased to make it available.

Thank you in anticipation of your continuing prayerful and practical support.

Richard Jackson (Revd)
International Coordinator CCILC

# 2006/3 OCT: MCSL ADMIN. COURSE PART 2

Our second Administration Training visit to Sierra Leone in October 2006 (12th – 26th) showed the value of taking the time in March to build relationships and of adopting a flexible approach to the training required.

The Team for visit 2:                    TEDDY BEAR MEETS 'MENDE TRAIN'

Revd Richard Jackson; Keith Philips; Revd Gilbert Hall; Mrs Sylvia Hall; plus Mrs Norma Krishnan (nee Beattie) re-visiting Sierra Leone with her 'SL fund-raising, School Teddy Bear' for personal reasons, and Mike Stapleford (Development & IT) preparing for the March input with regard to Conference Office equipment.

Despite the additional cost, the bringing together of most of the ministers (other than a few ageing or non-stipendiary ministers) from all three Districts of the Conference for the better part of four days proved to be a great success. The programme of biblical teaching focused on the Cross and, "Growing through conflict"; training given, in working together under a 'Connexional' umbrella; and a fruitful sharing around the perceived roles of key officers of the Conference provided an unexpected bonus.

The International Coordinator's sessions focussed around Edward De Bono's insights linked with "Six Thinking Hats" translated here with visuals as 'Caps' helped everyone reflect on their roles and responsibilities as leaders of teams with much to offer.

The ministers took it upon themselves towards the end of the programme to agree the text of a letter which was then signed by the three Chairmen of Districts, the President and Secretary of Conference. The ministers agreed to read the letter in every Methodist church on the following Sunday. In this letter they accepted their "share in the blame for the current deterioration in the interpersonal relationships among members of Christ's family" and committed themselves to "put all our differences behind us for the sake of Christ who is our peace and mediator".

Though not directly involved in our CCILC programme, Revd Richard Thompson, having travelled around reviewing the work of some of the Conference Institutions under the direction of the President of Conference was present with us for some of the time. His

preliminary feedback on this and talk on 'donors' was a helpful reminder to the circuit ministers of their own responsibilities in relation to these and other bodies. No doubt his report will have longer-term implications for the re-structuring (or re-establishing), proper lines of communication.

**REVD RICHARD THOMPSON AND DONORS!**

The course for ministers in Kenema was prefaced by a much appreciated day, on which Provincial District Circuit Stewards and ministers who had missed out in March caught up on the basic training given and it was followed on the Saturday by a similar meeting held at the Theological College in Freetown for Western District Circuit Stewards.

As arranged Revd & Mrs Hall were able to bring together from all three districts a group of designated 'trainers' of LP's and WL's for a three day course in Freetown. It is planned that these 'trainers' with others will work alongside the Hall's as they deliver a further training course in each of the three districts next February. Our hope is that this group will form the basis of a District Training Team who will continue this work on behalf of MCSL

Unfortunately, the second Monday of our October visit turned out to be a Public Holiday for the end of Ramadan, but we were able during the following days to continue our training with the Conference Office in Freetown. Many of the suggested improvements had been implemented. A changed environment was obvious to the eye and more positive attitudes and relationships were contributing to a sense

122

of well-being for everyone from the messengers/drivers (especially when they were presented with their promised 'MCSL Messenger Bags') through to the President of Conference.

We made further practical suggestions that could be implemented locally and filled out our practical review of IT (mainly ancient cast-offs with no two computers using the same software or printers the same cartridges!) and other needs now incorporated in a "Wish list" to be worked through before our final training visit in February 2007.

**"WAS THE FISH YOU CAUGHT REALLY THAT BIG, KEITH?"**

# CHAPTER 7 2007: CONTINUING IN NIGERIA & SL

*By February 2007, the Sierra Leone training in 'Administration' and the associated 'Lay Leadership' training was completed. Contact with the church there was maintained, but the main focus for the work of CCITC moved in the direction of a training partnership with the Methodist Church Nigeria, a much larger country. The Methodist Church has more than 2,000 workers active in ministry (ordained & lay) linked to the Methodist Conference through a hierarchical/episcopal organisation of Dioceses and Arch-Dioceses; Bishops and Archbishops; with the 'Prelate' as leader overall. As earlier in Sierra Leone, being engaged in the work related to the IDIAMM course meant that visiting lecturers, friends and sponsors generated funding also for improved student accommodation and water supplies, at Umuahia and Sagamu Methodist Training Institutions (MTI's). Support was given also to the pioneering college of Zonkwa, set in the strongly Muslim northern part of Nigeria.*

## 2007/1 JAN 3-18: MCN SECOND 'RESIDENTIAL'

### (IDIAMM 2006-08 PROGRAMME)

#### INTRODUCTION

The repositioning of the Methodist Church Nigeria (MCN) in relation to Evangelism alluded to in our July report has now been reinforced by a new (evangelism oriented) Constitution and the appointment for the first time in their history of a Bishop for Evangelism. This combination of initiatives alongside the invitation to the CCILC is a clear declaration of their intent. Obviously, these changes put the CCILC training programme in evangelism at the very heart of what our partner church is setting out to achieve.

Conversations were held with the newly appointed Head of the church: His Eminence, Revd Dr Ola S. Makinde; and the new Secretary of Conference, Bishop Chibuzo R Opoko; and later with the Bishop of Evangelism, Rt. Revd Dr Sunday N Onuoha; (who attended and spoke at the ILC Course in both of its centres). They made it clear that because of positive reports received locally on launch of the programme and the practical nature of the training being given, that they were planning for the CCILC course to become a 'rolling programme of training'. This programme would be undertaken by all ordained ministers working at all levels of the church. Whilst appreciative of this very positive response to the launch of this new programme in July, we encouraged our partners to discuss their plans with the Africa Secretary at World Church Office (WCO) at their upcoming meeting before formulating proposals for submission through the WCO to the Scholarship And Leadership Training (SALT) Advisory Group for ongoing funding.

MCN continued the appointment of the Very Revd Okon Ekerendu as the very able National Coordinator to liaise with the International Coordinator of the CCILC, Revd Richard Jackson. Once again regular correspondence between all the parties involved provided for a trouble-free journey to Nigeria on January 3$^{rd}$ and between the two centres by the visiting team which was made up of:

**THE CORE TEAM:**

Revd Richard Jackson MA BD International Coordinator CCILC Methodist Minister and former Postgraduate Tutor at Cliff College
Revd Dr Malcolm McCall MA        Methodist Minister in Shetland Isles, former teacher in Africa & Royal Navy Chaplain
Mrs Janet McCall BA (Hons) Methodist Local Preacher, & Former teacher in Africa: French, teaching English as a second language skill
Mr Keith Phillips Anglican, former VSO in Sierra Leone and Social Worker with Child Care expertise. CCILC Logistics and admin.

**SUPPORTING LECTURERS:**

Revd A Cameron Kirkwood, MA Methodist Minister & Lecturer with expertise in Community Development & Fresh Expressions of Church
Major Alan J Burns, MA Salvation Army Officer & Lecturer in Church Growth

The visiting team were again partnered by members of the Nigerian staff teams at the Sagamu & Umuahia Methodist Training Institutions.

*(A timetable used at both centres, largely adhered to, giving details of the teaching/training offered in January was appended to this document.)*

We reported in July an enrolment 57 students at Sagamu, near Lagos and 82 at Umuahia in the east. Despite the best efforts of both the local coordinator and tutorial staff a few students did not return for the second phase of the course. From what could be gleaned the main reason for non-continuation was the inability of those students to cope with the lectures in English and particularly the written work to be presented in English. As can be noted from the July report the visiting tutors had anticipated some problems along these lines and we built into the course for January a programme of English assessment tests prepared and supervised by Mrs. McCall with a view to grading the students according to levels of English. The suggested groupings will be of those able to do a Foundation Course, those capable of a Certificate Course (year 1 of a degree) and those who could cope with the course as originally designed at Diploma Level (year 2 of a degree).

The results of the assessments along with aural observations and the levels reached in the student's first submitted assignments are being evaluated and may lead to 'streaming' in the second year of the course. All students have been encouraged to take advantage of any courses being run in their local areas on 'Improving English' and we shall be providing some assistance with this within the time constraints of our own programme, but this will only ameliorate the difficulty rather than solving the problem. We shall continue to be flexible with this group. It may be possible for students to improve their written English to such an extent that they can be moved to a different level (or if the rolling programme becomes an actuality) add a further period of training to their course which will allow them to graduate at the higher level. We are being careful to communicate that the anticipated streaming is to do with the levels of English required for a validated course rather than a judgement about a student's capability as an evangelist, but we have been assured that those who come on future courses will have reached an acceptable standard in written English.

Despite changes to the staff, and even a change of Rector (Principal) at Sagamu, we were impressed by the work done since July by local tutors, many of whom had travelled more than once for tutorials/discussions with their particular group of students. The written work being presented bore the stamp of their inventive guidance and training upon it. Thanks to the Shetland District's release of Revd Dr McCall, he and his wife were able to stay in Nigeria for a further two weeks after the 'Residential' visiting students in and around Lagos as part of a strategy to encourage the students to put into practice what they are learning alongside their local colleagues and their own supervisors. This new initiative (a full report is available) which over the four 'Residentials' of the course should bring us directly into contact with most areas of the country in which our students are working was much appreciated and achieved its purpose. A helpful suggestion from the local tutors was that a 'CCILC Distance Learning Tutors' training leaflet should be produced which would spell out expectations for the tutors and give some guidance on ways of meeting those expectations that others have found helpful. Hopefully, we will be able to work with the local tutors in producing this booklet over the coming months.

**BOOKS AND OTHER MATERIALS**

As usual visiting lecturers were encouraged to provide full notes for the students which are being incorporated into their own (growing) training manual. Much work had been done by the National Coordinator in consultation with the International Coordinator as we explored the possibility of local sourcing at reasonable prices for the books that would be required for the students on the course. The generous commitment made by 'Feed the Minds' (subject to regular reports) means that funding is available for student books. We purchased English Dictionaries locally at reasonable prices but we wanted to make sure that the SPCK International Study Guides in particular could be provided locally without the logistical problems that were associated with the earlier programme when we had to arrange transport for the books to Sierra Leone.

UMUAHIA MTI RECTOR AND STAFF WITH CCITC

127

We travelled to have face to face contact with our prospective supplier Prof Lawrence at a bookshop in Onitsha and took delivery of our first load of 160 copies of some of the key books in the ISG series for students and local staff. Others books requested have been put on order and should be available before the students return in July. One of our visiting lecturers shared as a reflective highlight, 'the gratefulness of those-staff as well as students, in receiving books.' Something which we take so much for granted.

### OTHER RESOURCES AND ISSUES TO ADDRESS

There were several issues that arose during our visit to which further attention will need to be given. The first group relate to concerns raised, whilst the second group (as one might expect) are linked with fund-raising.

The status of senior sub pastors, evangelists and others on completion of the course. The Prelate indicated that providing the students are qualified also as Local Preachers, consideration would be given to upgrading some to the ordained ministry and others to become Conference, rather than Local Evangelists.

Consider some payment to local College staff, other than the small honorarium provided through the CCILC for additional work undertaken during what would normally be vacation time.

The possibility of a 'rolling programme' noted above, but also the venue and practical arrangements for the graduation of CCILC students in July 2008 (15th-22nd) which will be attended by the Prelate and MCN church leadership and the Revd Dr Martyn Atkins, Cliff College Principal, Director of CCILC and by then the recently retired President of the British Methodist Conference.

A CCILC Bank Account to be set up in Nigeria through which funds for payments for books etc. can be channelled.

Concerns that the visiting team have; about how much it is costing MCN to provide accommodation, food and travel within the country for such a large team working in two centres, when their own national church budget is so stretched.

At Umuahia progress has been made with student accommodation facilities. The Avenue Methodist Church, Sale is raising in excess of £5,000 to fund this work and the upgrading of their water tank which provides for both student and staff premises throughout the site.

Similarly at Sagamu, £5,000 is needed for the upgrading of the water tank to meet the growing needs of the site (£250.00 donated already by the Bramhall Methodist Church Thrift Shop). In addition this college still needs major funding of up to £20,000 for the project mentioned in our last report. (The college has built to roof height a large lecture room/conference hall/chapel, but it will need another £20,000 to complete this project.) Earlier buildings at this college were funded through the sale of Richmond College. We have approached some 'old boys' who are planning a 'Requiem for Richmond' and suggested that they might support the 'Resurrection of Richmond' College Chapel on this site at Sagamu in Nigeria.

**RICHMOND COLLEGE LIVES ON AT SAGAMU MTI**

Slowly the college libraries are being upgraded with additional books being supplied through trusts etc., but much more needs to be done to meet the academic requirements of universities to which the colleges are affiliated.

We will continue to seek funding and resources for these projects as part of the CCILC vision to build up local colleges for their continuing work. As we said last time, any offers of immediate support for these priority building projects or if any church or person would like to adopt a project it would be much appreciated. Early completion would facilitate the work that we are doing but it would also have a long-term impact on the development of these colleges. Further information with pictures can be provided on request.

129

Obviously, we as a team feel blessed to be sharing with the Methodist Church Nigeria in this way. To become beggars on their behalf is the least that we feel we can do in response to the unfailing friendliness, enthusiasm of both staff and students and as our thank you for the wonderful hospitality provided through the MCN in colleges and homes during our training visits there. If there is anything that you can do to help with these or other projects we would love to hear from you.

FINAL REFLECTION

I will leave the final thoughts in this report to the lecturer on his first visit with the CCILC to Nigeria who comments on, "The way in which we as a team worked together-each complementing the other. I found it amazing-some others might say it was the work of the Holy Spirit, that despite no discussion prior to the trip, our lectures and material seemed to drawing on similar sources and emphasising similar points." And having in mind the live issue in the UK of the BA member of staff in trouble for wearing a cross around her neck, what struck him was, 'The comment of the cabin crew member on arrival at Owerri airport, "May God bless you all".'

The words of that Nigerian cabin crew member will do to conclude this report on the pioneering progress of yet another CCILC project to which so many people in Nigeria and here at home have contributed, "My God bless you all".

**Richard Jackson (Revd)**
**International Coordinator CCILC**

We will keep our friends and sponsors informed as the programme develops in Nigeria, alongside the other programmes that the CCILC continues to be involved in. Experience suggests that if too much unsolicited information is sent out, it is rarely read and digested, but if there is any earlier report further information, documentation, photographs that anyone would like to see at this stage I shall be pleased to make it available.

Thank you in anticipation of your continuing prayerful and practical support.

# 2007/2 Jan 18-31: McCALLS-APPLIED EVANGELISM

IN THEIR LOCAL CHURCHES: (WITH RESPONSES FROM THEIR PRESBYTERS, CONGREGATIONS AND BISHOPS)BACKGROUND:

As indicated in the above report, Janet and Malcolm McCall stayed behind at Sagamu in January 2007 to visit the students, their Presbyters and local congregations in order to encourage the students in their application of the Course in their own ministry settings. About 17 students were visited (and/or their presbyters and churches) in 11 different Methodist Churches. Also: the Archbishop of Lagos; the Secretary of Conference; 3 other diocesan bishops; and Deacon Nancy Kennedy-Johnson (responsible for English Communication at MTI, Sagamu). Again to preserve confidentiality the student(s) name is replaced by a number

STUDENT 1:

*Ojoko Church (and Church Plant at Agoro Town, several miles away), Ota Circuit, Ogun State, (Lagos Diocese). Stayed with the Priest-in-Charge and his wife Shola. The Presbyter, was away, though we briefly met him after Sunday worship in the Ota Circuit Church, where he was very friendly. The Youth Fellowship at this church had worked hard to organise a Christian Youth Lending Library, of which they were very proud. Their books were appropriate for young people, but they need more. It would seem good if Student 1 could be available to work with these enthusiastic youngsters and encourage them into mission and evangelism.*

*Student 1 is pastoring a Church in Ijoko of 70 or so members, and is developing an evangelism-focused group within the church. He expects formally to start a church plant in Agoro Town on Easter Monday 2007. There is already a very eager informal group, meeting in the home of one of the Ojoko church members, which we were able to share into. Student 1 is clearly applying what he has been learning on the Course to his own situation. Very generously, with the approval of Very Revd. Okon Ekerendu, he also became our guide and helper from 18-31 January, showing his own organizational skills, and his serious commitment to the work of evangelism in the Lagos area generally.*

131

**STUDENT 2; STUDENT 3; STUDENT 4:**

*Freeman Cathedral, Ogbe, Abeokuta (Egba-Yewa Diocese) Somewhat disappointing, in that we had only limited time with the three students! Janet and I spoke briefly in the Cathedral during an Evangelistic Prayer Meeting, and were able to encourage the congregation to make use of what the students are learning on the IDIAMM Course. We also met the diocesan bishop, Rt. Revd Luke Odubanjo, Bishop of Egba-Yewa (and we met him briefly later at Methodist HQ, Marina) and with the Cathedral Presbyter. We trust that these meetings will encourage the best deployment of our three Course students, and also the development of "evangelism learning groups" around them. But in future, we must try to ensure that the programme for each visit to our students enables us to spend adequate time with them individually as well.*

**STUDENT 5; STUDENT 6**

*Oshodi Circuit English Church, Oshodi (Ikorodu Diocese) Student 5 and Student 6 seemed well-integrated into this lively church in terms of their role as evangelism enablers. We attended a Sunday morning Service led by the Priest-in-Charge, (we did not meet the presbyter), where about 300 were meeting for worship. Janet and I both spoke, and made an altar-call for people to dedicate themselves, in obedience to Jesus' Great Commission, to seek to make disciples, introducing people to Christ, being "Soul-winners" (a frequently-used expression in MCN). About 35 people responded with evident seriousness and sincerity in many. We encouraged the 2 students to set up "evangelism learning groups" with these 35, under the direction of their Priest. It was encouraging to learn 3 days later (when we visited Student 5 and his family for a meal) that these groups had already been organised and were "underway".*

**STUDENT 7**

*Student 7 at Abesan Methodist Church, Oshodi Circuit, Ikorodu Diocese. About 17 people responded to an altar-call to dedicate themselves to evangelism, and these were commended to Student 7, for him to take them on in training and action, under the presbyter. (Giving unstintingly of their own time and money, Student 7 & his wife drove us to and from various destinations – and we came to appreciate the potential in this couple to be a powerfully-used evangelistic team together.)*

132

*St. Peter's Circuit, Ikorodu Diocese Student 8 has wanted to pursue an evangelistic ministry in the local prison, but this has not yet happened. We spoke in depth to his Minister-in-Charge. He and Student 8 had begun a monthly open air evangelistic witness, but few of the church members had joined in. They came to the conclusion that unless the church members themselves have a real relationship with Jesus, they will have nothing to share with their neighbourhood community and will be unable to introduce others to Him. So, very humbly, The Minister-in-charge and Student 8 came to understand that "spiritual breakthrough" needed to begin with them! – and that is what they are now praying for. Both Minister and Evangelist need much encouragement and affirmation. While in Ikorodu, we also spent some time, profitably, with the diocesan bishop, Rt. Revd Olumuyiwa O. Odejayi, Bishop of Ikorodu (and his wife, Taiwo).*

**STUDENT 9; STUDENT 10; STUDENT 11; STUDENT 12:**

*Ago-Ijaye Circuit, The presbyter in this church is the Very Revd Sunday Aluko, who (until October 2006) was Rector of MTI Sagamu. He was very clear that his 4 students were thoroughly involved in the applied aspects of the IDIAMM Course. For example, Student 10 is involved with women's work and outreach and discipleship. Student 11 is growing a small church, and Student 12 is leading Monday evening Bible Studies. Also, they are starting, in February 2007, a weekly Church group on evangelism. And, once a month, they will be invited to lead worship. It was clear from all this activity that where the presbyter has a real understanding and sympathy with what the IDIAMM Course is about (as Very Revd Sunday Aluko clearly has from his time with us in Sagamu), then the application of the Course in the local church and Circuit becomes much easier and more effective both for the student and the local church.*

**STUDENT 13:**

*Okokomako Methodist Church, Olorunda Circuit, Lagos Diocese Student 13 came with his presbyter, to our hotel for a meaningful discussion. We were aware that this was a real breakthrough in a situation where the application of the course in the local church had not been proving easy. The Presbyter expressed an interest in joining any subsequent IDIAMM Course which we might provide for presbyters.*

STUDENT 14:

*Festac Circuit The presbyter, and the Priest, at Festac Church, were warm and welcoming. Sunday morning worship lasted over 5 hours. We attended separate English and Yoruba services. Youth Services and Sunday Schools (again, separate meetings for both children and youth in English and Yoruba) were conducted simultaneously with the adult services. In both Youth Services, several young people committed themselves to fulfilling the Great Commission, and, under the presbyter, were encouraged to establish an evangelism group with Student 14 to learn more about outreach and evangelism – and to do it! There was also a Circuit Ladies' Meeting afterwards (!) which Janet was invited to visit and speak at.*

STUDENT 15; STUDENT 16; STUDENT 17; STUDENT 18:

*Igbogila Circuit, Lagos Diocese We briefly met their presbyter when we stopped near his Church compound. Although this amounted to only a few minutes, we trust that he was encouraged to help his Evangelists apply the Course. Towards the end of our extended visit we were taken by Very Revd Ekerendu to meet and have discussions with the Right Revd O. Omotayo Babalola, Bishop of Lagos Mainland Diocese. We spoke about the possibility of having a second IDIAMM Course, designed especially for presbyters, starting in July 2008. The bishop was not only clear that this was right, but urgently encouraged us to consider having several residential weekends (both at Sagamu and Umuahia) for the wives of presbyters during the next 2-year Course, on the grounds that:*
*Presbyters' wives are often from other denominations and do not understand the ethos of MCN. If they are given no help in understanding their own area of ministry alongside their husbands, they cannot be blamed if they opt out. It is a waste of Human Resources if spiritually capable and willing wives are not given help and opportunity to exercise their own gifts within MCN. All four of us warmed to this possibility as we discussed it together; Janet would be thrilled to co-ordinate such weekends.*

*We also enjoyed a long interview with the Right Revd Dr Joseph S. Ajayi, Archbishop of Lagos in his Lagos Office. Dr Ajayi wanted to explain that he and some others in leadership in MCN had been trying for decades to encourage evangelistic initiatives in the church. He gave us some examples:*

*The formation of the Methodist Evangelical Movement (MEM). He had been the first organiser of this Movement, but had then passed on the leadership to the Very Revd Okon Ekerendu.*

*His evangelistic efforts in the Ogbomoso Diocese when he was diocesan bishop there from 1997 to 2006, which are detailed in his book Contending for Love (October 2006).*

*His seminal paper on the place of leadership in the evangelistic task for MCN, Leadership for Methodist Revival.*

*In an IDIAMM Course for Presbyters (beginning July 2008?), this document might be developed into a series of 6 lectures. Perhaps the Archbishop could be invited to come and deliver them? The Archbishop was aware how little MCN in general had been willing to "take up" the challenge of "making disciples" in past decades, and hoped that the latest initiatives might really be used by God to transform MCN.*

## 2007/3 JAN: McCALLS ENGLISH COMMUNICATION
**Background Thinking:**

It became obvious that clear communication in English was a challenge for (probably) a majority of the students on the Course. Janet was tasked (as qualified in teaching English as a second language) to develop a strategy (within the severe time-constraints of the Course) for improving the students' English Language communication skills. Malcolm was pleased to assist in this. During our extended visit to Nigeria in January 2007, we were able to speak with several Nigerian English Language teachers. We also spent time in the well-stocked English Language section of the CSS Bookshop in Lagos and settled on:

Swan, M. and Walter, C., How English Works (OUP, Oxford, UK, 1997; 12th. Impression 2002) ISBN 0-19-431456-1 with answers ISBN 0-19-431457-X without answers. However, discovered prices are prohibitively expensive, and CSS Bookshop would be unable to offer any price reduction on this book. Therefore, decided that during the short times available for "hands on" teaching, this book could be used for exercises and reference by the teachers. Although it is not specifically for use in Africa, it is designed for any students of English as a second language.

A STRATEGY FOR THE "ENGLISH COMMUNICATION" COMPONENT OF THE IDIAMM COURSE (DEVELOPMENTAL AND REMEDIAL WORK)

Keith Phillips kindly collated and analysed in detail each answer (90 answers) from each of the 125 students (= 11,250 answers!! Thank you, Keith). Janet has taken this analysis, and from it has divided the students into 3 "ability groups":

**Advanced:** those with language skills appropriate to Diploma level

**Intermediate**: those with language skills appropriate to Certificate level

**Basic**: those with language skills appropriate to Foundation Course level

Janet has done this analysis for both Umuahia and Sagamu. In both Institutes, the largest group is the Intermediate (Certificate) group. Therefore, within the time limits of the Residentials, we suggest the following strategy: Instead of Janet doing much lecturing (but reserving adequate time to share with the women on the Course), she would concentrate in the July 2007 Residentials on remedial and developmental work on English Communication. Malcolm, instead of doing much lecturing (but reserving, say, 3 "lecture spots" for the Spiritual Disciplines module), would share the English Communications work with Janet. Ideally, we would divide the students into 3 groups in each Institute, and give 8-10 hours of English Language tuition simultaneously to the groups. Clearly, it would be best for the efficiency of the timetable, if the 3 groups are taught simultaneously during the residential. However, this requires the provision of a third International (or National?), Team Member.

The idea would be, hopefully, to keep the "Basic" (Foundation Course) Group as small as possible to make maximum impact on the progress (we trust) of the ones with most need of help in English. We could expect the "Intermediate" (Certificate) Group to be the largest, and the "Advanced" (Diploma) Group to consist only of those who would otherwise be held back from forging ahead further in perfecting their language skills.

In January 2007, we spent some time at Sagamu speaking with Deaconess Nancy Kennedy-Johnson (Staff Member in the Institute)

136

who has been tasked with the improvement of the English Language of the regular ministerial candidates who are resident in Sagamu during term-time. We all wondered whether there might be some overlap between the Institute's Courses and the IDIAMM Course as we all face the same problem of inadequate English Language skills in our students. Presumably, the same would be true of the regular ministerial candidates in Umuahia.

# 2007/4 FEB 5-19: MCSL ADMIN. COURSE PART 3
INTRODUCTION

In the early days of the CCILC we listed among the qualifications required of visiting lecturers/trainers "A sense of humour and ability to adapt to changing circumstances". Both of these requirements were tested to the full as the core training team: (consisting of Revd Gilbert & Mrs Sylvia Hall; Mr Keith Phillips, Administrator; Revd Richard Jackson, Coordinator; and supplemented by Mr Mike Stapleford, recruited to set up computers and do some training in the MCSL Conference Office), returned to Sierra Leone for their final training visit in February 2007.

Towards the end of our October 2006 report we noted that in addition to the planned training programme we were hoping to re-equip the Conference Office with up-to-date IT equipment. This necessitated much preparatory work in the purchase, testing and local setting up of the computers/printers/laptops. Thanks to Bill McIntyre and students at Cliff College in association with Andy Seaton of Resolve IT solutions the 12 desktop, 5 laptops and 17 printers were purchased and made ready for transport to Sierra Leone by December.

**"ARE YOU SURE THIS IS ALL OURS?**

With time at a premium and figures of up to £3,000 being quoted for delivery we were again helped by Astraeus the airline and Parcelmove their agency in arranging for transport on the same flight as the team at minimal cost. With a generous baggage allowance of 60 kilos for each of the 5 passengers travelling and over 110 kilos of excess baggage packed in ten suitcases and 7 cardboard boxes the intrepid travellers and the computers survived all possible obstacles to arrive safely in Freetown, Sierra Leone. On arrival it became clear that the previously planned programme of training could not be adhered to. The programme planned for the Provincial Districts was disrupted by the rescheduling of Synods due to logistical problems, the hospitalisation of key people and the lack of transport fit for use. Problems with the main power supply in Freetown (virtually non-existent) and the breakdown of the Conference Office generator made the setting up of the IT equipment and training on it problematical to say the least.

In consultation with the President and Secretary of Conference revisions to the planned programme were made almost on a daily basis. An abbreviated diary of activities will perhaps best convey something of the difficulties experienced and share something of what was achieved.

MIKE STAPLEFORD: "NO PROBLEM!"

**Day 1** saw us transporting the computers to the Conference Office, greeting friends, sorting money, phones, passports and airline tickets and beginning to rearrange the programme.

**Day 2** Mike (assisted by the others at various points) unpacked the computers and set each up in a steamy basement room testing for casualties of transport. Amazingly, apart from a few dents, there were NONE! The coordinator cleared the redundant ILC store at the Theological College of materials left over from the IDIAMM course (the usable wheat was sorted from the chaff during the second week).

**Day 3** Messrs Jackson, Phillips and Stapleford travelled with the President to the Kailahun/Kono District Synod but the hospitalisation of the President's son delayed our departure until 1545. We arrived in Kailahun at 2300 to a great welcome (drums, shake-shake and singing) and a proper meal.

**Day 4** Synod started on time with District Chairman, Revd Peter Lebbie. The visiting team introduced themselves, greeted the members

138

of Synod and encouraged the 'Administration Course Trainees' to put into practice what they had learned. The visiting trainers then travelled with the President to the remote outpost of Sandaru-Penguia (where the International Coordinator had once been minister) to encourage the local members in their rebuilding programme of the church, clinic and the derelict manse.

**Day 5** After beginning the day with the Synod the 'Team' looked at the rehabilitation progress being made in Kailahun. One manse restored and one to do; Skills training Centre, (a North Lancashire District Project) almost completed; the Methodist Primary School fighting against encroachment on their land, but proud of the new classroom block rebuilt with the help of former pupils. The fully functioning Methodist Secondary School matched up well with the new buildings (built under Methodist Development supervision) of the Ahmadiyah Secondary School. Rather surreal contrast in the afternoon in a tarpaulin 'barrie' in remote Kailahun watching a Manchester United live game with their supporters on one TV screen whilst others were watching Chelsea on a second screen. The support was lively!!!

**Day 6** (Sunday) Team returned to Freetown with the President following up en-route, building projects and training done with people at Pendembu, Daru, Segbwema (Manse & Hospital), and in Kenema and Bo. Arrangements were made for the follow-up training being done by Gilbert & Sylvia Hall during the following week.

**Day 7** At the Conference Office the generator was still not working, so we were not able to set up any computers. The unreliability of a variety of 'power supplies', made the supply of 'Uninterruptible Power Source' units a priority (eventually 10 purchased locally at a cost of £800). We measured up and ordered six tables @ 5' x 2' x 2'6" for the 'computer room' which were produced locally but arrived a couple of days later than promised and with the varnish still wet!

**Day 8-Onwards**: Having organised the hire of a small generator, the Freetown visiting team dismantled (or moved) the old computers/printers and transferred files to the new computers. Individual training in Windows and Office XP was given to each member of staff using the new computers. The three Chairmen of

Districts, the President and Secretary of Conference were trained on their laptops which had the same software. Follow-up training in administration was provided and issues resolved towards the end of the two weeks.

**From Day One** Revd Gilbert & Sylvia Hall remained in Freetown reorganising their training programme. They liaised with The President & Secretary of Conference and others to come up with a revised programme of teaching linked with Local Preachers (LP) and Women Leaders (WL). They had to:
Cancel the planned for Connexional three day course for the L.P. and W.L. trainers and cancel a one day conference for L.P. and W.L. in the Kailahun/Kono District because Synod was meeting at the same time
Attend the Women's Fellowship/Network Annual Thanksgiving service
Prepare for and deliver a Saturday training day for the Western District which was attended by 26 local preachers and 12 women leaders.
Travel to Kenema and host a two day training course for 7 L.P's. and 11 W.L's.

Organise by District and through contacts a team of trainers who will become (subject to Conference approval) the Conference Training Committee (for which a training budget will be allocated.) This group will continue the training programme for MCSL. The proposed list consists of three ministers; three local preachers; and three women leaders from each District with the Revd Solomon Van Kanneh as the coordinator.

## SUMMARY OF THREE VISITS AND CONCLUDING REFLECTIONS:
We were invited by the MCSL to provide further training in 'Leadership and Administration'.

### THE FIRST TRAINING VISIT IN MARCH 2006 ALLOWED US TO:

Create and develop relationships with the Ordained Ministry and Conference Office staff through consultation, whilst providing basic training in styles of Leadership and Management, Administration, Communication, Training, Organisation, Office Work and Practice. Foundations were laid for the training of local 'training officers'.

Apart from the bringing together and continued training of the Ordained Ministry there were clear indications that most of the 'trainees', whether Ministers, Local Preachers, Women Leaders or Conference Office staff were beginning to put into practice what they had been learning. The changing attitudes and more settled programme made this feel like one of the most productive of the training visits.

## THE THIRD TRAINING VISIT IN FEBRUARY 2007-FOLLOW-UP NEEDED:

Due to many circumstances beyond anyone's control this final visit left the team with the feeling that, though much had been achieved in practical terms the overall programme, lacked 'completeness'. Despite the success in providing, transporting and setting up in the Conference Office the new IT equipment, we felt that more time for training of staff and rationalisation of working practices in relation to 'job descriptions' and delegation would have reinforced the 'academic' input and brought more practical benefits. Whilst attitudes are changing the freedom, independence, and ability of an outside 'consultant/trainer' working for short periods alongside local staff to accelerate the process of change is sometimes undervalued.

The work done by Revd Gilbert and Mrs Sylvia Hall with Local Preachers and Women Leaders in particular was much valued by the local church. The production of a list of District and Conference Trainers to be ratified by Conference might helpfully be reinforced by further work done by them alongside the appointed 'local trainers'. Perhaps support could be given to MCSL with a small supplementary training budget being provided through the SALT oversight group.

What should not be lost sight of in evaluating this programme linked with 'Leadership & Administration' are the spin-offs of 'Doing Training There' alongside and in partnership with the local church. Being there, helps to change attitudes in visiting trainers and trainees alike and relationships continue to be developed that bear fruit in countless different ways as we work together to strengthen the work of God in a variety of situations.

Despite the reservations expressed above we are of the mind that the £20,000 grant received through the WCO (which did not include the cost of IT equipment), has been well spent. It has provided training in Leadership and Administration for large numbers of key people in the Methodist Church Sierra Leone and through our activities prepared the way for the continuation of that training in the local church.

**Revd Richard Jackson,**        **29<sup>th</sup> March 2007**

## 2007/5 NOV NEWSLETTER 13: FRIENDS OF MCSL

### REPORT ON MEETING AT CLIFF COLLEGE IN AUGUST

The President of the MCSL, Rt. Revd Francis Nabieu, concluded our 24 hour conference 20/21 August at Cliff College, by:
asking us to pray for several Ministers who are unwell;
inviting us to visit and encourage the church in Sierra Leone;
and thanking us for our support.

With over 30 people due to arrive at Cliff it was discovered that Francis was not due to arrive in London until that day so a last minute flight change got him to Heathrow, he was met by car, carried north and had a night's sleep before we met. He had had a busy week as Returning Officer for Kailahun/Kono in the general election. The result had still not been declared when he left Freetown and was in the balance. The All Peoples Party was declared the winner and the subsequent election for a new President of the Country was reported by Reuters in these words:

'Ernest Bai Koroma was sworn in as President on Monday 17 September 2007 after winning polls marked by violence and some fraud, prompting celebrations and looting in which at least one man was killed. The 53 year old former insurance executive who came in second in the 2002 poll, took his oath in Freetown. The National Election Commission declared the APC candidate the winner despite a threat by the ruling Sierra Leone Peoples Party to challenge the result in court. "Let us begin the process of healing the wounds that suddenly appeared during the course of this political campaign. Let us endeavour to reconcile ourselves as one nation under God" said Koroma, a Christian from the mostly Muslim north. The NEC said Koroma had won with a 54.6% majority defeating Vice President Solomon Berewa on 45.4% '

It is understood that at the swearing in the defeated Mr Berewa pledged his peaceful support for the elected government, and that new ministers are now in post. The challenges include: high inflation with rice and palm oil prices up; government is late in paying wages; and much corruption in high places.

So what is the state of the CHURCH as the process of reconstruction continues? This year the rebuilding of manses and their dedication has seen those at Bandajuma Yawei, Sandaru and Segbwema completed with the outbuildings at Segbwema converted into a second housing unit. Eight MANSES still need to be done at a cost of about £8000 for each fully furnished manse.

**MINISTERS** Some are still without a manse and this may be deterring candidates; there were only 2 this year. Training is at the Theological Hall shared with the Anglicans and the United Methodist Church, and accredited by the University. Some of our older ministers are not well and there are only 2 women in a total of about 100. To serve the churches' needs a number of Conference catechists have been engaged. In many areas the people still cannot give enough to pay the ministers and the special fund donated via Revd Gilbert Hall has raised over £18,000.

**CHURCHES** have been restored or newly built and dedicated. York church was completed but lost its roof in a storm. St Augustine's, Bo, is now also a youth centre and a new worship area is planned. In Kenema a new church is going up near a college, as well as the planning and building of a conference centre there.

**SKILLS TRAINING CENTRES** to benefit young ex-soldiers, orphans and others have been planned. The Freetown centre has had an issue of leadership, but is now in the hands of the daughter in law of Michael Tengbe (a very able minister who died during the civil war). The Kailahun Centre, sponsored by the Lancs District, was opened in September. The Irish Methodist Church is sponsoring a new centre in Segbwema.

**CONFERENCE OFFICE** in Freetown has a development department, promoting 'livelihood' centres such as in Bo and Segbwema. This is a

Christian Aid sponsored programme to help in conflict reconciliation and finding new ways of living.

MCSL has been given responsibility for supervising school building schemes in the Kailahun District and in Bonthe. 'Sababu' is a World Bank fund for schools providing funds which are both helpful and confusing when the Methodist team has to supervise the building of a Muslim school in a town to the exclusion of the Methodist school!

EDUCATION policy is that every child should go to school but there is a shortage of teachers and classes remain very large. With a shortage of new buildings it is also necessary for the junior and senior secondary schools to follow each other on the timetable.
MCSL is in three Districts and is responsible for:
                55 primary and 11 secondary schools in Kailahun/Kono
        39        "        "    8        "        "    Bo/Kenema
        9        "        "    4        "        "    the Western
District.
In spite of late payment of salaries by the government teachers continue to teach.

NIXON MEMORIAL HOSPITAL, SEGBWEMA Is still undergoing a see-saw progress. In August a storm took the roof off the out-patient building which was recently rebuilt. It happened in a time of heavy rain and though government built, it will be 'our' money used to re-roof and was expected to cost about £5,000. On the other hand mission partners Michael and Joanna Tettey with baby Joelle went out early October. Michael will have responsibility for technical work and Joanna will be teaching in the Nursing School. Michael was present at Cliff and made notes on the background history as well as today's pressing concerns:

…funding is in hand for a HIV/Aids programme
…drugs are now available in Kailahun thus obviating a long trip to Freetown
…operating theatre still needs re-instating but waits on growth of need
…Nurses hostel has been completed using EU money
…the compound is fenced and is now fairly secure
…not enough income for salaries but not enough patients who can afford fees (numbers seem to increase when Dr Jenny Gibson is there!)

…a Doctor Hopkins will work at NMH for six months and a retired army doctor may go if funding can be found

…the primary 'care in the community' programme is still helping in 12 villages and there    are good reports of its effectiveness

…the plans for Michael Webb and his team to install pumps for a new water supply this  autumn did not happen. It is now expected in the new year and both Michaels, (Webb and Tettey) are eager that this should happen

In addition to the above, members had time to reminisce and share concerns about Sierra Leone, and on Tuesday also present were three local people concerned about asylum seekers. They brought Abdul with them, a Sierra Leonean asylum seeker. We heard his story, Francis promised to make some enquiries for him, and he left saying that he had not been in such an open and sympathetic group before.

MONEY can be a contentious subject! What has happened to all the money raised for Sierra Leone? A request had been made to the World Church Office and details of all monies donated since April 2005 for Reconstruction and for Nixon were received a few days after Cliff. This included monies sent by other churches and circuits as well as that channelled through FH and was a clear account of standing orders, recovered tax etc. and remittances to MCSL.

The agreement to keep separate accounts for MCSL in its special need is working. There is still money in hand but more is needed. Sent to me (FH) for World Church Fund ensures that it gets to the right place. The total received by Frank Himsworth since July 2005 to date is £16,360 for reconstruction and £44,300 for the hospital.  In addition a third gift of 10,000 US dollars has just been sent by friends who taught at Wesley School Segbwema in the 1960's.  MCSL is grateful for all that we can do.

The Cliff group also sent a letter to Church House concerned about the proposed reduction in staffing when so much needs to be done to provide the World Church of our Prayer Handbook with the support needed.  There has been no reply to that letter. Most of the material above is a report on our sharing at Cliff with a little updating.

For the record here is a list of the **PARTICIPANTS** at Cliff with dates when they served in Sierra Leone.

Janet & Stuart Clarke 84-89 P
Jenny Gibson over 30 yrs     M
Frank & Sheila Himsworth 59-68 P
Richard & Carole Jackson 69-79   P
Marcia & David Knights 61-67 M
Brian Lewis   71-75 P
Janet Mackinder 69-76 P
Francis Nabieu President
Monica Rhead 55-65 T
Mary 57-70 M & Colin Rowe
Glenys M & Roger P Smith 59-72
Mike Stapleford (visitor to SL)
Michael Tettey Admin Oct. 2007
Richard & Margaret Thompson 71-76 P
Gillian Webster80-82 M
Joan & Gordon Wynne 62-66 P
Mary Jefferson (SL visitor)
Pauline & Dick Drew 70's VSO

John Cochrane  73-76 M
Gilbert & Sylvia Hall 71-75   P

Rita King (Sierra Leonean)
Norma 77-79 & Jai Krishnan
Ralph & Elizabeth Mann 60-63 T
Agnes (Nan) Mumford 62-74 M
Keith Phillips 75-77   VSO

'NUFF SAID' ABOUT THIS ROGUES GALLERY

P=pastoral; M=medical; T=teaching; VSO=voluntary service overseas

PLEASE......if you get interesting information about Sierra Leone do send it on to me (FH) as I am told that many look forward to receiving this Newsletter but I need to know!!! Sorry this one is so late but personal circumstances have prevented me getting on with it.

And **FINALLY**, as usual please forward donations to me, payable to World Church Fund, and keep our support going for a few more years.

From: Revd Frank Himsworth

# 2007/6 JUL 3-19: MCN THIRD 'RESIDENTIAL'

(IDIAMM 2006-08 PROGRAMME)

**INTRODUCTION**

By invitation of the Prelate and Secretary of Conference of the Methodist Church Nigeria (MCN), the International Coordinator addressed the Conference Connexional Council (CCC) meeting on the final day of our training visit. In earlier discussions the Prelate and Secretary of Conference shared with members of the visiting team how much the work of the CCILC was appreciated by the MCN. After the International Coordinator's presentation, this appreciation was endorsed by the members of the CCC who passed a resolution to this effect. They submitted a new application to the Scholarship And Leadership Training (SALT) Advisory Group of the Methodist Church in London requesting further funding from 2008 for a rolling programme that would allow a second group of 150 presbyters and deaconesses to receive training on this programme over the next two years.

Conference Connexional Council (CCC)

**THE JULY 2007 VISITING TEAM**

As last year, divided into two and delivered the two-week training course at both centres with the two teams exchanging venues mid-week.

**The visiting lecturers included the core team of the CCILC**

Details as given in earlier reports:
Revd Richard Jackson MA BD International Coordinator;
Revd Dr Malcolm McCall MA & Mrs Janet McCall BA (Hons);
Mr Keith Phillips Logistics and administration.

**The support team** for this training visit delivering particular aspects of the course was made up of:

| | |
|---|---|
| Mr Peter Fleck BSc(Hons) BD(Hons) | Langham Partnership International. Biblical Hermeneutics |
| Mrs Mhairi Fleck BA (Hons) | Community Artist/Living Well Trust; Lay Resource facilitator |
| Revd Kehinde Olabimtan BTh MTh | Minister Mission Ed. Good News Baptist Church, Lagos |
| Revd Dr Stephen Skuce MPhil BD | Methodist Minister from Ireland, PG Tutor Cliff College |
| Revd Dr Michael Thompson MA BD | Retired Methodist Minister and Lecturer in Old Testament |
| Mr Peter Worrell | Methodist Local Preacher-retired violinist with the Halle |

The dates of travel varied according to the needs of the course and personal circumstances, but the McCall's again enjoyed an extended period with opportunity to visit course students and associated supervisors in their local areas concentrating this time on students in the north towards Jos. Also a small group from the visiting team were able to visit students and churches in the Calabar District.

**FRIENDSHIPS RENEWED IN WORKING TOGETHER**

Once again the visiting team want to pay tribute to our hosts in the MCN and to both Rectors (Principals) and Staff of the Colleges who could not have been more welcoming and supportive. An early 'friendship' meeting for renewal of relationships with local staff and introductions to visiting newcomers has proved invaluable and is being programmed into the arrangements for both centres. It was acknowledged by all parties that it was better where possible for the visiting team (most of whom had not met each other before) to be together in the same accommodation for the duration of the 'Residentials'. Practically it makes for easier and on-time transport arrangements. With a short and intensive training programme that

148

allows little space for orientation: to climate; conditions; or people; time spent together as a team provides opportunities for team-building and reflective conversation. In a social setting rather than in a 'meeting' context concerns can be aired and adjustments made to the programme with the knowledge and agreement of those directly involved.

**Very Revd Okon Ekerendu**

Again, special thanks to the: the National Coordinator for the hospitality organised and constant care and attention given to the concerns of the CCILC.

Sadly, due to a family bereavement Peter & Mhairi Fleck had to return home a little early having worked hard to complete their lecturing responsibilities before leaving. The practical help in facilitating their early return given particularly by the Protocol Officer of the church, Revd Raphael Idialu and the sympathy expressed by all involved was much appreciated.

**PROGRESS OF COURSE**

It may be helpful in building upon earlier reports to review the progress made with the delivery of the two-year course through to anticipated graduation in July 2008. The requirements listed below are summarised from the course booklet with the coordinator's brief comments in italics.

**2006   4$^{th}$ July – 20$^{th}$ July inclusive (*Registered at: Umuahia=90 students; Sagamu=70 students*)**

**Oct 31** Submission of NT Assignment (1,500 words)
*In final assessment 50% of NT marks awarded for assignment; 50% for examination.*
**Dec 31** Submission of Dissertation Proposal for evaluation with tutor during January residential. *Submitted and kept under review with local tutors until January 2008 assessment of those on track to complete a Diploma rather than a Certificate/Foundation Course.*

**2007   4$^{th}$ Jan – 9$^{th}$ Jan Umuahia-Submission/initial assessment-applied evangelism project**

149

**11ᵗʰ Jan – 16ᵗʰ Jan Sagamu-Submission/initial assessment-applied evangelism project**
*Still registered and continuing at Umuahia=72 students; Sagamu=57 students*

**Feb 28** Submission of Church History-Practice of Evangelism (Assignment-3,000 words)
**May 31** Submission of Being the Church: Spirituality & Mission (Reflective Journal-3,000 words) *Kept under review with local tutors but final mark awarded by Dr McCall on submission Jan 08.*

**2007 3ʳᵈ July –19ᵗʰ July (Preliminary assessment W & P portfolio) (OT & NT Examinations)**

*Still registered and continuing at: Umuahia=70 students; Sagamu=50 students*

**Sep 30** Becoming the Church-Church Growth in Church History (Assignment-3,000 words)
*Assignment set by Revd Kehinde Olabimtan in July 07.*
**Nov 30** OT Assignment (1,500 words)
*Assignment set by Revd Dr Michael Thompson in July 07*
*In final assessment 50% of OT marks awarded for assignment; 50% for examination.*
**Dec 07** *assessment made based on received marks that will stream those going forward to completion of Diploma/Certificate/Foundation Course before the January 2008 Residential.*

**Jan 2008        3ʳᵈ Jan–8ᵗʰ Jan (Umuahia-Submission of Draft Dissertation/Spiritual Journal)**
*W/e of Saturday 5ᵗʰ & Sunday 6ᵗʰ will include spouses training programme*
**10ᵗʰ Jan–15ᵗʰ Jan (Sagamu-Submission of Draft Dissertation/Spiritual Journal)**
*W/e of Saturday 12ᵗʰ & Sunday 13ᵗʰ will include spouses training programme*

**Feb 28** Submission Wp & Preaching Portfolio *(Marked by designated local tutor/Rector's review)*

*Should include insights gained from Sunday visits to growing churches of other denominations.*

**Mar 31** Submission of Dissertation
*(Marked by designated local tutor/Revd Jackson review)*
**Apr 30** Submission of Applied Ev. Portfolio
*(Marked by designated local tutor/Revd Dr McCall review)*

**Jul 2008 1ˢᵗ July - 17ᵗʰ July inclusive** *(amended to 30ᵗʰ June-15ᵗʰ July will continue rolling programme for 150 presbyters and deaconesses subject to funding)*

| **Wednesday,** | **16 July** | **CCILC Graduation at Sagamu MTI** |
| **Saturday,** | **19 July** | **CCILC Graduation at Umuahia MTI** |

**RESOURCES FOR THE TRAINING COURSE**

AT LAST THE BOOKS ARE IN THEIR HANDS!

Once again, despite a generous grant from Feed the Minds, we have experienced some difficulty in providing the course books to students on time. As indicated in our January report, visiting lecturers always supply full notes as a necessary resource for students engaged in this kind of programme. Help with the building up of a personal library as well as augmenting what is available through the college libraries has been an enduring function of this pioneering programme (of part-taught, part self-study; part research; part residential and part practical training) since its inception.

Hopefully, some of our delivery problems will have been resolved with the arrival in Lagos of student books supplied through the Langham Partnership, but delayed paperwork does cause logistical problems that can lead to significant demurrage charges. We are once again negotiating with African Christian Textbooks (ACTS) in Nigeria to try and set up a regular supply of required books delivered locally for what looks like being an on-going programme. This will gives us

151

access also to books produced and published locally from Nigerian and other authors which will augment what is already being provided.

The experiment of inviting a lecturer from Sierra Leone on Community Development and Mission last July and a Nigerian Baptist, Kehinde Olabimtan this July to teach African Church History proved popular with the students and added to the visiting team a friendly and culturally aware sounding-board for presentations. It also allowed a creative interaction to develop that was of benefit to everyone involved. Whilst the special contribution that visiting lecturers make is valued by both students and local staff, developing relationships in a longer-term programme offer much more scope for a similar interaction to be created through greater involvement of local lecturers in the residential teaching programme which benefits their ongoing college work.

**HIGHLIGHTS**

We welcome the enthusiasm of the students and their willingness to become involved in everything that was presented as being something that might enhance their evangelistic ministry. Whether being led by a tutor through a series of lectures on 'Encountering other Religions' or having a violinist prompt them to experiment in worship, students became totally involved. Perhaps their enthusiasm is best shared through an edited email from one student on the Course:

"Dear Revd. Jackson,
I have the pleasure to congratulate you on our recently completed session at Sagamu. We had a scintillating and useful time with Christ. Never thought there was so much to learn about evangelism. Thanks for everything.
We also enjoyed our time with the new couple Peter and Mhairi. They were lively; also Steve who blew our minds and showed us our ignorance concerning people of other faiths. Revd and Mrs. McCall were as usual wonderful. We are sorry for Malcolm's accident *(Ed. Note-a collision with an overhead air conditioner meant stitches in the head!)* and thank Jesus for making the pain bearable. He didn't even miss a lesson. You can trust a hyper-active old man, just like you (laugh)."

The closing Communion Service at Umuahia when ideas were put into practice was inspirational. Violin and African musical instruments played as one and rehearsed musical responses from the Methodist Worship Book were sung with none of the inhibition linked with singing hymns from the Methodist Hymn Book and all of the enthusiasm usually reserved for traditional African songs.

Obviously, with a course that bears the title International Diploma In Applied Mission And Ministry, (IDIAMM) we attach great significance to the 'Applied' aspects of the programme. Again, I use Revd Dr McCall's shared and authenticated testimony associated with two people on the course.

PERSONAL TESTIMONIES

*(Editor) Extracted and shared in this publication under:*
*2008/3 ARCHDIOCESE OF KADUNA: DIOCESE OF JOS*

PARTNERS IN DEVELOPING THE COLLEGES

It is encouraging to see how much self-help work is being done in rebuilding and renovating premises on the campus at Umuahia MTI as they work to provide adequate facilities for a growing number of longer-term residential students as well as for students attending shorter training courses like our own.

NOT THE CHEQUE TAKEN TO THE BANK

Despite what has been achieved already the Rector, staff and students moved into celebration mode when presented with a cheque for £5,000 raised by The Avenue Methodist Church, Sale towards the

153

completion of the student quarters and associated extension/enhancement of the water supply to all the college buildings. We look forward with our students to enjoying the benefits of this development programme in January 2008 and at all future residentials.

A similar work is going on at Sagamu MTI and we are hoping that by January 2008 we will be able to make a matching donation of £5,000 to the work planned there which will provide an improved water supply to the whole campus. Any contributions from interested friends and well-off churches will be appreciated, particularly as Sagamu needs a further £20,000 to help complete a larger lecture hall/worship/conference centre sadly lacking on this Methodist College Campus.

We continue to make some progress, but seek further help from all agencies in building up the college libraries at both centres. Outdated and testimony books are not the ideal resource for training the future ministry of the MCN.

### AN EPILOGUE-OUR (TOURIST) VISIT TO CALABAR

Calabar in eastern Nigeria is being promoted as a place to "Come And Live And Be At Rest" The difference that one person, a former State Governor can make was evident in the clean roads and helmeted motor-cyclists. His vision for "Tinapa", a large, modern development to the north of Calabar centre, featuring a business park, very large shopping area, film studios (Nollywood!), leisure facilities, hotel and waterpark with speedboat access to Calabar waterfront is even now taking shape and will be opened in December.

**A statue of Mary Slessor in Calabar** (she lived there from 1876 until her death in 1915) holding twins summed up the ministry of one who almost single-handedly changed traditional fears about twins and broke the custom of abandoning them to their fate in the bush. The legacy of the "White Ma" of Calabar lives on in the church and the social change that were a product of her ministry. As the team led worship in various churches on the Sunday we were very conscious of that heritage.

154

On the way to Calabar some members of the visiting team were able to call at The Methodist School in Oron where Albert & Judith Graham, two of our church members from "The Avenue" had served as teachers from 1961-5. We were warmly welcomed and met some people who had been taught by Albert Graham and had gone on to make a significant contribution to both church and society. Their personal tributes, among others, remind us all of the continuing value of dedication, education and training to the growth of a nation and the church.

**ALBERT & JUDITH GRAHAM (ORON & SALE)**

Nothing offered to God dies in the ground without bringing in God's time a harvest that is multiplied through God's gracious Spirit.

*Richard Jackson (Revd) International Coordinator, CCILC*
*Wednesday, 15 August 2007*

## 2007/7 JUL: APPEAL DIOCESAN LEADERS SUPPORT

### TO OUR FELLOW WORKERS IN SHARING THE GOOD NEWS OF JESUS CHRIST

Please let me introduce myself as Revd Richard Jackson, the International Coordinator of the Cliff College International Learning Centre (CCILC) working alongside your own Very Revd Okon Ekerendu in providing a training programme for evangelists. As many of you are aware the invitation to Cliff College given by your Prelate, His Eminence Sunday Mbang and the Methodist Church Nigeria has begun to bear fruit. Early in July 2006 the CCILC with its visiting team of tutors in partnership with local staff and tutors began the first of its 'Residential Teaching Weeks'.

There are 57 students registered at Sagamu MTI and 82 students at Umuahia MTI for a two year course leading to the International Diploma in Applied Ministry and Mission (IDIAMM). As you know this programme is intended to be just one aspect of the

Conference initiative that seeks to re-position the Methodist Church Nigeria and renew its traditional emphasis on evangelism/mission.

We had hoped that a large proportion of the students would be presbyters with practical experience and at least three years of full-time study in English at a theological college behind them. As it turned out few of the students registered fit into that category, but all are enthusiastic and gifted evangelists. As we worked with the students we became aware that despite the limitations of their written English, many of them were capable of thinking through the concepts being taught and applying them to their own situations. Adjustments to academic levels required in English may need to be made in the light of experience, but there can be no doubt that these students are fully capable of engaging with the issues being faced by the Methodist Church Nigeria and that with further training that they can become an invaluable resource for the church in its evangelism/mission. Over the next few months what the students have received through teaching, lecture notes, and involvement in the Residential will be backed up by a supply of appropriate books being given free to each of them individually and to the libraries at both centres.

The Course has been launched and all of us involved students, staff, local and international are enthusiastic about the possibilities. This is why I write to you as fathers, brothers and sisters in Christ seeking your help in encouraging those whom you have sent to be enrolled on what will be for many of them an arduous course of study before they can hope to graduate in two years' time. Every student has received a Course Booklet setting out the requirements and regulations relating to the IDIAMM course. As you will see from the extract set out below there is much work for the students to complete between the July and January 'Residentials' and some deadlines to be met which will keep them fully stretched over the next two years.

**DATES OF THE RESIDENTIAL TEACHING PERIODS AND SCHEDULE FOR PRESENTATION OF WORK TO TUTORS FOR MARKING/ASSESSMENT**

*(Editor's note: Dates as shown in report for 2007/6 above, are not repeated here.)*

Please accept these thoughts as my personal reflections based on past experience. Nevertheless, the comments I make have been influenced by the questions raised by students during the July 2006 'Residential'.

1. Students will appreciate any personal interest shown in them by those senior in the ministry whether Prelate, Archbishop, Bishop or Presbyter. There seems to be a general feeling amongst the students that 'evangelists' are not valued or given the respect that they are due in the Methodist Church Nigeria. My experience of Cuba, one of the fastest growing Methodist Churches in the world, suggests that where 'The Evangelist' is afforded the respect given to the pastor it makes a significant difference to the church and promotes an evangelistic/mission orientation for the whole church.

2. Some students will need help with books for assignments (particularly until they receive more of their own) and many will need some guidance with producing adequate academic work in English.

3. Students will need to be allowed 'study time' as part of their working schedule when they are employed by the church. The Rector at Umuahia suggested that to avoid disruption every effort should be made not to re-station any evangelist in training until they have completed the course.

4. Students whilst attending the 'Residential' have been required to attend and reflect upon different aspects of the Sunday worship enjoyed by other church groups, particularly those that are growing. They have been asked to take time out from attending their own church services locally and to do similar reflection/assessment of those church groups that appear to be growing in their own locality. Their reflections/observations will become part of their 'Worship & Preaching Portfolio'.

5. All students will need some local authorisation and encouragement as they gather together a group of people whom they will train (in English or the vernacular) as evangelists. An assessment of the training they give to others will become part of their 'Applied

Evangelism Portfolio' which will be submitted as a significant component in the second year of the course.

As you can see from this there is much work to be done by every student on the course. All students with geographically linked diocese(s) have been allocated to a local college tutor who will make arrangements to meet with their group in some central location, once between July 2006 and January 2007 and again between January and July 2007. Our hope and prayer is that all may work together locally and nationally to nurture and encourage the students who have committed themselves to this very demanding course.

Whilst this open letter to you is a somewhat immediate personal reflection, I am hoping that it will be countersigned by your own Prelate, the Secretary of Conference and the national coordinator for the CCILC programme and reach you during Conference. Already you will have received some feedback from those who you have sent on the course. I hope that you will feel able to encourage and support them and the programme in the ways outlined above.

Every blessing in your Conference deliberations and in your continuing work for God!

Richard Jackson (Revd) International Coordinator, CCILC

# CHAPTER 8 2008: REVIEW NIGERIAN LINKS

*Early in 2008, it became clear that the leadership of MCN was so impressed with the impact of the CCITC, that a 'rolling programme' beyond 2006-8 was expected. The innovative 'Spouses Week-end', introduced as part of the programme in January was appreciated. Graduates in July 2008 numbered 108 students and about 100 new students (with more promised) were enrolled for the 2010-12 programme. Ceremonies in Abeokuta, linked with the 19th Century death there of Mary Archer, the first wife of Revd Thomas Champness, the forefather founder of Cliff College, served to strengthen the historic 'ties that bind' us as partners in mission today.*

## 2008/1 JAN 2-18: MCN FOURTH 'RESIDENTIAL'

(IDIAMM 2006-08 PROGRAMME)

INTRODUCTION

Many factors contributed to making this training visit one of the most difficult yet rewarding experiences of the whole programme.

An armed break-in late one night in December at the Rector's house on the college compound in Sagamu threatened the lives of the Rector and his family. The thieves took everything of material value from laptops to tee shirts; they left the family distraught, but thankfully physically unharmed. Security has since been improved, but the hiatus following the break-in impacted upon the college, the staff and our own students' submission of work for marking.

We are grateful to the local tutors who overcame the difficulties caused by the late submission and marking of work at both Umuahia and Sagamu by receiving and marking scripts during their vacation time, a work that continued even whilst our students were in residence.

Course books supplied through the Langham Partnership (utilising generous funding from Feed The Minds) arrived in Lagos during our July 2007 visit, but due to circumstances beyond our control were not released from the docks until late December.

Hundreds of books had to be delivered to Umuahia and Sagamu over the Christmas period before being checked, sorted and distributed to our students during our January 2008 visit. Again it is thanks to the Secretary of Conference, the National Coordinator and other associates that the books were released (without any loss of books or heavy demurrage costs) and that they were transported to the two centres in time for distribution to the students.

**THE BOOKS BRING OUT THE SMILES**

On the positive side, with the dedicated involvement of both local staff and visiting tutors we were able to provide a full programme of lectures and incorporate a spouses weekend at both centres whilst the course administrator Keith Phillips and his team of helpers documented marks and distributed books. With almost all of our registered students returning for this the final residential week of the course; their work up-to-date submitted and marked; the release and the students' joyful reception of the remaining books finally delivered, we had achieved much that seemed unlikely on our arrival early in January.

### THE RESIDENTIAL TRAINING

Apart from the core team of Jackson, McCall x 2 and Phillips (see earlier reports) the team for January included:

Revd Pamela Bolas BA (Hons) Methodist Minister, Involved in HIV Aids awareness & Counselling
Revd Gilbert Hall Methodist Minister, Former missionary Nigeria & Sierra Leone, Lay Trainer
Mrs Sylvia Hall Methodist Local Preacher, " "     ", Teacher and Network Leadership, Lay Trainer

MCN at the outset of the course asked that we should include in our work with the students two sensitive issues important in the Nigerian context, 'Other Religions' and 'A Christian Leader's approach to HIV/Aids'. In July 2008 Revd Dr Stephen Skuce's lectures on 'Encountering Other Religions' were much appreciated. These were

160

supplemented in January by teaching and the provision of a text book on 'World Religions & Cults', dealing with concerns raised by the students about Mormonism and Jehovah's Witnesses.

**Revd Pamela Bolas'** sensitive but challenging presentation over six lectures made good use of stories relating to HIV/Aids sufferers and helped to change attitudes among the students quite dramatically. It was clear by the final lecture that the students had a far better appreciation of both the medical facts about HIV/Aids and the fiction that clouds people's judgment. More importantly, they have been encouraged as leaders in the church to preach and minister about this concern pastorally with compassion rather than judgmentally with self-righteous induced passion.

Revd Gilbert & Mrs Sylvia Hall were returning 'Home' to Nigeria after many years and were welcomed as 'belonging'. Whilst they provided focussed morning devotions at the beginning of each day and fitted in sessions during the week, they were instrumental in the success of yet another 'experiment'. With the encouragement of the Prelate of MCN the Halls were asked to organise a 'Spouses weekend' as part of the training course at each of the two centres. With 15 wives, 1 husband and associated children at Umuahia in addition to our students and 8 wives and 1 husband plus children at Sagamu they had their hands full, but the programme within a programme worked so well that it will now be incorporated into the two year programme on a regular basis.

### THE SPOUSES TRAINING WEEKEND

The spouses at each centre joined the course on Friday evening and were 'officially' present until and including Sunday lunchtime. On the Saturday Gilbert & Sylvia led sessions on: Christian marriage; Roles of men and women in the church; The Church as the Family of God and its mission; Worship; Revd Pam Bolas led a joint session on HIV/Aids which was followed by separate (Women & Men) group discussions. The Saturday closed with a session on Women in Leadership of Home Cell Groups followed by prayers, but the highlight of the weekend was the worship led on Sunday morning by three of the married couples who had participated in the training of the previous day. With the spouses, rather than the students taking the lead in worship, comments ranged from, "I have come to appreciate my wife" to "If Methodist worship was always like this many people would come". Later on the Sunday morning the participants joined together again to reflect upon the service and much that was positive was included in the students' worship portfolio.

**OTHER ACTIVITIES ASSOCIATED WITH THE PROGRAMME**

At Umuahia MTI we found that the July 07 donation of £5,000 from The Avenue Methodist Church, Sale for new student accommodation was being put to good use and the new water supply to every part of the compound improving hygiene and toilet facilities was 'in full flow'. We are grateful again to friends from The Avenue Methodist Church, The Shetland churches and other donors who

helped us make a further contribution of £5,000 in January to the college at Sagamu so that similar improvements can be made to the accommodation and water supply there. After their stressful time, the Rector and staff at Sagamu were particularly pleased to receive this reminder of continuing provision from the church and friends in the UK.

**£5,000: SHETLAND TO SAGAMU MTI**

Over the last eighteen months, Revd Dr Malcolm McCall & his wife Janet have undertaken to great effect an ambassadorial role for the programme which has seen them extend their two week 'training course' involvement for a further two weeks each time so that they could meet with students and their church 'supervisors' in different parts of the country. The generous hospitality provided by the MCN for their journeying has been appreciated. When we met up we shared in their sadness at the untimely death of the Archbishop of Calabar's wife and prayed together with shared concern as people learned of an accident involving a bus carrying the clergy and their bishop from near Port Harcourt to a meeting that the McCalls were addressing in Calabar. The Bishop and several other ministers were taken to hospital for treatment where one minister died. We continue to pray for them, their families and friends.

The McCalls' have been impressed by the number of new evangelism/mission projects initiated with the support of local leadership and being undertaken by students as a direct consequence of their involvement in the course. Full reports on their extended visits are available. Brief testimonies have been shared in earlier reports and others will be shared later, but the work of our students in one area that was visited in January has led to: 4 home fellowships which have attracted 15 new members to the church and regular evangelistic meetings; 2 home fellowships in Asanting Nkwongo and Asanting Asan providing 21 people for confirmation on 30th December 2007; a new church has been planted in Uyo which has grown to 56 attendees; one student is involved in outreach with students at Uyo University.

THE NORTHERN OUTREACH

*(Editor's note: Extracted to share under 2008/3*
*ARCHDIOCESE OF KADUNA: DIOCESE OF JOS)*

PLANS FOR THE FUTURE

The first two-year course in Nigeria will end in July 2008 with the likely graduation of up to 120 students. The President of the UK Methodist Church, Revd Dr Martyn Atkins (also Principal of Cliff College and Director of the CCILC) will attend the graduations at Umuahia on Wednesday 16th July and Sagamu on Saturday 19th July at the invitation of His Eminence Revd Dr Ola Makinde.

The MCN in its ongoing evaluation of the programme has deemed it so successful that already there are plans for a rolling programme which will have 150 ministers and deaconesses starting a new course early in July 2008. In a meeting this January with key people including the Secretary of Conference and the Bishop of Evangelism we reviewed what has been achieved and put in place plans for the July graduation and the new course. The basic funding for the course has been approved through the Scholarship And Leadership Training (SALT) advisory group of the Methodist Church UK and supplementary funding for books, materials etc. will again be sought from sponsors like Feed The Minds and other friends of the programme.

THE BISHOP OF EVANGELISM, RT. REVD SUNDAY ONUOHA WITH VISITING TEAM & PARTNER LECTURERS AT UMUAHIA

Plans for the future include promoting the concept of 'Doing training overseas in partnership with local churches' through leaflets, reports and DVD's. Some of these are available to interested parties/fund raisers now and we hope to produce a new DVD on the project in Nigeria during our July 2008 visit. Knowing that this report has a fairly general circulation as well as going to specific donors we limit it to two pages. Those who want or need to know more can contact me as indicated below. In the meantime thank you to all who will read this report in anticipation of your continuing prayers, your encouragement and where possible your practical and financial support.

**Richard Jackson (Revd)      International Coordinator CCILC**

**Fame comes at last with this footnote from a friend in Nigeria:**
"By the way you should be encouraged that one of the Nigerian newspapers has written up your story. I get a press summary collated by the British High Commission in Abuja. This was one paragraph in today's summary":

*Methodist Church Partners Cliff College UK: (Sunday Vanguard) Pg43: "As part of efforts towards repositioning the church and sustaining its leadership position in churches within Nigeria and abroad, the Methodist Church Nigeria has strengthened her partnership programme with Cliff College International Learning Centre, UK, for human resources and manpower development."*

# 2008/2 JAN 15: MCN/CCILC BRIEFING

Obviously, there have been throughout the programme ad-hoc planning meetings held with MCN leaders and College partners, with friendly, free and frank exchanges! (See also 2014/2)

## Present:

The Rt. Revd Dr C. Raphael Opoko, Secretary of Conference, MCN
The Rt. Revd Dr S. N. Onuoha, Bishop of Evangelism, MCN.
The Very Revd Samuel N. Nortey, Director of Administration, MCN.
The Very Revd Dr Okechukwu Ogba, Rector, MTI Sagamu.
The Very Revd Okon Ekerendu, National Coordinator, CCILC/MCN
Revd Richard Jackson, International Coordinator, CCILC.
Mr Keith Phillips, Administrator, CCILC.

Apology for absence was received from His Eminence, The Prelate, who has delegated full authority in these matters to The Secretary of Conference. Courtesies including presentation of books took place.

Main Agenda: 1. Graduation of students – 2006/08 Course.
2. Planning for 2008/10 Course.

## Item 1 Present Course

Richard Jackson (RJ) reported on the progress of the Present Course. There are 67 potential graduates from Umuahia and 50 from Sagamu. There is one (church planting!) student at Umuahia who, with the approval of his Bishop (Jos), is in attendance but, due to his extremely limited English, will not graduate.

RJ particularly paid tribute to the tutors at both Institutes for getting done a huge amount of marking of work submitted very late. Without their great efforts, it is doubtful if more than a small number of students would have been ready at this time to progress towards graduation.

Thanks largely to the efforts of the staff and international administrator as on 18th Jan 2008, there were 8 outstanding pieces of work awaited at both Umuahia and Sagamu (out of 476 at Umuahia and 350 at Sagamu). At the same time, RJ emphasised that there can be no further extensions for late submission and that the deadlines in the Course prospectus ending with the 30th April 2008 are not negotiable for students or their supervisors.

165

Some time was given to discussing the situation regarding the books ordered for the course. After a long delay, the books from The Langham Partnership are out of the docks and 10 titles, including 5 large reference books, have been distributed to students and staff. A further 4 titles, brought by air by the visiting team, have also been distributed to the students. Amazingly, no demurrage was paid on the Langham books and no excess baggage charge on the other books! Books ordered through ACTS at Jos, have not been delivered (apart from a few incomplete sets); Revd Dr Malcolm McCall is due to visit Jos and, with the Bishop of Jos, to follow up that potential source for the next course. The Secretary and the Bishop of Evangelism felt that this could be the best single source for all the course books, particularly with senior MCN "encouragement".

The Secretary also asked that information about any books coming from the U.K. should be shared with him at the very earliest opportunity. RJ explained why matters were not always in our hands when receiving grant aided book supplies. The confusion about the Form M was discussed. Although importers always ask for this form, it is apparently not required for importing books.

**Item 2 Graduation:**

The dates were confirmed as:

**Umuahia Wed 16th July 2008 & Sagamu Sat. 19th July 2008.**

The exchange of venues and dates is to accommodate the President of Conference, U.K. and make possible his presence in Lagos on Sunday 20th.

Coordination of the planning for the two graduation events will rest with:-

U.K.:                          Keith Phillips

Nigeria:                       Okon Ekerendu (at MCN HQ)
                               The Rector (at Sagamu)
                               The Registrar (at Umuahia)

166

Copies for information to:                The Secretary of Conference
                                          The Bishop of Evangelism
                                          The Director of Administration
                                          Revd Richard Jackson

**ACTION**: Keith Phillips to establish e-mail contact with all.

NOTE: this group is referred to as "The Contact Group".

**Objectives of Graduation**;

1.      Present awards to those graduating.
2.      Create awareness of the programme.
3.      Involve students' families.
4.      Involve local people and MCN generally.
5.      Encourage others in evangelism and study.
6.      Involvement of many others encouraged by the presence of His
        Eminence, the Prelate, and the President of Conference, U.K.

**Item 3 The Graduation event**:  Discussion about the format of the day(s) produced the following thoughts and decisions:

1. The graduation should be a single event, embedding the Graduation within the Service of Worship.  This is the normal practice at both Institutes and has served well in the past.
2.   The event should start at 10 a.m.; those coming a distance (families) would either start very early or arrive the previous day.
3. MTI MCN and CCILC would be responsible for entertainment etc. of the "invited dignitaries" only; students would be required to take care of their own guests.
4.  Revd Dr Martyn Atkins (President of Conference, U.K.) will be invited to preach and as the Principal of Cliff College and Director of CCILC he will present the certificates.
5. Mention was made of the possibility of attendance by the respective Governors of State.
6.  The Dress code for the students was discussed.  RJ indicated that students had been informed that national dress would be worn (moving away from the traditional black academic gowns & hoods associated with degree ceremonies).  The distinguishing and unifying mark would be the CCILC/MCN Preaching Scarves presented to each Graduate.

7. The production of the Preaching Scarves was discussed. Apparently there has been no response from the MCN Tailors. Okon Ekerendu was tasked with finding out whether that organisation can produce the 200 needed in good time, quality and price (Not more than £5.00 each). If not, then he is to take the job to someone else who can. The scarf will be in Cliff College colours (blue & gold), with the Cliff College badge embroidered on one end and the MCN badge on the other. Early action and careful supervision required.
**ACTION**:      Very Revd Okon Ekerendu as in 7 above.

**Invitations**:   The contact group (see above) are to share by e-mail and produce invitation lists for each venue.
**ACTION**:      Contact Group.

**Accounts**:    RJ stated that the full account for the 2006/08 Course would be needed for the SALT Committee soon but certainly no later than July 2008.
**ACTION**:      MCN

## Item 4. 2008/10 Course

**Agreed**:        That the next course should start in July 2008, and run for 2 years, (following the pattern of the first course). That the students should be ordained (Bishops?), Presbyters, Deaconesses, with at least 3 years of college study in English as their foundation for this course. RJ is to work on clear admission criteria.
**ACTION**:      Revd. R. Jackson

That, as far as is possible, local tutors should remain in post for the duration of the course. The same should apply to the post of National Coordinator who should be appointed to relate to the new course prior to July. (Okon Ekerendu is due to retire in 2008 but will remain national coordinator until after the graduation of the 2006/8 course).
**ACTION**:      MCN

That a total of 150 students should be enrolled spread more or less equally between the two Institutes. This may be affected by teaching space limitations at Sagamu, although completion of the new Chapel/Conference building would resolve this.

That consideration be given to a spread of students from each of the 9 Archdioceses with an equal number of nominations. The Bishop of Evangelism noted that there may be areas where the need for evangelism is greater, justifying a larger share of student places.

That the course study fee (£50 per annum) will be supplemented at a higher level for college accommodation, feeding, overheads etc. than for the first course, reflecting the financial status of the prospective students and circuits. The experience gained of likely costs locally in relation to the course should be used in setting a realistic overall figure. It was noted that N20,000 did not cover the local costs for 2006/8.
**EARLY ACTION:** MCN

The issue of gender (of students) was discussed with some recognition of the need for continuing female involvement.

The course was originally designed for Presbyters by developing a curriculum that majored on mission/evangelism and these modules will continue to be taught at an appropriate level for the students involved. The Diploma (2nd year University) teaching will be at the same level as that on the current course, but there will not be the need of a safety net of two lower levels (foundation & certificate) introduced as a possibility in 2007 to accommodate some less able (mainly linguistically) students among the present groups. Prospective students will pass or fail at Diploma level. All students will be encouraged to see this course as in-service training which will be expected to produce practical outcomes in relation to MCN's evangelism targets.

The use of Resource Persons from within MCN and additional invited lecturers was discussed, but time/financial constraints for all involved were noted. The supervising role of local partner tutors in the colleges was explained and acknowledged as vital.
The meeting closed with prayer.

Minutes by Keith Phillips          24/01/2008

# 2008/3 JAN: McCALLS APPLYING LEARNING TOUR

REVD DR MALCOLM & MRS JANET McCALL THROUGH EXTENDED VISITS: ENCOURAGE THE STUDENTS IN THEIR APPLICATION OF THE CLIFF COLLEGE IDIAMM COURSE TO MISSION PROJECTS.

## ARCHDIOCESE OF CALABAR

We were able to spend the last weekend of 2007 in Mary Slessor country: the Calabar area of Eastern Nigeria. Calabar was a major slave-trading centre: we were moved to spend the last Sunday of the year marking the abolition of British slave-trading with the Christians there! On Sunday morning we were involved in worship at Calabar Methodist Cathedral with a congregation of 300-400. The Archbishop, the Most Revd Efiom E. Ekpenyong, led the whole service powerfully, even though he was personally in the midst of the grief of his wife's recent death. Many responded to an "altar call" that our lives should be given to knowing Christ and making Him known. In the afternoon we met up with our Course students who live and minister in that area.

### STUDENT 1; STUDENT 2; STUDENT 3:

Student 1 was married in December 2007 to a Methodist Minister (who later joined us for the spouses' weekend in Umuahia). She spoke of an evangelistic programme with which she has been involved, reaching out into surrounding villages. Also, she was part of a church-planting initiative with 10-15 worshippers in it. As was always the intention, this church plant has been handed over to the responsibility of a neighbouring circuit which shared in its beginnings. It was good that Her Presbyter – and that of Student 2 & 3 came to this meeting for our Course students.

### STUDENT 4

Is now training for the Methodist ministry. As we travelled around in the next few weeks, we were amazed to discover that 6 or 7 of our students, partly encouraged by the impact of the Cliff College Course, had quietly candidated for the ordained Methodist ministry, been accepted, and started training! He described how his ministry has developed as he applied the Course through an evangelistic Discipleship Class numbering around 13. This has demonstrated the need for believers to practise evangelism – as he has been passing on to them the training he has received on the Cliff College Course. This Discipleship Class has conducted Open Air Evangelistic Meetings, joining with the Youth Fellowship, who would provide singing, dancing and drama. Also, a new preaching post has been established with about 15 worshippers.

**STUDENT 5** shared into our discussions

**STUDENT 6** Has been short of time to apply the Course because of his responsibilities as Senior Church Steward and as a Lay Preacher.

**STUDENT 7** Was unable to attend this meeting, but it was reported that he has been appointed as part-time Evangelist with a small financial allowance.

**STUDENT 8**

Has been limited in her application of the Course by ill-health, culminating in a major operation. However, she is looking to establish a Rehabilitation Centre for homeless youths in Calabar City. She has visited the Catholic Rehab. Centre for ideas and advice, and aims to incorporate into the new Centre a facility for teaching English reading and writing.

**STUDENT 9**

*Was unable to complete the Course because of being called up for a year's national service, helpfully joined in these discussions: she is the daughter of Engineer Okon Effretui, who has become well-known to the International Team, and who helped to arrange the return of the Dora Skipsey plate to MGHS Oron.*

**ARCHDIOCESE OF IKOT EKPENE**

We moved to the west of Cross River, and on Monday 31 December met the Cliff College students from UYO DIOCESE in Emmanuel Methodist Church, Itiam Etoi (see details below). From there we moved on to return to the Methodist Girls' High School, Oron, a large brass plate, originally presented to Miss Dora Skipsey in the 1960s. She had founded the school, and the ceremony proved to be a "richer" and more "inspirational" event than we had anticipated (a fuller email/"hard copy" report available on request). The Bishop of ORON DIOCESE, the Very Revd Elijah Udo Udo, entertained us for a meal, and it was a real thrill to pop in to the home of the Very Revd

171

Okon Ekerendu, who lives close to the school. Okon, who is the National Coordinator for the Cliff College Course, has become a dear friend, and it was a blessing that he shared our itinerary with us.

The Archbishop of Ikot Ekpene, the Most Revd Sunday B. Uko, gave us warm and generous overnight hospitality for 2 days. At the Methodist Cathedral, on New Year's Day, a large number of the several hundred present dedicated their lives, at the start of the new year, to personal mission and evangelism. It is so good that everyone in Nigerian Methodism seems aware of the Church's decision some 3 years ago, to "reposition for evangelism" to be central to the life and work of the Church.

The following day, we met with Cliff College students at the Cathedral (details below), following which the Methodist Archbishop of Ikot Ekpene had gathered all his ministers and deaconesses to a meeting concerning the Cliff College Course – about 140 of them in this strongly Methodist area. We spoke about the expected provision of a new Course for Presbyters and Deaconesses, beginning in July 2008. We were all very shocked to hear during this meeting that a bus carrying all the clergy and their bishop from one area near Port Harcourt to the meeting had been involved in an accident. Five ministers, including the bishop, were in hospital: one later, tragically, died from head injuries. Whatever else, this reminded us of the life-and-death spiritual battle we are involved in.

### THE DIOCESE OF PORT HARCOURT

The Bishop of PORT HARCOURT DIOCESE asked whether Cliff College would think of more closely partnering Methodist Church Nigeria in his diocese.

### STUDENT 10

Has recently been transferred to the Oku-Obon Circuit. There he has already organised Revival Nights throughout December 2007 for the 11 Circuit Churches, in consultation with his Presbyter.

### STUDENT 11

Has also recently been transferred - from Ikot Ediet Abiakpa Circuit. Before he left he ministered in 3 days of evangelistic meetings with the Priest-in-Charge, to establish a new preaching post at Ikot

Udo Oboro. At present, there are rather fewer than 20 members at this new post.

## STUDENT 12

Has opened about 4 home fellowships for "weekly prayers and Bible studies, which attracted about 15 new members to the church, and all of them have accepted Jesus as their personal Lord and Saviour," as well as conducting regular evangelistic meetings. He has candidated for ministerial training, and has already completed one year at Umuahia!

## STUDENT 13 and STUDENT 14

Attended the meeting, but had nothing specific to report.

## STUDENT 15

Has established 2 House fellowships as Asanting Nkwongo and Asanting Atan: through these House Fellowships, 21 new members were presented for Confirmation on 30 December 2007
organised a quarterly Crusade at Asanting Obot Obon village which, from 27 to 29 December 2007, attracted about 410 people
been appointed Youth and Children's Coordinator for his Circuit.
Student 15 says the Most Revd Sunday B. Uko, Archbishop of Ikot Ekpene, has been his supportive spiritual father: he also reported that his newly-born son has been named Malcolm!

## STUDENT 16 and STUDENT 17

Attended the meeting, but had nothing specific to report.

## STUDENT 18

Reported that out of a Bible Study in his local church, 7 individuals had confessed Christ and been born again.

## STUDENT 19

Has planted a church at 129 Aka-Etinan Road, Uyo, having used house-to-house evangelism as the starting point. A House Fellowship was started on 31 July 2007, and thereafter there has been "constant fellowship, teaching and faith-sharing." On 21 December 2007, 108,000Naira was paid as rent for a temporary place of worship, and the official opening and first worship service was held on Sunday 6 January 2008. A total of 56 people attended this service – 26 men, 16 women and 14 children. Dickson requests any help from British Methodism in provision of Bibles, hymn books, musical instruments and (by far the biggest financial challenge) land for a permanent site.

## STUDENT 20

Has been reaching out to students at Uyo University, training about 15 Methodist Campus Fellowship members in evangelism and discipleship. "The Fellowship programme is richer and . . . has increased to about 80 members. But the University Administration intends to derecognise campus fellowships, hence the problem of space has become a threat."

## STUDENT 21

Reached out to the community in Ekpen Nsukara, where a new church was started. He arranged an anniversary programme in 2005 with only 15 members: now there are about 82! He has also been coordinating a radio evangelism programme.

## STUDENT 22

Has been busy as Assistant Church Steward. She has shared in evangelistic Bible Studies and Praise Evenings. Through a crusade, a new preaching post has been established in the last year at Ekpri Nsukara. More than 500 people from the area attended a Praise Night.

## STUDENT 23

Was made Coordinator for Baptismal and Confirmation Classes at the Methodist Cathedral of the Cross, Oron Diocese. He was able to prepare 34 candidates for Baptism on 23 December 2007 and 62 candidates for Confirmation on 6 January 2008

These visits were followed by the residentials at Umuahia and Sagamu reported elsewhere.

## ARCHDIOCESE OF KADUNA: DIOCESE OF JOS

*(This part of the Report is an amalgam of our 2 visits to Jos Diocese and Plateau State, one in June 2007 and one in January 2008. The second visit was a response to an official request that we should explore the possibility, as a Cliff College Team, of providing some help at Zonkwa Methodist College, which is the third of the*

174

*Conference-supported Methodist Colleges in Nigeria: Umuahia in the East; Sagamu in the West; and Zonkwa "looking North.)*

**ZONKWA MTI: BUILDING FOR NORTHERN OUTREACH**

At the end of the Residentials in Umuahia and Sagamu, Janet and I again had the enormous privilege of travelling to where our students are ministering, in order to identify how the course is being applied in their own churches and circuits, and to offer them encouragement, as we had done in the Calabar area before the Residentials. How we have loved, over the last 3 visits to Nigeria, living in the homes of our Nigerian sisters and brothers, enjoying our communal life together in Christ. We were in **Jos** from 17 to 21 January, where the mainly "Christian" South and the mainly "Muslim" North meet. The Methodist Bishop of Jos took us to Zonkwa, about 2 hour's road-journey from Jos. Here there is a Methodist Theological College, which in some ways might be considered similar in ethos to Cliff College itself. There are around 30 students and 3 members of staff, the latter being all Methodist ministers.

**FACILITIES IN THE COLLEGE ARE VIRTUALLY NON-EXISTENT!**

No electricity or running water. Indeed the "water supply" is a deep solitary rough-hewn well with a small pool of dirty-looking water at the bottom: all that is available for washing, cooking and drinking!! 26 male students are accommodated in a leaky-roofed room which has 8 sets of two-tier bunk beds (=16 places); the other 10 sleep on mats on the floor between the bunk-beds!! But what a vision: to reach the North with the Good News of Jesus, in Hausa, the indigenous language, with Methodist emphases and Methodist church pastoring. The Principal, the Very Revd Shettima Chibok, is a convert from Islam, from the far North of Nigeria: his wife came to Christ after him. Janet and I were moved, thrilled, and caught up in the vision. With no financial provision as yet, Shettima has started redeveloping a fine permanent site for the College, which the Methodist Church owns just outside Zonkwa.

There were other encouragements in Jos. We visited the Anglican Archbishop, wanting to stand with him after a group of men had entered his home in the night in July 2007, intent on murder. He and his family were miraculously saved from death, though the 17-year-old son was badly beaten. This sort of thing has happened to this family on a number of occasions. But we were able to meet his son, looking fully recovered, and full of the joy of the Lord! The Archbishop has said, **"I am continuing with my work, as I have decided that preaching the gospel is worth living for and it is worth dying for."**

STUDENT (NORTH) 1

Came to visit us in the home of the Bishop of Jos with the question, "What happens after the course is finished? How, really, are we going to reach out to those people in the far villages beyond my home who have not heard the Gospel, and do not know who Jesus is?" With shining face, and resolve clear and focused, he warmed to the thought of Zonkwa Methodist Theological College developing further as an evangelistic training centre looking to the North. Calvin himself is a Hausa-speaking indigene, and from an ecumenical background, is concerned that the blessings of the Cliff College Course should be shared with other denominations.

In particular he mentioned the Anglican Church in the Jos area, and the Church of Christ in Nigeria. (The latter is a fairly small, orthodox denomination which is spread mainly through Plateau State.) We were struck by how important it rightly seems to the Methodist Church for Hausa-speaking indigenes to be involved in any evangelistic enterprise in the North. Student (North) 1 is another who has candidated for the Methodist ministry, and has already started training in Ibadan: he broke his journey back to Ibadan to share with us his zeal for further evangelistic development in his own home area. He does not have an income now he is studying full-time at Ibadan: his wife has been generously helping with the finances from her own teacher's salary.)

176

On Friday 30 June 2007 we visited a large number of churches where our students are active, the highlight being our visit to the church at Gengeri Gyel. Student (North) 2 provided a report on how this new church has been planted within the last 12 months.

During a Course lecture in Umuahia in July 2007, this student "felt a burden in my spirit to reach out in evangelism at Gengeri Gyel. As I returned to Plateau State on 27th. July 2006, I and my wife, by His grace, moved into evangelism using (the) house-to-house method. The few that accepted the Lordship of Christ in their lives teamed up with me and we started a house fellowship meeting in one of the brethren's houses." This group of 25 people first met on 10 August 2006, and they agreed to become a church. His minister, gave the "go-ahead," and provided some chairs. "On 25th November," The student writes in his report, "the church started its first worship services as a group, and we are still worshipping here . . . and as the Lord is helping us we had 56 worshippers on Sunday 24.6.07 to the Glory of God." Janet and I were deeply moved to visit this church as daylight faded on Friday evening 29th. June. Student (North) 2 and his wife were there, together with many of the 56 worshippers. Bishop Jaja, (the then Bishop of Jos, moved to be Bishop of Kano in late 2007) encouraged this new church plant (all Igbo, Yoruba or Iduma-speaking people) to reach out to the Hausa-speaking "indigenes." (Indigene is a much-used word in Nigeria now, meaning the original inhabitants, the natural owners of the country, the people 'born and bred' in that district.) The Church was meeting in half of a rough barn with earthen floor and no facilities. John said he was looking to build a Methodist church building, a manse, and even a primary school.

While Janet preached elsewhere, I was able to return to this church plant in Gengeri Giel in January 2008. I shared worship with about 55 participants. The student, the Pastor at Gengeri Giel, later came to see us at the home of the new Bishop of Jos, the Rt. Revd Ibrahim Chindo. He came with his wife, who shares with him in this evangelistic project. Their vision continues to expand! They now have land enough for a church building, a manse and a Primary School (The student's wife is a trained Primary School teacher.) They want to name their Church "Cliff Good News Church" out of appreciation for the Cliff College programme being used of God to plant this church! Janet felt they had got to the heart of the matter when they said that they go out into neighbouring villages and preach Christ. When their listeners have become excited about new life in Jesus, then they invite them to "Cliff Church." Understandably, John appealed for any financial help which might be available from the British Methodist Church.

STUDENT (NORTH) 3

Is a special person. Limited in his use of English, but powerfully effective in his native Hausa, he said in July 2007 that he felt he could not reach the standard of written work required by the IDIAMM Course. But since he has found the Course such a help and encouragement, he eagerly asked if he could continue to be part of it to its conclusion, without doing the written work, and therefore not receiving a diploma: his request was granted. He oversees all the four Hausa-speaking churches in the Cathedral Circuit, and has himself planted 3 churches in the last 12 months. In June 2007, we visited Miango Methodist Church, which had virtually ceased to exist as a congregation, and found a vibrant group of over 50 people there. This group also included the Church Stewards of 2 newly planted churches which are beyond Miango, and were too far distant for us to visit. These churches now have viable congregations of 20 or more worshippers each. Student (North) 2 is bubbling over with Holy Spirit enthusiasm to do more. As we spoke with him in January 2008, he was longing to plant a church in his own isolated village.

Out of all this, you will not be surprised that Janet and I have acquired a deep yearning to partner the Methodist Church (if we are asked by Methodist Church Nigeria, and if the Cliff College programme allows) in "looking north" to this huge and challenging mission-field, where great sacrifice is required to proclaim the Gospel. (Methodist ministers have been murdered, buildings burnt down, and the official introduction of Sharia law in some States has threatened the security of Christians in their life and work.)

ARCHDIOCESE OF LAGOS: DIOCESE OF LAGOS WEST
STUDENT LAGOS 1; STUDENT LAGOS 2:

Our last few days in Nigeria in January 2008 were spent in Lagos West where two of our lady students had produced a well-organised visit for us. In 2 days we spoke in 5 churches, in some cases several local congregations combined. For me, the highlight was a

178

service in the Cathedral where a dozen or so adults committed themselves "to know Christ and to make Him known." But also, 9 young children came forward to ask Jesus into their lives, the first youngster to come forward being the daughter of the Cathedral's Presbyter. Afterwards we made paper boats together, singing, "With Jesus in the boat we can smile at the storm," and similar choruses. (Janet had spoken on the first verses of Luke 5 – Jesus in the boat with Peter.)

Student Lagos 2 immediately took the names of the children and agreed to meet up with them for a children's discipleship class, starting in the Cathedral on the following Saturday afternoon! She is a Sunday School teacher in the Cathedral, and is writing her Cliff College Diploma dissertation on child evangelism. We could not have seen a better example of the Course theory being immediately and practically applied in local church ministry! The young bank clerk who interpreted for us into Yoruba at the Cathedral sent us an email in mid-February 2008 to confirm that the children's ministry in the Cathedral is already "yielding tremendous results," and that among the adults, "the fire of revival has started to burn . . . zealously." We would see this as a result of much prayer on the part of our two students and others; the warm support of the Bishop of Lagos West, the Rt. Revd Isaac Ayo Olawuyi; and the involvement of the local Methodist ministers of the diocese. It was a most encouraging visit for us.

The International Diploma In Applied Ministry And Mission (IDIAMM) is basically a two year academic course but we have established that the key to a successful training outcome is the 'Application'. For the course in Nigeria every Diploma student is required to demonstrate their own 'application' through an 'Applied Evangelism' portfolio which they will submit as their final piece of work. What has been included in these portfolios has been reviewed by their local tutor as the course has progressed. The current indications are that most of the students are applying what they are learning in very practical ways and making a difference to the mission of the MCN.

Janet and Malcolm McCall,
February 2008

# 2008/4 JUN 20–JUL 20: MCN GRADUATIONS & ?

(IDIAMM 2006-08 PROGRAMME)

INTRODUCTION

The basic funding for the new two-year course (2008-10) has been approved through the Scholarship And Leadership Training (SALT) advisory group of the Methodist Church UK and supplementary funding for books, materials etc. is again being sought from sponsors like Feed The Minds and other friends of the programme. Knowing that this report has a fairly general circulation as well as going to specific donors we limit it to two pages. Those who want or need to know more can contact me as indicated below. In the meantime thank you to all who will read this report in anticipation of your continuing prayers, your encouragement and where possible your practical and financial support.

We tried to save time for the participants and money for the ILC programme by combining several activities in this month long training visit to Nigeria. Our media men recruited for this purpose, James Atkins and Michael Claye, were able to record over 20 hours of video footage of:

Exciting developments at the northern training college in Zonkwa;
The enthusiastic beginning of a new two-year programme with a fresh batch of students at Sagamu and Umuahia;
A moving memorial service at the graveside of an early missionary with Cliff College connections in Abeokuta;
And showing the colourful graduation ceremonies of the 2006-08 students, with celebrations at both Umuahia and Sagamu Methodist Training Centres;
After editing, (which is a time-consuming task), DVD's and pictures will be available on request.

Despite preparing as much as possible in advance of our visit, the increased pressure of finalising arrangements for all these events whilst working with the new intake of students within a strictly limited time-scale meant that an always hectic programme became almost unmanageable at times. Tribute must be paid, not only to our travelling team for their hard work and unfailing good humour, but also to our partners in the MCN who worked tirelessly with us to achieve the successful outcomes shared in this report.

**THE COLLEGE AT ZONKWA**

ZONKWA MTI: WATER SUPPLIED

The college at Zonkwa (see earlier reports) set in the predominately Muslim north of Nigeria was not part of the original CCILC programme. Fortunately, with the help of donations and team visits we have been able to respond to the MCN request of the Prelate and the Principal at the college that we should help build up the training work being developed at Zonkwa. Revd Dr Malcolm & Janet McCall share this brief report,

*"The developments at Zonkwa over the 6 months since our last visit in January of this year were truly amazing. The longed-for borehole has been sunk, linked with a generator, and is now producing good, clean water on the permanent college site. Our friend Very Revd Shettima Chibok, the College Principal, has built rudimentary student accommodation and a chapel with mud blocks, and has moved the whole college on to the permanent site. For our short 5-day input of lectures, 68 people turned up, and the chapel was used as our assembly-room."* It is particularly encouraging that the Very Revd Shettima had enrolled as a student on the new course with us this July in Umuahia.

**MCN GRADUATIONS FOR COMPLETED (2006-08) PROGRAMME**

Distance Learning Programmes are difficult to monitor and bring to completion in any setting but the huge distances to be travelled and the problems with communications even when many Nigerians seem to have cell phones glued to their ears make life very difficult for students and local staff. Despite the best efforts of all involved there was still much work to be done in linking marks on a spreadsheet to actual work that could be reviewed and moderated in ways that satisfied academic integrity and made allowances for the problems faced by all involved. After much hard work, particularly by our administrator, Keith Phillips and through the cooperation of the college registrars we achieved much more than had been anticipated at the outset. It quickly became clear that all of the students who had completed and submitted their work for marking had shown much improvement in their English writing skills and ability to formulate answers to questions.

Many later submissions belied the students' earlier difficulties and a judicious reassessment of their work overall meant that all the students who completed the course gained a pass mark at Diploma Level, making redundant earlier thoughts about grading at Foundation or Certificate levels. What was particularly gratifying was to see how so many students had taken very seriously the 'Applied Ministry And Mission' aspect of the course and produced portfolios that demonstrated a great deal of ingenuity in applying their studies to their local situations. The portfolios suggest that planting new churches by students has become almost commonplace and this is backed up by reports from Bishops and others who have noted the spread of this work. To read how students have responded to the need for what some might describe as social work or community development as part of engaging in mission/evangelism is heart-warming. These very practical portfolios will be used as training aids for future courses.

**THE NUMBER OF STUDENTS TO GRADUATE OUT OF 57 WHO STARTED THE COURSE AT SAGAMU WAS 46**

(5 of these with merit-averaging 60% or above) and from the 82 who began at Umuahia, 62 graduated (15 with merit). A further 10 students may graduate later if their remaining pieces of work are submitted through the local registrar and receive a pass mark. Overall then, this means that of 139 students who began the course in 2006, 108 have earned a diploma (including 20 with merit) but more importantly every student

has been resourced with lecture materials, books and practical training that will continue to enhance their ministry for many years to come. Once again we are reminded that it would cost more to bring two students to the UK on scholarship for two years than it has cost to train and resource over 100 students in Nigeria.

A cause for celebration, and celebrate we did, with the students at the Umuahia graduation on the 16th July, and the students at Sagamu on the 19th July. Both of these packed celebrations were graced by family and friends and a glorious 'Technicolor' gathering of the leadership of the MCN along with local and international tutors involved in the course.

The Principal of Cliff College, Revd Dr Martyn Atkins preached and presented to the successful students the 'International Diploma In Applied Ministry And Mission' (IDIAMM). The International Coordinator, Revd Richard Jackson draped each of the graduates with a blue and gold Cliff College Preaching scarf tailored in Nigeria. The MCN motto "Worthy is the Lamb" on one face of the scarf being balanced by the evangelistic thrust of the Cliff College motto, "Christ for All: All for Christ." on the other. The National Coordinator, The Very Revd Okon Ekerendu, then offered each of the graduates back to the MCN for a blessing by the Prelate and his representatives as, "trained evangelists of the Conference of the MCN".

183

# 2008/5 JUN 20-JUL 20: MCN FIRST RESIDENTIAL

(IDIAMM 2008-10 PROGRAMME)

2008-10 ENROLMENT AT UMUAHIA MTI

We were concerned that despite the promise of 150 students (85 at Umuahia; 65 at Sagamu) nominated to undertake the new programme; the numbers at the outset were much smaller than had been anticipated. A number of factors seem to have contributed to a breakdown in communications between those being nominated and those doing the nominating and there appears to have been some misunderstanding about the payment of locally levied fees to offset the feeding and other costs of the residentials. Intervention by the Prelate, His Eminence Ola Makinde, the Secretary of Conference, the Bishop of Evangelism and others soon changed the situation. 56 new students were enrolled at Umuahia and 40 at Sagamu.

As the numbers originally agreed by the Conference Connexional Council had been organised on a 'quota' basis through the Archdiocese and Dioceses of MCN, we discussed how the 'latecomers' might be allowed to join the course. It was agreed with the Prelate and the Bishop of Evangelism, Sunday Onuoha that the numbers at both centres would be made up to at least 85 at Umuahia and 65 at Sagamu. Those joining late will be required to undertake a supervised 'reading week' at the college in September 2008 (after the August Conference of MCN, but before the regular students of the colleges return). The July Residential lecture notes, Course Booklet and books (delivery of which are still presenting problems!) will be provided for them. They will be expected to undertake the same assignments (for submission by end of September and October) as the other students. By the time all nominated students attend the January 2009 Residential, they will have reached the same stage in the course.

This is not ideal, but the high calibre of the students chosen for the new course, (many with a first degree and most having completed

184

a 3/4 year college course of training at degree level) means that they will start this new course in Applied Ministry and Mission with a good academic foundation in English as well as other studies. The visiting lecturers found lecturing to this new group of students challenging. The visiting team can be identified from this picture taken with the Bishop of Evangelism, the Rector at Umuahia and the National Coordinator. They included:

**THE CORE TEAM:**

Revd Richard Jackson MA BD International Coordinator of CCILC, former Postgraduate Tutor at Cliff College
Revd Dr Malcolm McCall MA Methodist Minister, former teacher in Africa and Royal Navy Chaplain
Mrs Janet McCall BA (Hons) Methodist Local Preacher, qualified to teach English-as-a-2nd-language
Mr Keith Phillips Anglican, former VSO in Sierra Leone CCILC Logistics and administration

**VISITING TEAM WITH BISHOP OF EVANGELISM:**

Mrs Audrey Hensman MA Methodist Local Preacher and former Social Worker
Revd Dr Michael Thompson MA BD Retired Methodist Minister and Lecturer in Old Testament
Mr Peter Worrell Methodist Local Preacher and retired violinist with the Halle Orchestra
Revd Kehinde Olabimtan BTh MTh Director of the Institute of Mission Studies, Good News Baptist Ch. Lagos

**COMMUNICATIONS:**

Mr James Atkins BA (Hons) Television Production-experience of filming in Sierra Leone and Sri Lanka
Mr Michael Claye Level 2 Key Skills award in communication and interested in filming

**GRADUATION DISTINGUISHED VISITOR:**

Revd Dr Martyn Atkins BA Principal, Cliff College, Immediate Past President & General Secretary Designate of UK Methodist Conference

Revd Thomas Champness is known to many as the forefather founder of Cliff College. In the 19th Century he began to gather around him and train evangelists under the banner of the Joyful News Newspaper which he first published in 1883. These evangelists travelled the UK and eventually to different parts of the world as "Joyful News Missioners". As this group of trainee evangelists outgrew Champness' homes in Bolton and Rochdale they were housed eventually in 1903 in the newly established Cliff College.

What is less well known is that earlier in his ministry in 1857, Thomas Champness responded to a call to serve as a missionary in Sierra Leone. After three years he returned home in poor health. Whilst on furlough he married Mary Archer and returned with his young bride in 1860 to West Africa, but this time to Abeokuta in Nigeria. Mary Archer Champness died there on the 23rd September 1862, less than two years after her marriage to Thomas and she was buried in Abeokuta. Revd Thomas Champness was invalided home in 1863 and the rest as people tend to say is 'history'.

### RE-DEDICATION MARY ARCHER CHAMPNESS GRAVE

The International Coordinator, Revd Richard Jackson's own ministry involvement for ten years with the Methodist Church in Sierra Leone (1969-79), more recently in Cliff College and now through the CCILC in Sierra Leone, Cuba and Nigeria has served to keep the 'history' alive in at least one heart and mind. Through our friends/partners in Nigeria, we were able to locate in an old cemetery at Abeokuta and refurbish with a new headstone the grave of Mary Archer Champness. It was particularly appropriate that: the present Principal of Cliff College, Revd Dr Martyn Atkins (who earlier this year as President of the Methodist Church UK unveiled a blue civic plaque commemorating Thomas Champness on his former Bolton home); Revd Richard Jackson and the CCILC team; and the

Head of the Methodist Church Nigeria, His Eminence Dr Sunday Ola Makinde should be able to link past missionary sacrifice and service with our present and continuing partnership by sharing in a service of remembrance; a most moving ceremony at the graveside of Mary Archer Champness.

His Eminence announced that at the upcoming Conference in August, a resolution would be brought to confer a posthumous award as a 'Knight of John Wesley', the highest award given to a lay person, on Mary Archer Champness. His Eminence, in addressing those present paid tribute not only to Thomas and Mary Champness and the continuing partnership through the CCILC with Cliff College and the 'Mother Church' in the UK but also to those indigenous servants of God from Sierra Leone, who shared the gospel down the west coast of Africa and who have meant so much to the church in Nigeria.

**CONCLUSION**                    **"WILL YOU GO TO AFRICA?" "YES, IF YOU SEND ME."**

Perhaps, our remembrance of Mary Archer and Thomas Champness does more than anything else in this report to highlight the DNA link between past missionary service, our present CCILC partnership and the future mission of the worldwide church. The challenge to Christians today is no less demanding than that made to the first disciples and to Thomas Champness who when asked in 1857 by the President of his church, '"Will you go to Africa?" replied, "Yes, if you send me." "Will you go to Sierra Leone? Before you answer, let me tell you that Sierra Leone is the white man's grave. In front of the Freetown Chapel there is a row of graves on each side of the walk, and a young missionary lies in each grave; some of them lived only a few months. Will you go?" With the greatest calmness imaginable he courageously replied: "Yes if you send me".'

**Richard Jackson (Revd)**          **International Coordinator CCILC**

# CHAPTER 9 2009: A GROWING RESPONSE

*The 2009 residentials were exciting models of enthusiastic participation but they were overshadowed a little in January by the even more exciting evangelistic convention at Sagamu that brought together over 10,000 Nigerian Methodists for refreshment and renewal. In July, the student 'Residential' was followed by an 'Episcopal Consultation' held in Lagos which allowed the MCN Leadership and the CCITC team to share fellowship and personal experiences of growth within the church, some associated with the training being done through Cliff College. In November several ITC team members were able to return to Sierra Leone, to renew relationships and revive the training partnership there.*

## 2009/1 JAN 5-21: MCN SECOND 'RESIDENTIAL'

### (IDIAMM 2008-10 PROGRAMME)

#### INTRODUCTION

Following on from the success of our first two-year programme in Nigeria (2006-8–see earlier reports) the Methodist Church leadership advised us that some of their key people would be enrolled for the 2008-10 training programme. What we had not anticipated was that having begun the programme in July 2008 two of our students and one of our partner lecturers would be made Bishops of the Methodist Church Nigeria (MCN) by the time we returned for the second 'residential' this January. It was good to be able to celebrate with them during our visit.

It was good also to see how well the local teams of lecturers led by the National Coordinator, the Very Revd Okon Ekerendu and the Bishop of Evangelism, Right Revd Sunday Onuoha had incorporated the 'added students' from July by organising special 'residentials' during September. At both Umuahia and Sagamu centres these students were able to catch up on those who had been present in July. The additional students had been given the Course Booklet; been present for lectures; and received the July lecture notes/study books. Most of them had completed the required assignments before arriving with us for the January residential.

These MCN Conference directed arrangements meant that for our January 'Residential' we had 77 students in residence at Umuahia and 57 students at Sagamu making a total of 134 students in all, roughly the same number as began our 2006/8 programme. The 'Chapel/Lecture Hall' accommodation at Umuahia can cope with larger numbers, but the lecturing accommodation at Sagamu is more limited at present. Plans are afoot and the money has been raised locally for the completion of the large chapel/lecture hall at Sagamu. In the meantime the use of the refurbished former 'dining hall' (with fans) as a lecturing space made it possible to cope with 57 students plus staff with less of a 'greenhouse' atmosphere. Judicious lecturing moves to the fresh air outside in the afternoon/early evening kept both students and lecturers 'with it' throughout the long teaching days.

The MCN continued the appointment of the Very Revd Okon Ekerendu our very able National Coordinator beyond his retirement last September in order to train up his successor the Very Revd Paul Olukunga in liaising with the CCILC. Regular correspondence between all the parties involved provided for a trouble-free journey (via London by British Airways -whose charges were for the first time competitive with their European rivals!) to Nigeria on January 5th and between the two centres. The regular 'core' visiting team (see earlier reports for details) of Revd Richard Jackson, International Coordinator, Revd Dr Malcolm & Mrs Janet McCall, Student support/supervision and Mr Keith Phillips, Administrator was supplemented in January by:

Revd A Cameron Kirkwood, MA     Methodist Minister & Lecturer in Community Development and Fresh Expressions of Church
Revd Dr Jennifer Smith, BA MPhil   Methodist Minister (from USA serving in the UK) Lecturer in Methodism, Holiness and Social Action

Dr Carole Jackson, Methodist Conference Medical Committee; Psychiatrist, special interest in adult learning disabilities
Mrs Janet Kirk, MA (CQSW) Methodist Local Preacher with Social Work, Lay Leadership, Groups and LP training experience

The visiting team were again partnered by members of the Nigerian staff teams at the Sagamu & Umuahia Methodist Training Institutions. The two key lecturers for January linking mission to community outreach and social responsibility were: Revd Cameron Kirkwood and Revd Dr Jennifer Smith from Kettering. Cameron, the minister of a community church in London was well received when he lectured in Nigeria two years ago and again his lectures prompted stimulating discussions as students were challenged to apply what was being shared to their own situations in ministry. This was even more the case with the lectures given by Revd Dr Jennifer Smith. Lectures on Wesleyan Holiness applied to the African Social Context delivered by a vivacious American woman working as a Methodist Minister in Britain (whose previous association with Nigeria was visiting medical and caring institutions) had the potential to be a highlight in the whole programme and so it proved to be. The conversations about issues raised went way beyond the lecture rooms and 'Jen' had to be rescued again and again in time for food and drink.

**HONOURING MARY SLESSOR**

As usual our accompanying (at their own expense) friends, this time Dr Carole Jackson and Mrs Janet Kirk, apart from a pilgrimage to Calabar of Mary Slessor fame and visits to a Leprosy Village and an Orphanage, made their own very personal contributions to the training and to the cohesion of the team as a whole.

**BOOKS AND OTHER MATERIALS**

Visiting lecturers are encouraged to provide full notes for the students which are then incorporated into their own substantial training manual. Much work had been done by the National Coordinator and college Rectors as we have worked towards the local sourcing of books at reasonable prices. As yet the relationship with ACTS in Jos has not proved to be a workable solution. Logistically, it has proved difficult to have the large number of books required delivered on time and accounted for and the SPCK International Study Guides sourced through India by ACTS are unfortunately of a much inferior printing/paper quality to those sourced from the UK.

The generous commitment made over several years by 'Feed the Minds' to CCILC has come to an end, but FTM have now arranged to register both Umuahia MTI and Sagamu MTI on the 'Books For Life' scheme through which every new full-time student on their residential courses will receive 10 International Study Guides delivered to the colleges free of charge. It was good to share in the Sagamu Rector's happiness at the first delivery of these books.

Fortunately, the Methodist Missionary Society (Ireland) has come to our aid and has agreed to provide some funding for books to be bought for students on the programme. Once again the Langham Partnership has agreed to provide key books at much subsidised prices. Shipping and Lagos dock controls permitting these books should be distributed to the students in July. Each time we distribute books we realise afresh how valuable a commodity they are to those in ministry who have so little access to the resources that we take for granted. Even where the internet is available in Nigeria there is no guaranteed access without considerable delay and my own experience of time-consuming 'lost connections' remind me of pre-broadband use in the UK.

### ACKNOWLEDGEMENTS AND PLANS FOR THE FUTURE

Once again our thanks must go to the Head of MCN, His Eminence, Revd Dr Ola S. Makinde, the Secretary of Conference, Bishop Chibuzo R Opoko and the Rectors and staff of the two Colleges for their encouragement and for the hospitality/travel arrangements made locally with the help of the newly appointed Protocol Officer, Very Revd Agunbiade Busuyi. Our good friend the Right Revd Babatunde Taiwo, the Bishop of Remo once again provided the accommodation for the whole of the visiting team at Sagamu and entertained us with an afternoon visit to his home village.

The Prelate and the <sup>Bishop of Evangelism, Rt. Revd Dr Sunday N Onuoha,</sup>

(who again made time to attend and speak to the ILC students in both centres) have made it clear that it is because of positive reports received locally and the evidence seen of new churches being planted, local church training being given and community projects being started by students of the first course that they are asking CCILC to organise some similar training for the leadership of MCN and its Archbishops and Bishops in July 2009.

In conversations with MCN the dates have been set for this event with participants travelling to the Sagamu Centre on Monday 13<sup>th</sup> July and returning home on the 17<sup>th</sup> July. From Tuesday, 14<sup>th</sup> through to Thursday, 16th inclusive there will be a consultation on Mission/Evangelism. Whilst this programme will be run in parallel with the continuing two-year CCILC programme for 134 Presbyters/Deaconesses, further donations/funding will be welcomed by the CCILC as we provide resources and books for up to 60 Bishops and others who will be attending this additional but separate consultation.

Many Pastors and Evangelists have undergone training (2006-8); now Presbyters and Deaconesses are involved (2008-10); sharing with this strategically significant leadership group in July will give a fresh but shared impetus to the challenge of repositioning the MCN in relation to Mission/Evangelism.

As part of the overall repositioning emphasis, though not directly related to our CCILC programme, Revd Dr Malcolm and Mrs Janet McCall during their extended visit were invited to attend the first National Convention of the Methodist Church Nigeria at Sagamu from Tuesday 27 to Friday 30 January 2009. Speakers from Nigeria and overseas addressed the convention on "The Church in a Troubled World." See full report below.

192

We continue to seek funding and resources for associated projects like libraries and the pioneering college of Zonkwa in the north, as part of the CCILC vision to build up local colleges for their continuing work. Our experience in fund-raising suggests that if too much unsolicited information is sent out, it is rarely read and digested, but if there is any earlier report further information or documentation and photographs that anyone would like to have, particularly for fund-raising purposes, I shall be pleased to make it available. The new CCILC-DVD mentioned in the last report is still 'a work in progress' but we hope to be able to release it to our friends and supporters shortly.

### CONCLUDING REFLECTION                    "YES, WE CAN"

The international coordinator was fortunate to be present in the small town of Dunedin, Florida, USA for a Barack Obama rally prior to Obama's election as President of the United States. Obama as a speaker and the event itself were both impressive. I bought the tee shirt and it seemed like a good idea to use it as a visual aid with our student enthusiasts for change in Nigeria.

On the front of the shirt above the 'iconic' picture of Barack Obama is written the campaign slogan, **"Change we can believe in."** The words on the back of the tee-shirt **"Yes We Can"** echoing around that stadium and the Washington inauguration celebrations in January allowed many millions of people throughout the world to identify with a locally inspired lay movement with **"The Audacity of Hope"** at its heart. Whatever the future holds for Barack Obama and his vision in the huge challenges that he faces, I commend his writings to you and invite your prayers for this new leader and his nation.

The changes made to help with the repositioning of the Methodist Church Nigeria (MCN) in relation to Evangelism alluded to in earlier reports were reinforced in 2006 by a revised; book sized; large print;174 pages; evangelism oriented Constitution; and the appointment for the first time in their history of a Bishop for Evangelism. This combination of initiatives alongside the invitation to the CCILC was a clear declaration of their intent and put the CCILC training programme in mission and evangelism at the very heart of what our partner church is trying to achieve.

The World Church Office (WCO) of the UK Methodist Church has responded positively to these changes. Through its Africa Secretary and the Scholarship And Leadership Training (SALT) Advisory Group they have continued to give support to the innovative CCILC programme that is playing a vital role as the national leadership of MCN sponsors a 'movement in mission' of great significance.

The Barack Obama vision for change that inspired a vibrant movement of ordinary people in the USA to believe and respond; **"Yes, we can"** provides a contemporary challenge to the church. If we each add our own personal commitment of, **"With God's help we will"**, the church movement towards change that we are seeing in Nigeria might be replicated in our own church.

Thank you once again in anticipation of your continuing prayerful and practical support as we continue to pioneer new ways of working in partnership with our friends in the world church.

**Richard Jackson (Revd)**
**International Coordinator CCILC**

# 2009/2 JAN: McCALLS-MCN "KAIROS MOMENT"

A MESSAGE FROM THE McCALLS' FOR THE METHODIST CHURCH NIGERIA (MCN) –WITH IMPLICATIONS FOR THE WORLD-WIDE METHODIST FAMILY.

## 1. BACKGROUND

Between July 2006 and January 2009, my wife Janet and I had the most wonderful privilege of visiting very many Methodist diocese and circuits as we partnered the Methodist Church Nigeria (MCN) in "repositioning for evangelism." We are part of the Core Team of the Cliff College International Learning Centre (CCILC), and our responsibility was to observe and encourage the application of a "sandwich course" for Methodist leaders in mission and evangelism. This gave us a unique opportunity to visit dozens of local churches as we encouraged our Cliff College students in Nigeria to apply what they had been learning in their own situations. We were able to share hundreds of conversations with Methodist members in these local churches.

Whilst engaged in this task, we were invited to attend the first National Convention of the Methodist Church Nigeria. It was held at the Methodist Theological Institute, Sagamu (an hour's drive from central Lagos) from Tuesday 27 to Friday 30 January 2009. The theme for the convention was "The Church in a Troubled World."

## 2. "GOD IS NOT A METHODIST."

In the opinion of many Nigerian Church leaders, the Methodist Church, in the last half of the 20$^{th}$ Century, stagnated in terms of numbers, and lost its "dynamic" (though not with the same catastrophic decline as British Methodism). With great determination and honesty, the Church faced this situation and produced a slogan: "Repositioning for evangelism." This became more than a set of "good ideas" or Conference resolutions as representative committees fed ideas into a new church constitution. This new constitution, produced in 2006, set evangelism at the centre of the church's life and work. The CCILC was invited to provide further training in evangelism and mission for evangelists and presbyters in Nigeria. At the same time the Right Revd Dr Sunday Onuoha was appointed as the first ever MCN

Bishop of Evangelism & Discipleship. He was given the task of encouraging the whole church in its primary task of mission.

MCN recognised that it was losing many young people, who largely gravitated to the "new generation" or so-called "Spirit churches" (Pentecostal and charismatic churches) rather than ceasing to attend church at all. These young people give various reasons for leaving Methodism:

a)     Church worship is "outward form," lacking a lively sense of God's presence.
b)     Exuberance, spontaneity and participation are largely excluded from Methodist worship.
c)     There is little feeling of "belonging" to a warm, loving, caring community church.
d)     Signs and wonders and miracles are apparently missing in Methodist meetings.

We feel that these criticisms may not be entirely fair. Nevertheless, the young people, in many local churches, have voted with their feet, and left behind a more elderly and "traditional" group of worshippers. The sad epigrammatic but challenging comment of some youngsters was, "God is not a Methodist." In the last 2 or 3 years, under the direction of the Prelate, His Eminence, Sunday Ola Makinde and with motivation engendered by the Bishop of Evangelism the Methodist Church Nigeria has seriously and courageously begun to respond to this challenge.

### 3. SAGAMU JAN 2009: THE LARGEST GATHERING EVER OF NIGERIAN METHODISTS

The Bishop of Evangelism, Sunday Onuoha encouraged the 2008 Methodist Conference to plan for a National Methodist Convention in January 2009. This Convention –the first of its kind – was an amazing success. It was wonderfully well organised by the Evangelism and Discipleship Directorate of the Church, led by Bishop Sunday Onuoha. It was preceded by a Ministers' Retreat, attended by the vast majority of Nigerian Methodist Ministers and Deaconesses. It was a truly remarkable experience to see Sagamu Methodist Cathedral overflowing with over 2000 ministers and deaconesses, most dressed in pristine white cassocks! The entire national leadership of the Methodist Church attended both this retreat and the main convention which followed, making it a truly significant event for Nigeria. By the end of the first day of the main convention, around 10,000 Methodists had registered, and more arrived later (together, surely, with some who were "unregistered"!), swelling the numbers to around 13,000 to 15,000. This represented the largest gathering of Methodists in the history of Nigeria. There were thoughts that it might also have been the largest gathering of Methodist people ever witnessed in the African continent. Certainly, in terms of numbers and enthusiasm, it was a truly awesome event.

The World Director of Methodist Evangelism, the Revd Dr Eddie Fox, placed the Convention in a global perspective during his keynote addresses to the Convention: he is convinced that the Nigerian Methodist Church has a large responsibility for the whole of the African continent (together with the Kenyan and South African Methodist Churches). Indeed what happens in Nigeria will have a profound impact on the whole worldwide Methodist family. Dr Fox's remarks caused serious reflection: Nigeria is Africa's most populous nation, and the largest "black nation" on the planet. In terms of the wider church, it was noted that, already, the largest local church in the UK is Nigerian led!

#### 4. "THE LOST KEY".

With honesty and humility, the Convention brought before God the sense that in the last half-century, Methodist Church Nigeria had lost something essential in its mission and ministry. The keynote speakers addressed this challenge "head on".

The Revd Dr Eddie Fox told a number of stories which together made the same point: Methodism often has a good organisation with everything in place, but it is as though we have "lost the key." What is that key? The key is Jesus Himself. Eddie went on to demonstrate from Scripture and Church history that only by the power of the Holy Spirit may that key be found and used to unlock closed doors. Amazingly, although there had been no opportunity for consultation between the main speakers, the same theme was underlined time and again by almost every speaker: "When the Spirit of truth comes . . . . He will glorify Me" – as Jesus promised (John 16. 13-14). Only the Holy Spirit can do it – but He can! This became the main thrust of the teaching at the Convention.

197

One of the most memorable teaching sessions was led by the Very Revd Dr Mike Oye – a mature and deeply spiritual Nigerian Methodist minister. He took as his theme, "Signs and wonders – God's business." His teaching was "inclusive" and not divisive, as he encouraged us to shout out together "all" from Joel 2.28 and Acts 2.4. He encouraged us all to seek such a fullness of the Holy Spirit as would result in the Lord confirming His word by the signs that accompanied it (Mark 16. 20). Likewise, Eddie Fox's final address encouraged us to believe for an outpouring of the Holy Spirit upon us. He suggested that those who wanted should "cup" our hands together; holding them out in front of us, and, through this visible sign, ask for the Holy Spirit to be poured out into us. It seemed that the majority of people in that vast assembly followed Eddie's suggestion.

It is difficult to convey an adequate impression of the impact of the teaching on the convention crowds, and the sense of God's Presence moving among us. Personally, it was the nearest experience I have known to what I read in Acts of the Apostles. The Eighteenth Century revival in Britain, and the preaching of Wesley and Whitfield seemed more real and relevant than I have ever known.

There was much spontaneous praise and dancing in the meetings, culminating in an all-night praise Celebration on the Friday, the last day of the Convention. We also witnessed generous acts of love and service. For example, after a Bible Study on I Corinthians 13, the Archbishop of Ibadan, the Most Revd Michael Kehinde Stephen, spontaneously suggested that we should take up a freewill offering in support of Ebenezer Church in Jos. (Their church building was burnt down during violent troubles in that city in late 2008.) It was a wonderful moment when thousands of convention members came forward to place their gifts of money into large bins which were hurriedly put in place inside the central meeting-ground.

### 5. IMMEDIATE RESULTS: "GOD VISITED US."

It is early days to assess the impact of the Convention on Methodist Church Nigeria (writing only a week after the event), but one anecdotal incident will always remain in our memories: the day after the Convention we travelled to Ogbomosho and preached in the Cathedral on Sunday 1 February, and later, in Oni-keke Circuit, two hours journey away. Around 100 people from the Cathedral had been

198

at the Convention with, of course, the Cathedral ministerial staff. In the main service, the Cathedral was packed with around 1,700 people. When the altar-call was made at the end of the preaching, over 1,000 people came forward and knelt in the Sanctuary and down the aisles to the back of the building! This was in striking contrast to our experience 18 months ago in the same cathedral. On that occasion when I made a similar altar call only 3 people had responded out of a congregation of maybe 350! I asked our friends and hosts, Professor "Ade" Aderinto and his wife "Dele," what had made the difference. (They are long-term Methodist members of the Cathedral, and a mature spiritual couple.) Ade simply replied, "God visited us this morning."

This sense of God's Presence was evident not only in the "main service", but also in the earlier (mainly young people's) service at which my wife Janet preached, as well as in Oni-keke later in the day. In Oni-keke, around 250 people asked to receive more of the Holy Spirit in response to Janet's preaching, and many came forward, at the suggestion of the minister of the circuit, to be anointed with oil.

This Sunday in the Ogbomosho area was very moving in its own right: but we are praying that it represents just one example of a move of the Holy Spirit in local Methodist Churches all over Nigeria!

### 6. WIDER IMPLICATIONS: "WHY NOT NIGERIA?"

Evidence from Methodism in Cuba and South Korea (to mention only two other countries) points in the same direction as the Spirit's thrust for Nigerian Methodists at Sagamu: the "lost key" is the glorifying of Jesus by the Holy Spirit (John 16.14).

Dr Fox movingly told us the story of the only memorial he knew, worldwide, to a visitation of the Holy Spirit in power. Apparently a small group of Tongan Methodists met near a little village for a prayer meeting soon after the initial conversion of the islands in the nineteenth century. They prayed something like this: "LORD God, we have heard how the Spirit came in Jerusalem at Pentecost. We have heard how the Spirit came in England at the time of John Wesley. We have heard how the Spirit came at different times in different places. Father, why not Tonga?" And the Spirit fell upon that group in an amazing way. One of the results of that empowering was that the Tongans paddled canoes to Fiji – not to make war, as in the past, but to share the Good News. In the longer term, Tonga remains the most "Methodist" land in the world, with more than half the population belonging to the Methodist Church.

So, Eddie Fox encouraged us to ask the LORD, "Why not here? Why not Nigeria?" – not for the sake of Nigeria alone, but for the sake of the whole African continent. As the only two Europeans in that great Convention, we were amazed to think that this gathering represented a whole national Methodist Church and we longed that its results might indeed not be just for Nigeria, nor even for the African continent alone – but also for Britain.

The Revd Dr Malcolm McCall,

## 2009/3 JUN: McCALLS GOING & GROWING VISITS

**2009 JUNE 19-29    McCALL REPORT ON EXTENDED 'ENCOURAGEMENT' VISIT TO NIGERIA BY REVD DR MALCOLM & MRS JANET McCALL.**

Our extended visit was greatly facilitated by the Methodist Prelate, His Eminence Ola Makinde, who kindly arranged for transport throughout our travels. He also enabled the Very Revd Paul Olukunga (Cliff College Programme National Coordinator) to accompany us: Paul was a great blessing, and provided us with much assistance at every level.

**OYO CIRCUIT, IBADAN ARCHDIOCESE, SATURDAY 20 JUNE 2009**

The Circuit Superintendent is the Very Revd Joel Akinola, who is also the President for the Sagamu Section of the Presbyters' 2008-2010 Diploma Course. We were privileged to stay for an all-too-short visit in his manse with him, his wife and his lovely family. The manse has been newly-built in the church compound. We felt that Joel, as he introduced us to members of his circuit team and showed us various church premises, had a clear and mature understanding of repositioning his Circuit for evangelism. In discussion, he outlined his strategy in the area of mission and evangelism:

The whole congregation in his Circuit-church needs to "re-orientate" to focus on evangelism. One practical way in which Joel has sought to implement this priority is by providing warm hospitality in his own manse for his Circuit leaders and ordinary members. The building of trust, with a shared evangelistic vision for the Circuit, are by-products of this approach.

"Tent-making" ministers need to augment the number of "full-time" paid ministers in his circuit, in order to provide adequate ministerial resources for evangelistic outreach. In Oyo Circuit there are now 2 "full-time" paid ministers and 8 "tent-making" ministers. This is in line with a development which Archbishop Michael Stephen urged upon Methodist Church Nigeria at the Sagamu Convention in January 2009. ("Tent-makers" are non-stipendiary Methodist ministers who are given local ministerial appointments, and who are to be regarded in every way as exercising the same ministry as "full-time" ministers.)

Joel has encouraged several of his evangelists to train as full-time ministers, and has sponsored them through theological college. One has already finished his training, and has returned to the Circuit as a full-time minister. During the last 2 years, 2 churches have been reopened in the Circuit, and 2 new church-plants established.

The visit to Oyo concluded in an amazing way for us. We had promised to go from Oyo to Ogbomosho Methodist Cathedral for a special act of worship in which our friend Dr Tolani Olumide Oluwode was being made a Knight of John Wesley, in recognition of his many years of Christian service within the Methodist Church. Dr Tolani had stitched up Malcolm's head when he had his accident 2 years ago in Sagamu.

On the night before going to Ogbomosho, Malcolm was asked by the Methodist Prelate to preach at this service! It was wonderful to see perhaps the majority of the 2000 or so worshippers in the Cathedral respond to an invitation that we should commit ourselves to returning home to "tell how much God has done for you" (Luke 8.39). (It was estimated that perhaps as many people again as were in the Cathedral stood outside, listening to the service over loudspeakers!)

**ZONKWA METHODIST THEOLOGICAL COLLEGE: MONDAY 22 TO THURSDAY 25 JUNE**

It was a great joy to return to Zonkwa for another "teaching visit". 35 people gathered for 3 full days of teaching and sharing. These 35 included some of the students at the College (though some of

201

the students had returned to their far-flung homes throughout the North for the summer vacation, which had begun a couple of weeks earlier). Others among the 35 were church leaders from the Zonkwa area; but some were ministers from as far as Kano (4 hours' drive away from Zonkwa) and Igede (even further!). It was very moving to see older Methodist presbyters eagerly and humbly seeking by all means to develop their ministries. Various opportunities were offered to the students in these 3 days:

Return of written work completed in January 2009, which we had marked, paying particular attention to English communication of the Gospel. All the subjects which we had asked them to write about were central to sharing the Good News. This method proved, in answer to much prayer, a most fruitful means of teaching – as was to happen later with the Diploma Course students at Sagamu and Umuahia. Janet simply went through their corrected work and drew out English points that occurred in a number of scripts and which needed attention. This approach meant (a) the corrections were those with which the students personally required assistance (b) the corrections dealt with the heart of communicating the Gospel, and (c) the students were encouraged in a non-threatening environment to ask about further problems and difficulties they were encountering in presenting the Gospel and leading worship in the English language. Several students made the undeniable observation that they had been poorly-taught from primary-school level, and these few days in Zonkwa represented their first opportunity to gain help from teachers whose "first language" is English.

Provision of booklets on *Christian Spiritual Disciplines* (which we hope to give to the Umuahia and Sagamu students in January 2010). We could do no more than dip into this resource – but we made the point that Christian ministry requires a strong discipline in our personal life. (This requisite had been underscored during the ministerial session of the Sagamu Convention last January.) Several seminal Bible Studies were led by Janet. Morning devotions were ably conducted by the Very Revd Paul Olukunga.

We had met with the Methodist Prelate at Methodist HQ in Lagos the previous week, to speak with him about Zonkwa, and he had strongly supported the idea that it would be good if we could go to

Zonkwa during term time to major on a 2 weeks' "crash course," teaching *English for Gospel Communication.* The Prelate recounted his experience in MTI Sagamu years ago, when a key for some ministerial candidates' development was one-to-one remedial English tuition.

Since the Zonkwa students are scattered all over Northern Nigeria, it is impracticable for them to return to the College in the middle of their vacation (which is when the Cliff College team always comes to Umuahia and Sagamu for the "Residentials"). The Prelate agreed that the last week in February 2010 and the first week in March would be ideal for such a "crash course," (before the diocesan Synods later on in March). When we were in Zonkwa, this suggestion met with the warm approval of the Principal, the Very Revd Shettima Chibok. So Janet and I committed ourselves to return for those 2 weeks in 2010 (possibly funding ourselves on this occasion).

**CHURCH-PLANTING IN KAKAU, KADUNA NORTH CIRCUIT: THURSDAY 25 TO SUNDAY 28 JUNE**

One of our students in Umuahia, is the Circuit minister of Kaduna North Circuit. For over a year he had been thinking and praying with his church leaders about planting a church in the village of Kakau, a place with a growing population, over-spilling from Kaduna City. A Methodist member in the village said he was willing to offer the parlour in his home as a gathering place for a new church plant. The preparations were very prayerfully and carefully made. It was decided to organise a set of open-air meetings on the local primary school field, as a "launch-pad" for establishing the church, on Thursday, Friday and Saturday evenings, 25 – 27 June. (Although this was the middle of the rainy season, much prayer was made that there would be no rain, and God answered, PTL!) On Sunday 21 June, a lorry had gone round the village, playing gospel music and giving out invitations to these meetings.

Crowds of between 300 and 400 came on each of the 3 evenings, drawn partly by music from a rousing Christian band, which resulted in much joyful dancing in praise and worship. The Methodist Archbishop, the Most Revd Oche Job, attended and shared into the meetings. On the Saturday evening, a Christian Youth Drama Group provided a gripping presentation which drew some extra youngsters from the village to come and look and listen. An "altar-call" was made each evening, and altogether over 100 people responded – including a goodly number of children. Also on each evening, it was announced that the first worship-time of the new Church would be held at the same venue at 8am on Sunday 28 June.

It was a great thrill to have around 200 people turn up for this event, including around 80 children, who were provided with their own lesson and activity. The Minister announced that a former student (2006-8 course) would temporarily be pastoring this new church plant during his long summer vacation. Like very many other students from that first course, he subsequently candidated for the presbyteral ministry, and is presently studying at Emmanuel College, Ibadan. Wonderfully, temporary accommodation was provided for him within Kakao village, to help him in his pastoring of the new church.

We had asked that our Prayer Partners should join us in praying for "More, LORD," for this visit to Nigeria. We joyfully joined the rest of our colleagues on the International Lecturers' Team, for the remainder of the June/July residential programme, fully assured that prayer had been gloriously answered!

Janet and Malcolm McCall, Wednesday 29 July 2009

## 2009/4 JUN 29-JUL 19: MCN THIRD 'RESIDENTIAL'

### (IDIAMM 2008-10 PROGRAMME)

#### INTRODUCTION

As usual Revd Dr Malcolm McCall setting out on the 17th June acted as our John the Baptist preparing the way with his wife Janet for the arrival of the larger team of lecturers who travelled to Nigeria on the 29th June. Malcolm's role as a visiting encourager of students in their home locations has expanded as he has become an evangelist at large and advocate/trainer for the pioneering Methodist Training Institute at Zonkwa in the north (separate report available on request).

As regular readers of this ILC programme report will know, the July residentials are for a longer period than those that we have in January. We utilise a larger group of visiting lecturers who are divided into two teams, exchanging venues and students between Sagamu and

Umuahia mid-way through the two week residentials. We had the added 'complication' this time of fitting in a 'knighthood' ceremony on the 12th July at the Methodist Cathedral in the capital Abuja (not Lagos!) and a three day 'Episcopal Training Consultation' of which more later.

Patience, flexibility and a sense of humour on the part of everyone involved in the programme continue to be key factors in the success of this programme and our thanks go out to all who have contributed to making this visit one of our most rewarding in so many ways. The new National Coordinator, Very Revd Paul Olukunga and Protocol Officer, Revd Agunbiade Busuyi facilitated our safe arrival by Air France/KLM (the cheapest this time!) and onward air travel to and from the more distant eastern college of Umuahia. Once again our thanks must go to the Head of Methodist Church Nigeria (MCN), His Eminence, Revd Dr Ola Sunday Makinde, ably backed by the Secretary of Conference, Bishop Chibuzo Raphael Opoko and the Rectors (Principals) and staff of the two Colleges for their encouragement and first-class hospitality.

**THE JULY 2009 'RESIDENTIALS'**

After the usual slow start due to delayed arrivals, payment of fees and return of assignments we had 71 students in residence at Umuahia and 54 students at Sagamu making a total of 125 students in all. As noted previously the 'Chapel, Lecture Hall' accommodation at Umuahia can cope with larger numbers. Now with money raised locally they have begun roofing the large chapel/lecture hall at Sagamu. This will improve the facilities at Sagamu but in the meantime we continue to use an inadequate building with no lights, fans and little ventilation.

The regular 'core' training team (see earlier reports for details) of Revd Richard Jackson, International Coordinator and Mr Keith Phillips, Administrator headed up Team 1 which began in Umuahia and Revd Dr Malcolm & Mrs Janet McCall, led Team 2 at Sagamu:

**Team 1**

Very Revd Deji Okegbile MA Presbyter MCN; Cliff PhD Research Student) Lecturer on Fresh Expressions
Revd Dr Stephen Skuce MPhil BD Irish Methodist Minister; Cliff Director of PG Studies & CCILC
Mr Peter Worrell Methodist LP and retired violinist with the Halle Orchestra; Lecturer on Adult Learning

**Team 2**

Revd Dr Peter Ensor MA          Methodist    Minister,    Director    of Undergraduate Studies: Lecturer in New Testament
Revd Usman Habib MA          Cliff    Postgraduate    Research    Student; Lecturer on New Generation Churches
Revd Dr Kehinde Olabimtan BTh MTh Baptist Minister of Mission Education

The visiting team were again well-supported by members of the Nigerian staff teams at both Sagamu & Umuahia Methodist Training Institutions, but for the first time we had three Nigerian ministers on the 'visiting' team. To have African Church History scholar Kehinde Olabimtan (now Revd Dr) with us has always been a joy, but to have added two of our Cliff College research students proved to be inspirational. With a renewed emphasis on practical outcomes the Very Revd Deji Okegbile was returning to share with old friends in MCN 'Fresh Expressions' for the Nigerian context and was welcomed by the students; Revd Usman Habib converted from a Muslim background, but now a leading pastor in the 'Church of God Mission' presented the challenge of the New Generation Churches not only through his lectures, but also as the students at Sagamu and Umuahia experienced Sunday worship with hundreds of people at the 'Church of God Mission' churches in Lagos and Umuahia. These experiences of worship outside the Methodist Church (and other traditional denominations) not only contribute to the students' 'Worship Portfolio' but they are proving to be a seed-bed for fresh thinking in repositioning the MCN.

Our only significant problem with the programme this time was that the large consignment of books generously provided through the Langham Partnership and with funding from MMS (Ireland) and Methodist Insurance failed to arrive on the Lagos dock in time for them to be cleared and distributed to our students during the residentials. The documentation has now been completed and the hope is that they will be cleared within the next couple of weeks. Arrangements have been put in place for the books to be distributed through the colleges to the students without further delay once they have been released from the docks. As we noted last time and reiterate now, "Each time we distribute books we realise afresh how valuable a commodity they are to those in ministry who have so little access to the resources that we take for granted. Even where the internet is available in Nigeria there is no guaranteed access without considerable delay and my own experience of time-consuming 'lost connections' remind me of pre-broadband use in the UK."

### KNIGHTS IN THE MAKING

We were thrilled during the last few months to learn of the MCN's intention to make posthumously the late Mary Archer Champness a 'Knight of John Wesley' and to honour one of our lecturers the music-maker Peter Worrell (very much alive) as a 'Knight of Charles Wesley'. These honours are given by MCN to lay-people who have made an outstanding contribution to the life of the church.

### THE CHAMPNESS FOLDER PRESENTED TO MCN

We learned that the ceremony was to be at Abuja on the 12th July. I had tracked down the Champness family and was able to meet up again with Richard Champness on the Friday before we travelled to Nigeria. Mary Archer Champness, as some of you know, was the first wife of the forefather/founder of Cliff College who died after less than two years of marriage at Abeokuta on 23rd September 1862. We reported on the ceremony that took place at her refurbished grave last July. Amazingly, the Champness family had managed to track down some additional personal information about Mary and even a photograph, which is almost certainly her from a century and a half ago. The family had made up a presentation folder of this information which I was able to hand over to the Prelate of

MCN, His Eminence, Revd Dr Ola Sunday Makinde at the ceremony in Abuja. The Methodist Cathedral in Abuja was packed with over a thousand people for the service and presentation of these awards along with others. Peter Worrell, Keith Phillips (Photographer!) and I enjoyed, rather than endured a 4 hours plus service of worship, the highlight of which was the decoration of the recipients. I was strangely moved to represent the Champness family in receiving the Mary Archer Champness award of a bible, certificate and medallion, but particularly because historically it meant so much to the Methodist Church in Nigeria as well as to those of us from the UK who have served as missionaries overseas in much more hospitable times.

My own mood changed quickly into celebration as Peter Worrell, retired from the Halle Orchestra, fully robed as a KCW was invited by the Prelate to 'prove' that he was a musician by playing his violin at the lectern before receiving his award. The sound of Peter playing Finlandia to a packed Nigerian cathedral congregation, most humming the tune along with him, will live long in the memory. As will the upgrade to Club Class for 'Sir' Peter (as he will be addressed in Methodist gatherings in Nigeria) and his lowly entourage on the flight back from Abuja to Lagos!

**SIR PETER WORRELL, KNIGHT OF CHARLES WESLEY**

**THE EPISCOPAL TRAINING CONSULTATION (14-16 July inclusive)**

Some months ago we were asked to partner MCN in bringing together the whole of the clerical leadership of the MCN with its 9 Archbishops and up to 50 Bishops for a training consultation, at which they would learn more about the CCILC and our programme and we would discover how much impact the programme was having through people that had been or were being trained in their dioceses. The logistical arrangements raised problems because we were involved in this programme which took place in Lagos whilst the main course with 125 students in Umuahia and Sagamu was being concluded. Mutually agreed changes to timetabling, travel etc. made a positive outcome possible. Few of the bishops took advantage of a dispensation by the Prelate to be absent.

In preparation for this consultation we applied for and received an additional grant of £5,000 through the SALT Advisory Group of the Methodist Church in the UK. This was used to provide key books (some from Langham, still on the docks in Lagos!) and resources which included a book of sample lectures (300 plus pages put together for the occasion) that have been presented by an international group of highly-qualified lecturers in both Sierra Leone (2002-4) and Nigeria (2006-8; 2008-10). This book and the notes were used to ground the whole consultation as Revd Dr Malcolm McCall led devotions related to Spiritual Disciplines. Revd Richard Jackson led challenging sessions with the Bishops on Methodism & Ministry; Making Disciples; whilst Revd Dr Stephen Skuce laid the Biblical and Practical foundations for Encountering Other Religions. As The Prelate presided over our deliberations and the Bishop of Evangelism, Rt. Revd Dr Sunday N Onuoha guided the Consultation the positive response from the participants means that we are making headway in a shared understanding of mission and ministry. It became clear that the leadership of MCN will continue to give wholehearted support to evangelists, ministers and presbyters who have undertaken the full programme as together they experiment with the kind of changes that the re-positioning of MCN is requiring of them.

**DANGER! BISHOPS AT WORK!**

Interspersed throughout the Consultation were presentations by the bishops of each of the nine archdioceses that looked at the ways in which their diocese was becoming involved in 'evangelism and church planting'. The large number of presentations and the difficulty that presenters had in highlighting what was significant for mission from each of the reports meant that this was less useful than anticipated.

The fact that we now have written reports, means that we are in a position to analyse what is being accomplished overall by the MCN and respond accordingly, with our ILC programme. The very positive response to the continuing work of the ILC and the 'Episcopal Training Consultation' led the Prelate to encourage us to explore the possibilities of providing a full-blown training programme for the Bishops at Cliff College possibly in October 2010.

I must return to thoughts of Mary Archer Champness and in closing share some of the poignant words written by Richard Champness on behalf of the family to the Secretary of Conference, MCN.

*I and my Sisters are deeply touched by the great honour that the Conference has bestowed posthumously on our great grandfather's first wife in recognition of her services to the Methodist Church in Nigeria all those many years ago. Like the wives of other Christian Missionaries of her generation Mary was prepared to risk and sacrifice all in the cause of the Gospel. By making this Award, Conference rightly acknowledges Mary's personal sacrifice in obedience to the Lord's call on her life and, in doing so, salutes her publicly as a role model for those Christian women of our own generation who would follow her example. Whilst I greatly value my Christian heritage and ongoing links with Methodism, I cherish even more the personal relationship with Jesus Christ that I am privileged to enjoy together with the wider fellowship of Christian believers through His sacrifice on the Cross.*

*My thoughts and prayers will be with you all as you meet in the Methodist Cathedral of Unity on Sunday the 12th July 2009 to celebrate the life and work of Mary Champness as the first Wife of my illustrious great grandfather Thomas Champness. It is gratifying to know that his memory is kept alive by those who have reaped the harvest he sowed so tirelessly and effectively both in England and Nigeria three generations ago.*

*May the Lord bless you and protect you. May the Lord smile on you and be gracious to you. May the Lord show his favour and give you His peace now and always.*

*Warmest regards*

Richard S. Champness

**Richard S Champness**

We continue to seek funding and resources for associated projects like college and school libraries as well as funding for the pioneering college of Zonkwa in the north, as part of the CCILC vision to build up local colleges for their developing work. Our experience suggests that if too much unsolicited information is sent out, it is rarely read and digested, but if there is any earlier report further information or documentation and photographs that anyone would like to have, particularly for fund-raising purposes, I shall be pleased to make it available. The new CCILC-DVD mentioned in an earlier report is almost complete. With the addition of January and July 2009 material we hope to be able to release it to our friends and supporters shortly.

**Richard Jackson (Revd)**
**International Coordinator CCILC**

## 2009/5 JUL: MCN EPISCOPAL CONSULTATION

**METHODIST CHURCH NIGERIA HEADQUARTERS**
**DIRECTORATE OF EVANGELISM AND DISCIPLESHIP**
*in partnership with the*
**CLIFF COLLEGE INTERNATIONAL LEARNING CENTRE**
**(CCILC)**
*And*
**THE WORLD CHURCH OFFICE OF THE UK METHODIST**
**CHURCH**

Date: Arrival-Monday 13 July, 2009 – (through to) Friday 17th July, 2009-Departure
Venue: Mei Hotels limited, 27 Kaara Street, Off Osolo Way, Off Muritala Muhammed Int'l Ajao Estate, Lagos.

**PURPOSE: TO RESOURCE AND STRENGTHEN THE EPISCOPAL LEADERSHIP OF THE METHODIST CHURCH NIGERIA.**

*The Episcopal Consultation provided the opportunity for aspects of the CCILC programme and some materials to be shared with the wider leadership of the Methodist Church Nigeria. Pre-prepared Archdiocesan reports presented by every archdiocese highlighted the interaction that was already taking place between those being trained and the re-orientation towards evangelism that is being generated by the MCN.*

**TUESDAY-INPUT & SEMINARS-METHODISM AT WORK IN A MISSION TRAINING PARTNERSHIP**

8:30   Devotion
9:15   Declare Open: The Consultation - The Prelate, MCN
9:45   Address – The Bishop of Evangelism, MCN
10:30  Tea Break
11.00  Methodism in a Mission Partnership 1 - Revd Richard Jackson
12.00  Reflection in groups
1pm   Lunch
2pm   Methodism in a Mission Partnership 2 - Revd Richard Jackson
3pm   Reflection in Groups
4pm   Brief Closing Devotion
6:30   Dinner
7:30   Informal evening – Social gathering

**WEDNESDAY-INPUT & SEMINARS-ENCOUNTERING OTHER RELIGIONS**
**REPORTS-GOD AT WORK TODAY IN THE ARCHDIOCESE: NORTHERN; IBADAN; UMUAHIA; CALABAR**

8:30   Devotion–Holiness & Mission - Revd Dr Malcolm McCall
9:15   God at work today in Northern Archdiocese
9.45   God at work today in Ibadan Archdiocese
10:30  Tea Break
11:00  Encountering other Religions 1 - Revd Dr Stephen Skuce
12.00  God at work today in Umuahia Archdiocese
1pm   Lunch
2pm   Encountering other Religions 2 - Revd Dr Stephen Skuce
3pm   God at work today in Calabar Archdiocese
4pm   Brief Closing Devotions
7.30   Informal Evening

**THURSDAY-INPUT & REFLECTION ON SPIRITUALITIES, HOLINESS AND MISSION**
**REPORTS-GOD AT WORK TODAY IN THE ARCHDIOCESE: ABUJA; ENUGU; IKOT EKPENE; LAGOS; ILESA**

8:30   Devotion–Spiritualties & Mission - Revd Dr Malcolm McCall
9:15   God at work today in Abuja Archdiocese
9:45   God at work today in Enugu Archdiocese

10:30  Tea Break
11 am  God at work today in Ikot Ekpene Archdiocese
12 am  God at work today in Lagos Archdiocese
1pm    Lunch
2pm    God at work today in Ilesa Archdiocese
3pm    Closing-Secretary Of Conference
Friday Departure

Materials, several larger reference books and 300 page booklet of CCILC lecturing (specially prepared for the consultation) resources were made available free of charge to all participants.

## 2009/6 NOV 1-17: MCSL TRAINING & REFRESHER
VISITING TEAM

The visiting training team, Revd Ken Todd, Revd Dr Malcolm and Mrs Janet McCall and Revd David and Mrs Sylvia Griffiths minus Revd Gilbert and Mrs Sylvia Hall travelled from London on Sunday Nov 1st and stayed overnight at Javouhey House on Leicester Peak, Freetown. Gilbert and Sylvia arrived in Freetown on Wednesday 4th. Despite the difficulties experienced whilst in Sierra Leone which largely related to limited transport, funding and unavoidable last minute rearrangements regarding venues, the whole team paid tribute to the leadership of the MCSL for the hospitality provided and the support given. Their personal reports noted below as events from their diaries speak also of being encouraged by the faith and commitment of friends old and new who continue to serve the purposes of God in Sierra Leone.

NOV 3RD (TUESDAY) REVD MALCOLM AND MRS JANET McCALL

METHODIST SECONDARY SCHOOL, KAILAHUN

Travelled to Kenema and the following day on to Kailahun (one of the hardest hit areas in the troubles of the 1990's) reconnecting on the way with many ex-pupils from their teaching days in the Methodist Secondary School, Kailahun. They were thrilled by the testimony of a boy from a Muslim back ground, Stephen Vandi Tarawalli who had joined the school Boys Brigade run by Malcolm so many years ago, but who is now the Principal of the Methodist Secondary School in Kenema, and the Vice-President of MCSL. Malcolm and Janet encouraged the Kailahun Methodists working in church, schools and the community before travelling back to Segbwema to provide similar encouragement in schools and to some staff at the Nixon Memorial Hospital. On Saturday they led a Lay Training course with about 40 leaders present and Malcolm preached at worship in Segbwema on Sunday 8th before travelling back to Bo on the Monday.

### NOV 4TH (WEDNESDAY) DAVID AND SYLVIA GRIFFITHS

Travelled to Bo. Led a seminar for 15-20 Ministers, Preachers & Teachers on Thursday at St.Augustine's, Bo before travelling the rocky road to Sumbuya on Friday to provide training for 20+ lay leaders (including 5 of the 25 strong Youth Fellowship) there on the Saturday. As with the other 'area training' given by members of the team, the renewal of old relationships and the encouragement (one to one) given to those being met for the first time was found to be as important as the actual training programme. Many groups stressed the urgent need for further training in Church Leadership, Sunday School resources, and further training for evangelistic outreach. David and Sylvia both took part in the 4 ½ long (the length of the service was not down to him!) Sunday worship service St Augustine's Church, Bo before they met up again with the team on Monday.

### NOV 4TH (WEDNESDAY) REVD KEN TODD
### "ARE THERE DIAMONDS IN THERE SOMEWHERE?

Travelled, by 'good roads!' to the diamond mining centre of Koidu. Whilst being involved with the people in Koidu he visited the less-accessible outpost of Kainkoidu to provide encouragement, training at a course on Thursday 5th. Ken preached in the worship service on Sunday before travelling on Monday 9th via junction 51 where he joined the minister travelling from Freetown with the new mission partners (arrived in Freetown Nov 2nd) Revd Peter and Mrs Janice Clark for the journey to Bo.

214

Travelled to Kenema via Bo with the President of Conference Rt. Revd Francis Nabieu (no other transport available!) and arrived 5pm. Arrangements for the Lay Training course in Kenema were not in place but following phone calls and visits it went ahead on Saturday 7th. Gilbert & Sylvia preached at two acts of worship in Kenema, one at the College Chapel and the other at Sidney Groves Memorial Church. On Monday Nov 9th after visiting two Methodist schools, whilst Sylvia attended the Methodist Pre-School, they travelled with the President to Bo for the Ministerial Retreat. The 'booked' venue for the Ministerial Training Retreat, the Catholic Pastoral Centre in Kenema advised MCSL that they could not host this event which meant that hectic last-minute arrangements had to be made to move to the less-suitable Catholic Pastoral Centre in Bo.

**NOV 9TH-13TH MINISTERS' TRAINING RETREAT IN BO**

The visiting team came together from their 'area training responsibilities' to meet with the ministers in Bo. More than sixty ministers attended including two or three Anglican ministers and partners in ministry serving in Sierra Leone from Ghana, and the UK. It was recognised that this was the key consultation in the programme and it was intended to provide both training and encouragement for Methodist Ministers as well as reinforcing relationships between the ministers of isolated congregations and Districts of the Conference.

The training course went as planned with the usual minor adjustments made in response to the needs of the ministers attending. Lectures on aspects of ministry and mission were interspersed with Bible Study, prayer and seminars related to local concerns. The retreat closed with a lively, but moving service of Holy Communion led by the Conference Secretary (and President Designate), Revd Arnold Temple.

The ministers provided the following evaluation of the programme and suggestions as to what might follow:

**1. Positives**-Good spiritual food; inspiring impact on us; very encouraging;
Fellowship bonding across the connexion; Prayers excellent-opportunity to pray together
Teaching sessions meaningful; interesting; inspiring; touching and appropriate for the church today
Prayer partners much appreciated; Speakers very friendly and zealous
Valued opportunity to clear misunderstanding and doubts on ministerial appointments (some seen as a sort of punishment!) and other matters in a shared fellowship environment.
Question regarding wives? Wives bitter about the Methodist Church moving their husbands around so frequently. They can't follow

without taking children out of school which is very unsettling. This is the cause of rifts between husband and wife and possible break-down of the family. Therefore they want stationing for a longer term.

FOOD AND FELLOWSHIP APPRECIATED BY ALL

**2. Negatives**-Time for discussion too short; Management of the Retreat-information too late;
Accommodation not up to standard. Water a big problem. Food sufficient.

**3. Suggestions for future Training Retreats**
a. Workshops on Accounting; School chaplaincy; Counselling; Appraisal; Circuit Twinning; Ecumenical relationships; Leadership training;
b. Renewal of ministerial vows.
c. Visiting team to partner with ministers

d. Increase the length of the Retreat by one day Monday to Friday
e. Opportunity for the training of spouses
f. Friday; Holy Communion service

The team of trainers felt that the 3 full days of the Ministerial Programme was well received by the group as a whole. The visitors and the MCSL Leadership were able to respond to practical and spiritual concerns not only in the open sessions, but in counselling and prayer opportunities that arose throughout the week. We trust and pray

that in all that took place participants were, encouraged, re-envisioned, empowered and reminded that unity between all the different tribes, groupings and backgrounds in the Church is essential if the work of the MCSL is to be fruitful for God's Kingdom.

**"WE ARE IN THIS TOGETHER, BUT TIRING FAST."**

**Nov 13<sup>th</sup> (Friday) The Visiting Team** travelled to Freetown in a very old mini bus! On Saturday Gilbert and Sylvia as planned led Western District Lay Training course in Zion Methodist Church whilst other members of the team renewed relationships in Freetown through personal visits.

**Nov 15<sup>th</sup> (Sunday) Ministers of the visiting team** were invited to preach at the morning worship in four different circuits. The team plus

the Clarks, the President and Secretary of Conference then toured the Skills Centre before enjoying a meal prepared by Lillian Lahai. The group visited the grave of the Revd Michael Tengbe for prayers with his widow Sarah before spending time the

widow of the Revd Dr Leslie Shyllon, who had died in hospital on the Saturday evening. The training team returned to the UK overnight on Sunday.

## 4. Specific Visiting Team Reflections about training/outreach (In no particular order)

Methodist Ministers in Sierra Leone seem generally convinced that unity within the Church and among them is the key issue if the Church is to advance. The visiting International Team would certainly endorse this understanding of the spiritual situation.

Perhaps some thought should also be given to include husbands/wives in future courses/retreats.

The presence of 3 Ghanaian Methodist Ministers was a good encouragement at the Consultation; and the Revd Kwame is already proving a blessing in Segbwema. Next connexional year, there may also be an exchange programme instituted with Methodist Church Nigeria. We believe these are right Kingdom initiatives. But there will need to be a deeper appreciation by everyone that there are large cultural and spiritual differences between Sierra Leone, Ghana and Nigeria. The Methodist Church looks very different in these 3 different nations. Skin colour naturally indicates that there are such differences between Africans and Europeans. But there are also big differences within West Africa, which the Methodist Church will need fully to recognise, and know how to handle, if the greatest benefit is to be gained from this spiritual cross-fertilisation.

### The Bo Methodist Youth & Community Resource Centre,

uses its well-developed premises to offer IT training, sports activities and provides HIV/Aids awareness through teaching and visuals.

The paid and voluntary staff use drama, dance, music to take their message to the young people of Bo, surrounding towns and villages. They are currently supported by a Christian Aid worker. The Centre could also offer an ideal base for imaginative evangelistic outreach to the Young People of Bo, & urge that careful & prayerful consideration is given to this.

The training visit overall was considered by visiting team members to have been a most valuable and rewarding experience both for themselves, the ministers and the lay-leaders with whom they were able to meet. Clearly, the devastation caused to the church and the country in the ten years of conflict in the 1990's cannot be dismissed even after a decade of rebuilding and reconciliation.

As Roland Allen ('Missionary Methods: St Paul's or Ours' & 'The Spontaneous Expansion of the Church') recognised so many years ago we have left behind us overseas a legacy of a paid ministry, an expensive Conference organisation, large institutions, (Hospitals, Schools etc.) that can hardly be supported by local funding and limited leadership even in the longer term. It will be many years before the MCSL (like most other churches in Africa and even now in the UK) can move from its western inherited traditions towards a manageable economic structure and streamlined organisation more in keeping with its culture and capabilities.

The leaders of the Methodist Church in Sierra Leone, CCILC and the visiting team want to express their thanks to their partners in the UK Methodist Church, World Church Office and members of the Scholarship And Leadership Training (SALT) advisory group whose grant of £10,000 contributed to the success of this training programme in Sierra Leone.

In conclusion, perhaps we should recognise again that any support and encouragement that we can give to the MCSL and other churches overseas through personal sharing, training and funding should not be viewed as charitable but as a responsible continuation of our partnership of the past which has left such a burdensome legacy that they must carry into their future. We continue to welcome further donations from individuals or organisations who wish to support the kind of training work overseas that we are doing through the CCILC. Further information and specific reports are available through:

**Richard Jackson (Revd), International Coordinator CCILC**

# CHAPTER 10 2010: PARTNERSHIP IN NIGERIA

*The July 2010 graduations of 129 trainees from the 2008-10 CCITC programme provided opportunities to reinforce relationships, not only with our MCN partners, but also with New Generation Church Pastors. They and their church leaders have so generously hosted our trainees' explorations as they have worshipped with them on the Sundays of the Residentials and sought answers to questions about the growth of their churches. In June 162 new trainees were registered and began their first residential of the 2010-12 programme.*

## 2010/1 JAN 3-19: MCN FOURTH 'RESIDENTIAL'

**(IDIAMM 2008-10 PROGRAMME)**

INTRODUCTION

Revd Ken Todd MMS (Ireland) and I were encouraged during a three hour consultation with the Prelate of the Methodist Church Nigeria (MCN), His Eminence Revd Dr Sunday Ola Makinde, to hear that, **"Cliff College has become a household name in the Methodist Church Nigeria."**

As the second of our programmes in partnership with MCN draws to a close in July 2010, we learned from the Head of the Methodist Church in Nigeria about the contribution being made by students past and present who have taken part in the programme as community projects have been started; new churches planted and evangelistic outreach initiatives taken in many parts of the country. We were pleased to receive from the Prelate the positive affirmation that the CCILC is providing much-valued training as MCN repositions itself in relation to mission/evangelism. The Prelate was enthusiastic about planning together for a future that may provide similar opportunities of further training for both lay leaders and the episcopate.

### THE TRAVELLING TEAM AND OUR SHARING

As usual our January travelling team was made up of smaller numbers, with Revd Ken Todd from Ireland, Revd Dr Jen Smith from London and Revd Gilbert & Mrs Sylvia Hall being added to two members of the core team Keith Phillips and the Coordinator, Revd Richard Jackson. In July the larger team is divided into two with both teams taking turns in delivering a one week training programme to large numbers of students in both of our centres at Umuahia and Sagamu, but the January team travelled first for one week in Umuahia MTI and then for the second week to Sagamu MTI.

**Gilbert & Sylvia Hall** (former mission partners in Nigeria and Sierra Leone) shared responsibility for five deeply challenging morning devotional sessions based on passages in the Book of Revelation that examined the pastor's relationship with the Lord Jesus Christ. They led also four sessions on practical preaching which covered the preparation of the preacher, the sermon and aspects of communication both verbal and visual.

During outdoor group tutorials **Gilbert and Sylvia Hall** responded to concerns about such diverse issues as relationships in a hierarchical church structure; frequency of transfers dividing families; demands for church tithes; and inter-religious crises, particularly in the north of Nigeria. During the spouses weekend, which was poorly attended in Umuahia but  attracted more partners at Sagamu the Hall's used scripture to explore the positives and possible pitfalls of a Christian marriage when couples working together in ministry were subject to both cultural and church pressures to conform to a 'church image' of perfect pastors and the role of women and children in family life.

Our Sunday worship at both centres flowed out of the spouses' weekend, and under the guidance of the Halls' was prepared and led by those present at the weekend, female and male. Later discussions about aspects of this worship and the Umuahia College Community service at which Revd Ken Todd was invited to preach was lively, to say the least!

Throughout the training week at both centres **Revd Dr Jennifer Smith** provided lecture notes and led informative sessions on the government's response to HIV/Aids. She highlighted the influential role of church leaders in changing attitudes and providing teaching and practical guidance within the church and community life.

For Umuahia MTI, Jennifer (using the internet) had recruited a Nigerian, **Mr Jude Munaonye**, Project Director of a community based support group 'Living Hope Organisation', to share with us from personal experience. We learned that Jude a husband and father, has lived for the past 10 years with the knowledge that he was diagnosed as HIV positive. He and his wife, who is blind, have 4 children of their own and have welcomed into their family 6 children orphaned by AIDS.

The students learned from a man, who had tested positive but demonstrated a zest for living backed by a deep and practical concern for others similarly affected. Jude's honest, open, transparent testimony declared how it is possible to survive the stigma and discrimination surrounding those suspected of having, or living with HIV and AIDS and to still have dignity and a quality of life. His story, showing how these barriers can be broken down, was punctuated by poignant stories of men and women who, having been diagnosed HIV positive, suffered rejection, condemnation and isolation which sometimes resulted in suicide.

SENSITIVE SUBJECTS BETTER SHARED IN SMALL GROUPS

Jude, in concluding, called on the ministers and deaconesses present to be well informed about the current health initiatives concerning HIV/AIDS; the whereabouts of suitable clinics (the sufferer may prefer to be referred to a clinic some distance from home); and to show understanding, care and compassion. Though Jude was unable to be with us at Sagamu, the impact of his presentation continued and his testimony overflowed into the spouses' weekend at both centres, during which the women (wives and deaconesses) valued a separate very practical session on the issues relating to HIV/Aids with Sylvia and Jennifer.

**Revd Ken Todd,** former missionary in Sierra Leone and past President of the Methodist Church in Ireland used his teaching

sessions on Elijah to address many of the personal issues faced by church leaders as they remain faithful to God in ministry and mission. To be led through, 'Elijah and the False Gods'; 'Elijah's hostile environment'; 'Elijah: what it means to be God's person'; etc. in the context of Nigerian political and religious life was for many of the students an opportunity to gather together what has been learned in academic terms and work through in a personal and practical way the challenges that they find in their own ministry.
(Ken's book on Elijah was given to all students to add to their personal library of several hundred pounds worth of books and lecture notes provided for them free as part of the course and subsidised by MMS (Ireland), Methodist Insurance, grants and the Langham Partnership)

**Revd Richard Jackson** and the administrator, **Keith Phillips** found themselves (as usual at this stage of the two-year programme) fully stretched in moderating the marks given for assignments and updating marks spreadsheets. Typically with distance learning programmes in a large country where communications of any kind are difficult and travel comparatively expensive in terms of

time and money, student submissions can go astray or be lost completely. Allowances have been made for the five students who have become bishops since the course began and some will still complete the course.

Once again the Rectors and staff of the colleges have gone above and beyond the call of duty (in what is always their own vacation time) to supervise student work and to facilitate the marking of late or lost submissions. Thanks to the patience of the staff and their hard work (with a few exceptions or required re-submissions) most students have fulfilled the requirements of the course to date and are left with an 8,000-8,500 word dissertation to complete by the 28<sup>th</sup> February 2010. Arrangements are being put in place for the graduation of 50+ students at Umuahia (7<sup>th</sup> July) and 70+ students at Sagamu (17<sup>th</sup> July), hopefully as part of a two year programme with newly recruited students which will begin in July 2010 and complete in July 2012.

**PERSONAL RELATIONSHIPS STRENGTHEN PARTNERSHIPS**

Through numerous casual and planned contacts we were reminded on this visit of how important relationships are to our current partnership with the Methodist Church Nigeria. Outside the colleges with which we are involved and the programme itself, but related to it were the official, but always friendly meetings with the Prelate, The Secretary of Conference, and the Bishop of Evangelism. At different times during our training visit we were greeted as old friends by Bishops who had attended the July 2009 training consultation and received the books supplied through the Langham Partnership with funding through the World Church Office in London. One Bishop, now become Archbishop of Umuahia, invited the team to an evening reception at which he shared how the books provided had seemed like God's gift in replacing those lost to him in a fire that destroyed his home.

COMPASSION AND COMFORT SHARED

Four of our team, Gilbert, Sylvia, Jen and Ken were able to visit and encourage the people still associated with the leprosy Colony at Uzuakoli. To quote: (from a longer report that is available to interested parties about the Colony and long-term Mission partner Ros Colwill's new project.)

*"People will remember the work that was done in years past at Uzuakoli, and the thousands of leprosy patients who began new lives there. Recently, a programme of resettling families in their home villages has meant that only a few dozen residents remain, including nine very elderly persons, the 'weak line.' Deaconess Matilda took us pastoral visiting and we walked around the camps, pausing to pray and visit with each resident. We were overcome with the welcome we received, as when one very elderly lady literally danced to meet us, though she could barely walk.*

*A highlight was the group all coming together for an impromptu gathering with prayers and greetings, pictured under the trees together. Being remembered by the world church was a great encouragement to these people, who often feel forgotten amidst all the rush of changing church priorities!"*

On the final Sunday, at the invitation of the Prelate, we were involved in the enthronement of the new Archbishop of Ilesha and once again (as throughout the visit at various events) Ken Todd was able to bring greetings, not only from Ireland, but also from the WCO and Methodist Church in the UK. People present on all of these occasions shared with us memories of past missionaries and told us about present links with family and friends living in the UK and the USA

CONCLUSION

During the past few years, our personal hosting in the UK of friends from Sierra Leone has been almost superseded by the relationships being developed with friends from Nigeria. When Bishop Babatunde Taiwo and his family (who host the whole of the visiting team(s) at Sagamu) stayed with us shortly before Christmas, a 'Nigerian evening' allowed former missionaries and many Manchester based Nigerian Methodists to meet up with the Bishop and his family in our home. We are in contact with Nigerian students studying in the UK at Cliff College and elsewhere. Raphael Idialu, recently returned to Nigeria after completing an MA in Birmingham. He was posted to Sagamu MTI as a tutor and is now a supervisor on the CCILC programme. Family members linked with MCN who now live in the UK have created a flourishing network of relationships that should

225

remind all of us of how small our (still very large Methodist Church) world has become.

As we concluded our programme(s) in Nigeria by praying together in prayer triplets with the students we were deeply moved by the concerns expressed one for the other. Only on our return to the UK did we learn of the violent disturbances taking place in the north of Nigeria. How important might our prayers be for Nigeria as a nation as well as for our pastor students as they return to their place of service?

The new Governor of Lagos, despite the huge task being undertaken, is leading the way in showing what can be done to improve the conditions for travel and cleanliness for the teeming millions that call the great city of Lagos their home.

What has become a welcome tradition (If we do things more than once in Methodism it can quickly become a tradition!) for our team has been lunch on the final day of our visit at the Secretary of Conference's home in Lagos. In what has become a more accessible and much improved environment, Raphael Opoko and his wife Alice, provide the hospitality for what might be termed a 'working lunch' as we exchange final thoughts on the kaleidoscope of experiences that have both touched and challenged the visiting team during our stay.

Our thanks go out to them and countless friends in Nigeria and many other parts of the world who keep reminding us that people do matter and that everyone of us can make a difference to the ways in which people throughout the world relate to one another.

Despite the publicity given to Facebook, twitter and all the blogs on the web, nothing is quite so productive for us personally or society as a whole, as nurturing relationships across creed, colour and clan through meeting together.

We grow as God's people even more quickly when we work in partnership with others to achieve some great purpose: and that after all is our Christian calling.

**Richard Jackson (Revd)**
**International Coordinator CCILC**

We continue to seek funding and resources for associated projects like college and school libraries as well as funding for the pioneering college of Zonkwa in the north, as part of the CCILC vision to build up local colleges for their developing work. If there is any earlier report further information or documentation and photographs that anyone would like to have, particularly for fund-raising purposes, I shall be pleased to make it available.

## 2010/2 FEB 2010: 'RELATIONSHIPS MATTER'

As Coordinator of the Cliff College International Learning Centre (CCILC) I have just finished writing my report on our recent (Jan 2010) training visit to Nigeria. In writing this 'Good News' article for the Methodist Recorder I was prompted to speculate on how important personal relationships (past and present) have been to the successful development of the CCILC programme.

I remember well the frustration I felt as a mission partner in Sierra Leone when I waited for the first time in a queue, the length of which was determined by how much time the serving civil servant took with each person as they gossiped about families and friends. It took me some time before I became de-westernised and began to value their interest in, and concern for, each other.

One of my concerns about the future of our relationship with our partner churches overseas is that in reducing the numbers of people employed here we make it impossible for those who continue in ministry locally, nationally and even internationally to have time for the kind of personal relationships/friendships that oil the wheels of every organisation.

I am well aware of the proliferation and value of the 'modern' means of communication. Even in Lagos we see so many people wandering around with mobile phones glued to their ears. The justification in Africa is that landlines which work are few and far between, but with mobiles for different networks people can usually make a connection. The CCILC would be well-nigh impossible to coordinate without access to emails, websites and less expensive communication internationally using Skype. Everyone is becoming more aware of the so called friendship sites, the aptly named: Blog; Facebook; and Twitter. Yes, even we use the videocam to keep in touch with family in the USA and some friends who have the same equipment, but I do question whether all of these modern methods for communicating are personal enough.

We contact each other in so many ways, but real communication between people takes place and lasting friendships are re-invigorated when we meet each other with a smile, a hug, or a kiss depending on the relationship. Familiar voices and faces alive with friendship lighten our world wherever we are. During our team's training visit to Nigeria in January we were reminded again of how important relationships are to team bonding, to our partnerships with the world church, and perhaps increasingly to the world in which we live. To be hugged and almost lifted off your feet by the MCN Secretary of Conference, who is a large man in every way, is like being greeted by a friendly bear. To be sent on our way to return to our CCILC programme duties with a hug of farewell from a smiling Prelate in all his finery during a special service enthroning the Archbishop of Ilesha is to be publically accorded the status of 'friend'.

In our travels overseas we enjoy the respect given to us as representatives of the 'Mother Church of Methodism'. People share with us in personal ways the affection felt by so many of our mission partners for individuals in the UK who have contributed something, either in Nigeria or in the UK to their own growth in discipleship.

Alongside the constant enquiries about friends who have served overseas in the past, tributes are paid to Area Secretaries of the World Church Office, so-called official representatives from the UK, friendships engendered at Conferences and Scholarship Committee Secretaries who have been pastors as well as paymasters to students visiting these shores. Everywhere we go tributes are paid to all of those here, who through local churches or on a personal basis have done something to respond to the expressed needs of churches overseas or for friends or families living and working in the UK.

Cliff College itself is one institution that has a long history of receiving students from overseas and being a 'sending agency' as part of this World Church which is Methodism. Within that whole body we, and the UK Methodist Church, are fortunate to be the recipients of so-much good will.

We may have to find new ways of partnering Methodist Churches overseas, who with the enthusiasm of youth are outpacing the older generation in mission and evangelism, but what we should be careful not to lose as we seek to 'balance the books' is time and opportunities for maintaining face to face friendships that are the bed-rock of any fruitful relationship.

Wherever our regular responsibilities as friends of Jesus lie, in local church; place of work; Cliff College or Conference Offices; here or overseas; let us make the time to create and maintain personal relationships through meeting together, (even on exotic holidays!) both here and there, with friends in the church throughout the world.

**THE SMILE SAYS IT ALL!**

Richard Jackson (Revd) Coordinator, Cliff College International Learning Centre

## 2010/3 FEB: REV'D PUBLICITY-IRISH DEPUTATION

WE HAVE TRIED TO KEEP IN PRINT UPDATED EDITIONS OF A GENERAL PUBLICITY LEAFLET FOR THE CCILC. THE LEAFLET WAS UPDATED AND THE NAME CHANGED TO CLIFF COLLEGE INTERNATIONAL TRAINING CENTRE (CCITC) EARLY IN 2010, IN TIME FOR DISTRIBUTION AT THE IRISH DEPUTATION.

## *CLIFF COLLEGE INTERNATIONAL TRAINING CENTRE (CCITC)*

### *PARTNERS IN TRAINING FOR MISSION & MINISTRY*

### *A PROGRAMME FOR THE 21$^{ST}$ CENTURY*

Cliff College is a Methodist institution with an evangelical and mission ethos. It has a proud history of giving training to Christian lay-people of all denominations from many parts of the world for over 100 years. More recently it has become a chosen centre for the further training of both ministers and lay people through its pioneering and popular distance learning courses validated by Manchester University and offered from Diploma through to Masters Level.

Learning and reflection linked with praxis has become the hallmark of these part-taught (during residential weeks), part -self-study (reading and assignments) and part-research/placement assessed courses which are usually completed over two-years. During the past eight years Cliff College through its International Training Centre has used this basic template to pioneer, pilot and develop successfully a visionary training concept in association with partner churches in Sierra Leone and Nigeria.

## TRAINING IN SIERRA LEONE

In 2002 the British Methodist Church provided primary funding of £20,000 a year for two years and we began to explore what would be involved in using this well-proven template to do training overseas in partnership with local churches and Christian Councils. At the invitation of, and in partnership with, the Christian Council of Sierra Leone (CCSL) Cliff College ran a very successful ecumenical pilot programme at the Theological College in Freetown. This resulted in 73 of the 99 trainees who began the two-year course in 2002 completing and being awarded by Cliff College an International Diploma in Applied Ministry and Mission (IDIAMM) in 2004.

**Once underway the project attracted additional support from a variety of sponsors,** including MMS (Ireland), UMC (Germany), SPCK/Feed The Minds, Methodist Insurance and the Langham Partnership. This support meant that during the pilot programme in Sierra Leone and later in Nigeria all trainees, including those who were not successful, received lecture notes and contextualised teaching (from a partnership of local and international lecturers). Every trainee was given large numbers of books to study (retailing at  several hundred pounds sterling). They will continue to enrich their ministry in the years that lie ahead. Associated with the CCITC programme in Sierra Leone, training was given to Local Preachers and key Women Workers.

**A positive evaluation of the two-year pilot project in post-conflict Sierra Leone** prompted the Methodist Church in Sierra Leone (MCSL) to request further training in 'Leadership and Administration' for those in ministry and for Conference Office Staff. This training of key personnel involved in the community re-building and reconciliation programmes of the church was undertaken by a visiting team who made three visits in March 2006; October 2006; February 2007. In November 2009 a follow-up refresher programme was undertaken, which brought the ordained ministers together for a training consultation and encouraged the locally appointed trainers at regional events. (Separate reports are available.)

In 2005 the Methodist Church Nigeria (MCN) asked us to develop an IDIAMM course, similar to that piloted in Sierra Leone, but with a special emphasis on training 'evangelism trainers' as the church re-positions itself with a fresh focus on mission. This programme began in July 2006 at two Methodist Colleges in Nigeria and saw 108 trainees graduate in July 2008.

A further programme (2008-10) with 120+ key presbyters expected to graduate in July 2010 has been so successful (5 trainees having been made bishops!) that further funding sought by the MCN for 2010-12 has been approved by the UK Methodist Church.

In July 2009 we felt privileged to be invited to lead a three-day 'Episcopal Training Consultation' on ministry and mission attended by the Prelate, 9 Archbishops and 40+ bishops of MCN. Again thanks to our sponsors we were able to supply key books and lecture notes to all those attending the Consultation.

The IDIAMM programme with books provided, is flexible enough to meet changing circumstances and specific concerns. Usually it includes modules on:
Study & Research Skills;
Adult Learning and Training in Communication;
Mission in the Old Testament; Evangelism in the New Testament;
Encountering other Religions &Sects; Applied Ministry & Leadership (incl. Pastoral);
Worship & Preaching (incl. visits to and assessment of local growing Churches);
Christian Spirituality (& journal writing);
Church Growth in (African) Church History (including teaching on Methodism);
Applied Evangelism; Aids Awareness etc.

In Nigeria it was agreed that we should incorporate in the IDIAMM programme a requirement upon the trainees (mainly evangelists, deaconesses and ministers) that trainees should be involved also in new mission initiatives: planting churches; starting community projects; training evangelists (especially in the vernacular); in their local situation, throughout the two year course. Their success (or otherwise) with this is assessed through the submission of an Applied Evangelism portfolio and with a research project (8,000-8,500 word) as part of the overall course.

**'DOING TRAINING OVERSEAS WITH PARTNER CHURCHES' WORKS!**

Basic funding of around £20,000 a year from the British Methodist Church for each course has attracted further donations and funding from elsewhere. Sponsors have helped to resource trainees, local staff and college libraries associated with each of these courses.

Our partner churches in Sierra Leone and Nigeria have contributed to the course costs by providing buildings, local lecturing resources, and hospitality for the visiting team.

Outside the programme budget, many thousands of pounds continue to be generated through visiting lecturers, for projects as diverse as Manse rebuilding in Sierra Leone and College water supplies in Nigeria.

Highly qualified visiting lecturers/trainers, many with previous experience overseas have offered their time and particular expertise free. The cost of travel, visas and out of pocket expenses for a visiting team of 6-8 people utilised for the 2-3 weeks residentials, twice a year are met from the budget.

The visiting lecturers, who are partnered with local lecturers, engage in a mutually profitable exchange of insights, lecture notes and other materials that enriches their continuing ministry.

Several hundred full-time church workers have received (further) training and resources (at a cost of £500 per trainee per annum) through tailored courses that address their own concerns and contexts whilst they continue with their own ministry.

Whilst every effort is made to maintain the courses and training at appropriate academic levels, the Cliff College validation, has freed the course from the additional costs and constraints that would be imposed by affiliation to a British university. The CCITC concept of 'Doing training overseas with partner churches' has proved itself economically viable, practically possible and adaptable to differing situations and circumstances (including a brief but enriching training visit to Cuba). The door has been opened to a different kind of relationship with our partners in our mission to the world. This programme has been developed through Cliff College with the larger part of the funding being provided by the UK Methodist Church.

Our hope is that its success will inspire general recognition on the part of all churches (and former missionary societies) that 'Doing training overseas with partner churches', and with all the associated benefits in terms of renewing personal relationships for all parties concerned, is a worthwhile investment for the future of the church worldwide. CCITC welcomes donations made through Cliff College from individuals or organisations who wish to support any aspect of the work that we are doing overseas.

**CCITC Graduation Preaching Scarf**
**(Locally made with church and Cliff College emblems)**

**MC NIGERIA**
Symbol with words

*WORTHY*

*IS*

*THE LAMB*

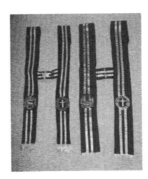

**MC SIERRA LEONE**
Symbol with words

*UNITY,*

*FREEDOM,*

*JUSTICE.*

**CLIFF COLLEGE:** *CHRIST FOR ALL╬ALL FOR CHRIST*

**Cliff College Website** www.cliffcollege.org    *(Revised and updated February 2010)*

234

# 2010/4 FEB: McCALLS-ENGLISH COMMUNICATION

**REPORT FROM ZONKWA: REVD DR MALCOLM & MRS JANET McCALL (Feb 21-Mar 6)**

As promised in 2009 we started our "English for Gospel Communication" Course at Zonkwa MTI on Monday 22 February, and taught throughout the whole of the working week, then rested on Saturday 27th. The Revd Emmanuel Bakuzo, Minister of the Hausa-speaking Methodist Church in Zonkwa, was part of our Course, and on Sunday 28th he invited Malcolm to preach.

We were kept busy throughout the following week until our Course finished on Friday 5 March, when the Methodist Bishop of Jos, Bishop Chindo, came to present "Awards" to those who had successfully completed the Course. The violence in Jos had left him with much to do around the city. However, he said that if we had come all the way from the UK to deliver this English Course, he should at least take time to make the 3-hour journey from Jos to celebrate the conclusion of the programme. (We were later horrified to hear of further serious violence in the Jos area – with rumours of up to 500 Christians massacred – on Sunday 7 March, just after we left the area!)

Another dear friend who met with us briefly at Zonkwa during our Course was Bishop Jaja, Methodist Bishop of Kano (formerly Methodist Bishop of Jos): he blessed us in fervent prayer. The Very Revd Shettima Chibok, College Principal, did everything he could to make our time comfortable and profitable, including meeting us at Abuja Airport as we arrived in the country. He also drove us to Kaduna on Saturday 6 March. It was good to speak and pray personally with Shettima, and with his 2 Methodist Minister colleagues on the College Staff – Revd Gabriel Adah and Revd Habila Ansah

We certainly felt the intensity of the programme when there were just 2 of us to conduct the whole programme. (We are used to operating as a larger Cliff College team during our regular teaching residentials at Umuahia and Sagamu). However, the 22 College students were a joy to teach and we shared with them at many different levels. Spiritually the students were very responsive, and we found it a great privilege to share our hearts with them, and to cry out to the LORD together in fervent prayer.

The Course also included some visitors. Among these were The Revd Sunday Ibrahim, Chairman of the Zonkwa Christian Association of Nigeria Chapter. Deaconess Rhoda Dunioh, whom we had previously known as a student at Zonkwa, returned to enter fully into the Course: she has been appointed by the Methodist Conference to Sokoto in the extreme North-West of Nigeria. We also had visitors from Maiduguri in the extreme North-East; Kano in the North; some came from Abuja in the central belt of Nigeria. It was therefore very moving to be teaching a group whose "home-bases" covered the whole of Northern Nigeria.

### ENGLISH TEXT BOOKS AND INTERACTIVE TEACHING

The English books we took with us entitled "How English Works" had been gifted and prayed over individually by Methodists of the Shetland Methodist District. They were received with excitement and gratitude by the Zonkwa students and the visitors, and were very well used by Janet on each day of the Course. She employed a variety of teaching methods:

1. The English textbook itself was an enormously valuable resource, and we helped the students to experience (a) the "test yourself" section, (b) follow the main explanations and exercises with students actually doing a selection of the exercises "in class," (c) noting the formal grammar summaries, and (d) learning to use the "answers" section at the back of the book. We tried very hard to make sure that each person could leave the Course confident in using their book as a self-tutor and a working reference book. (We had been careful to choose an edition which contains answers, so that students can correct their own work when no teacher is available.)

2. As a help to oral communication of the Gospel, we did several "One Minute Please" sessions, where each student was given the opportunity to "speak out" a short monologue on such subjects as "What Christ means to me," and "My heart's desire".

3. From these "oral" sessions, Janet quietly noted the students' slips and mistakes. She then (naming no names!) sensitively

introduced several "Corrections Sessions". The students showed great eagerness and a mature humility in wanting to get the most out of these sessions, which were amongst the most productive in terms of improvement in English. (It is interesting that we have noticed the same productivity through these "Correction Sessions" at Sagamu and Umuahia over the past 4 years.)

**4.** As a help to aural comprehension, Janet engaged the students in personal stories and testimony.

**5.** As a further – and rather more lively and light-hearted – means of enhancing oral communication skills, Janet arranged for all the students to be involved in a dramatic presentation of the Book of Esther.

**6.** Malcolm complemented this "classroom work" with written homework (which most of the students took very seriously) as well as sharing in the main English lectures. Towards the beginning of the 2 weeks, Malcolm set a piece of homework which he marked for each student. It was a great thrill to discover that those marks, compared with another set of marks later on, showed the English of virtually every student had improved; in some cases, quite exceptionally!

Malcolm also presented the Morning Devotions at the beginning of each day, and introduced a basic Gospel theme, crucial in any evangelistic presentation. "Grace" was the key word. We started from the father in the Prodigal Son story: grace is "love that runs to meet us". Grace gives us the best robe – a "robe of righteousness" – which is Jesus Himself  (Rom. 13. 14: "clothe yourselves with Christ"). We were very excited by these themes, and about grace as the "Gospel heartland."

The Course members were also encouraged, in sessions led by Malcolm, to explore the TNIV Study Bibles, kindly donated to each student by a British Methodist Circuit in Leicester, and obtained at greatly subsidised prices through the Langham Trust Literature organisation. As part of the Cliff College programme, Zonkwa students had also received copies of the African Bible Commentary. So we felt encouraged that they each had in their possession books providing the basic resources for effective "Gospel Communication in

English". (Malcolm found the TNIV Study Bible a great treasury of information, but quite complicated and challenging for the students to use. However, we are confident that this particular Study Bible is one of the best available, and that the students will be able to use it, each "at their own level".

The philosophy behind our 2 weeks' Course was that improved Gospel Communication in English would "cascade" into improved communication in Hausa (the lingua franca of the North), and from Hausa into the numerous smaller language groups that are "heart languages" for many in the North. The aim is for improved Gospel Communication in those "heart languages."

Among our own students, as many as 20 such languages were known and used. This is a huge vision – but we have a great God! It was a tremendous privilege to lead this "English for Gospel Communication" Course. Our great heartache was that, as one mature man said, many of the students had been poorly taught in English from Primary School onwards. A whole year of intensive remedial "one-to-one" tuition might be needed by some of the students. Yet the amazing improvement amongst some students in just 2 weeks was little short of miraculous.

We thoroughly agree with the Methodist Prelate's assessment that in the environment of Northern Nigeria, nothing could be more helpful for our Methodist Students than remedial English tuition. We only longed to do more!

STUDENTS AT WORK

In the course of our 2 weeks in Northern Nigeria, we were thrilled to share with 3 of our students at present engaged in the Presbyters' Cliff College Diploma Course at Umuahia.

1. The Very Revd Shettima Chibok - it was a great joy to see him so active in his own ministry, translating theory into practice as College Principal at Zonkwa.

2. The second student is ministering in a Methodist Circuit in a suburb of Abuja. He asked us to preach in his church on Sunday 21st. February. It was good to see the Methodist building packed to capacity

(and beyond!), and to visit the site purchased to provide for a larger church building. A manse has already been built, and the student and his family are already living in it.

3. Finally, we were graciously entertained by the Archbishop of Kaduna for the last weekend of our visit (6 – 8 March), and thereby were enabled to meet up again with the Superintendent of Kaduna North Circuit. In this visit we continued following the progress of a church plant in Kakau, a suburb of Kaduna, which we had seen started in July 2009.

On Saturday 6th March, about 100 people gathered for a Rally. The following day there were perhaps 70 at Morning Worship. The new congregation is still using the side veranda of a house belonging to Samuel, a key founding member of the new church. The Superintendent took us to a possible site for a new church building: the owner is willing to sell it to the church for £12,500. We prayed over the site, and asked God to provide the finances. We also prayed for this new church to have a strong and good leadership team, and a missionary heart.

So we left North Nigeria grateful not only for the Zonkwa Course, but also for opportunity for renewed contact with 3 of our Umuahia Cliff College Course Presbyters, all expecting to graduate in July 2010.

Janet and Malcolm McCall
Easter 2010

# 2010/5 JUN 27-JUL 19: MCN GRADUATIONS & ?

(IDIAMM 2008-10 PROGRAMME)

INTRODUCTION WITH VISA CONCERNS

The only serious cause for concern in relation to the planned programme of graduations and the launch of a further two-year programme in Nigeria developed into an energy-sapping crisis in the weeks leading up to the travelling team of lecturers planned departure date from the UK. Visas were applied for in good time with passports and the appropriate documentation one month ahead of the travel dates but administrative changes at the Nigerian High Commission meant that the (normal) 3-4 days for obtaining visas in London became two weeks (awaiting confirmation from Abuja), then three, then four. Our flights were booked for Sunday, 27th June, but by Friday the 25th we were making preparations for the likely cancellation of the July programme.

The intervention of the Head of the Methodist Church Nigeria (MCN), who happened to be in the UK at that time; person to person lobbying of officials in Abuja by the Secretary of Conference and the Bishop of Evangelism in Nigeria; the patience and persistence of our administrator who waited at the visa office in London for a second full day (and much prayer from all who were aware of the situation) saw the 9 passports stamped with visas by 4.00pm on the Friday afternoon. We breathed a sigh of relief and made final preparations to travel as planned from Manchester to Lagos via Paris early on Sunday morning.

As usual the July travelling team became two groups on arrival in Nigeria (team 1 to Sagamu and Team 2 to Umuahia), only meeting up as we exchanged venues and for the graduations.

THE TRAVELLING TEAM AND THEIR ROLES

## Team 1 led by:

The International Coordinator, Revd Richard Jackson; included Administrator, Keith Phillips; Cliff College Principal, Revd Dr Chris Blake; former Director of Evangelism UK Methodist church, Revd Phil Clarke; and Miss Amy Parker sharing in Student Liaison and

Course Evaluation. Whilst there was a full programme to be adhered

to, opportunity was given to the Principal, and other newcomers to Nigeria to say **prayers at the refurbished grave of Mary Archer Champness in Abeokuta,** and to visit Immanuel College, Ibadan, Schools and the Methodist Centre at Uzuakoli.

**Team 2 led by:**

Core Team member, Revd Dr Malcolm McCall; included English teacher, Mrs Janet McCall; Lecturer in Old Testament, Revd Dr Michael Thompson; and Methodist Local Preacher, (Sir) Peter Worrell KCW.

# 2010/6 JUN 27-JUL 19: MCN FIRST 'RESIDENTIAL'

### (IDIAMM 2010-12 PROGRAMME)

Advance warnings of large numbers of trainees pre-registering for the planned 2010-12 programme proved not to be unfounded, though the pre-registration and funding through Dioceses with advance copies of timetables supplied did not stop some trainees from finding fresh excuses for arriving late at both centres after the course had begun!

#### 2010-12 PROGRAMME:TEAM 2 AT UMUAHIA

Eventually, 89 trainees were registered on the course at Umuahia and 73 at Sagamu, a total of 162 in all, which is many more than we have coped with on any previous course either in Nigeria or Sierra Leone. Whilst most of the trainees are presbyters seeking further training in

241

ministry and mission, the one disappointment is in the reduced number of women attending, an indicator perhaps of the cultural bias that women face even when serving the church in Nigeria.

Having said that, both teams reported an improvement in the atmosphere at both centres as the new students demonstrated a real enthusiasm for learning and the interaction with both local and visiting lecturers stimulated everyone involved. This may have been helped by the distribution of lecture notes in booklet form which allowed the trainees to be better prepared for the subject being taught and able to respond in more productive ways. As visiting trainers we try not to forget that we are learning too and changes made in the programme since its inception reflect that.

### RESOURCES AND BOOKS

Apart from the lecture notes provided, books are a key resource for the trainees undergoing this programme. We acknowledge again our indebtedness to our sponsors from the UK Methodist Church, MMS(Ireland) and Methodist Insurance as well as to local churches

and donations that help to fund the books provided free to our trainees. We are helped in this also by the generosity of SPCK, the Langham Partnership and friends at 'How to books' who supply the books so appreciated by our trainees at well under the commercial rate.

**HAPPY RECIPIENTS WITH TEAM 1 AT SAGAMU**

The logistics of supplying these from the UK in time, direct to the students in our two centres can be a nightmare (visiting lecturers complain of stretched arm muscles) but the joy with which these books are received and the enthusiasm for studying the books make the effort worthwhile. (More pictures for publicity are available.)

### NEW GENERATION CHURCHES

New Generation Churches (largely Pentecostal inspired), many with exotic sounding names are added to daily in Africa and many of them flourish in the Nigerian context. Not without some difficulty we have begun to help our trainees, largely pastors in the traditional  Methodist denomination, to attend some of these churches (on Sundays as groups during our programme and individually in their home situation) and to learn what lessons they can about why/how these churches grow in Nigerian communities.

Over the past four years these visits to a variety of church situations (written up in worship portfolios) have become a feature of the programme and an important learning experience. Churches visited have welcomed the trainees as learners, rather than 'critics' and have responded by asking if their own pastors might benefit in some way from the programme. Spontaneously, we promised to invite the 'New Generation Churches' pastors with whom we are involved to an open training day in January. Only now are we beginning to explore the possibilities of returning their hospitality and perhaps providing an Africa Bible Commentary for each attendee (however many that may be!). This excellent commentary might help to share a nuanced African but more balanced insight as these churches continue to grow.

**MCN GRADUATIONS FOR COMPLETED (2008-10) PROGRAMME**

7th JULY AT UMUAHIA & 17th JULY AT SAGAMU

The graduations have much in common, even sharing the same brochure this time, but the larger worship centre in the college at Umuahia provided a more spacious setting for the 76 graduates, 3 of whom obtained distinctions and 16 with merits. A further 53 graduated in an adjacent church at Sagamu, 6 of who gained distinctions and 14 with merits. As a tribute to the hard work done by our partner tutors in Nigeria in supervising and marking the work of trainees on the course, each one was pleased to receive a Cliff College certificate acknowledging their involvement in the training programme.

Presided over by the Prelate at Sagamu, and with the Archbishop deputising at Umuahia, the graduations are great occasions of celebration, with everyone from family and friends through to the lecturers and dignitaries dressed in colourful regalia, but the focus as always is on the trainees, most of whom have battled through many geographical and other challenges to receive their certificates and the International Diploma In Applied Ministry and Mission scarf.

**REVD DR CHRIS BLAKE, PRINCIPAL**

The Cliff College Principal presented the certificates; the International Coordinator put on the scarves; the Charge was given by the MCN Secretary of Conference at Sagamu and the Bishop of Evangelism in Umuahia. This was associated with a resounding rendition of 'Glory to God' by the trainees as the ceremony came to a moving climax when the trainees were commissioned back into the MCN and the congregation prayed for their ministry as trained evangelists.

We appreciate, but have grown more used to, the welcome and the generous hospitality that we receive on our regular training visits, but in talk of celebrations it would be remiss of me not to mention the

response made by our friends there to Amy, our youngest team member, not only hearing the news of her BA (2.1) whilst in Nigeria, but also arriving at the grand old age of 21 on the 12th July. The gifts and celebrations associated with their 'daughter, Nigerian dressed and hair styled' will not have been bettered when she returned home to a second celebration in the UK.

As indicated earlier the only major problem faced this time was linked with obtaining visas. That we hope will be resolved by the church and authorities in Nigeria before the team travel again for the January 2011 residential. After eight years of devoted service by so many dedicated people our on-going concern is for the future of the CCITC programme beyond the year 2012.

The vision that prompted a few jottings made on a sick bag as we returned by air from a devastated Sierra Leone in 2001 has become a tried and tested programme of partnership in training that has proved its worth in undertaking and completing several two-year programmes in Sierra Leone and Nigeria. Alongside these longer programmes this resource (at minimal cost) has proved flexible enough to contribute to the training of pastors in Cuba; and provide training in administration to Conference Office Staff, Local Preachers, Women Workers and other personnel in Sierra Leone.

In July 2009 at the request of the MCN we shared in a 3-day 'leadership training consultation' provided in Lagos for the 50 Archbishops, and Bishops of the Nigerian Methodist Church. This report is not the place to rehearse again in detail the add-on value/benefits of 'doing training there in partnership with the national church(es)', but it is an appropriate place and time to stake a claim for an agreed proportion of the budget made available through the World Church Office to be set aside to fund the training being done in countries like Nigeria, whether that training is being done through CCITC, Mission Partners or other organisations.

The success of these practical training programmes and the impact being made by graduating trainees has been evaluated and is attested to by the leadership of the churches where we have been involved for the past eight years. With an annual budget equivalent to that needed to train two people on scholarships 'here' in the UK, we have resourced with materials/books and shared in giving further training 'there' in leadership, ministry and mission to literally hundreds of full and part-time workers in Sierra Leone and Nigeria.

Our hope is that during the next two years our church will not only acknowledge the value of this training resource alongside others and but also fund its continuation as a conduit through which partner churches can solicit the kind of support for their own training programmes tailored to meet their needs. At a time when reduced funding and cuts in staffing in London threaten to undermine our shared mission, we have the opportunity to build into our ongoing relationship with our partners in the world church a proven resource for training ministers/evangelists that could be broadened to include specialist lay training through short courses in children's and youth work.

We close by saying thank you with a photograph (on the left) of some of those trained in Sierra Leone and (on the right) with greetings from some trainees beginning the new course (2010-12) in Umuahia this July.

**Richard Jackson (Revd)**
**International Coordinator CCITC**

PS ON OTHER PROJECTS

Apart from fund-raising for CCITC, as part of the vision we try to build up church training centres for their developing work. So we solicit funding and resources for associated projects, especially college and school libraries as well as helping the pioneering college of Zonkwa in the north. An updated CCITC DVD 2002-2010 produced by James Atkins and narrated by the General Secretary of the Methodist Church, Revd Dr Martyn Atkins is available on request. If there is any earlier report further information or documentation and photographs that anyone would like to have, particularly for fund-raising purposes, I shall be pleased to make them available.

# CHAPTER 11 2011: PARTNERS IN NIGERIA

*With no visits planned for Sierra Leone, 2011 saw the continuation of the IDIAMM training in Nigeria. Regular visits there and some reciprocal visits to Cliff College and our homes here have strengthened the partnership. Relationships have been nurtured through mutual respect and reciprocal engagements as we have shared with MCN leaders and the Rectors and staff of its colleges. This has enriched everyone associated with the programme. As the reports show, the regular and continuing involvement in a programme leads to progressive sharing that encourages both personal and church growth.*

## 2011/1 JAN 4-20: MCN SECOND 'RESIDENTIAL'

### (IDIAMM 2010-12 PROGRAMME)

#### INTRODUCTION

Following the success of earlier two-year programmes in Nigeria with Evangelists, Deaconesses and Presbyters (2006-8; 2008-10;) many key leaders were enrolled by their diocese for the 2010-12 training programme. Since our last visit in July two more of our trainees and one of our partner Rectors (Umuahia MTI) had been designated as Bishops of the MCN. The Leader (not the Head, as he explains, in re-defining the Prelate's role) of MCN, His Eminence, Revd Dr Ola S. Makinde; made it clear that those people (including the newly appointed Director of Administration at Conference Office) who have begun would be expected to complete the two-year programme.

#### THE JANUARY 2011 'RESIDENTIALS' AT UMUAHIA AND SAGAMU MTI'S

The MCN-directed arrangements meant that for our January 'Residential' we had 84 trainees of the 89 registered in July in residence at Umuahia and 73 trainees, the same number as registered originally at Sagamu making a total of 157 in all. The visiting team of 'regular' facilitators included:

Revd Richard Jackson MA BD          International Coordinator of CCITC Methodist Minister and former PG Tutor at Cliff College

Revd Dr Stephen Skuce BD, MPhil, MEd    Irish Methodist Minister, Cliff College Academic Dean & Director CCITC

Mr Keith Phillips CQSW, Cert Ed    Anglican, former VSO in Sierra Leone and Social Worker with Child Care expertise

Revd Cameron Kirkwood MA (CNAA) Methodist Supt. Minister, Brixton Cct, London, Community Development & Fresh Expressions

Revd Dr Jen Smith BA MPhil        Methodist Minister
Lecturer in Wesleyan Holiness & Mission, Politics and Religion

Revd Dr Heather Morris BSc BD (nee Kingston) Methodist Minister/Director of Ministry, Edgehill Theological College, Belfast Mission & Pastoral Care

The visiting team were again partnered by members of the Nigerian staff teams at the Sagamu & Umuahia Methodist Training Institutions (MTI's). The visiting lecturers for January were asked to link the mission of the church to community development and social responsibility; also to respond to the religious and political tensions found in Nigeria.

Revd Dr Heather Morris, was returning to her birthplace in Umuahia. Both her grandfather, the Revd Paul Kingston, who translated the 'Ogoni' Bible and her father Revd Paul Kingston (past President of the Methodist Church in Ireland) served in Nigeria. Heather provided the foundation by expounding and expanding the 'Pastoral Role of the Church. Revd Dr Stephen Skuce challenged pre-conceptions as those present as they; 'Encountered Other Religions' in a learning context. Revd Cameron Kirkwood, the minister of a community church in London that numbers many Nigerians in the congregation prompted discussions on the role of the church in community life. These thought-provoking presentations coalesced as Revd Dr Jen Smith challenged participants to ground Wesleyan Holiness in the African Social Context. The cross fertilisation and interaction between topics meant that discussions became livelier (and noisier) as enlightened trainees focused on an appropriate Christian response to the very real questions surrounding the impending elections in Nigeria. The conversations about issues raised went way beyond the lecture rooms and all fed into the January residential focus of developing the church's understanding of 'mission' in the Nigerian context.

BOOKS AND OTHER MATERIALS

Visiting lecturers are encouraged to provide full notes (in booklet form) for trainees which are then incorporated into their own substantial training manual. Much preparatory work had been done by the National Coordinator and College Rectors as we have worked towards the local sourcing of books at reasonable prices. Logistically, both here and in Sierra Leone, it has proved difficult to have the large

number of books required, delivered on time. Once again the SPCK International Study Guides sourced locally in Nigeria through Onitsha were fewer than ordered, though the Langham Literature delivery this time from Carlisle through Manchester Airport organised by Luke Lewis and the team there worked well.

**RAPID READING:FRONT & BACK; FIRST & LAST**

We are grateful to all of our regular discounting Book Sponsors: in particular Langham Literature; How To Books; and SPCK but we acknowledge too MMS(Ireland) and other donors for the grants provided, with which we purchase these books and build up college libraries. For those of us who are there to distribute, and I hope for all our sponsors, the smiles on the faces of these recipients and the knowledge that they will continue to be used in our partner churches overseas by people who care about the community as well as the church will be an encouragement to all donors.

ACKNOWLEDGEMENTS WITH THANKS

To quote from a recent official letter of appreciation from the Secretary of Conference, (SOC) Bishop Chibuzo R Opoko, "I write on behalf of his Eminence, Dr S Ola Makinde, GPJ, CON,, Prelate

249

Methodist Church Nigeria and the Methodist people in Nigeria to express profound gratitude to you and other members of the Cliff College team for your deep commitment and passion for capacity development of Methodist Church Nigeria ministers. The impact of the Cliff College programme on the life of the Methodist Church Nigeria

cannot be over-emphasised." In response, our thanks must go to our MCN partners and good friends: the Prelate; the SOC; The Bishop of Evangelism, Rt. Revd Dr Sunday Onuoha; the new Rectors and staff of the Colleges; and for the hospitality/travel arrangements made by the ever-efficient Protocol Officer, Very Revd Agunbiade Busuyi; and the joy-full National Coordinator, Very Revd Paul Olukunga.

**PRELATE'S GIFT FOR UMUAHIAN DAUGHTER**

Paul Olukunga gives written testimony about an evangelist, a former student who, "In his college graduation stole, mounted the pulpit, and gave a wonderful sermon on the theme of 'Restoration'. I could not believe that the programme can make such a great impact on Methodist Church Nigeria preachers until I witnessed it." We too are thrilled to see MCN goals being realised as new churches are being planted, local church training given and community projects being started by those who have been trained and resourced through this programme.

**VISA CONCERNS AGAIN**

As in July 2010, what seemed like a minor cause for concern about visas developed for many of us into another, time-consuming, energy-sapping crisis in the weeks leading up to Christmas. Administrative changes at the Nigerian High Commission in London and with the authorities in Abuja meant that they wanted to issue the visiting unpaid lecturing/facilitators 'single entry work visas' at a cost of £300 for each visa rather than the usual £90. The leaders of MCN took time out of busy schedules trying to resolve the crisis, but, despite representation being made in Nigeria and our best efforts in London, it became clear that if the programme was to proceed on time in partnership with the lecturers and trainees at the two MCN colleges in Umuahia and Sagamu, we would have to pay what was being asked and make further representation whilst in Nigeria.

On the plus side, our flights from London to Lagos booked for Tuesday, 4th January went without a hitch. For the first time we flew internationally with the Nigerian based airline, Arik Air (the cheapest flights!), and were impressed with of their service (particularly leg-room; stand-up bar area; magazine and 60 kilos baggage allowance in two suitcases). Some of our travelling team found the increased baggage allowance a mixed blessing because it allowed the coordinator to add a significant number of books etc. to the weight that they were carrying already!

### PLANS FOR THE FUTURE

Much of what follows in this report is shared as growing out of that relationship of mutual respect and caring concern about the team and its activities. Though it may be read and understood in that light MCN is moving forward in such a way that a separate report could be produced about their own initiatives. They have supported the CCITC programme; helped fund and train church leaders/ministers from other parts of Africa; built on their own re-focusing of the church in relation to evangelism (backed by a revised, simplified constitution with a proper focus on their agreed priorities and highlighted in the photographic record of the 'Journey so Far'); supported church growth initiatives in planting churches and special evangelistic events; and begun to realise their potential as one of the leading Methodist Churches in Africa.

Their initiative in proposing a visit of MCN leaders to Methodist Churches in Britain and Ireland post-Easter 2013 was inspired by a CCITC/WCR funded 2009 'Episcopal Consultation' in Lagos, but it is also a clear sign of a growing maturity. Such a visit (properly prepared and utilised) could be a completely new cross-cultural learning experience for many Methodists in the 'Mother Church' as well as well beneficial to our visitors. Methodism in our partner churches overseas may be different, but Wesleyan faith, spontaneity, innovation and pragmatism may yet prove to be their liberating gift to us.

The MCN Conference, on the recommendation of the leadership of the church acknowledges the notable contribution of its lay-people (not the ordained ministry or their partners) at an awards ceremony usually associated with the Wesley name. (Sir) Peter Grubb (Nigeria Health Care Project) led the way for personnel from overseas as a Knight of John Wesley some years ago. This was followed by the (posthumous) award to Mary Archer Champness and to our own (musical) Knight of Charles Wesley, (Sir) Peter Worrell, at a ceremony in Abuja reported on in 2009.

We were pleased to learn that once again the MCN Conference has acknowledged the work of lay-members of the CCITC team. The 'Anglican' administrator/logistics/tackle anything, Keith Phillips, is to become a Knight of John Wesley, and Mrs Janet McCall (English Communication and now 'Mama' to many throughout Nigeria) is to receive the Susanna Wesley Award at a ceremony to be held in the Revd Mellor Methodist Cathedral, Sagamu (the seat of our good friend the Right Revd Babatunde Taiwo, the Bishop of Remo who provides accommodation for the whole of the visiting team) on Sunday 26th June 2011.

### THE 'MELLOR MEMORIAL METHODIST CENTRE'

Is a 'concept' now approved by the Prelate and the leadership

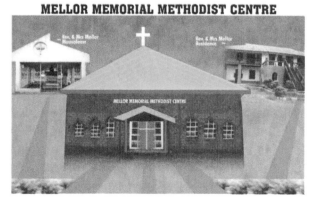

MELLOR MEMORIAL METHODIST CENTRE

of MCN with which we are pleased to be associated. As far as we are aware Chief Revd William Frederick Mellor, born in Stoke on Trent on March 13 1892, has no family ties with the (more familiar to Cliff College readers), Revd Dr Howard Mellor our former Principal. Revd W F Mellor was ordained at Wesley's Chapel, London in 1921 and set sail for Lagos in that same year. As a dynamic and forward-thinking missionary of his generation, Mellor is a much revered, particularly in the Sagamu area of Nigeria. The mausoleum on the Sagamu MTI campus houses the final resting place of his wife, Cecilia (20th September 1956) and Revd W F Mellor (7th February 1977).

THE MELLOR MAUSOLEUM: SAGAMU MTI

The 'concept' of a 'Memorial Centre' will be written up in detail with an appeal for funding but in embryo it translates the historic 'missionary significance and schools development' associated with the name of Mellor into a far-sighted vision of a multi-purpose College Chapel/Lecture Hall, Youth and Community Centre for the Sagamu MTI Campus, Schools and Neighbourhood. As the building already begun is roofed we trust that it will generate further donations of up to £30,000 at home and overseas towards its completion. Coincidentally (or God-incidentally), along with the published primary research on Mellor and Remoland written up by Chief Olu Ayodole, the family of Bolaji Idowu (1913-93) (Former leader of MCN and author of 'Towards an Indigenous Church') have entrusted some of his books to Sagamu MTI's library. Arrangements are being made to house them securely in an air-conditioned environment suitable for research.

### FRIENDS OF THE METHODIST CHURCH NIGERIA

The church in the UK has responded to the pastoral needs of those from other countries now living in our larger cities partly by appointing Chaplains funded through our mission budget. Some countries like Sierra Leone have benefited from the interest and support of another ad-hoc network made up largely of former mission partners who have served in that country. Unfortunately, no such network has nourished the many one-to-one relationships and contacts made between the friends who have served with the Methodist Church in Nigeria.

We have been asked by the leaders of MCN to share in rectifying that situation by exploring the possibility of hosting an inaugural meeting of such an association in the UK which would bring together such friends on a date(s) when the some leaders of MCN could be in attendance to share 'Fellowship' and respond to the interest being expressed by a number of former mission partners. During a fortuitous meeting overnight in Lagos between the new Coordinator of the UK sponsored, Nigeria Health Care Project, Dr David Cundall and the CCITC Coordinator, Revd Richard Jackson, we were reminded (despite Jen Smith & Ros Colwill's association with both programmes) of how much was being done and how little was being shared between the 'friends of MCN'. As requested by the Prelate and after consultation with others we will be inviting interested parties/persons to share in exploring possibilities. We will be pleased to add to our list of contacts anyone who would like to be part of such a 'Friends of MCN' network and will make contact during the next few weeks.

### WORLD METHODISM, METHODIST CHURCH NIGERIA & CLIFF COLLEGE ITC

Methodists from around the world will meet in South Africa for the World Methodist Conference during August this year. MCN, as a large and growing church will be well represented. Our hope is that CCITC will be present too not only physically in the WMC Exhibition Hall in Durban, but also in and through the large number of people attending that Conference who have been impacted in some way by the pioneering work of 'Doing Training There' in a practical partnership with churches overseas. Revd Dr Martyn Atkins, now General Secretary of the British Methodist Conference and one of the key-note speakers in Durban, was the first (encourager!) Director of the Programme when it began in 2001.

Revd Thomas Kemper (then General Secretary of the UMC in Germany-now General Secretary of the UMC Board of Global Ministries in the USA) wrote up the concept in their 2002 Yearbook as they provided resources and scholars for the pilot project in Sierra Leone. Many other people with key roles here and overseas in 'World Church Relations' have responded, bought into the programme in practical ways and helped bring the vision to fruition, but funding for the longer-term future of this and similar partnership programmes is uncertain. Articles, regular reports, evaluations and DVD's provided since 2002 are full of testimonies to the positive impact made on everyone associated with or involved in this kind of programme (available on request).

254

Much more could be written (Jn.21.25-would it be read?). Please forgive my 'pioneer's' appeal for the future of what has sometimes been seen as a personal or Cliff College programme, rather than as a visionary response to a training/resourcing need. In a recent submission seeking recognition for the 'concept' and longer-term funding I wrote:

*"Personally, I cannot doubt that God's direction was given to me as I returned from the 2001 Conference in conflict-devastated Sierra Leone and jotted down on a 'sick-bag' the outline of what has grown into the Cliff College International Training Centre. Nor can I doubt the direction given to countless people, named and un-named, who have helped us in so many ways to realise this vision and become a blessing to everyone involved both in the UK and in the countries where we have shared in training leaders."*

This economically viable and proven concept which provides so many practical and personal 'added-value benefits' needs your support if it is to become a better-known option for further training, and continue making its unique contribution to our relationship with, and the mission of, our partner churches throughout the world.

## 2011/2: MAUSOLEUMS, MEMORIALS & MISSION

**The reminders received during our January training visit to Nigeria about the importance of relationships prompted the writing of the following article on MAUSOLEUMS, MEMORIALS & MISSION TODAY, as my Cliff College Joyful News contribution (before editing!) for the 10 March 2011 edition of the Methodist Recorder.**

## HISTORY OF 'JOYFUL NEWS' AND THOMAS CHAMPNESS

Regular readers of the Methodist Recorder, Cliff Today magazine or the Cliff College International Training Centre will need no reminder that the 'Joyful News' headline for Cliff College articles published in the Methodist Recorder dates back to the 19th Century. Revd Thomas Champness, known to many as the forefather founder of Cliff College, a returning missionary from West Africa began to mentor and train evangelists under the banner of the 'Joyful News' Newspaper which he first published in 1883. The "Joyful News Missioners" helped revive the tradition of Methodism throughout the world as a 'lay movement for mission', a tradition continued by Methodism's Cliff College on the present site since 1903.

What is less well known is that in 1857, Thomas Champness responded to a call to serve as a missionary in Sierra Leone. After three years he returned home in poor health. Whilst on furlough he married Mary Archer and returned with his young bride in 1860 to West Africa, but this time to Abeokuta in Nigeria. Mary Archer Champness died there on the 23$^{rd}$ September 1862, less than two years after her marriage to Thomas and she was buried in Abeokuta. Revd Thomas Champness was invalided home in 1863.

Mausoleums and well-tended missionary graves in Africa should remind the 'Mother Church of Methodism' that the 'Missionaries' (whether expatriate or African), with all their idiosyncrasies and sometimes because of them, were appreciated as 'living epistles' embodying the message through their mission in  education, agriculture, medicine and ministry. Those blessed by their endeavours are less willing than we may be to forget the sacrifices they made. Whilst at Cliff College we continue to welcome students from Nigeria, as well as from many other parts of the world studying with us, we have learned from our partners overseas to honour our heritage as we have shared experiences through the CCITC in Nigeria.

In turn they have asked us, and through us, you, to share with them in two new projects that celebrate the past whilst building for the future of the Methodist Church Nigeria.

### THE 'MELLOR MEMORIAL METHODIST CENTRE'

Being built on the campus of Sagamu Methodist Training Centre, it is an exciting new 'concept' approved by the Prelate and the leadership of Methodist Church Nigeria (MCN). **Chief Revd William Frederick Mellor, born in Stoke on Trent on March 13 1892,** is not related to a former Principal, of Cliff College, Revd Dr Howard Mellor (who is alive and still kicking!).

In 1893 two 'Joyful News Missioners': Evangelist, Overs and medical worker, Bond, helped establish Methodism in Remoland of which Sagamu is the centre. Revd W F Mellor would not have been out of place in the entrepreneurial tradition of Champness and his 'Joyful News Missioners'. Following medical service in WW1, Mellor trained at Didsbury College, Manchester and Handsworth College, Birmingham, before being ordained as a Methodist Minister in Wesley's Chapel, London in 1921. Revd Mellor was accepted by the Methodist Missionary Society for service in West Africa and arrived in Lagos in October of that same year.

Here in the Methodist Recorder there is little space to share much about an enlightened and fruitful ministry (a separate leaflet will be made available). A contemporary of Mellor's, Dr Tai Solarin is quoted in Ayodele's, 'Methodism in Remoland' as saying:

*"I have known the Revd W F Mellor for forty years. He is the hardest working white man I have ever come across. He is a straight dealer. Very scrupulous. Very Honest………*
*He is a teacher, a painter, a farmer, a carpenter, a bricklayer, a singer, a community development officer, a nurse, a psychologist. For every human problem in the tropics, Mr Mellor has an answer."*

The mausoleum on the Sagamu Methodist Training Institute campus houses both the final resting place of Revd W F Mellor (7th February 1977) and his wife, Cecilia (20th September 1956). In embryo the 'concept' of a 'Memorial Centre' translates the historic missionary significance and schools development associated with the name of Mellor into a much-needed multi-purpose focal point on the Campus for the College, the Schools and the Sagamu Community.

The Mellor Methodist Memorial Centre will be roofed before the 'rainy season', but estimates indicate that further donations of up to £60,000 (Naira 15,000,000) will be needed to complete this exciting project. *Donations may be sent to Cliff College ITC, but should be clearly designated for the Mellor Memorial Methodist Centre.*

**METHODIST CHURCH NIGERIA (MISSIONARIES/FRIENDS) ASSOCIATION**

Secondly, at the request of the MCN leadership and some former mission partners, we have been asked to explore the possibility of organising a network, similar to that enjoyed by the friends of Methodist Church Sierra Leone (MCSL) that will provide a friendship link through a mailing, circulars, and perhaps occasional meetings in the UK with the MCN leadership.

To quote from an MCN letter of appreciation to the CCITC Coordinator dated 17th January 2011, from the MCN Secretary of Conference on behalf of the Prelate writing of their desire, 'to set up Methodist Church Nigeria Missionaries Association in the United Kingdom and Ireland-a network of missionaries who worked in Methodist church Nigeria but are currently resident in the United Kingdom and Ireland. The goal of the Network is to build on the relationship these worthy servants of God had established with Methodist Church Nigeria with a view to keeping them abreast of the development in our church as well as enrich our cross-cultural experiences and share ideas on continuous basis.'

As a first step we have begun to put together a list of people who have expressed some interest in responding to the MCN request. Names with contact details (and offers of help) may be forwarded to:

*Revd Gilbert and Mrs Sylvia Hall, (Editor: Details edited out)*

This 'Joyful News' from a growing and maturing Methodist Church Nigeria, will continue to inspire our contemporary Christian experience and witness. Reminiscing takes us back to the past, but we cannot live there. Remembrance brings our past into the present to inspire and renew us. It is our personal Response that can make such a difference to the future. Jesus set his seal on this 'Transforming Friendship' by saying, "Do this in remembrance of me". Through our Relationship with God and in partnership with each other we will continue the work and witness of the 'Joyful News Missioners' in a changing world.

# 2011/3 JUN 24-JUL 16: MCN THIRD RESIDENTIAL

(IDIAMM 2010-12 PROGRAMME)

As we move into our 10<sup>th</sup> and quite possibly our final year of pioneering and perfecting this highly effective programme of training in partnership with overseas churches we have several more firsts to report.

## NEW TRANSPORT ARRANGEMENTS

For the first time most of the travelling team of visiting lecturers gathered at Cliff College, sorted loads and piled into Tony Nemeth's 'door2destination' Chauffer driven luxury, seven seat Mercedes Viano mini-bus. Tony's efficient service in both directions meant that we journeyed together more cheaply and with much less hassle than when carrying the airline's generous luggage allowance of 60 kilos per passenger in addition to our hand-luggage by train and through a network of London Underground obstacles to Heathrow Airport.

As usual the coordinator tried to persuade each member of the team to restrict themselves to one suitcase of 30 kilos which included their lecture notes for 180 trainees and staff. This meant that before we left Cliff College we were able to fill the trailer accompanying the mini-bus with our optimum luggage allowance and include books for libraries and friends in Nigeria; with enough copies of an excellent new work-book on: Exploring Theological English, for our trainees and partner college lecturers in Nigeria.

At least we didn't have to haul a 'Trek Cart' manually like those of an earlier generation at Cliff College. After a little juggling of weight allowances (luggage, not people!) when we met up with Keith Phillips, coming from the south, at Heathrow Airport, we joined the overnight flight with Arik Air, the modern and efficient Nigerian based-airline to arrive in Lagos early in the morning on Saturday, 25<sup>th</sup> June.

Our Saturday arrival in Nigeria meant that the whole team could be together at Sagamu for the MCN Awards ceremony on the Sunday, at a glorious celebration service where **(Dame) Janet McCall** and **(Sir) Keith Phillips** our core team course administrator along with other MCN awardees were honoured by the Methodist Church Nigeria for a life-time of service to the church world-wide. (See Jan 2011 report for details-a 'long' video is available!). This event more than made up for some of us having to miss out on the annual graduation ceremony at Cliff College which did not take place until the following Wednesday.

Unexpectedly, but with encouragement from the leaders of MCN present: the Prelate, His Eminence, Dr Sunday Ola Makinde, the Secretary of Conference, Bishop Chibuzo R Opoko, and the Bishop of Remo, Babatunde Taiwo, the awards service provided an opportunity for local fund-raising in relation to the proposed:

**MELLOR MEMORIAL METHODIST CENTRE FUND RAISING**

The designated fund-raiser, a former Lay President might well have embarrassed a British congregation with his direct and very personal approach, but in this context, he and the giving was applauded as the total raised in gifts and pledges at this one event added up to the Naira equivalent of £18,000. This is almost half the target figure for the completion of the whole project. The roofing will soon be completed and funds are in hand for moving forward with this exciting project. **We will leave that figure of £18,000 raised locally to make its own appeal** to interested parties in the UK who may be willing to make donations through Cliff College or raise funds here for this worthy tribute to a much loved and respected former missionary in Nigeria, Revd William F Mellor (1892-1977).

The separate 'Research Unit', housing the Bolaji Idowu (1913-93) books and other research materials in the main MTI library complex has already been completed and is being furnished with the help of donations.

LIBRARY: BOLAJI IDOWU (1913-93)

THE JULY 2011 'RESIDENTIALS' AT UMUAHIA AND SAGAMU MTI'S

After the 'High' of the Awards Ceremony in Sagamu on the Sunday, we might have anticipated the usual 'Low' prompted by poor attendance on registration day as the visiting team separated to continue with the regular programme in the two centres. Early on Monday morning the Jackson group travelled via Lagos and the airport at Owerri to Umuahia MTI whilst the McCall group continued with the prepared timetable in Sagamu.

In the event, earlier notice given by the National Coordinator of MCN, **Very Revd Paul Olukunga,** and his new, but very able assistant **Bukola**, followed by personal letters from the Prelate to Archbishops and Bishops, meant that many more of the students at both Umuahia and Sagamu MTI's turned up in time for us to begin the programme proper on the Tuesday morning at both centres.

Inevitably with such a programme in a proper 'Nigerian Rainy Season', there were some comings and goings and adjustments to be made in the light of local circumstances, but with 81 trainees continuing at Umuahia and 70 at Sagamu any feeling of anti-climax after the awards ceremony was soon caught up into the fresh enthusiasm of meeting up again with trainees, local staff and supportive leaders in the local churches and centres.

The fact that some members of the visiting team used in both centres were Nigerians and others, no strangers to those involved with us generates a unique sense of community in which we learn from each other. Once again, the subjects being taught whilst focusing on mission as part of the programme can give only a hint of the fun and fellowship that is enjoyed rather than endured within the kind of interaction taking place throughout the programme, but particularly during the residential weeks with inspirational visits from the Bishop of Evangelism and local leaders, clergy and lay.

VISITING LECTURERS AND THEIR GIFTS

Those who know Revd Dr Malcolm & Janet McCall will recognise that lectures on subjects like New Testament Mission and Theological English and Communication respectively provide not only intellectual stimulation, but very lively spiritual inspiration from a couple who preach what they practise. Many of us are still a little concerned that the tall Malcolm in his enthusiasm for preaching will one day lose a flailing hand to the cutting edge of a lowered ceiling fan!!!

His team was supported by another of our MCN-MA students currently studying at Cliff College, Very Revd John Eze, from Port Harcourt. The experience gained by (even taller than Malcolm-but few flailing arms!) Revd Dr Peter Ensor of Cliff College in many parts of Africa, feeds into Church Growth in Mission through Roger Bowen's, "So I Send You". This dovetails well into the (His)story of western missionaries and their pioneering African counterparts involvement in African Church History as presented by Revd Dr Kehinde Olabimtan (a Nigerian Baptist protégée of Prof Andrew Walls) working in Lagos.

Regular lecturer (Sir) Peter Worrell's role this time was to share thinking on the theme of Adult Learning. As a Local Preacher and violinist extraordinaire Peter is the epitome of his subject, always learning, but enthusing others with his unique contribution and in the process recruiting a legion of volunteers who want to learn to play his 200 year old (second!) violin in one week!

The International Coordinator's lectures on Mission and Ministry challenge much of the traditional mode of learned ministry and (ad)ministration that is more likely to control the thinking and activities of the church than convert through mission. Interesting, how it is always the 'one above us' who is responsible for our failure to change as a church. In MCN, as in many traditional churches, the

262

ordinary Member blames the Evangelist; the Evangelist blames the Priest; the Priest-the Presbyter; the Presbyter-the Bishop; the Bishop-the Archbishop; which means that there is no one left for the Prelate (the leader of the church to blame) except 'the one above' -God!

A participatory training game of 'Follow My Leader' concluded the lessons learned in this lecture series on leadership with a very fit, Usman Habib, (instead of an unfit International Coordinator) in the lead leaving most of the trainees puffing and panting in his wake. This ageing leader sat back, and took some photographs whilst praying for responsible but risk-taking leaders at all levels of church life.

### YOUTH WORK WITH REV DR STEVE EMERY-WRIGHT

An even greater challenge was identified by the participants in responding to Revd Steve Emery-Wright's humour and reflections on Contemporary Youth Mission. From his own research done in many parts of the world and some parallel research that he was undertaking with young people, (much of it seemingly

undertaken introducing the Umuahia Rector's young family for the first time to the adjacent hotel pool!) whilst he was in Nigeria. Steve was able to bring into focus for the trainees many issues (not all of them relating to young people) that the main-line churches in Africa will need to address if their appeal is not to be lost on the increasingly internationalised generation of the communications-aware younger generation.

### OUR RESPONSE TO NEW GENERATION CHURCH PASTORS/LEADERS

Regular readers of these newsletters will know that one of the 'Applied' characteristics of this programme has been developed through involving all of our trainees in what are increasingly being termed, 'New Generation' (NGC) rather than simply 'Pentecostal' Churches every Sunday for worship during the programme. This has provided trainees with the opportunity to be present at non-Methodist services and in their Worship & Preaching Portfolio's to reflect together upon aspects of their growth that might contribute to changes being made within Nigerian Methodism as it repositions itself as a church committed to evangelism, mission and growth. Without exception the NGC's, with exotic sounding names, that we have attended over the past five years with our different groups of trainees have welcomed us and been generous in their hospitality even when we must have seemed like an invading army of Methodist Inspectors of their Sunday Worship styles.

**PASTOR USMAN HABIB LEADS LIVELY WORSHIP**

As our response to a request from NGC Pastors we arranged another first when we invited our Sunday Worship NGC hosts to join us at a Saturday 'Open Day' in both centres. We were pleased to have with us on our visiting team (for the second time) Usman Habib a lively and prayerful NGC Pastor from Nigeria who is studying for his PhD at Cliff College. As well as helping change perceptions among Methodists through his leading of worship, counselling individual trainees and his lectures on the New Generation Churches and Mission, he followed up contacts made with the College Chaplains/Registrars to issue a personal invitation to the NGC Pastors concerned. Usman led the inspiring worship and lectured along with others at both of the Open Days in Umuahia and Sagamu. He has produced a full report which is available on request, but in the limited space available here we use his words to sum up the overwhelmingly positive response to the First New Generation Church Pastors Open Day at both Centres:

*The summary of their comments was that - in all the fellowship was unique, first of its kind, and a dream come true. In particular, one of them said, "What our grandparents could not achieve or be able to do in their lifetime by bringing the mainstream Church ministers' and Pentecostal*

*ministers' together" he has witnessed in his own life time. They were overwhelmed by the gift of the African Bible Commentary and the Holy Spirit books, and expressed their thanks for the gesture.*

Hopefully, this 'first' will not be the 'last' as the NGC Pastors and the College Staff at both Centres maintain the 'friendship' links established and offer more open events for training and fellowship.

**FAREWELLS: PRELATE & SECRETARY OF CONFERENCE**

Once again we express our thanks to our own hosts and now friends in the Methodist Church Nigeria who in countless different ways make it possible for this programme to achieve all that it has achieved in the past five years of working together in Nigeria. The leaders of MCN have led the way in personally welcoming the group(s) despite busy schedules of their own. They have been followed in this by Rectors, College Lecturers and their families who have not only offered hospitality, but fitted into flexible timetables whilst we are there and provided supervision, marking and guidance for the trainees when we have moved on.

Less obvious are the very important people (VIP's-working behind the scenes), lightly rewarded **cleaners and cooks** who provide food for the trainees on time with a smile on their faces (even when the trainees don't arrive!). The commitment that everyone gives to this additional college activity during their vacation time is invaluable when coping with adaptations and additions like the NGC Open Days as part of an already hectic programme.

At home there are so many sponsors and supporters that it would be invidious to name names. Individuals, spouses-horrid word for loving partners!, friends, colleagues, organisations and churches in practical and prayerful ways make sacrifices so that the different teams who travel for each residential are supported during the busy time of preparation and blessed by telephone calls, emails, texts and the encouragement given. Thank you to all who are in any way associated with us as friends of this programme.

**AND FUTURE PLANS**

As for future plans about which we wrote at length in January, interesting information has been shared by some of the people who knew the Mellor's in Nigeria. More photographs have been taken of projects, buildings, and medical centres begun by Revd W F Mellor. As indicated earlier further progress is being made with the building of the Mellor Memorial Methodist Centre At Sagamu MTI, but we are still trying to track down any family links with forbears in the Stoke-on-Trent area where Mellor was born (13/03/1892) or any obituary that might have been published in the UK or Nigeria where he died (7/02/1977).

We have begun to put together a list of Methodist Church Nigeria Friends (MCNF) largely, but not exclusively former missionaries in Nigeria. Revd Gilbert Hall (01697-742885) will be glad to receive additional names for that list. The leader of MCN, His Eminence Ola Makinde is hoping that we can organise a reunion sometime next year which he and possibly other friends may be able to attend.

**ROS COLWILL, WORLD METHODISM, MCN AND CLIFF COLLEGE ITC**

Many of us will be praying for Methodists from around the world who will be meeting in South Africa for the World Methodist Conference during August. MCN will be well represented as dedicated mission partner and friend, **Ros Colwill** receives her Methodist Peace Award. Other friends of the CCITC will be sharing in a personal way about the work that we have been doing over the past 10 years with partner churches in Sierra Leone, Cuba, and Nigeria. Though we have received little encouragement from the Conference Organisers to be represented, we know that CCITC will be present in and through the large number of people attending that Conference who have been impacted in some way by the pioneering work of 'Doing Training There' in a practical partnership with churches overseas.

These are uncertain days economically for the church as well as for society as a whole and the future of the CCITC programme beyond August 2012 remains unclear. Many people both here and overseas are committed to its continuation and even its expansion as a proven 21$^{st}$ Century partnership model for sharing in training for mission in the world-wide church. Whilst many avenues for funding an International Coordinator, at least half-time as part of a settled secretariat (to supersede the Dad's army look of the unpaid 'core team' who pioneered the programme) are being explored, we will value your prayers for a positive outcome.

The future of this economically viable concept which provides so many 'added-value benefits' in terms of world church relations needs the support of those who value the concept if it is to continue making its unique contribution to the mission of our partner churches throughout the world.

As we reminded people in January, articles, regular reports, evaluations and DVD's provided since 2002 are full of testimonies to the positive impact made on everyone associated this kind of programme. They will be made available to you on request.

**GOODBYE TO FRIENDS: WE ARE ON OUR WAY**

# CHAPTER 12 2012: A YEAR OF HIGHLIGHTS

*2012 began in a troubled Nigeria with the bombs of Boko Haram and a national strike, but ended with a celebration of so much that had been achieved through the completion of the 2010-12 training programme in Nigeria. 'Refreshing training visits' provided fresh resources for earlier trainees in both Sierra Leone and Nigeria. These training visits were linked with attendance and presentations at both the MCSL and MCN Conferences. The Conferences paid tribute to the work of Cliff College and its International Training Centre in giving further training and supplying resources for ministry and mission. They welcomed also plans for a Lay Training programme and a 2013 Study/Heritage Tour.*

## 2012/1 JAN 3-20: MCN FOURTH 'RESIDENTIAL'

(IDIAMM 2010-12 PROGRAMME)

A DISTURBED AND DISTURBING TIME

Regular readers of these CCITC reports will know that we do not normally share with you a chronological order of our activities. But then our 'residentials' in Nigeria are not normally undertaken at a time when an Islamic terrorist group 'Boko Haram' are bombing indiscriminately and when a national strike has been called. Country-wide demonstrations were already taking place against the Nigeria government's decision (made over the holiday period), to remove the fuel subsidy supported by Nigerian oil revenues from the beginning of 2012, thus more than doubling the cost of fuel for vehicles and light/power producing generators, from 65 Naira (25p) per litre to N141 at the stroke of a President's pen!

THE BEST-LAID PLANS BECOME A DIARY OF HAPPENINGS: LAGOS TO UMUAHIA MTI

*Jan 3ʳᵈ Tuesday* The travelling team of Revd Richard Jackson, (Sir) Keith Phillips, Revd Gilbert and Mrs Sylvia Hall and Revd Dr Jen Smith came from different directions to congregate at Heathrow airport largely unaware of more recent events taking place in Nigeria. We travelled comfortably and well (as usual) with Arik Air to the International Airport in Lagos arriving in the early hours of

Wednesday morning. We were met by the National Coordinator of CCITC, Very Revd Paul Olukunga and the Protocol Officer for MCN Revd Agunbiade Busuyi who had stayed overnight near the airport. On transfer to the national airport for the 8.30am onward flight to Owerri we were joined by Revd Dr Deji Okegbile who had travelled earlier to Nigeria. Over breakfast our Nigerian friends and the newspapers made us aware of the disturbed situation and the pending national strike. Our (one-hour) flight to Owerri in the east was delayed by 'Harmattan' weather until lunchtime.

We were in good company as we met with the Methodist Archbishop of Ibadan, **Most Revd Dr Michael Stephen,** also delayed in travelling to Abuja. **Gilbert & Sylvia** who have known him and his family from when he was 'nowt but a lad' in 1960's Nigeria enjoyed the chance meeting. We were picked up at Owerri airport and arrived at Hotel Roy next to the college late in the afternoon. We were pleased to find that our partner lecturers in Umuahia Methodist Training Institute (MTI) had made good use of the time in preparing our trainees for a prompt start with the timetabled programme on Thursday morning.

*Jan 5<sup>th</sup> Thursday* Most of the trainees had travelled to Umuahia for the final residential of the two year programme (2010-12) through road-blocks and some demonstrations. Despite their own family concerns about the troubled situation they responded positively to: Gilbert & Sylvia's morning devotions on characters from the Bible, backed up by guidance on Practical Preaching.

**Deji's lectures on 'Fresh Expressions'**; and Jen's sensitive presentation (enlivened again by Jude Munanonye's personal experience testimony) relating to Aids Awareness. The International Coordinator's Seminars on team leadership using Edward De Bono's, 'Six Thinking Hats (Caps)' followed by prayers rounded off each day.

By that first evening as we met with the Secretary of Conference and our Nigerian Colleagues it became clear that the worsening situation with demonstrations and the threat of a national strike closing down everything from the following Monday meant, that for the safety of both staff and trainees some curtailment of the programme (timetabled through till the following Tuesday) in Umuahia was necessary. Unfortunately, one of the casualties of the curtailment was the 'spouses weekend', led by the Halls' though we were able to organise a truncated version on the Saturday for the eleven wives and three deaconesses who were able to join us.

*Jan 6/7ᵗʰ Friday/Saturday* Having made the decision that the programme at Umuahia would complete on Saturday, so that everyone could travel on Sunday, before the national strike proper began on Monday, the next two days were a blur of prioritised activity: as lecturers (fortunately with notes to distribute) crammed what was required into the time available. Keith Phillips, our administrator with the help of the Registrar and our College Staff partners, filled out his spread sheet of marks received and made clear what was required from every student by the closing date of 28ᵗʰ February (as well as the completion of their work-book on, Exploring Theological English), if they were to be sure of graduating later in the year.

On Friday **Jen Smith,** accompanied by Richard fulfilled her (additional) liaison role for the **Nigeria Health Care Project (NHCP) Uzuakoli Support Group** by sharing with staff and viewing the new Maternity Ward, and the Laboratory as well as other building projects at the Royal Cross Methodist Hospital, Ugueke, followed by a well-received visit to the 'Motherless Baby Unit'. Our indefatigable friend Paul Olukunga with college staff support moved here and there in re-arranging flights for our  return to Lagos and travel to Sagamu on Sunday, rather than Tuesday.

***Jan 8<sup>th</sup> Sunday*** Flights from Owerri were full but thanks to Paul's efforts the team, accompanied by some of our trainees from that area, travelled by road early in the morning to Port Harcourt without major incident. Clearly there was some tension at road blocks manned by police, army and occasional vigilantes, but the presence of clergy and expatriates in our two vehicles meant that little effort was made to extract 'a new year gift' from us on the road. Our Nigerian friends saw us through the chaos of check-in at the busy airport into the relative calm of yet another waiting period before boarding. Jen Smith met (as you do!) with the family of the mother whose funeral she had conducted in Ealing, London just before Christmas.

Apart from the delay on arrival in Lagos whilst our baggage was returned, the onward journey to Sagamu was uneventful as the Protocol Officer, Busuyi Agunbiade, **Driver Emmanuel**, and Paul with the additional help of Ms Bukola Mustapha from MCN HQ smoothed our way into the vehicle and on to the much improved main road to Sagamu MTI. Text messages sent in advance by Paul to trainees linked with the Sagamu residential inviting as many as possible for their own safety to travel on Sunday meant that many were already in residence at the college when we arrived; others arrived later and some were turned back. As usual we were hosted on the compound adjacent to the college, by the Bishop of Remo, Rt. Revd Babatunde Taiwo. Our regular hosts, the Bishop, along with his wife Abimbola, The Prelate, Secretary of Conference and the Bishop of Evangelism with other MCN representatives were waiting to hear whether they would still be able to travel to the World Methodism Evangelism Conference in Jerusalem in the early hours of Tuesday morning.

**BISHOP BABATUNDE & ABIMBOLA TAIWO WITH GRACE, JOSHUA & DANIEL**

***Jan 9-10<sup>th</sup> Monday/Tuesday*** It was quite eerie to wake early on Monday morning in Nigeria to the 'Sound of Silence' on the nearby road instead of hearing the sound of beeping vehicles and noisy lorries!' The national strike had begun! It was to be maintained by a 'common community will' to reverse the decision about the 'removal of the fuel subsidy' and through the surveillance conducted by groups of committed individuals in each community who made it clear that breaches of the 'common will' would be responded to by direct action against the offenders. Alongside this local and almost universally observed strike, peaceful demonstrations took place in many parts of the country. This meant that everything was closed down from early morning to early evening when shops were allowed to open and people as well as vehicles (where fuel could be bought) were able to move about freely. Weekends also were strike free times of movement, though there was always the possibility of being caught up in one of the many demonstrations that were taking place.

Sadly, as the media was quick to report, some of these protests turned violent with lives being lost and people being injured in the clashes that took place. Unfortunately, the media, both in Nigeria and in the UK struggled to help their readers and listeners to differentiate between these largely peaceful and national political activities and the terrorists of the Boko Haram sect who have used the hiatus to continue their bombing campaign as they try to de-stabilise the northern states of Nigeria. These atrocities are abhorred and condemned by right thinking Muslims and Christians alike. But as with the historic troubles linked to Northern Ireland such condemnation from within the situation does not easily sever the supply lines of extremist support that come from outside of the country to fuel the fire of perceived wrongs among disaffected groups who live in the predominately Muslim northern areas of Nigeria.

The well-organised nature of the strike overall meant that the MCN group were able to leave for Jerusalem early on Tuesday as planned, though there were reports of Bishop Etim Ekong's (recent scholarship student in England) car being attacked and damaged en route to the airport. The MCN group returned inspired and safely a week later.

***Jan 11/14<sup>th</sup> Wednesday/Saturday*** Once again our shared reading of the political situation and the likely continuation of the national strike and demonstrations led us to plan for a revised programme that would allow our trainees at Sagamu to return home by Sunday. In the meantime, as at Umuahia, (see above) we were able to continue with much of the lecturing programme planned through from Wednesday to Saturday. Though it was clearly impossible in the deteriorating circumstances for spouses with children to travel any distance at all, we made ad hoc arrangements through Deaconess Nancy Kennedy-Johnson, a lecturer at the college, for Gilbert, Sylvia and Jen to meet with the wives of tutors and some of the women leaders living nearby on Saturday morning and Monday afternoon. Overall, the disappointment of not having the spouses together with their partners was assuaged a little by the positive

response to the smaller group meetings where training was given and in-depth conversations were shared with a variety of women leaders, numbering more than thirty between both centres. All of the participants received free books and a few children were blessed with the gifts that were taken to occupy the many!!!

A MELLOR PILGRIMAGE

### Jan 15<sup>th</sup> Sunday

The earlier departure of the trainees left the visiting team free to attend the English service at the Mellor Methodist Cathedral at 8.00am and to visit some of the sites at and near Ikenne associated with the name of the much revered missionary Revd William F Mellor. We were thrilled to be greeted by many of our:

**trainees leading inspiring worship with packed congregations** at the churches as we travelled around the area on Sunday morning.

We had the added bonus of discovering a broken down pulpit from an original Mellor Church building that we hope will be renovated in time to join the lectern (already recovered) in the Mellor Memorial Methodist Centre at Sagamu MTI.

## A GRADUAL RETURN TO NORMALITY

*Jan 16/18<sup>th</sup> Monday/Wednesday* Once we had confirmed that the cost of changing our (cheap!) tickets to travel back to the UK early was prohibitive and that we were likely to be 'confined to barracks' by the continuation of the strike we found plenty to occupy our time. I was able to work with a good friend and lecturer, Raphael Idialu on his book related to Mission and Church Growth through Church Planting. Keith Phillips used the time to clarify the situation regarding registered trainees Umuahia (82) and Sagamu (71)-(lecture note packs delivered to absentees). Apart from the meetings with the women described earlier, Gilbert, Sylvia and Jen were involved in much coming and going with individuals. Deji with members of the Nigerian support team catered for our every concern with background information and up to date news about what was happening in the country. A weekend amelioration of the situation that prompted the strike was provided as the government with promises of controls reduced the price of a litre of fuel to N95.

By Wednesday children were returning to school, businesses were re-opening and it was clear that most people were ready, at least for the time being, to accept this compromise. Traffic was moving freely and we were able to move from Sagamu into a hotel in Lagos in preparation for a meeting with The Prelate and The Secretary of Conference at MCN HQ on the Thursday.

## RENEWING RELATIONSHIPS AND REVIEWING OUR PARTNERSHIP PLANS

*Jan 19<sup>th</sup> Thursday* As previously arranged, the team were graciously received as they joined in prayers with HQ staff; celebrated Sylvia's ?? birthday with Mrs (HQ) Phillips birthday cake; and shared lunch at the office with the Leaders of MCN, His Eminence, Dr Sunday Ola Makinde, and Rt. Revd Dr Chibuzo Opoko, the Secretary of Conference. The Coordinators and Administrators met together with the leaders also for a more formal business meeting at which issues affecting the future work of the CCITC in partnership with the Methodist Church in Nigeria were discussed. Our shared vision for a continuation and diversification of the training programme in Nigeria noted the possible impact of the far-reaching and widely publicised 'Fruitful Field' proposals relating to British Methodist Training Colleges being discussed by the British Methodist Church, but apart from questions about visas etc. our focus was upon the more immediate issues relating to:

Graduations for the current programme (2010-12) which are likely to be held at    MMMC-building progress in association with the MCN Conference (6-13th August) in Lagos and linked with the hoped-for completion (*further donations gratefully received*) and dedication of the Mellor Memorial Methodist Centre at Sagamu MTI.

A 2012 Evaluation of the training programme to be developed at Regional Centres (in Nigeria and Sierra Leone) as all former trainees and tutors involved will be invited to receive updated Mission & Ministry DVD's and to complete an evaluation questionnaire highlighting the practical impact of aspects of the programme on their ministry.

Plans for possible new (short-term) programmes beginning in Jan 2013 should make provision for: lay training; church growth through church planting; women, youth and children's work training.

Planning continues for a Post-Easter 2013–Episcopal training and Methodist Heritage exposure through MCN funded (two-week+) programme at Cliff College and with Districts of the Methodist Church in Britain and Ireland. No fewer than 14 of these new Bishops have been involved in the CCITC programme.

Was-2008/10 Trainees President Now-Bishop Joel Akinola

The current list of 'Friends of MCN' was warmly received. These friends may be linked with a Chaplaincy that is likely to be developed amongst the 'Diaspora' of MCN friends living in Britain and Ireland.

*Jan 20/21st Friday/Saturday* An early start for Lagos International Airport, straightforward check-in and boarding of the flight was followed at 11.00am by a six hour delay sitting on the aeroplane as a fault in the cockpit was being dealt with before guidance/clearance was received from the manufacturer of the plane. Text messages advised those waiting at home about the delay on the ground but later in the middle of the 6-7 hour flight to London a medical emergency arose which had to be dealt with at Heathrow by police and paramedics before we were able to disembark. Fortunately, Revd Dr Jen Smith and her husband Keith epitomise the 'flexibility with a sense of humour' required of participants in the programme as at 11.30pm the travelling team were treated to Pizzas and a bed for the night at their home in Ealing before travelling on to their own homes on Saturday morning.

The final day of travel with its frustrations being offset by the resigned but friendly acceptance that comes from 'everyone, being in the same boat (aeroplane!)' provided a fitting climax to a most unusual period of travel and training. Once again, when tested by particularly difficult circumstances we were reminded how important personal relationships are to the partnership in which we share. As the visiting team we can only give thanks to everyone for the care, prayer and encouragement that our friends here and in Nigeria have given to us all.

**OUR HOSTING BISHOP BABATUNDE TAIWO SAYS FAREWELL**

*Just before we left for Nigeria my attention was drawn to an article by Bim Adewunmi of the Guardian (4 Jan 2011) which is worth reading in full. The Banner Headline-" is not something with which we would disagree!*

## "NIGERIA: THE HAPPIEST PLACE ON EARTH"

*Nigeria is beset by poverty, corruption and violence – but a poll says it is the world's most optimistic nation. To quote: "In a 53-country Gallup poll, Nigerians were rated at 70 points for optimism. By contrast, Britain scored a deeply pessimistic -44. Why so glum, Britain? And what in the world makes Nigerians so happy?"*

We continue to pray that God will work together with all its people for the good of the Country of Nigeria and the Continent of Africa where we have found not only the 'happiest' but some of the 'friendliest' people on earth.

As we shared in our last report, these are uncertain days economically for the church as well as for society as a whole and the future of the CCITC programme beyond 2012 remains unclear. Many people both here and overseas are committed to its continuation and even its expansion as a proven 21st Century partnership model for sharing in training for mission in the world-wide church. The future of this economically viable concept which provides so many 'added-value benefits' in terms of world church relations, needs the support of those who value the concept if it is to continue making its unique contribution to the mission of our partner churches throughout the world. Articles, regular reports, evaluations and DVD's provided since 2002 are full of testimonies to the positive impact made on everyone associated this kind of programme. They will be made available to you on request.

# 2012/2 MAY: MCSL CONFERENCE & REFRESHING

REPORT OF REVD RICHARD JACKSON, BRITISH REPRESENTATIVE TO THE METHODIST CHURCH SIERRA LEONE (MCSL) CONFERENCE HELD AT BUXTON MEMORIAL METHODIST CHURCH, FREETOWN 22ND TO 27TH MAY 2012.

### INTRODUCTION

Ten years on from the elections that confirmed the end of the 'Blood Diamond' fuelled conflict that has seen Charles Taylor sentenced recently at the Hague for crimes against humanity, the Methodist Church in Sierra Leone continues its work of reconciliation and restoration. Though not without its problems as reported to the Conference, the MCSL under the able and sensitive leadership of its President of Conference, Rt. Revd Arnold Temple; the Secretary, Revd Musa Jambawai and a gifted group of lay-people continues with its re-building programme despite limited resources and funding.

Conference visitors from the UK: Revd Richard Jackson as the British Representative; Revd Ken Todd from Ireland and Mr Peter Worrell, Cliff College International Training Centre (CCITC) lecturer; (and recently arrived Mission Partner Revd Dr Wendy Kilworth-Mason); are pleased to express our appreciation of the generous hospitality provided by MCSL and to say thank you to those friends who hosted us in their homes and responded to every request made by us: Mr Moshe Roberts; Ms Marcella Davies and

MS ANDRINA COKER HOSTING PETER WORRELL

### REDISCOVERING OUR EVANGELICAL HERITAGE

The chosen theme for the Conference: **"Rediscovering Our Evangelical Heritage"** inspired reports that:

**reflected** on lessons to be learned from their past history of 220 years of Methodism in Sierra Leone;

**reviewed** immediate but diverse concerns about recruitment for the ministry through to land encroachment;

**responded** positively to good news being shared and looked forward in faith and hope to future growth.

For the first time, the MCSL Conference followed a recent tradition begun elsewhere of having a separate 'Lay Session' on the opening day meeting at the same time as that of the traditional 'Ministerial Session' of Conference. The 'Lay Session' later reported back their concerns to the main sessions of Conference accompanied by a request that the Ministers also should report back in future. This plea was 'noted'! The shared Conference opened in the Buxton Methodist Church in Freetown under the watchful eye of **Sierra Leonean Methodism's saints of old commemorated in their treasured stained glass window.**

The opening devotions led by the Chairman of Kailahun/Kono District reminded us that 'Methodism was a Movement before it became a Church'. This was followed by an inspirational and wide-ranging Presidential address (subsequently published). Expanding on the Conference Theme the President led us from the historic 'Deed of Foundation' to consider some challenges that might lead us into a contemporary expression of 'Our Evangelical Heritage' in the MCSL.

The shared closing session on Methodists in Mission linked with the Wesley Historical Society was led by Revd Ken Todd, invited guest from the Irish Methodist Conference. Revd Todd helpfully linked the Theme of the Conference with the historic coming to Sierra Leone of George Warren and friends in 1811. He was able also to dovetail in reflections on the life and witness of Revd Leslie Wallace, long-time missionary in Sierra Leone shared in the recently published book 'Pa Wallace', which was made available to the Conference.

279

Here is not the place to rehearse again all that is written up in the reports and later the journal of Conference. With several very full days at Conference sharing excellent food, fellowship and hospitality with friends old and new followed by meetings each evening, this supposedly brief report might soon become a book.

As the Secretary of Conference made clear 'land encroachment' and the consequent time-consuming conversations and/or legal action relating to this issue is becoming a major concern of the church in all three Districts. Obviously, the situation has been exacerbated by the ten years of conflict but even long-standing institutions like the Nixon Memorial Hospital and some of our Methodist Schools are struggling to protect their rights to land which is not being used at present. Whilst the Conference Office does what it can with limited resources of time and money, it seems clear that much more will need to be done if land that was gifted to the MCSL in earlier years is to be preserved for future generations. A full-time appointment of someone who has the legal background to assess the documentation that is available and negotiating skills to take time over such issues may help to alleviate the situation and the work-load for the Conference Office.

The agreed 2010 edition of the Constitutional Practice and Discipline of the Methodist Church Sierra Leone was actually printed, published and a copy presented to the British Representative by Dr Sama Banya, a friend and former Vice-President, towards the end of the 2012 Conference. When the time came for designations to be made for the President and Vice President of the 2014 Conference confusion reigned!

It became clear that legislation made in a hurry as a reaction to immediate circumstances and personalities, even when written up with the positive intention of promoting inclusivity and unity, can in fact unintentionally become the trigger for the kind of controversy that it was meant to eliminate. After much heart-searching and prayer the concerns expressed from all sides were referred to the General Purposes Committee of the Conference for further consideration and for guidance to be given during the two years before the next Conference.

Other controversial issues that might at times have derailed the Conference were dealt with, largely through the 'good humour' of all present. The President's gracious releasing at times of the 'chairing' of the Conference to the former President (now Emeritus) Rt. Revd Francis Nabieu, the Vice-President and chosen visitors helped to maintain an experienced light touch with little sense of business being rushed or delegates being denied the opportunity to make their contribution. The helpful Sierra Leonean tradition which allows representatives and those from the various institutions to 'hang heads=discuss' together outside of the Conference itself and move towards a rapprochement may not please all, but it does allow the Conference to make progress.

Again the value of having others chair the Conference generated insights from elsewhere. The Presiding Bishop of the Ghana Conference, Revd Prof Emmanuel Asante, in particular proved helpful with background information provided about issues of common concern. MCSL expressed its appreciation to Ghana for the gift of three Ghanaian ministers who have been serving in Sierra Leone, but who will be returning home soon and they expressed the hope (and invitation) for others to come and take their place. The ordination service, for three new ministers received by the Conference, appropriately on the 24th May, at which Revd Prof Asante preached, drew attention to a concern expressed in Conference about a perceived and growing imbalance in ministry.

There are fewer ministers offering for full-time 'stationable' ministry than those 'non-stipendiary' ministers whose opportunities for service may be limited geographically or by personal circumstances. On the other hand, as Revd Roland Allen in his book 'Missionary Methods: St Paul's or Ours' pointed out 100 years ago, full-time paid ministry (and multiple mission pioneered institutions) can be impossible to maintain without outside support when 'younger' churches like MCSL and some 'older' churches in decline are struggling to maintain their ministry and mission.

281

MCSL expressed its thanks also to the Methodist Conferences of Britain and Ireland for the support given and noted the continuing strong relationships, particularly as the Designated Presidents & Vice President of those Conferences have enjoyed long and strong associations with the Methodist Church in Sierra Leone. Revd S Kenneth Todd and I, (both former missionaries with MCSL) were able to respond on several occasions at Conference and in public evening meetings as we brought greetings and renewed contacts with old friends like Dr Sama Banya and Ms Lillian Lahai reinforcing the strength of those relationships.

**WORSHIP TOGETHER**

The final service held in the afternoon of Conference Sunday (most people having attended worship for several hours in the morning) included the sermon of the British Representative on the words of Jesus, 'This Do in Remembrance of Me' shared in the context of a service of Holy Communion. Our first time visitor to

Sierra Leone, Peter Worrell, who earlier took two days out of Conference and carried our greetings during sight-seeing travel in Bo, Kenema and Segbwema proved to be 'at home' on his violin with a mini-recital and as he accompanied a duet sung by the President of Conference and the Chair of the Western District.

**THE HALLE OR HALLOWED TRIO**

By general consensus, their violin accompanied singing of 'Amazing Grace' by John Newton who was a slave-trader in Sierra Leone, followed by a joyful sing-in of the 'Hallelujah Chorus' led by the massed choirs from the Freetown Methodist Churches, provided a fitting climax to the Conference proper as we ended on a celebratory and joyful note of thanksgiving to God.

On Monday, 28th May, a training day at the Theological College with a representative from Tear Fund (at which we were observers) proved to be the beginning of a new relationship, which may lead to joint projects being undertaken in the future.

We used the Tuesday (before ministers returned to their up-country stations) to run a pre-planned Cliff College International Training Centre (CCITC) 'Refresher Day' for former students/trainees who had completed the pioneering pilot programme in Sierra Leone several years ago. The intention behind this new initiative (which will be repeated in Nigeria) later in the year was to have those involved in the programme complete a 'reactionnaire' following-up in the longer-term on earlier evaluations. The 27 forms completed, when analysed, will provide fresh data direct from our trainees on how the training given and the books and resources provided through the Cliff College validated 'International Diploma In Applied Ministry and Mission' (IDIAMM) course have impacted on their ministry.

An open invitation was issued for lay leaders and ministers to attend the 'Refresher Day' of lectures and activities in the Buxton Methodist Church Centre. The President and the Secretary of the Conference, plus the Principal of the Theological College were in attendance, and up to 90 people were present for some or all of the sessions. We were able to project and distribute to everyone present DVD's of this pioneering programme's development in both Sierra Leone and Nigeria. In addition 200 CD's were distributed for use of lay and ordained leaders of MCSL.

These CD's contained 1400 pages of Ministry & Mission Lecture Notes; whole books on Preaching; and PowerPoint presentations on everything from working with children through to learning lessons from 'New Generation Churches'. This kind of resource, easily produced, carried and accessed will be helpful to leaders of our partner churches in countries where books are expensive to buy and internet access continues to be spasmodic and unreliable. Revd Ken Todd through MMS(Ireland) was able to provide copies of a study book on Biblical Concepts to participants along with the recently published 'Pa Wallace' in which he shares something of the mind, memories and ministry of the much-loved former missionary (1949-87).

The greetings of the father of the Sierra Leone and Irish Methodist Conferences, Revd S Leslie Wallace MBE, CR along with such memories were shared with all and it seemed appropriate for Revd Ken Todd and me that our final morning should be spent with two outstanding, but ageing mentors and friends from our early days of service with MCSL. The 96 year old, E L Coker and comparative youngster, G L Thomas, gracious as ever, with their family around them welcomed us into their homes with tears in their eyes and we took photographs so that we too might revive precious memories for families and old friends back at home.

**GEORGE THOMAS & FRIENDS**

**ATROCITIES, DIAMONDS, DIPLOMACY AND MISSION!**

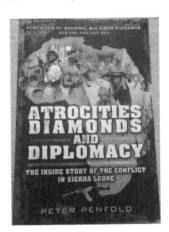

As we settled into our seats for our return flight home, I put the book launched during our stay by Peter Penfold, the former British High Commissioner into the seat pocket in front of me. As I turned away from the brightly coloured cover of **'ATROCITIES, DIAMONDS AND DIPLOMACY'** subtitled, **'The inside story of the conflict in Sierra Leone'**, I looked across the aisle to my left and saw the same book sitting in the rack in front of a young Sierra Leonean lady sitting there. In conversation, proudly she showed me pictures from the book of her late father Chief Sam Hinga Norman, described there as a true hero of the Sierra Leone conflict, who led the resistance to the rebels, but who in 2003 was indicted for war crimes by the Sierra Leone Special Court and died in detention following an operation in 2007.

The convicted Charles Taylor, the censured British High Commissioner, Peter Penfold, the indicted defender, Hinga Norman and many others with mixed motives caught up in a conflict, the consequences of which still impact upon a nation! Ten years on from the end of this devastating conflict and the rights and wrongs of action taken by key participants in the troubles continue to be debated. This is the confused cultural context within which the Methodist (and other churches) in Sierra Leone continue to rebuild a shattered nation and church.

To those who have loved and served in MCSL, it has been an historic jewel in the crown of mission among our partner churches overseas. In recent years it has become a parable illustrating the difficulties that face a church continuing on a journey. 'Rediscovering Our Evangelical Heritage' in the MCSL will lead it again into the complexities of church hopes and dreams set against a confused political and desperate economic background that will not make it easy to discern how, "To serve the present age, My calling to fulfil."

Let those seeking easy and early solutions to the problems that face the Methodist Church in Sierra Leone, look elsewhere. Those who care, will continue in prayer and give practical support and encouragement to those seeking to maintain their witness in a country that has moved from being labelled in missionary parlance the 'White Man's Grave' to being seen in the 1990's and early 20th century as one of the 'Most dangerous places on earth'.

Our recent and past personal experience reminded us that its people at peace are among the most welcoming to be found anywhere in the world.

**Richard Jackson (Revd)**
**Wednesday, 06 June 2012**

*(Editor's note: The concerns expressed here in 2012 are even more relevant as I write in November 2014, when Sierra Leone is again being devastated by the scourge of 'Ebola'.*

# 2012/3 JUL 30-AUG 15: MCN GRADUATIONS & ?
## IDIAMM 2010-12 PROGRAMME

For the past six years CCITC teams have travelled to Nigeria in January and July each year with graduations held at our two centres Umuahia MTI in the east and Sagamu MTI, just outside Lagos in the west. To save travel and other expenses related solely to the graduations we have started a new two year programme of training every second year (2006-8; 2008-10; 2010-12;). This year was different! A team of five people travelled in August intending to: round off the current programme with graduations; distribute updating disks of lectures and obtain completed questionnaires from present and former trainees; dedicate the Mellor Memorial Methodist Centre at Sagamu MTI; attend the week-long MCN biennial conference celebrating 50 years of autonomy and 170 years since Methodism adventured into Nigeria through Badagry; and make plans for future training and linked programmes in association with the leadership of MCN. No pressure then!

VISA PROBLEMS YET AGAIN

Though much was different, one problem remained the same! Once again obtaining Nigerian visas for the travelling team proved to be a most frustrating exercise. Despite the new and much vaunted on-line system, applying individually, not one out of the group of five of us went through the system unscathed. On-line application is made through the Nigerian High Commission to a company in the USA called SW Global who process the forms and to whom you make payment on-line. They are supposed to receive your payment and issue on-line a confirmation of your payment with a reference number indicating to the Nigerian High Commission in London that this has been done. At this point you are given a date on which to take this with passport etc. into the High Commission who then take a few days to process the application before returning the visa stamped passport to you at a later date. All of us individually had money taken from our account, sometimes twice, with no confirmation received and no personal response to our queries other than a complaint reference number received by email! Without going into further details here, the whole process was a shambles, largely attributable to SW Global, which left us waiting for visas until the last few days before we travelled to Nigeria. By way of contrast, two months earlier, we obtained visas for Sierra Leone, with everything done on-line and no visit to London required within the promised time of three days!!!

Fortunately, such frustrations fade from the mind, if not the memory, when the actual journey is underway. The team of five people, Revd Richard & Dr Carole Jackson, Administrator (MCN-Knight of John Wesley) Keith Phillips, lecturer (MCN-Knight of Charles Wesley) Peter Worrell, and camera/video producer Chris Jackson travelled from different directions to meet up at Heathrow for the overnight flight with Arik Air from London to Lagos. Travelling out when the Olympic crowds were coming in, had its advantages. The timing of our visit meant that we saw the fantastic Opening Ceremony with our visiting family, but missed out on their return to the USA, United Kingdom successes, and 'Lightning Bolt' etc. With snippets seen on TV there, it did allow us to empathise more fully with our Nigerian hosts who were unhappy at their own failures in the hoped-for medal count.

### REFRESHING AT UMUAHIA MTI AND 'REACTIONNAIRES'

After our early morning arrival we were welcomed at the airport in Lagos by our friends, the Protocol Officer, Revd Busuyi Agunbiade, and the National Coordinator, Very Revd Paul Olukunga, with driver Emmanuel in the newly purchased Cliff College bus, (the first one was wrecked in the north before we had chance to see it, but the insurance came through). We flew on to Owerri, accompanied by Paul, to be met by our friends from Umuahia MTI. With the usual courtesies observed, we began to review and moderate locally marked assignments for the International Diploma In Applied Ministry & Mission (IDIAMM) programme and to ensure that our graduations lists tallied. Despite everyone's best efforts, the distances travelled and communication difficulties experienced by the trainees and staff of the colleges make such vocational distance learning programmes an exercise in pastoral relationships as well as an examination of academic ability. It is that pastoral and practical concern for continuing support of our trainees that has prompted our new pioneering initiative, largely funded by MMS (Ireland). This project trialled in May in Sierra Leone saw 'us' (actually Carole, my wife!), collating material, buying disks, reproducing and writing on well over 1,500 copies of a DVD about the CCITC for Sierra Leone and Nigeria.

In addition we have distributed a CD with over 1400 pages of lecture notes, Methodist Evangelicals Together (MET) books on preaching, PowerPoint presentations and photos of graduations made available by lecturers and friends of the programme for use in our programmes with partner churches. Leaders, lecturers and trainees in Sierra Leone and Nigeria, expressed their thanks to those of you who provided funds and to others who responded so willingly to a pressurised deadline in providing this material for their use. Our 'hold' baggage this time weighed less than books, but it is surprising what spindles of 100 disks along with packets for individual distribution weigh. The completed evaluation forms gathered at the 'Refreshing Days' in Sierra Leone and in Nigeria have yet to be collated and analysed, but there are clear indications within the overwhelmingly positive responses that the CCITC programme is helping to change lives and the ministries of those who are called to serve God in this way.

### DEDICATION(S) AT SAGAMU MTI

After the time spent in Umuahia preparing for the joint graduation to be held in Sagamu on Monday, 6th August and sharing in the 'Refresher Day' for past and present trainees, we returned to Lagos on Friday and then on to Sagamu MTI to make similar preparations for the much-anticipated celebrations to be held there. First though, on Sunday the team accompanied Bishop Taiwo in leading worship to round off a youth training weekend at Irolu in the Remo diocese.

**Monday 6th August,** the date chosen by MCN for the Dedication and Graduation, was a travelling day for those coming to the Methodist Conference in Lagos, which meant that a number of people with services to lead on Sunday could not make it to Sagamu on time. Nevertheless, it was being seen as a celebratory launching pad for the Conference itself which was to begin (as is their custom) with separate ministerial and lay sessions on the Tuesday. That Monday began with reports of significant hold-ups on the road from Lagos to Sagamu, but a very early start by the Prelate and other dignitaries saw us being involved first at 9.00 am in the Dedication of the Prelate's Guest House, newly completed on the MTI campus.

**MELLOR MEMORIAL METHODIST CENTRE (MMMC) DEDICATION**

This was followed by the Dedication of the Mellor Memorial Methodist Centre with its refurbished 'original Mellor Pulpit and Lectern' and the CCITC Graduations for both Colleges in that same building. Regular readers of these reports will know that we have been helping to raise funds for the long-awaited completion of a larger building started many years ago. The

fresh impetus given just twelve months ago through the new concept of the Mellor Memorial Methodist Centre part-funded and developed by the CCITC in consultation with the MCN leadership has seen this building almost completed.

**"DOES IT BITE?"**

The dynamic leadership of the Bishop of Remo, Right Revd Babatunde Taiwo: supported by the Rector of Sagamu MTI, Very Revd Joshua Adeogun; and financially by contributions of the Lay Leadership and the Centre Committee, plus generous Builders and Contractors of Remo had helped to make great progress. With continuing encouragement from the Prelate, His Eminence, Dr Sunday Ola Makinde and National Church Leaders; they have produced a magnificent building for Community, Church and College use which is almost completed. Even with the offices, bookshop, toilets, seating, curtained sanctuary area yet to be funded and completed at a further cost of up to £10,000 (all donations welcomed!), it provided a superb venue for the activities of the day.

**MCN GRADUATIONS FOR COMPLETED (2010-12) PROGRAMME**

**UMUAHIA & SAGAMU GRADUATIONS FOR COMPLETED (2010-12) PROGRAMME** held at the Mellor Memorial Methodist Centre, Sagamu on Monday, 6th August 2012.

The impressive opening ceremony and dedication led by the Prelate, was followed by the graduation of trainees in 'Ministry and Mission' from both Umuahia and Sagamu Centres, led by the International Coordinator, Revd Richard Jackson (in the unavoidable absence of the Cliff College Principal, Revd Dr Chris Blake who sent greetings).

The presentation of certificates to our 141 graduates was enhanced by the presence of my wife:

Dr Carole Jackson

(The Secretary of the Conference, Rt. Revd Dr Raphael Opoko who gave the Charge insists that you have to acknowledge your wife if you want to eat!)

Fortuitously too, the Chair of the Sheffield District (in which Cliff College is located), Revd Vernon Marsh, arrived in Lagos just the day before to represent the British Methodist Church at the MCN Conference. Together they managed to drape the CCITC preaching scarves around the necks of the graduates without strangling any of them, though it was touch and go at times. Unfortunately, the pre-Conference timing meant that the Prelate and many of the MCN leaders involved in the Conference had to return to Lagos at lunchtime, but joyful celebration continued for those who had invested so much time effort and money in making this impressive Centre available for the occasion and for the 141 graduates present with their families and friends. In a matter of weeks, Chief Olusegun, a Methodist author and Sagamu Community Leader, produced a 100 pages long book on the much-revered missionary Revd William F Mellor. This was being sold with profits and other donations solicited by our experienced fund-raiser and twister of long arms (for more alms!), Sir Remi Omotoso to help off-set the outstanding debt and funds needed to complete the building.

**THE MCN CONFERENCE**

After many congratulations and photographs with the graduates the visiting team left Sagamu by road late in the day for Lagos to be accommodated with other overseas delegates from Togo and Zimbabwe at the Mainland Hotel, quite close to the Conference and associated venues at Hoare's Memorial Methodist Cathedral, Sabo, Yaba, Lagos State. The Methodist Church Nigeria Conference (preceded by breakfast served to several hundred representatives in the huge basement hall) opened officially on Tuesday morning at 8.30am with a shared communion service, before lay and ministerial members met in separate venues for two days before joining together again on the Thursday morning to continue though until Sunday evening. What can we say (without going into too much detail) about attending with hundreds of delegates this hugely important biennial Conference in Lagos.

The opening ceremony presented **a kaleidoscope of colour** with the Prelate, Archbishops, Bishops, Presbyters and Priests along with MCN Knights and lay-leaders in their colourful finery, but also there was a muted cacophony of conversation in this huge church as old friends greeted one another. Many of them made sure that we as visitors did not feel that we were being left out.

Our thanks again go to those friends in Nigeria who greeted and treated us (as always) like honoured guests. Mention only had to be made of a particular concern or a need for one of our Nigerian friends sitting nearby to respond helpfully. I have to say though that one thing they could not cope with was the full breeze of the standing fans cooling us in what to them was already a very cool time of the year. Fortunately, though it was their rainy season, we did not have too much rain outside of our time in Umuahia, but it was noticeable that nearby seats in the pews emptied, even in the afternoon when 'our' fans were going full blast! The CCITC team regulars were impressed with how many of our former trainees were attending Conference in one capacity or another and again by the increasing number of them who have been involved in the programme in some way as college tutors or trainees and are now leading the church as Bishops.

Unfortunately, we do not have space to report in full the activities of Conference. (Revd Vernon Marsh, the official delegate, will be giving a fuller report and our intrepid video man Chris, will hopefully produce an edited video in the weeks to come!) Whilst some aspects, like Stationing and Memorial Services for those who have died were recognisably Methodist this was far from being a UK Methodist Conference. We began with an Agenda of a couple of hundred pages at both the Lay and Representative sessions of Conference, but we were given later a large number of hefty supplementary documents that illustrated (often with pictures) many aspects of the work accomplished by the Methodist Church Nigeria and its committees since their last gathering two years earlier.

I am not sure how many members of the coffee/lunch and tea oriented members of the UK Conference would appreciate waiting, and wading through several hours of business before breaking at tea time for lunch. Having returned to Conference after the Prelate's Party with guests on Saturday evening they would certainly have joined in the singing of the fabricated ditty 'Please, Let us go home' at 9.30pm.

My personal highlight of the Conference week was to be involved in the Sunday ordination service for 121 Priests (both Tent-makers with other careers and full-time ministers). But then I did not have to return after the Ordinations at 8.00pm on Sunday evening for a further session of Conference stationing and designation of Bishops, which reportedly carried on until 2.00am on Monday morning!!!

**ORDINATIONS FOR THE FUTURE**

Having said our goodbyes to our new-found friends from overseas Conferences and others who had looked after us so well, the CCITC team travelled back to Sagamu. By that time we were tucked up in bed in readiness for the training 'Refresher' which would bring a number of former trainees together on Monday at Sagamu MTI to complete 'Questionnaires' and receive the updating DVD's and CD's.

Despite their sleep deprivation, the pressures of Conference and the Press, the Prelate and the Secretary of Conference, met with us as planned at the Conference Office on the Tuesday before we left for London. Once again, our easy relationship turned a business meeting into a conversation as we celebrated together the successful shared venture that had resulted in the completion of the Mellor Memorial Methodist Centre and shared our thoughts on the completion of the IDIAMM with 74 trainees graduating from Umuahia and 67 from Sagamu. The conversation then followed up on plans for a post-Easter 2013 training and Methodist orientation visit by the Bishops (at MCN expense) to Cliff College and the Districts of the Methodist Church in Britain and Ireland. It is hoped that the agreed theme of 'Leading by Example' will inspire reflection on Leadership: Scriptural; Methodist; Organisational; and MCN Leadership for Today and Tomorrow.

This follow-up to the Episcopal Consultation held in 2009 will be linked in theme and content with an MCN/CCITC partnership in Lay Training initiative to begin in February 2013. Having been involved in training MCN Evangelists, Priests and Presbyters from 2006-12, some of whom have since become Bishops, the Prelate and his national leadership team are planning now to provide opportunities for very capable lay leaders to share in a similar programme of resourcing and refreshing. The experimental pattern (Friday to Sunday) for this Pilot Lay Training Programme beginning in February 2013 (with follow-up later in the year) will be undertaken initially with the three Archdioceses of Umuahia; Riye (Sagamu MTI) and Lagos. As they say, mission accomplished, but much more is yet to be done in planning for the future.

For Methodists with the phrase 'Fruitful Field' still echoing in minds from our own Conference, I can think of no more 'Fruitful Field' available to us than that with which we are engaged through training programmes with our partners at home and overseas. Please join us and our partners!

# CHAPTER 13 2013: AN EXPANDING PROGRAMME

*In April, we responded to a request from the MCN leadership to provide for their Episcopal Leadership (as a follow-up to the 2009 Episcopal event in Lagos-see 2009/5): a Study Course at Cliff College; followed by two by two fellowship visits to most Districts of the British Methodist Church; and an associated Methodist Heritage tour of the UK. In August, we said farewell to the retiring Prelate, Sunday Ola Makinde and welcomed the newly elected Prelate, Samuel Uche who had been in the UK with us for the Heritage Tour earlier in the year. Later in the year we launched Part 1 of our first Training programme in both Sierra Leone and Nigeria intentionally focused on lay leaders at local, diocesan and national levels of the church.*

## 2013/1 APR: MCN EPISCOPAL RETREAT-UK

Report on The Methodist Church Nigeria (MCN) Leadership visit to their: 'Mother' Methodist Church in Britain for an historic Episcopal Training Retreat (23rd April-10th May 2013)

MCN EPISCOPAL RETREAT & UK METHODIST HERITAGE TOUR

After 170 years of Methodism and 50 years of autonomy, the two million plus member Methodist Church Nigeria is growing as it responds to its own (2006) Mission Statement: "To consistently win more souls for Christ, to develop spiritually fulfilled members and remain very active in serving humanity."

During the past eight years at the invitation of the MCN Leadership, Cliff College, through its International Training Centre has shared in the further training for 'Ministry & Mission' of several hundred Evangelists, Priests and Presbyters in Nigeria. As a follow up to the autonomy celebrations held last year in Nigeria, a further partnership programme for training lay leaders is being piloted in three arch-dioceses during 2013. In addition, this growing church decided that its 'Episcopal Leadership' should be given the opportunity to share in a programme of training at Cliff College followed by some cross-cultural exposure to British Methodism and our common Wesleyan Heritage while visiting the UK at its own expense.

The current leaders of MCN: **The Prelate, His Eminence Dr Sunday Ola Makinde;** the Secretary of Conference, Rt. Revd Dr

Raphael Opoko; and the Bishop of Evangelism, Rt. Revd Amuta Edoka; asked for this programme to be organised as a structured spiritual retreat and training programme. This they saw as building on the work done together during an 'Episcopal Training Consultation' enjoyed by many of us in Lagos in July 2009.

### THE INTERNATIONAL COORDINATOR & THE DIRECTOR OF CCITC, REVD DR STEPHEN SKUCE WITH THOUGHTS OF THE PROPOSED EPISCOPAL HERITAGE TOUR

The overall theme "LEADING BY EXAMPLE" will feed into the further training programme planned for Lay Leaders in Nigeria later in 2013. Both Episcopal and Lay Leaders have received in advance of these practical training programmes their own personal copy of the CCITC Training DVD and a CD of 'Ministry & Mission' resources distributed in August 2012.

Intending episcopal participants were asked to: Submit a detailed (Arch-)Diocesan Report analysing the past five years with statistical details; Share a paper outlining the Diocesan leader's personal vision for mission in their own (Arch-)Diocese; and to keep a personal (confidential) Spiritual Journal in the style of John Wesley from the beginning of January 2013.

### BEGINNING THE STUDY RETREAT/METHODIST HERITAGE TOUR AT CLIFF COLLEGE

The detailed practical preparation for the programme in Nigeria and in Britain began to bear fruit as most of the travel-weary passengers (two-thirds of whom had not visited England previously) were picked up by a chartered coach from Heathrow in the early hours of the morning on Wednesday, 24th April and transported to Cliff College. The final number of 42 Bishops and 5 facilitators along with the CCITC support team were literally squeezed into the last available room space at Cliff College. Rested and fed, I found it difficult to believe that these same leaders on that same evening were enjoying so wholeheartedly the welcoming 'Working Together' activities led by Piers Lane with strange names like 'Tarpaulin Turn' and 'Gutterball'!

Despite a cool start, good food, a fellowship of fun, good weather and an excellent programme of lecturers (yes, perhaps in that order) meant that the next few days flew by for everyone directly involved. A noisy Nigerian welcome was given to the visiting President-designate of the Irish Conference, Revd Dr Heather Morris, born of the Kingston family in Umuahia in Eastern Nigeria and acknowledged as one of their own. Having noted Heather's unique contribution, it would be invidious to  name-drop or pick out from the Cliff College staff and visiting lecturers what were deemed by many to be significant contributions to the theme of, 'Leading by Example'. A copy of the timetable can be

 provided for interested parties. Suffice to say that break times, once 'The Taskmaster' (= one of my more polite earned titles) had convinced all the would-be questioners that the time-table needed to be adhered to, were punctuated by positive comments about every lecture as the conversations continued.

Invited friends of MCN and former mission partners, included 90 year old Enid Kingsley-Johnson from Stockton-On-Tees whose books on 1950's missionary work with her late husband in Nigeria were made available. Friends visiting on the Saturday 'Open Day' reminiscing together, shared hugs, memories and poignant celebrations that brought tears to many an eye. An unexpected feature of the whole programme was that of relationships renewed by our Nigerian visitors through spontaneous telephone calls or visits arranged in the limited time available between families and old friends.

Purposely, the Sunday at Cliff College was kept low-key with most of our visiting Bishops sharing in the normal worship of many smaller churches in the near-by circuits. The 'normal worship' experience did not stop many of their hosts from providing generous hospitality, with sight-seeing in the grandeur of the Peak National Park and challenging conversations about the church in Britain and Nigeria. The Prelate, Sunday Makinde and the Secretary of Conference, Raphael Opoko joined the small Crumpsall Church in north

Manchester where Sunday's son, Toyin and his family worship. There were many murmurs of affirmation as the leader of the Methodist Church Nigeria in responding to questions, shared in a very positive way what he owed to the Methodist Church.

The highlight of the programme for many of our visitors was enjoyed on the Monday as we left Cliff College for Epworth. (If any of you Christians, Methodists or not, have never visited or at least not recently, it is time that you did!) It would be even better if you could visit with a group from our partner churches overseas who give life to the experience as their presence makes it a pilgrimage of prayer and spiritual renewal for all involved. Competent guides, warm hospitality and a true reverence for our Methodist heritage, treasured by our partners from overseas, challenged us all to celebrate with thanksgiving those links with our past in ways that impact on our present church activities. Many of us were touched to hear prayers being said at Epworth by the MCN leadership, seeking guidance on the retirement of the present Prelate in October this year (at the age of 70), that the new leader should be imbued with the spirit of John and Charles Wesley.

REMEMBERING THE WESLEYS AT EPWORTH

A final series of lectures on Tuesday morning, followed by an afternoon of rounding up and group photographs took us into a deeply moving evening communion service led by the Principal, Revd Dr Chris Blake and the Prelate, His Eminence, Sunday Makinde. Truly a foretaste of the 'Heavenly Banquet' prepared for all people!

### TWO BY TWO TO THE DISTRICTS OF METHODISM

Reality set in again the following morning. The planned practical arrangements for the 'two by two' travelling of Bishops by road, train and plane to British Districts as widespread as Scotland and the Isle of Man in the north through to the Channel Islands and Cornwall (and the Isles of Scilly for some) in the south, were tested to the limits. Thanks to the patience, good humour and flexibility on the part of those acting on behalf of the Districts and the activity of several people, including the Principal, responding to late taxi emergencies at Cliff College everyone arrived at their destination, though not always the originally intended one!

**REV DR KEITH DAVIES, MANCHESTER & STOCKPORT DISTRICT CHAIR WITH THE PRELATE & SECRETARY OF MCN AT 'THE AVENUE METHODIST CHURCH SALE**

The Districts who received two Nigerian visitors will have their own stories to tell, but in the reporting back of the 47 sent out, like the 72 of old, they 'came back in great joy' sharing with each other the positive experiences enjoyed in every District. There is little space in this report to do anything other than record our appreciation of the time and effort that so many people put into planning visits. These District programmes allowed our visitors to: learn more about their Wesley heritage; meet and discuss with members the local church at work here and overseas; respond to questioning and share in Sunday worship; and for light relief to attend significant places of secular worship, like Old Trafford, home of the Champions (again!), Manchester United, in our own District! For any who might question the inclusion of such sporting theatre visits, please note that worldwide TV coverage

has made Premier League football enthusiasts with differing allegiances of most of our friends throughout Africa and beyond. Thank you again to the participating Districts for your hospitality, friendship and care in returning our guests safely to London for their final two days of visits.

**LONDON: WESLEY'S CHAPEL; METHODIST HOUSE; ST. PAUL'S; WESTMINSTER & WALWORTH (CLUBLAND)**

After such a kaleidoscope of fresh experiences we were concerned that the visit to London should not feel like an anti-climax. We need not have worried! The impact of the programme prepared under the guidance of Dr Olubunmi Olayisade (WCR-Partnership Co-ordinator Africa) and the recently appointed Nigerian chaplain in London Revd Dr Deji Okegbile surpassed all expectations. There was time on the way by coach from the Premier Inn near Heathrow, Terminal 5 into Central London for people to exchange stories of their District visits and loud laughter was never far from the surface of conversations as they shared experiences. The Wednesday tour of Wesley Chapel and surrounding sites; the welcome at Methodist Church House and an impromptu barbecue organised by the MCN Secretary of Conference will live long in the memory.

**ST PAUL'S ON ASCENSION DAY**

The Thursday itinerary, which included a guided tour of St Paul's and reserved seats at the Ascension Day sung Eucharist, a bus tour of the sites/sights of London and a visit to Westminster Central Hall, was rounded off by fellowship and African food provided by friends of the Nigerian and Sierra Leone fellowships at:
**Walworth Methodist Church (Clubland).**

On Friday morning we were privileged to be at Heathrow Airport saying our good-byes to a group of Nigerian leaders who were so full of their experiences that they repeatedly responded-"Thank you! Thank you! Thank you!"-to us, and through us to all who have been involved in creating a very special kind of learning experience for our friends and partners in the Nigerian Methodist Church.

Despite the occasional clashes of culture and Methodist practice, might we not also be saying "Thank you!" to our visitors. For being a refreshing embodiment of the scripture that instructs us to, "Be joyful always *(laughing out loud is included)*, pray at all times *(even early in the morning, when others in Cliff College or your household are sleeping)*, be thankful in all circumstances *(positive thanksgiving in trying situations)*. This is what God wants from you in your life in union with Christ Jesus. Do not restrain the Holy Spirit; do not despise inspired messages. Put all things to the test: keep what is good and avoid every kind of evil."
1 Thess 5: 16-22

### FORWARD TOGETHER

MCN designated the Bishop of Remo, Rt. Revd Babatunde Taiwo, who bore the brunt of the preparatory work in Nigeria, as their national coordinator for this 'Episcopal' programme to liaise with Revd Richard Jackson, Coordinator of CCITC at Cliff College. Our visitors' programme of training will not be completed until their learning experience has been translated into a personal paper (3,500-4,000 words) on: Forward Together: What action should we take to apply what has been learned and stimulate church growth in our own (Arch)-Diocese? This will be followed in August by the presentation of a Cliff College International Certificate in Methodism, Leadership and Mission (ICIMLM) to those who have fulfilled the requirements relating to the whole programme.

FAREWELL TO CLIFF COLLEGE

As a coordinator, who is old enough to remember the conclusion to Bob Newhart's, 'The Driving Instructor', I must admit to a twinge of doubt when the Prelate suggested that we should coordinate a similar pilgrimage of Wesley heritage sites for the MCN Lay Leaders. It sounded to me like the chaotic learner's comment, "I must make sure that I get you again next time!" We shall see, but for me, the suggestion made by their leader was testimony to how much has been achieved in personal, ecumenical and international relationships through this visit. Thank you again to all who in different ways have contributed so much to making this training retreat such an enriching experience for everyone involved.

May God continue to bless the Methodist Church in Nigeria and bring refreshing through our overseas partners to the Methodist Church at home!

## 2013/2 AUG 22-SEP 2: FAREWELL & WELCOME

*REPORT ON AUGUST 2013 VISIT (22nd August to 2nd September)*

**Nigerian Visas for this special visit arranged at the invitation of the retiring Prelate of MCN, His Eminence Dr Sunday Ola Makinde,** were in our hands early-available two days before we travelled! 'Sir' Keith Phillips KJW, 'Sir' Peter Worrell KCW and I travelled well by Arik Air (allows a generous 2 suitcases of 30 kilos each-made up largely of books, plus 12 kilos of hand luggage) from Heathrow arriving in Lagos at 4.50am on Friday morning the 23rd August. We were met in the early hours by the national coordinator, Very Revd Paul Olukunga and the Protocol Officer, Revd Agunbiade Busuyi. Following a hastily revised itinerary we were carried by road to Sagamu Methodist Training Institute where once again we were hosted by The Bishop of Remo, Bishop Babatunde Taiwo and his family. Reviewing our plans with friends and colleagues before leaving the UK we thought that we would be involved in:

1. Reviewing and moderating the final submissions by the Bishops of their 3,500-4,000 word dissertations on "Forward Together: What action should we take to apply what has been learned and stimulate church growth in our own (Arch)-Diocese."

2. Official presentations of Cliff College Diplomas to the Episcopal Leaders who have completed the required work, following on from their UK training visit.
3. Consultations with the Lay Leadership of MCN about the dates, venues and programme planning for the Lay Training programme due to begin in November 2013.
4. Consultations with the MCN Leadership about future training programmes.
5. Further discussion on the possibility of a Wesley Heritage Tour being organised for May 2014.
6. A Special Conference to say thank you and bid farewell to the MCN Church Leader, His Eminence Sunday Ola Makinde.
7. Praying together with MCN for the Prelate's successor as the new leader is designated.

In addition, on some appropriate occasion, we shall be making an official presentation to Very Revd John Eze, on behalf of Cliff College of his Manchester University MA certificate. He was unable to be present at this year's Cliff College graduation ceremony earlier this year.

As usual due to circumstances beyond our control, some of what was planned, we were unable to accomplish, but additional unplanned activities combined to make this visit an especially rewarding and fruitful experience for us all.

LOCALLY SPONSORED NEW BUILDING AT SAGAMU MTI

**On Friday afternoon, we delivered our books to Sagamu MTI** and discovered that the Mellor Memorial Methodist Centre completed (with your support) last year has helped inspire a local donation of hundreds of millions of Naira (£2 million plus sterling) to develop fresh student accommodation and other college buildings on the campus. This donation will be used also to renovate the original Mellor Mission House and create a museum with associated artefacts in this historic building alongside the plans for a first-class research library. Donations of appropriate books (and funds) for this and

302

Umuahia MTI library will be welcomed by Cliff College ITC as we (in faith) fill a container on our campus for delivery to Nigeria next year.

**It was a particular joy for our (representative!) team to return to Lagos on Saturday to share with Bukky (Bukola Abiola) and Kola (Kolawole Peter) in their wedding** at the Foursquare Gospel Church and the reception that followed. Both Bukky and Kola work in the MCN Conference Office. Bukky was a facilitator with the group that visited the UK earlier this year. We were warmly welcomed by the Pastor, who invited us to take part in the ceremony, and their family thanked

us for accepting their invitation to be there with them for this special occasion.

**On Sunday, I preached at the Mellor Methodist Cathedral shorter service** (under two hours) beginning at 8 am. This was followed at 10.00 am by an Association of Methodist Brigades Inauguration and Investiture Service supported by an enthusiastic band etc. which lasted through to almost 3.00pm. Our team did not last quite that long! On Sunday afternoon, we received hospitality at the home of Ayo, who provided secretarial support for the Episcopal Retreat in the UK and sharing refreshments with her husband Taiwo and their two children.

These events and later descriptions of our 'social calendar' in Sagamu caused my wife Carole to respond to my telephone call with, "You are really on holiday there, aren't you?"

A Monday morning drive with Bishop Taiwo to Abeokuta allowed us to visit Archbishop Odubanjo of RIYE Archdiocese and again share prayers at the refurbished grave of Mary Archer-Champness. We arranged for continuing care of the grave and its surrounds before moving on to visit the impressive State Government Offices. An early evening meal followed at the invitation of the family descendants of Chief Oba William Christopher Adedoyin, who granted some Remo land and title to Methodist missionary Revd (Chief) William F Mellor. The extended family, all of them impressive leaders of the community and the church in their own right, provided good food, stimulating conversation and helpful insights about Nigeria and its development. Unfortunately, the later football match seen on TV with Manchester United 0 v Chelsea 0 was much less interesting!

At a meeting on Tuesday with the MTI Rector, Very Revd Joshua Adeogun and some college staff we discussed the plans for the college and the continuing support; staffing; maintenance etc. of the new buildings.

We moved on to the home of Elizabeth & Adutola Osilesi (our hosts from 2008) where a thanksgiving service was in progress for the **98th birthday** of Elizabeth's mother. Friends of the Nigeria Health Care Project will be pleased to note that **Dame Chief Victoria Wende Awoseyi Osilesi,** beaming brightly, was born 27th August 1915, completed Nursing Training in 1934 and started work with Dr Ludlow as a midwife at Ilesha. She delivered Michael Kehinde Stephen (now Archbishop) and his twin sister. Victoria retired from active nursing at the Wesley Guild Hospital in 1973, but looks fit enough to begin again.

We visited also Chief Ayodele, Remo's church historian and prolific author. Chief Ayodele had excused himself from a meeting and returned home to greet us. When we dropped him back for his meeting at the police offices we were welcomed by the District Police Officer, Adebuwale Lawal. It may be not what you know, but who you know that matters!

Wednesday the 28th dawned with a return journey by road to Lagos for a number of meetings with key personnel of MCN, including The Prelate, Secretary of Conference and the Lay President, Sir Jimmy Coker. As a result of these meetings and a presentation made on the following day to the Conference Connexional Council, plans for the

Lay Training Programme with four people from each diocese (to include the Lay President; at least-one woman and one younger person) were finalised and approved with dates as follows:

**Nov 2013:** 15-17 (Umuahia MTI) & 22-24 (Sagamu MTI): Registration: Thursday 14 & 21
**Mar 2014:** 21-23 (Umuahia MTI) & 28-30 (Sagamu MTI): Registration: Thursday 20 & 27

It was agreed that the possibility of a 10 day Cliff College/Wesley sites 'lay pilgrimage' in 2014 should be explored if sufficient applications with £1,000 deposit are received by 31st October 2013.

On Friday the 30th we as honoured guests accompanied by the Africa Secretary from World Church Relations in London, Dr Olubunmi Olayisade were involved in the main event of our August programme taking place at the spacious Muson Centre, Onikan. It was **the Prelate's Send-off Party and what a party it was!!!** From 10am

through to late afternoon many friends lay and clerical among the thousand or so guests greeted us as we shared in an extended programme, that allowed the Methodist Church Nigeria and Community dignitaries gathered to pay tribute and say farewell to their leader for the past seven years, His Eminence, Dr Sunday Ola Makinde. The 22 items on the day-long programme included hilarious speeches by the Chief Guest of Honour and former Head of State, His Excellency, Chief Olusegun Obasanjo, church fun presentations, worship & prayers, and many tributes to their friend and ours, Sunday Ola Makinde, who rounded off the event with his own personal response.

A more relaxed Saturday of sight-seeing at the National Stadium and socialising for some of us, allowed the dust to settle on this great event, before we moved into the Sunday ordination at Williams Memorial Methodist Cathedral of up to 150 Priests and Deaconesses. **This five hour Ordination service of celebration,** which included the planned-for presentation of an MA Certificate & Manchester University Hood to Revd John Eze, and was followed by many photographs taken with the retiring Prelate.

  **Later in the afternoon the Electoral College met to elect the new Prelate** due to take office on the 70th birthday (10th October) of Sunday Makinde. Stamina and prayer for those directly involved in the Electoral College was of the essence as they deliberated late into the night. There was no smoke, white or black, sent out from the Electoral College, but there was thanksgiving all around as news began to circulate that in response to much heart-searching prayer and fasting, **the Archbishop of Enugu, Most Revd Samuel Chukwuemeka Kanu Uche had been chosen to lead the Methodist Church Nigeria.**

  Our late-night and early morning packing for the Monday flight home to the UK was punctuated by news of further changes of station and roles that were being proposed. Our thoughts and prayers continue to be with our many friends left behind in Nigeria at the dawn of a new era. As with all such momentous occasions there will be disappointment for some as changes are taking place, but as we sang spontaneously to close the ordination service,

**This, this is the God we adore,**
**Our faithful, unchangeable friend,**
**Whose love is as great as his power,**
**And neither knows measure nor end:**

**'Tis Jesus, the first and the last,**
**Whose spirit shall guide us safe home;**
**We'll praise him for all that is past,**
**And trust him for all that's to come.**

  So we say farewell to one leader believing that God has chosen an inspired successor in **Archbishop Samuel Uche.** MCN will continue to be blessed: through one who will acknowledge what is past, but not live in it; build on what is present, but not be tied to it;

and through whom the church will be given a vision for future change to meet the challenges that face it. So we pray with him and the church: "God grant me the serenity to accept the things I cannot change, courage to change the things I can, and wisdom to know the difference."

As for me and the visiting CCITC team, we express our thanks to all who made us feel so at home during a busy time. They helped us achieve 5 out of the 7 objectives listed earlier. We are quite relieved that the presentation of certificates to Bishops who have completed their submissions on 'Forward Together' linked with the UK visit earlier this year has been postponed until our next visit. In November the submissions can be given the attention they deserve as MCN with its Lay Leaders, Priests, Presbyters and Episcopal leaders move 'Forward Together' with God into an exciting future of ministry and mission.

## 2013/3 OCT 18-25: MCSL ADMIN. TRAINING PART 1

INTRODUCTION TO 'EFFECTIVE MANAGEMENT & ADMINISTRATION TRAINING' PART 1

An interesting journey by car, plane, car ferry and road saw the visiting team of: Reverends: Dr Stephen Skuce; Richard Jackson; Peter Clarke; Gilbert Hall & his wife Sylvia along with Keith Phillips our administrator meet up at various points en route to Kenema in Sierra Leone. He (Stephen Skuce) who was lost overnight was found! Eventually, we met together with the President of the MCSL Conference, Right Revd Arnold Temple at Hastings Methodist Church, Freetown, where on Sunday morning, quite appropriately, we were commemorating with a worship service and a plaque (one year on from his death) the life of Elkanah Coker, an outstanding lay leader and committed member of the Methodist Church Sierra Leone.

HONOURING THE LATE ELKANAH L COKER

From Hastings we travelled in a convoy of two vehicles on improved roads to Kenema in the Eastern Province of Sierra Leone arriving in darkness at 7.30 in the evening. The visiting team were hosted in the former manse now converted into a Guest House on Combema Road in Kenema. There was a lasting sense of déjà vu for those of us who had lived there as mission partners in time past. Buckets filled with water and an unreliable town power supply, boosted on occasion by a small, but noisy generator reminded us that development was not uniformly progressive, but we were well cared for throughout our stay.

### THE TRAINING COURSE

By 9.00am on Monday morning we gathered as planned on the timetable for prayers in the recently built College Chapel of the Eastern Polytechnic. By lunchtime, most of the 35 participants from Circuits and the Conference Office were in attendance, though as anticipated, time was taken in meeting and greeting old friends and new (Sierra Leonean style), throughout the day. It quickly became clear that there were not the facilities available for the relaxed longer break at lunchtime that had been planned, so everyone agreed to a shorter lunch-break (as soon as the food was available!) and an earlier finish in the evening.

The wife of the Methodist Principal, **Grace Bockarie and Mrs Mary Kamara of the Kenema Methodist Church** led the team of people who cooked and catered for the whole of the training programme. In the event a 9.00am to 5.30pm time-tabled day for the week took place, largely as planned, and proved to be ideal. The earlier finish allowed people to return to the homes in which  they were being hosted with time to reflect on the day and to socialise with each other and their hosts.

In preparing the course of training on Effective Management and Administration, we tried to strike a balance between the larger issues relating to Leadership and Management in the church and the more detailed practical concerns required of all Superintendents and Desk Officers relating to accounts etc. etc.

Revd Dr Stephen Skuce painted a picture of the larger background of Methodism with reference to its pragmatic leader, John Wesley, indigenous participants in world mission and relationships with other religions. Revd Richard Jackson looked at management/leadership teaching, secular and sacred; and earthed accounting in the integrity of the individual and the detailed work required to achieve accountability at all levels of church life. Interactive sessions led by Revd Peter Clark on Development from the strategic planning stage through to dealing with Aid Agencies kept the participants very involved in the post-lunch sessions. Keith Phillips, the CCITC administrator shared something of the learning process that is part of the 'Doing' within a development programme, like the CCITC.

Gilbert & Sylvia Hall, in their own gracious way, through the devotional times and personal sharing epitomised what it means to be leaders who are sensitive to all, but who through caring pastoral relationships, minister rather than manage; as they helped put the 'ministration' into ad-ministration.

The MCSL President, Secretary of Conference, District Chairs and Desk Officers shared how they thought that Circuit Superintendents might help them fulfil their own responsibilities. If there was a prize for the fastest writer on a Flip Chart, it would have to go to:

**The Training Officer, Revd Solomon Van Kanei** (the son of teacher, late S. S. Kanei), who did an excellent job of coordinating the event with the help of the Kenema Superintendent Minister, Revd Leonard Yemi.

OTHER ACTIVITIES

'Out of Course' activities allowed the Sierra Leone newcomer, Stephen Skuce and Keith Phillips to join the President on a pastoral visit to Segbwema, surveying a new road in the making, whilst visiting some schools and the Nixon Memorial Hospital en route. Donations sent from Darlington through Mrs Norma Krishnan were delivered to the Kenema Primary School and the growing 'Jackson Secondary School' at Hangha was enriched through a personal visit. All of us involved in the programme were grateful for the hospitality shared throughout, but especially for the 'drinks social' donation from the former Vice-President of Conference and Methodist Secondary School Principal, Vandi Tarawalli. It made a fitting 'Au Revoir' until February for all of us who travelled by roads old and new to various destinations. Road building and renewal proceeds apace in Sierra Leone and the visiting team were able to go direct to Lungi Airport from Kenema for the flight home.

Conversations shared indicate that much of what had been hoped for on this first visit has been achieved. The participants will be doing 'homework' relating to their own situations before February, when there will be more opportunity for feed-back and response that we trust will embed the teaching given into their on-going learning experience of Effective Management and Administration.

**Richard Jackson (Revd)**               **International**
**Coordinator CCITC**

*Author's note October 2014: Part 2 of this MCSL training has been delayed by a change of leadership during the 2014 Methodist Conference and as a consequence of the continuing 'Ebola Epidemic'. Hopefully, the training partnership with MCSL will continue in 2015 with an added focus on training young people.*

# 2013/4 NOV 13-26: MCN LAY TRAINING PART 1

**INTRODUCTION TO TRAVEL ARRANGEMENTS**

As regular readers of these reports will know, travelling to our training destinations in West Africa is never without incident or interest. Once again with this visit to Nigeria we were left without visas until two days before we were due to travel. We will not go into details about the whole sorry saga, but frantic emails/telephone calls and last gasp Nigerian High Commission visits in London were all part of the emergency retrieval operation! This, backed up by James Bond style handovers, of visa-stamped passports on remote railway stations two days before travel, meant that Prof David Dunn-Wilson and Administrator, Keith Phillips travelling from London; the Coordinator Richard Jackson and Peter Worrell leaving Manchester; and Malcolm & Janet McCall from Glasgow met up in Amsterdam as planned on Wednesday 13th November for onward travel with KLM to Lagos.

**PROF. DDW, SOC & FRIEND**

Despite the confusion caused by the late arrangements, our hosts did not let us down and we were met by an enthusiastic deputation on our arrival at Lagos airport. After an overnight in Lagos, we travelled on by air to Owerri to begin the first of our two-part (Nov 2013 & Feb 2014) Lay Training sessions at Umuahia Methodist Training Institute (MTI). We were accompanied by the Secretary of Conference (SOC), Bishop Rafael Opoko, who like most of the leaders of both church and nation was attending a memorial service in the east of Nigeria relating to a national figure and military leader. Fears about lack of accommodation and absentees from the programme were alleviated in typically Nigerian fashion by SOC; our national coordinator, Very Revd Paul Olukunga; and the Rector (Principal) of the College, Very Revd I K Tasie whose combined efforts made it possible for us to stay in our usual Villa Roy hotel, which is conveniently situated alongside the college.

In the event, we had **fifty enthusiastic Lay Leaders** from a large number of dioceses in attendance. Many had taken time off work to undertake the Friday, Saturday and Sunday training programme. We had asked that each diocese should try to send at least one younger person and one woman in their  group of lay leaders. As a team, we were impressed by the calibre of the trainees and multiple roles in the church undertaken by those leaders registered for the course.

With limited time available, the lecturing programme on Methodism, Lay Leadership and Mission was intense, beginning at 8.00 in the morning and continuing through to the evening meal at 6.00pm, with just a brief break mid-morning and one hour for lunch. To compensate for the shorter lunch break, and to keep both the trainees and us awake in the sweltering heat during the post-lunch session, we introduced what proved to be highly successful Group Tutorials, within which the Lay Leaders in groups of ten, were able to share with the visiting lecturers their own concerns and receive encouragement and support from each other.

During these sessions it became clear that the issues relating to leadership being addressed by the visiting lecturers were stimulating the trainees own thinking about leadership in relation to their own context and the challenges facing the Methodist Church in Nigeria. Clearly, there are many issues relating to the hierarchical model and cost of leadership that are being addressed by the lay and ordained leadership of MCN, but the overwhelming impression given was that those that were undertaking the training sensed a significant change of mood. This was attributed to the 2006 constitution re-orientating MCN in relation to mission and evangelism; the inter-related 'Cliff College Training' of evangelists, priests, presbyters, bishops; and the recent transition of leadership that was encouraging them to 'take a lead' in their own situation. Concerns were expressed both in Umuahia and later in Sagamu at the overspending on leadership in many areas of the church's life. The leaders gathered acknowledged that lavish expenditure on ceremonies relating to funerals, birthday thanksgivings, multiple worship offerings new dioceses etc. etc. right through to 'gifts acknowledging service' took money away from priorities in the local situation that relate to mission.

**LAY LEADERS MEETING AT SAGAMU MTI**

We were blessed too as so many leaders at Umuahia and Sagamu shared testimony as to how local initiatives were helping them and the church to move forward in mission and ministry. Clearly, the motivation was there and several testified as to how new programmes relating to diocesan evangelism training, church planting and work with young people was growing. One leader's testimony here must suffice for many. Refusing to be constrained by lack of support and finance one leader has put together a 'Youth Orchestra'. She has encouraged those in her own situation who have the resources, but not the gifting for youth work to pay for the instruments as she generates interest amongst those who work with her in training musicians and keeping their young people in the life of their church!

**GIFTS OF CD'S, BOOKS AND RESOURCES**

In addition to the lecturing programme, we supplied every trainee with a CD filled with additional lectures, materials and books that will be helpful not only for their own studies in leadership, but also to link this programme with those studies undertaken in previous years by ordained MCN trainees and with leaders sharing in the Episcopal Training programme. A recently completed DVD of the history of CCITC (2002-13) which illustrates the training programmes undertaken in Nigeria and elsewhere was distributed also. As usual assignments relating to the programme on vision, church growth and becoming an invitational church, some requiring personal practical initiatives, were set to be completed in time for our next visit in February. Photographs were taken throughout and moving concluding devotions were followed by noisy farewells which saw most of the leaders returning home on Sunday evening in time for work on Monday morning.

On that same Monday morning the visiting team travelled again by road to Owerri airport, by air from Owerri to Lagos and again by road to Sagamu MTI. En route we met up at Owerri with the recently installed **Prelate, His Eminence Dr Samuel Uche,** who having spent time with us during the visit of Nigerian Bishops to Cliff College earlier this year greeted us as old friends.

### LAY TRAINING PART 1 AT SAGAMU MTI

In Sagamu, we were generously hosted once again on the Bishop's compound by our friends Babatunde and Abimbola Taiwo, and catered for by the National Coordinator Paul Olukunga and his team of two Kemi's. After the usual courtesies and meetings with the Rector, Very Revd Joshua Adeogun and lecturers who have become our friends, we repeated the Umuahia programme with **forty-one leaders attending the Friday to Sunday training programme in the Mellor Memorial Methodist Centre at Sagamu MTI.**

We encountered similar enthusiasm and responses from the participants, though changing venues (due to regular activities, including weddings and Sunday worship) within both centres created changes in atmosphere for both lecturers and trainees. It is interesting how the involvement of HQ staff and proximity to a larger centre like Lagos changes the dynamics and occasionally causes more disruption for the committed trainees. Nevertheless, with the exception of one or two, the trainees maintained their own admirable discipline within what were sometimes hot and trying conditions throughout the whole programme.

Four of the visiting team had experienced how hot and trying the conditions could be on the Wednesday previous when we accompanied our friend, the Bishop of Remo, on an early morning journey four hours by road to the Diocese of Edo-Delta to which he will be moving within a few days. We visited: the recently dedicated Wesley Cathedral, with its associated school, in a noisy but lively Benin City; met up with a New Generation Churches College Principal and current Cliff College PhD student, Pastor Usman Habib; and surveyed with the Bishop the virgin site purchased for a Bishop's house and training centre (on an aptly named Recreation Drive, which we quickly hyphenated and renamed as Re-Creation Drive). This will become, in time, his new home located on the outskirts of Benin City. The return journey was marked and marred by the breakdown of the vehicle air conditioner and oncoming traffic choosing to divert on to the better side of the supposed dual carriageway at their own discretion!!

## LAGOS PLANNING FOR WHAT LIES AHEAD

Our final day in Nigeria was spent in Lagos allowing the visiting group to see the sights, and the team together with the Prelate and the Secretary of Conference, to spend several hours in Conference Office reviewing reactions to the programme. We shared too in planning for what  may lie ahead in February and again in June when we are being asked to organise a heritage tour similar to that organised for the visiting Bishops in May this year. Provisional dates, subject to sign-ups were set for the $10^{th}$ to $22^{nd}$ June 2014 with the first few days being spent at Cliff College (including a visit to Epworth) followed by visits to Bristol, via Mow Cop etc. and London, via Oxford.

The training visit was concluded in what has become our traditional way with food and fellowship shared at the home of Bishop Raphael Opoko, the Secretary of Conference. It was particularly fitting on this occasion, because Alice, Bishop Opoko's wife and our hostess on many

315

earlier visits, had shared with us and other trainees during the training at Sagamu her 50th birthday celebration which took place on the Saturday of our training programme, with cake and prayers!

We ended the day on the final Monday as we began, at Lagos airport with concerns about a delay in arriving back in Amsterdam with engineers working to change the front wheel on our scheduled aircraft. We were delayed in Lagos, but fortunately, the team and just as importantly our luggage, arrived in time at Amsterdam early on Tuesday morning to be transferred to our connecting flights to London, Manchester and Glasgow. Spare a thought and a prayer for Malcolm & Janet McCall who through the vagaries of flight security

had to return to Glasgow with KLM before returning back immediately to Amsterdam for a next day flight to South Africa to spend time with their family there!

The Lagos statue set in the attractive gardens dedicated to Madam Efunroye Tinubu, an opponent of slavery and colonialism, who died in 1887, **symbolises the empowerment that learning and knowledge can bring.**

**This set alongside the verbal and visual beauty of the Beatitudes upper window in the Tinubu Cathedral,** seat of the Prelate in Lagos, seems to sum up for us what we are working to achieve through the Cliff College International Training Centre.

Our own prayer is that those to whom we go are as blessed as we are through our sharing together in a practical partnership that is mutually rewarding.

# CHAPTER 14 2014: SPONTANEOUS EXPANSION

*2014 heralded the completion of the first lay training programme in Nigeria with 83 leaders graduating from the course at the two centres of Umuahia MTI and Sagamu MTI. Part 2 of the Management & Administration course was postponed in an Ebola threatened Sierra Leone. We organised a June UK study/heritage tour for MCN lay leaders and in July/August a new training (ad)venture was pioneered in Uganda. The CCITC Coordinator was welcomed as both a friend and the Delegate from the British Conference at the MCN Conference held in Port Harcourt during August.*

## 2014/1 FEB 12-25: MCN LAY TRAINING PART 2

INTRODUCTION TO COMPLETION & GRADUATION

The success of Part 2 of our partnership training programme with the Methodist Church Nigeria can be summed up with the simple statistics that show:

LAY LEADERS 'CERTIFIED' AT UMUAHIA MTI

On Monday, 17<sup>th</sup> February, 47 Lay Leaders (9 Women & 38 Men) out of the 50 enrolled in November at Umuahia Methodist Training Institute who were in attendance at the February residentials and had completed their assignments graduated with a Cliff College: "International Certificate In Methodism, Leadership and Mission" (ICI-MLM).

Again on Monday, 24<sup>th</sup> February, 36 Lay Leaders (10 Women & 26 Men) out of the 41 enrolled in November at Sagamu MTI, graduated to the sound of great celebrations. We were pleased to have our hoped-for mingling of age groups as well as gender with 13 of the participants under the age of 30; 17 aged between 31-40; 40 aged 41-60 and just 8 leaders over the age of 60 and 5 who were 'age-less'!!

Many of those completing the course are professionally employed and had to arrange time off from their place of work to attend the programme. Most have multiple responsibilities for leadership in the life of their churches ranging from Children/Youth Workers through to Lay Presidents/Preachers and Evangelists. About half of the MCN Dioceses had at least one representative attending the programme. Though the numbers enrolled were fewer than originally intended, what was lacking in numbers was more than made up for in the quality and diversity of the participating groups at both centres. Younger and more seasoned leaders learned to listen as well as speak to each other and they themselves insisted that we should make provision for having their contact details (email addresses & mobile numbers) shared so that they could remain in touch with each other.

### A COMMENTARY ON THE COURSE BEING CONCLUDED AT BOTH CENTRES

These shared statistics may allow you to feel that you need read no further, but then you would miss out on the colourful diversity of the relationships being developed between the Methodist Church Nigeria and the British and Irish Methodist Churches through the work of the Cliff College ITC. Thanks to the support received from the British Methodist Church, MMS(Ireland) and the generosity of other sponsors our 'Partnership in Training' programmes undertaken within Nigeria since 2005 have seen further training in mission and ministry being given to several hundred Lay Pastors, Evangelists, Priests, Presbyters, Bishops and more recently these courses for Lay Leaders. This backed up by friendships created during the 2013 visit of 46 MCN Bishops to Cliff College, UK Districts and the Methodist Heritage Tour means that wherever we go in Nigeria we are received as friends who belong to the Methodist Church in Nigeria rather than visiting strangers.

318

The regular visiting team of: Revd Dr Malcolm & Mrs Janet McCall; Peter Worrell (MCN Knight of Charles Wesley); Keith Phillips (MCN Knight of John Wesley); and the Coordinator, Revd Richard Jackson; supported so ably on this occasion by Prof David Dunn-Wilson, was pleased this time also to have a former Mission Partner & President of the Irish Methodist Conference, Revd S Kenneth Todd sharing lectures on Leadership in Methodism.

**LEARNING TOGETHER TO READ THE BOOKS**

The lecturing input on all of our programmes is augmented by the provision of books for trainees (For Lay Leaders: Africa Bible Commentary; New Bible Dictionary and Commentary; African Christian Theology; and Norman Shields, Christian Ethics for Africa). For the first time we provided also a memory stick with up to 1.3 GB of supplementary teaching (including several books) on mission and ministry for each of the participating leaders. As might be expected the leaders were thrilled to receive the books and materials provided, and the experiment of generating discussion with the books in their hands on relevant topics to be found in these books proved its worth.

Whilst the shared worship, Bible Studies and lecturing input was appreciated, it was in the interactive discussion sessions that the real issues affecting the church were given a voice. The MCN Leadership's focus on growth was applauded but serious questions were being raised about the cost in time and money of sustaining the ceremonials associated with the hierarchical nature of MCN ministry that seems to belie the original concept of 'Towards an Indigenous Church'. There was recognition that in some areas money meant for mission was being diverted to maintaining ceremonial visits and services with all the associated expenses. Again sensible concerns were being raised about the short-termism of much of the ministry with too many in ministry at all levels being moved on just at the point when they were becoming more effective leaders in mission with outreach and adding numbers to the church.

319

The Lay Leaders' were most appreciative of the involvement and support of the Rectors, Staff and the regular students of the colleges, most of them in training for the Methodist ministry. At Umuahia the returning students traditionally pray through the College Grounds and join in their own Covenant Service on the Sunday afternoon. On this occasion, that service was enriched by the participation of the Lay Leaders from our programme and the preaching of Revd Ken Todd as they celebrated together, with the college staff, ministerial trainees, and visiting lecturers in an inspiring Covenant Communion cum Celebration Service on Sunday evening. This was followed by everyone supporting the Lay Leaders in their Monday Graduation Service and presentation of certificates with the Archbishop of Umuahia, Most Revd Sunday Agwu. The learned experience at Umuahia was repeated at Sagamu MTI, as the shared service on Sunday evening paved the way for a celebratory occasion on Monday morning attended by the college **Rector and staff, with Bishop Michael Akinwale and Sir Chief Awofala as special guest,** encouraging the trainees and receiving them with their Cliff College Certificates on behalf of MCN.

### BENIN CITY AND ENTHRONEMENT OF BISHOP TAIWO

When we set up the two week programme with timetables and timing of flights etc. there seemed to be some leeway built-in, but the 'best-laid plans of …..!' Adjustments were made for the Coordinator to share in the Saturday evening building dedication of the new Bishop's House, and the Sunday enthronement of our friend and support, Rt. Revd Babatunde Taiwo as the Bishop of Edo-Delta. This meant a four hour drive for lecturer Revd Dr Ekebuisi who took Revd Richard Jackson from Umuahia MTI, via Owerri and over the Niger at Onitsha to the Cathedral in Benin City on Saturday afternoon. The journey felt worthwhile as friends old and new made their appreciation of Cliff College and its training known and this visiting (former Sierra Leonean Chair of District from 1975=Nigerian Bishop) was given the honour of sharing with MCN Archbishops in making sure that Bishop

Taiwo was properly enthroned securely in his seat. The afterglow of the Sunday celebration with the journey broken by a brief courtesy visit to Rt. Revd Dennis Mark, the Bishop of Owerri and his family, made the afternoon return journey to Umuahia seem much shorter.

### HOSPITALITY & ROYAL CROSS METHODIST HOSPITAL

A Sunday evening invitation at Umuahia to share a meal with the former Rector, now Bishop Igwe and his wife Udoh in their new home provided a helpful social context for wide-ranging conversations that included shared thinking about the planned revision of the MCN Constitution.

**MMS (Ireland) support for the Royal Cross Methodist Hospital, Ugwueke, prompted an hour-long journey led by Revd Ken Todd to the hospital** on the Monday afternoon after the Umuahia graduations. We shared in a fascinating tour of the developing hospital guided by the administrator, Sir Chief Paul Okorie and in conversation over food with the devoted Medical Director, Dr Hans Van Den Corput, we (and through Ken, MMS Ireland), were made aware of both current positive growth and continuing concerns about future developments. A Monday evening fellowship meal at the home of Archbishop Agwu and his wife Elizabeth incorporated the traditional greeting 'kola' ceremony that others may need to explain to the un-initiated!

### CONFERENCE OFFICERS CONSULTATION IN LAGOS

Our plans for next few days on our return to Lagos en route to Sagamu MTI changed several times. Eventually, we found a time when it would be possible to meet up with the Prelate of MCN, His Eminence Dr Samuel Uche. The Prelate made available a very small 'window' in his travelling schedule. After his meeting with the Governor on Tuesday afternoon we met with him and his wife at his home on Tuesday evening before he travelled again on Wednesday to the east of Nigeria for a family wedding and other meetings that would keep him out of Lagos until we had returned to the UK.

 During our relaxed conversations with food and drink provided, The Prelate made it clear that he and the Methodist Church Nigeria were pressing through the Methodist World Church Relations office in London for the continued involvement of Cliff College ITC with its training programmes. The Prelate invited the CCITC Coordinator personally (at MCN expense) to be part of the MCN Conference due to take place 4-11th August 2014 and to share with the Conference aspects of the further training programme.

Apart from the proposed 'Lay Leaders' training visit to Cliff College and UK tour of Methodist Heritage sites planned for 10-22nd June 2014, the Prelate would like us to run a further two-part Lay Training programme beginning in November 2014 and concluding by March 2015 as well as beginning a new two year programme for Presbyters beginning in January 2015. Obviously, the planning and funding for these programmes is in the early stages of negotiation, but the Prelate is convinced that this kind of further training in mission and ministry is making a difference to the church as a whole and he wants to see it built into their further training programme.

The Secretary of Conference, Revd Dr Raphael Opoko, who had just returned from 12 days at the WCC HQ in Geneva, joined us briefly that evening, but then hosted us in his Lagos Conference Office on Wednesday morning, before he too headed off east for Episcopal Enthronements and further meetings. The new Prelate (as with the recently retired Prelate) and the Secretary of Conference are at one with the MCN church as a whole in enthusiastically commending the training work being done in partnership with Cliff College ITC.

Our friend, the administrator of MCN, the Very Revd Dr Sunday Onadipe, kindly provided an updating tour of the progress being made with the church planted as the 'Wesley Chapel' Lekki in Lagos. The rapid growth in numbers attending  the partly built worship centre, are being matched by the grandiose nature of the concept and the rapid progress being made with the building. A vision for mission indeed!

As we travelled on from Lagos to Sagamu MTI for the final phase of our training visit we met in a college that is almost unrecognisable from that which was in existence just three years ago. The CCITC sponsored improvements to the water supply and the long-delayed completion of the Mellor Memorial Methodist Centre last year seem to have inspired a generosity locally with a family influenced by Mellor that is spending millions of Naira to make this Methodist Training Centre into a fantastic, but functional centre for further training.

The 'Lay Leaders', meeting at Sagamu, like those at Umuahia, had taken seriously the requirements of the course and the assignments submitted on topics as diverse as Growing a Church; Mistakes being repeated in MCN; and Becoming an Invitational Church, were generally of a good standard for this kind of course. **The smile on the face of the wife of the Secretary of Conference, Mrs Alice Opoko,** who managed to balance responsibilities with another programme for Minister's wives and  the care of her family, with her commitment to this course, says all that needs to be said, about what it has meant to so many to share in such a programme and achieve the hoped-for result.

A youthful Nigerian violinist (not Sir Peter Worrell) helped us celebrate as "One Body", with spontaneous shouts from MCN worship of "Worthy is the Lamb, Hallelujah!" and Cliff College's, "Christ for All, All for Christ."

*"Worthy is the Lamb. Hallelujah!"*        *"Christ for All, All for Christ."*

*"One Body"*

# 2014/2 FEB 18: SIGNPOSTS TO FUTURE PLANS

Obviously, there have been throughout the programme ad-hoc planning meetings held with MCN leaders and College partners, with friendly, free and frank exchanges! (See also 2008/2) Shared below is a non-confidential example of notes of meetings held between the Prelate of Methodist Church Nigeria (MCN), Revd Richard Jackson, Coordinator of Cliff College International Training Centre (CCITC) and other key people. This meeting was held at the Prelate's home, on Tuesday evening, 18th February 2014 and shares something of the business discussed and the relaxed atmosphere within which such meetings have taken place..

The Prelate graciously welcomed and provided hospitality for the CCITC team, before Revd Ken Todd, joined the Prelate and the CCITC Coordinator for a brief business meeting and time of fellowship.

Concerns were again raised about the Nigerian visa situation for the team and the Prelate promised to follow this up personally in Nigeria (Abuja and Lagos) seeking longer term multiple entry visas provision for key members of the CCITC team.

Revd Jackson, backed up by Revd Todd, provided a positive report on the recent training programmes being undertaken by the Lay Leaders. Full report to follow! (Already circulated-RJ). Revd Todd shared on behalf of MMS(Ireland) aspects of our visit to, and sharing with staff at, the Royal Cross Methodist Hospital, Ugwueke

The Prelate invited Revd Jackson to come to the Part Harcourt Conference (August 4-11th 2014) at MCN expense (in addition to the WCR Delegates) to address the Conference with regard to 'Training Programmes'. The Prelate will be consulting with WCR representatives about the funding and support for the continuation of the current Lay Training programme from November 2014 with Part 2 in March 2015 and a new beginning for the two-year CCITC programme beginning in January 2015.

We agreed that the Prelate/SOC would send out 'final reminders' to all Episcopal Leaders reminding them that their submissions on 'Forward Together' needed to be in the hands of the

Secretary of Conference by the end of June if they are to receive their certificates at Conference in August.

The Cliff College training and Heritage Tour, primarily for Lay Leaders, scheduled for June 10-22 will proceed with a minimum number of 20 people, but at least £1,000.00 non-returnable deposit per person should be received at Cliff College before the end of March 2014 if the Tour is not to be postponed. Prelate/SOC and Bishop Babatunde Taiwo to follow up!

The Prelate, and SOC who was able to join us part way through the meeting were pleased to make provision for gifts with some reciprocation on behalf of the team by Revd's Todd and Jackson.

Despite the busy schedule of both the Prelate and the SOC, we once again enjoyed our time together and felt completely at home with our friends that evening and with SOC, the following morning in his Lagos office.

**Richard Jackson (Revd)     Coordinator CCITC**

## 2014/3 JUN 10-22: CLIFF & UK HERITAGE TOUR

INTRODUCTION

Following on from the much appreciated visit by a large number of MCN Episcopal Leaders, who were also hosted in UK Districts last year, the newly elected Prelate, His Eminence (Dr) Samuel C K Uche JP; backed by the Secretary of Conference, Rt. Revd (Dr) Chibuzo Raphael Opoko TPG asked that a similar pioneering programme be arranged in 2014 for a small number of Lay Leaders. The arrangements made coincided with the official inauguration of the Nigerian Methodists Chaplaincy which took place in Wesley's Chapel in London on Sunday, 8th June 2014. The Prelate was the preacher at the well-attended celebration service where

**Very Revd Dr Deji Okegbile a graduate of Cliff College & Manchester University was commissioned as Chaplain.**

The larger group of those enrolled for the Training Retreat/Heritage Tour, joined by others already in the UK, were picked up at Heathrow Airport and transported to Cliff College on Tuesday the 10th June. Inevitably, adjustments were being made on all sides as necessary business meetings in London and elsewhere were attended by the Prelate, the Secretary of Conference and key leaders who were in Britain as part of the programme.

Eventually, a group of 14 key leaders, among who were: The Prelate's wife Mrs Florence Uche and the Lay President of the MCN Conference Sir Nathanael Jimmy-Coker, and his wife, Virginia, gathered together at Cliff College for a full programme of timetabled activities as outlined below:

**THE LAY PRESIDENT & HIS WIFE**

CLIFF RESIDENTIAL: "GREAT EXPECTATIONS"

## (Tuesday June 10th to Monday, June 16th)

From the beginning of the programme with Piers Lane's interactive (fun) learning games about leadership through to the deeply moving final communion service led by the Principal, Revd Dr Chris Blake we sensed that God was at work amongst his people gathered in this way at Cliff College.

Revd Dr Malcolm (in his usual demonstrative style) & Mrs Janet McCall (more sedately) linked their morning devotions with studies that reminded us of our Biblical Heritage and the consequences for our Discipleship.

Prof David Dunn-Wilson revived our understanding of Matthew's Gospel with fresh insights as he explored with the group how Matthew might be interpreted as 'A Gospel for the Vulnerable'.

On Saturday morning Revd Dr Ben Pugh introduced the group to the Biblical Metaphors relating to the Atonement and Revd Dr Stephen Skuce majored on a significant topic for present-day Nigeria providing 'An Authentic Wesleyan Response to People of Other Faiths'.

The distribution of free books and CD's of additional lectures was welcomed by those participating, but they would have little enough time to examine them in detail until their return home.

Nearby Chatsworth and Eyam competed for interest with 'shopping expeditions' during the 'free' afternoons. The Coordinator's evening lectures, prayers and social conversations in the pleasantly refurbished Broadbelt/Eagles buildings provided some linkage between our anticipated Heritage visits; the life story of the Wesleys; and the growth of Methodism.

Obviously, the highlight for most of the lay leaders who had never been there before was the Friday visit to Epworth with the shared opportunity of walking where the Wesleys walked, worshipping and praying together in what they acknowledged and appreciated in typical African fashion as hallowed places.

Once again our thanks must go to all the staff at The Rectory and Revd David Leese and his team at the Wesley Memorial Methodist Church who so ably guided our visitors through a day of devotion and re-dedication in that historic setting.

For Sunday worship, the group of Lay Leaders was broken down into car-loads of worshippers as they ventured out to attend near-by churches. As last year, the visitors commented on the friendliness of the welcome at Totley Rise, Eyam and Calver, and the quality of the worship enjoyed but there were comments too and concern expressed at the age profile and the small numbers of regular worshippers in these churches.

### HERITAGE TOUR: POTTERIES, BRISTOL, OXFORD & LONDON

It would be invidious (and a little boring) to repeat our thanks for the hospitality given by everyone throughout the extended Heritage Tour with overnight stays at the Premier Inns in Bristol, Oxford and London.

En route, we took in visits to the home of **Primitive Methodism and climbed Mow Cop,** followed by a visit to the Mow Cop church and Englesea Brook Museum.

We will let a few pictures from the places visited speak for themselves about the learning, fellowship and fun enjoyed by the whole group as experience after experience was shared with the group and then through the group became a challenge to honour the commitment of the past by our own activities in the present and the future.

Bristol, under the guidance of David Worthington, took us through the **oldest Methodist Chapel in the world at the New Room (1739)** and the associated museum followed by a tour of Charles Wesley's house.

Oxford was introduced to us by its renowned Wesleyan Scholar Revd **Dr Martin Wellings, stationed at Wesley Memorial Church and his Anglican friends associated with Christ Church and Lincoln College.**

During our last few days in London we arranged structured visits, tours at Wesley's Chapel and Westminster Central Hall, (with its BBC Balcony viewing area for recent great national events associated with Westminster Abbey-see picture below).Experience gained from the

visitors with us last year meant that, having mastered the mysteries of the 'Oyster Card' we allowed much more free time in London for 'tourist' activities and meeting up with friends/family at church and other events being held in and around the capital.

REVD DR LESLIE GRIFFITHS &
REVD JENNIFER POTTER

It would be inappropriate for me to share here what was in their communique to the Methodist Church Nigeria. Nevertheless, the fact that the visiting group were recommending to their Conference that a, "Cliff College Retreat and Heritage Tour", be made a bi-annual programme for laity and clergy during the non-conference years, commencing from 2015, says enough about the impact of these programmes to justify a more direct involvement by our own Conference in sponsoring and supporting such programmes for partner churches. Our partners from overseas continue to value the 'Heritage' shared through their 'Mother Church'.

But then, I am well aware of how often 'expensive' tours to the UK and Methodist Heritage sites are arranged for our friends from the USA. I find that I am challenged to do more (perhaps with the help of the Methodist Heritage Trust and our World Church Relations officers) to facilitate such visits from less well-off areas of Wesley's World Parish!

We shall see, but for me, the suggestion made by this group under their new leader was testimony to how much has been achieved in personal, ecumenical and international relationships through this visit.

Thank you again to all who in different ways have contributed so much to making this training retreat such an enriching experience for everyone involved. May God continue to bless the Methodist Church in Nigeria and bring refreshing through our overseas partners to the Methodist Church at home!

# 2014/4 JUL 29-AUG 2: UGANDAN PATHFINDING

INTRODUCTION

Cliff College International Training Centre (CITC), with encouragement from Dr Olubunmi Olayisade (Africa Secretary, World Church Relations (WCR), responded to an initiative taken by Revd Dr Tom Kisitu, a Ugandan minister serving in Scotland by arranging for a team of lecturers to provide an introductory training course for the Methodist Church Uganda (MCU). As a Ugandan, the Revd Dr Tom Kisitu was overall Team Leader. The trainers were: The Revd Dr Peter Ensor who used his annual "main leave" from Kenya Methodist University Campus, Meru, to travel and give his services free of charge. The Revd Dr Usman Habib, former Cliff College student, was given permission to attend from the CGMI Bible School in Benin City, Nigeria. He also claimed no expenses from any church or institution; bearing personally his total costs of around 1000 British pounds. The Revd Dr Malcolm and Mrs. Janet McCall represented the CCITC Core Team. The Team leader Tom asked Malcolm to take responsibility for the Introductory Course itself.

RESPONDING IN UGANDA

SUMMARY STATEMENT: "The LORD your God carried you all the way" (Deut1:13).

Sixty-six participants completed this Introductory Course, including all 5 ordained ministers and probationers who are connected with the Kenya-related Methodist Church of Uganda. The General Superintendent, the Revd Amooti Bagambi provided encouraging support by attending every session. The other participants included: pastor-evangelists; church stewards, and treasurers; youth and children's church workers; local preachers; and prospective ministerial candidates.

There was an almost equal mix of men and women and the average age was under 30 – a youthfulness which was reflected in the vitality and enthusiasm of the group as a whole. The students' eager commitment to the course was quite remarkable. For example, the original lunch break of 2 hours was shortened to 1½ hours (and thereafter to 1¼ hours) by popular demand, in order to provide more

time for teaching and discussion. On at least one occasion the students were **spontaneously worshipping** together in a lively praise session, even before the trainers arrived to start morning devotions.

TEACHING AND TRAINING

Monday afternoon was reserved for Welcome and Registration. Tuesday to Friday became full teaching days. Dr Usman Habib introduced each day with lively and powerful praise and worship, which was followed by a series of Bible Studies on foundational subjects led by Revd Dr McCall. Revd Dr Peter followed up with a brilliant series of lectures on "Leadership in the New Testament." Mrs Janet McCall divided her sessions between "English for Gospel Communication" and exegesis of "All one in Christ Jesus" (Gal 3.28) In addition, Dr Usman provided 3 lectures on the work of the Holy Spirit in the life of the Christian leader.

On Friday morning, Tom also opened up the Course to Christian leaders of any denomination in Jinja to join the Course for two hours of challenge by Revd Usman Habib on "Accountable Servant Leadership." About 10 leaders took advantage of this invitation. The whole group hung on his every word, and in a huge response at the end of the session, many people publicly committed themselves to a transformed life of humble service, financial transparency and obedience to established church authority.

Saturday morning was reserved for Worship, Celebration and Commissioning. We used the central part of the Covenant Service in this inspiring act of worship – many of the students had never shared in this precious Service before – and the celebration concluded with the Lord's Supper, led by Revd Tom Kisitu.

LOCATION

MCU had no suitable venue combining sleeping and catering facilities with an adequate conference infrastructure. However, the YWAM campus on the edge of Jinja provided all that was required on all these fronts. Mr. Antoine and Mrs. Cissie Kabanga, the campus wardens, were excellent hosts at both material and spiritual levels: we cannot thank them enough. The conference facilities included permanently-fitted power-point projection equipment, which Dr Usman used to good effect. The YWAM centre is a "prayed-in-place" with a peaceful spiritual atmosphere, overlooking Lake Victoria: a better setting would be difficult to imagine.

As regards accommodation for the visiting lecturers, Miss Anne Muyanga (Tom's sister-in-law), with great generosity, provided rooms in her brand-new "orphan-oriented" home. We were greatly blessed by this provision, including meals when necessary. During the week's course we shared meals with our students on the YWAM campus.

**TOM KISITU & JOSEPH KYEGOMBE**

The challenge in this arrangement was transport: without the virtually non-stop help of Mr. Joseph Kyegombe and his Land Cruiser, the situation would have been impracticable. We owe a great debt of gratitude to Joseph, who works for the Uganda Methodist Relief and Development Support Agency. Also, Peter had driven the Meru Campus Methodist 4x4 all the way from Kenya to Jinja, and so was able to provide extra lifts in his vehicle. Transport, apart from Joseph and Peter's kindness, would have been a real logistical nightmare!

**LECTURE NOTES AND BOOKS:**

All the trainers had prepared lecture notes. The photocopying of the notes in Jinja was not a problem in itself, but the day we wanted to buy reams of paper to do it turned out to be a public holiday for Eid-Al-Fittr! We had hoped that most students would have access to a PC, enabling the use of memory sticks. Sadly, it quickly became apparent that very few had computer access, and almost none owned their own computers. Providentially, we were able to take with us 75 copies of one book, A Guide to Interpreting Scripture, which had been recommended to us by our long-standing friends at the Langham Trust

Literature headquarters in Carlisle. Its author, Michael Kyomya, turned out to be the present Anglican Bishop of the Jinja diocese! Langham Literature HQ noted that the exporting of books to Uganda was usually trouble-free, efficient and speedy. Perhaps in any future visits, we will not need to carry a huge weight of books in our personal luggage! (The book we carried with us was paid for from CCITC reserve funds.)

## FINANCE

Without any allocated grant for this visit, finances were "on a shoe string" from the beginning. However, the inevitable challenges of the situation were compounded by several unexpected problems. Two hospital-visits were needed in connection with members of the Course, and Tom had to spend much time and endless visits to Jinja town centre in order to address the various financial issues. Unlike the Nigerian and even Sierra Leone Churches, MCU is new, small and financially challenged. However, the sheer verve and dynamism of the young people who came for this CCITC training hopefully heralds better times ahead.

## CLIFF COLLEGE NATIONAL COORDINATING GROUP:

MCU, under the Revd Amooti, took an initiative in forming a small National Cliff College Coordination Group. (Dr McCall tried to insist that any future visits were conditional on the agreement of Cliff College, a SALT Committee grant, and Dr Olubumni Olayisade: but everyone else insisted on prophetically planning for the future!) The Coordinating Group, under the supervision of the Revd Amooti, consists of the Revd Moses Dikange and the Revd David Ntogonya, together with Mrs. Jane Bagambi, Amooti's wife.

## ENGLISH LANGUAGE PROFICIENCY:

Before the beginning of the Course, an *ad hoc* team had travelled round the Ugandan Methodist Churches, aiming to discover those who could best profit from the Training Week, and making arrangements for them to join. (Joseph had been instrumental in enabling this "screening group" to travel round the various churches.) One key criterion for this group was whether any possible student could handle teaching, conversation and written work in English, without the need of an interpreter. At the beginning of our week, Janet

333

provided tools for assessing competence in English through (a) a "basic points" multiple–choice grammar test, and (b) a short piece of written work on the subject, "How Jesus led me to Himself." When Janet has marked these, it should be possible to provide an objective indication of how many students would meet the demands of a CCITC Diploma Course. Anecdotal evidence during the introductory week suggests that all but a small number have (at least) adequate conversational English and good English comprehension.

CONCLUSION:

Sadly, the hoped-for observers from the Rwanda Methodist Church were not able to come to the Introductory Course. But the sixty-six Ugandan participants took full advantage of the course, showing great appreciation and a huge eagerness to pursue a full two-year  Diploma Course - though no promises were made. This eagerness is led by the Revd Amooti himself, with the support of the presiding Methodist Bishop in Nairobi.

The introductory course participants were provided with a 1500 word assignment, to be submitted by 19th January 2015. The title of the assignment is: *"Prayerfully undertake a Spirit-led evangelistic initiative, either personal or church-based. Explain your goals and methods, and summarize the outcomes of this initiative."* With typical drive, enthusiasm and faith, Revd Dr Usman sent out the participants at the end of the week with this message: "By the end of the year, let us see MCU establish 5 church plants". We do believe that the Holy Spirit was powerfully moving amongst us all during the sessions of our Introductory Course. Whatever the longer–term future holds, we earnestly expect that by God's grace, the goal set by Dr Usman Habib will be met!

***Report presented by Revd Dr Malcolm McCall: Core Team Member CCITC***

# 2014/5 AUG 4-11: MCN CONFERENCE

The International Co-ordinator of CCITC, Revd Richard Jackson, found himself invited to the August 2014 MCN Conference, not only representing Cliff College, but also the British Methodist Conference. Though no stranger to Nigeria, I flew with Air France from Manchester to Port Harcourt for the first time and again a first, found that one of my suitcases did not arrive. To say that the suitcase took from the Friday to the following Wednesday to catch up with me is to minimise the efforts through constant calls and visits to the airport by my hosts that eventually re-united me with my suitcase. I was welcomed at the airport by Revd John Eze, a friend and former student of Cliff College with a policeman escort: a reminder of a very different attitude to security in the oil industry centre of Port Harcourt and showing an awareness of the threat of Boko Haram terrorists to such large church Conferences, wherever they are held. Security and the less obvious threat posed by the spread of the Ebola epidemic to Nigeria were never too far from the thoughts and prayers of the 500 or so Methodists attending the Conference from every part of Nigeria.

As a Fraternal Delegate I was accommodated in the Rachael Hotel just across the road from Wesley Methodist church where I preached on the Sunday before the Methodist Conference proper began on Tuesday, 5th August 2014. The MCN Conference is structured with a shared (Ministerial & Lay) gathering for the joint opening Eucharist and the Prelate's address on the first day (Tuesday). This is followed by separate Lay and Ministerial Agendas, until Thursday morning when the whole Conference meets together for the Representative Sessions and associated events through till late on Sunday evening.

**THE 2014 METHODIST CHURCH NIGERIA CONFERENCE**

The theme of the Conference based on Exodus 14 v15 was, "Let my people move forward".

This set the mission tone for the Conference and was returned to in Bible Studies, Prayer and Preaching throughout. The Bishop of Evangelism, Rt. Revd Edoka Amuta, used Hebrews 12 v1-3 during the Opening Eucharist to address the issue of required change by, "Dealing with bottlenecks to our moving forward."

After the Opening Ceremony, the Prelate, His Eminence, Dr Samuel Emeka Kanu Uche JP, leading his first MCN Conference (of what is likely to be a ten-year tenure) took up the theme in a wide-ranging address. Dr Uche led us from an exposition of the biblical journey of Moses and the mixed response of God's people to highlight many of the issues being faced by MCN at the present time. His keynote address looked at aspects of church life and its growth and raised 'domestic' concerns

about sustaining the continuity of institutions like the Wesley University of Science and Technology (WUSTO) and the Theological Colleges. The Prelate moved on to address issues regarding the 'State of the Nation', Boko Haram, and the pastoral support that is being given to those who are hardest hit by the insurgency and the kidnap of the girls in the north of the country. He then closed his address by looking forward with hope to the General Election planned for 2015 and appealed for free and fair elections that should not be marred by coercion of any kind, but should be marked by the integrity of everyone who will be involved.

The traditional administrative corrections, presentations, rules of debate and courtesies etc. were observed as the Ministerial Session of Conference was constituted under the guidance of the indefatigable Secretary of Conference and 'Guardian of the Narrow Gate' Rt. Revd Dr C Raphael Opoko. The conference greeted, not one, but two 'Prelates Emeritus' as the immediate past **Prelate, Sunday Ola Makinde was joined on the front pew by Sunday Mbang, the first in line.** Given names are significant for Nigerians and much play was made about Sunday being followed by Sunday, but the tradition being broken by Prelate Uche, whose initial 'S' refers to Samuel rather than a third Sunday!

The fraternal delegates were welcomed and the greetings from the Methodist Church in Britain, Benin and Zimbabwe were conveyed to the MCN Conference. For those conversant with the confidential sessions of Ministerial Synods and Conferences the process of dealing with matters relating to the retirement and discipline of ministers would be nothing new, but to see 162 ordinands examined by a lottery of numbering was an experience not often shared. To have the same 162 ordinands, received on stage at the Saturday afternoon, uniquely African concert in the middle of the 'Prelate's Party', when they were accepted into full connexion by the Representative Session was unusual but celebratory to say the least.

**The sight of that same group of people receiving ordination at the hands of the Prelate and the Methodist Episcopacy at the Methodist Cathedral on Sunday afternoon was the climax of the whole Conference, but I am moving ahead of myself.**

On Thursday morning, it felt a little like déjà vu as we began again with another shared Eucharist at Wesley Methodist Church bringing the two sessions of Conference together as one Representative session. The Conference Delegates then moved in organised chaos by mini-buses, cars and coaches to the huge Civic Centre where we were to meet for the next three days.

**Providentially, the Lay President of the Methodist Conference for a number of years, Sir Jimmy Coker, a Knight of John Wesley,** *(Leading MCN Laymen can be made a Knight of either*

*John Wesley, awarded for outstanding service or Charles for their musical contribution)* is a leading member of the Port Harcourt

Archdiocese in which the Conference was being held. Sir Jimmy, with the organising committee had arranged the seating in the Centre in such a way that the hierarchical model of earlier conference seating arrangements with Archbishops, Bishops and Clergy (with Lay Knights and Trustees) predominating in the front seats, was broken down. Instead, we found a large number of small tables at which delegates from the same dioceses whether Lay or Clergy were grouped together. To the three-time observer of the MCN Conferences this change seemed to nurture relationships and improve participation in the debates from microphones set up around the centre. As is the case with most large Conferences the pre-preparation done with those due to attend who are unfamiliar with procedures can help them to be part of the democratic process in church as well as state.

MCN AND BRITISH METHODISM

A report of the Conference being circulated to so many people is not the place to go into detail about every aspect of a very full agenda, so I will content myself and at least some of my readers by mentioning three highlights with UK linked connections.

**1.     Associated with the Directorate of Evangelism Report** on a variety of Nigerian 'Mission' and training initiatives there were indications of the knock-on effect of outreach and support being given in turn by the British Methodist Church through MCN to some of the smaller churches in West Africa. Following on from the support given to the Methodist Church Sierra Leone

as five of their ministers completed their MA's in Nigeria, fraternal delegates and reports spoke of the work being supported in The Republic of Benin, Equatorial Guinea, Togo and Gabon. This bodes well for a West African partnership in mission that reaches well beyond the borders of Nigeria and should be encouraged in every way possible.

**2.     Under the Health Secretary, Deaconess Iboronke Oworu's Medical Report,** appreciation was expressed for the continuing support given through the Nigeria Health Care Project (NHCP). Reports were shared of the January 2014 visit of the Trustees and developments that were taking place. Long-term mission partner Sister Ros Colwill who attended the Conference presented her report on the expanding work of the Amoudo Centre and increased  attendance at courses associated with Mental Health Awareness.

**3.     A full report on the recent CCITC training programme for Lay Leaders** (already seen by many of our readers) was included in the Representative Session Agenda. The plans for further 'partnership in training' initiatives in Nigeria and a 2015 UK Wesley Study and Heritage Tour were welcomed by the Conference. The Prelate from the chair of Conference led the plaudits of those who have benefitted from both the Nigeria based training and the Study/Heritage Tours. The countless personal greetings and thanks of Conference attendees who usually began a conversation with, "I attended the 2006-8 (or some other course)" made me even more aware of how much these courses on Leadership, Ministry and Mission and the books, materials, CD's supplied have meant to so many people.

Much more could be said about attending with hundreds of delegates this MCN biennial Conference in Port Harcourt. The ceremonial occasions presented a kaleidoscope of colour with the Prelate, Archbishops, Bishops, Presbyters and Priests along with MCN Knights and lay-leaders in their colourful robes, but perhaps more importantly there was a background buzz from the table groupings. There and at mealtimes in this impressive centre, conference deliberations were translated into relevant conversations that will enhance the future mission of the Methodist Church Nigeria.

The theme of the Conference based on Exodus 14 v15, "Let my people move forward" lived up to its name in words. How the documents produced and many words spoken inspire the 'Acts of the Holy Spirit' in Nigeria over the next few years will determine how effective our meeting together in this way has been! My thanks go to the British Conference for inviting me to represent our church and Cliff College in Nigeria and to the Leadership of MCN and those friends in Nigeria who made me feel so at home by treating me as one of their own rather than as an honoured guest.

My return journey via Paris to Manchester was uneventful apart from finding on arrival in Manchester that my second and larger suitcase had gone walkabout! Back down to earth after a foretaste of heaven!

PS Thursday-Missing suitcase delivered! Answered prayer or were the suitcases lost because we failed to pray?

# CHAPTER 15 2015: THE END OF THE BEGINNING

THEIR THOUGHTS NOT MY THOUGHTS

Much has been written here about the impact of the programme on the people and the places to whom we go, but we move towards a conclusion of this history by sharing some unsolicited reflections from our Visiting Lecturers on teaching Leadership, Mission, Evangelism, Community Development, HIV Aids etc. in another culture and context.

"The CCITC 2 year course offers men and women in the active ministry opportunity to: reflect and evaluate their ministry; refresh their biblical knowledge; open their eyes to the church's mission and evangelistic responsibilities; share in fellowship and wrestle with faith, family and social issues."

"Because the visiting tutors are refreshed by the cross cultural teaching experience, the local tutors see a different way of delivering, the relevance of cross cultural mission in the UK and across the globe is clear to all. UK Missioners need to learn from African models (where the church grows) not from Western ones (where the church shrinks). Engaging with models that work is energising! What we need to move on to, and can perhaps offer best as Western church, is an approach to faith which is not only personal or worship based but which challenges structures and builds community - I would see this as a development of the work begun - TLC: Transforming Lives and Communities."

*"It strikes me that meeting student ministers, deacons and presbyters in their normal metier is to be available to them and to meet them where they are in their regular environs we get a sense of the day to day issues they are dealing with as ministers and Missioners. As you know my visit was a huge eye-opener for me (which was why I was glad to be invited). Though I came to do HIV awareness, while I think they learned much, I learned much from them, especially when their spouses arrived. Working with other nations is a partnership and if we go to them we have to learn about and from them in a way which would not happen if they always came to the UK. I guess we have all met African students in college, but nothing beats going to their*

*country to forge deep relationships and mutual respect. Thanks for the opportunity to experience that. PS ..............and of course it has to be cheaper!*

"I am a much better pastor in my London churches; breaks down stereotypes about theology held by different 'camps'; new resources - books are good!; safe space for outsiders to reflect things that would be costly for local tutors to reflect; costly to see how different theology is, and culture; may introduce new teaching methods in Nigerian theological colleges; engagement with different cultures requires much more than niceness, and the programme does it; (baptismal!) water is thicker than blood. We have to work it out and make it so - not just sing a song together and smile at big ecumenical councils and then go home. Work in partnership in the CCITC model means we have cultural difference in the course without presumed cultural privilege - which deepens the reflection on the relation of culture and Gospel for all participants, where work alone does not."

"I think I'd summarise CCITC as an amazing and intense programme, which not only teaches the ministers further about applied evangelism, but also gives both the visiting team and students the opportunity to share in their culture and traditions in their normal day to day experiences and following Christ."

LEARNING FROM EXPERIENCE DURING THE PAST THIRTEEN YEARS, AT HOME AND OVERSEAS, THROUGH THE CCITCWE HAVE SHARED WITH FRIENDS:

Regular reports highlighting the 'course residentials' and related developments;
Updating articles in the Methodist Recorder, Cliff Today and other journals;
Several revised editions of the original 'course booklet';
An abundance of updated publicity leaflets;
A 300 page booklet of lectures delivered, organised by module for the MCN episcopal consultation in 2009.
Cd's sharing lectures and books with trainees and partner lecturers involved in the programme;
DVD's updating the development of CCITC. These have been produced and distributed widely for Sierra Leone in 2004; updated with the inclusion of Nigeria in 2010 and again in 2013.

Some of what has been achieved is shared in this history. It is a tribute to all those men, women, leaders and organisations who have contributed in so many ways by their: giving; praying; going; lecturing; and by their participation as students/trainees/leaders; in this 21st Century partnership. Through the CCITC, you have made the 'vision' written on an aeroplane 'sick bag' a reality as we have shared with so many friends in partner churches their training for ministry and mission. Thank you!

For those of you who are happy to read the story of how the vision written down on an aeroplane sick-bag, has now been written into the lives and experience of so many people, this history may end here.

Others may want to read on into the Appendices, 'The Trainers Workshop), and engage with some of the 'nuts & bolts' of producing and maintaining such a programme as the Cliff College International Training Centre (CCITC).

If you are then encouraged to develop similar programmes of doing training there with our partners overseas, your initiatives will be welcomed and advice will be readily available. If others want to lend their support to what is already being undertaken through the CCITC, contact can be made direct to Cliff College or through:

***Richard Jackson (Revd)***
***International Coordinator, CCITC***
***Home/Office 2, Almond Drive,   &  at Cliff College, Calver,***
***Sale, Cheshire, M33 5QZ          Hope Valley, Derbyshire S32 3XG***
***+44 (0) 161-718-2548             +44 (0) 1246-584-200***

***Email:*** *rev.rj@ntlworld.com*        *r.jackson@cliffcollege.ac.uk*

On behalf of those associated already with the Cliff College International Training Centre, I can say that we look forward to 'GOING' again to Sierra Leone, Nigeria, Uganda, and as the Lord leads being available to go elsewhere, 'AND GROWING TOGETHER IN TRAINING' during 2015 and beyond.

## "WE'LL PRAISE HIM FOR ALL THAT IS PAST, AND TRUST HIM FOR ALL THAT'S TO COME."

**REVD RICHARD JACKSON**
**INTERNATIONAL COORDINATOR,**
**CCITC**

# APPENDICEES (1-12): TRAINERS WORKSHOP

*An original 'rationale' (See 2002/1), with minor amendments has continued to provide a focus for the work of CCILC/ITC. With this philosophy in mind and using the readily offered experience and expertise of Cliff College staff, we prepared the following introduction to the 'Pilot Scheme' in Sierra Leone which was intended for sponsors of the programme.*

## CLIFF COLLEGE INTERNATIONAL LEARNING CENTRE (CCILC)
### Programme leading to the award of an
### INTERNATIONAL DIPLOMA IN APPLIED MINISTRY & MISSION (IDIAMM)

This Pilot scheme to be funded by the: World Church Action Group of the Methodist Church and planned in co-operation with: The Christian Council of Sierra Leone was presented to possible sponsors/supporters with the following introduction.

### INTERNATIONAL LEARNING CENTRE-PROGRAMME INTRODUCTION FOR SIERRA LEONE

Cliff College (1904) from its earliest days has been of service to the church worldwide. It began by training workers for mission overseas and more recently has found itself equipping increasing numbers of church workers from overseas for service in their own country. This long-standing tradition is being built upon and extended as we establish our International Learning Centre, (ILC) which will work in tandem with our Open Learning Centre (OLC). The ILC has been established in response to a need expressed by the war-ravaged churches of Sierra Leone.

The practical outcome of this philosophy developed out of several discussions and through regular contact with the churches in Sierra Leone is that a team of five lecturers associated with (but not all from) Cliff College will visit Sierra Leone for about a month from the 15th July 2002. During this time they will share as a team with five lecturers from Sierra Leone in delivering a two-week concentrated refresher/training course for about 100 church designated students from all denominations, most of whom will already be active in ministry.

The residential fortnight will be repeated in 2003 as part of a two-year course during which students will be required to tackle IDIAMM distance learning modules in ways that will help them apply what is being learned to their own ministry. Their work will be marked/assessed locally with standards/supervision being maintained through direct e-mail access from the capital Freetown to tutors in the UK and at Cliff College.

This two-year Diploma Course focussed around two weeks of intensive residential study each year will begin as a pilot scheme in July 2002. With its emphasis on 'Applied' the course will major on working through a pastoral response to issues related to justice, reconciliation and hiv/aids in a way that will supplement the foundation teaching/training that students received some years ago on the Theological Hall Course. It will seek to equip students for the changed situation in post-war Sierra Leone. The Course will have the advantage of being locally delivered in a culturally sensitive way at a reduced cost to a much larger number of students than would be possible for the churches in Sierra Leone undertaking a piecemeal further training programme. If successful the scheme could be extended elsewhere and the level/nature of courses being delivered multiplied.

#### ECUMENICAL SUPPORT

The outline proposals have received the unanimous backing of the Theological Hall in Freetown and the Christian Council of Sierra Leone. Bishops: J. C. Humper (United Methodist Church); J. O. Lynch (Sierra Leone Church); A. F. Kulah (Principal, Theological Hall); and the Rt. Revd F.S. Nabieu (President, Methodist Church Sierra Leone & Chairman, Board of the Theological Hall) are enthusiastic about the Project and have graciously agreed to act as patrons.

The Methodist Church (UK): World Church Office meeting on the 8$^{th}$ November 2001 has approved the proposals and agreed to fund the major part of the budget allocating £20,000 per annum for two years. Further offers of funding are being followed up and we are receiving some help in relation to the provision of course books at reduced cost from SPCK and others.

Please pray for this exciting new venture. If successful the scheme could be extended elsewhere and the level/nature of the Cliff College courses being delivered overseas multiplied.

*(Editor's Note) This introduction was followed by the circulation of the original 'course booklet' (Appendix 2) which has been revised for every programme.*

### APPENDIX 2 (2002) CIRCULATED 'COURSE BOOKLET'

This early Combined Prospectus and Business Plan for a World Church Partnership in Training Initiative was based on existing documentation for distance learning courses linked with residentials at Cliff College. It was updated (27th February 2002) following the visit of Revd Francis Nabieu, President of the Methodist Church Sierra Leone and Chairman of the Theological Hall Board in Freetown, Sierra Leone. Since 2002 it has been revised several times, but the fundamentals of the course requirements have remained the same.

AIM:

to facilitate in a Local Context, Refresher Courses/Further Training, for those engaged in Ministry in our Partner Churches throughout the world.

to undertake a two-year pilot scheme in partnership with the Christian Council of Sierra Leone (CCSL) from July 2002 to July 2004

# CLIFF COLLEGE INTERNATIONAL LEARNING CENTRE
## (IN PARTNERSHIP WITH THE WORLD CHURCH)

## THE CLIFF COLLEGE
## INTERNATIONAL DIPLOMA IN APPLIED MINISTRY
## AND MISSION (IDIAMM)

is designed for people:

* engaged in some form of Christian ministry - lay or ordained
* wanting to study and reflect on mission and ministry particularly in relation to the development of their own work and ministry
* who have formal theological training and several years of relevant work experience

The courses are part time delivered during short periods of residency at a 'local' College.

### THE INTERNATIONAL DIPLOMA

Is a part taught, part self-study and researched two-year course, with a compulsory two-week residential period at a 'local' College each year.

### Foundation Course for Further Studies.

The IDIAMM is a 'level two' undergraduate course, complete in itself. Outstanding Students on this course may be encouraged by the sponsoring bodies to continue in further studies to graduate or postgraduate level.

**Validating and Awarding Body: Board of Collegiate Studies at Cliff College** validates the course and awards the diploma

### PARENT INSTITUTION-CLIFF COLLEGE

Cliff College is situated in the heart of the Peak National Park, one of the loveliest parts of England. It lies in the Derwent Valley, ten miles from Chesterfield and twelve miles from Sheffield. Since 1883, Cliff has been training people for evangelism and Christian service. Although part of the Methodist Church, students come from a wide range of denominations and from overseas as well as from Britain and Ireland.

The ethos of the College is one of teaching evangelical theology, which is biblically rooted and related to contemporary life and culture, as informed by personal experience. There has always been an emphasis on the Spirit-filled life, evangelism and holiness, in both teaching and practice. As a result, vital issues facing the church and society are constantly being addressed.

Cliff College is an institution validated by the Board of Collegiate Studies of the University of Sheffield. The College, together with the Urban Theology Unit, the Wilson Carlile College of Evangelism, the Hallam Pastoral Centre and the Biblical Studies Department of the University is a founder member of the Sheffield Federation of Centres for Theology and Mission.

### ECUMENICAL AND DENOMINATIONAL SUPPORT

The College and its courses are open to Christians from all traditions. In recent years members of Cliff College postgraduate courses have received the encouragement and support of various denominational networks of continuing ministerial education and development.

A good relationship exists between the course directors and the CME networks of the Church of England and the Formation in Ministry Office of the Methodist Church. Students representing the United Reform Church, the Salvation Army, and a number of other denominations, in Britain and overseas, have also been encouraged and supported to undergo these courses.

### ABOUT THE COURSE

Because the **IDIAMM** is a part-taught, part self-study and researched course, the knowledge and experience course members bring to the course is valued and welcomed. Good practice is a fundamental part of the learning process. Course members will:

Attend the two-week long designated residential periods at a 'local' College each year. Lectures, seminars and tutorials are used to introduce the main areas and themes relating to course units, enabling course members to engage in informed reflection.
Read key texts, and other sources as appropriate from a reading/resource list.
Produce pieces of course work each year of the course, from a list of topics based on course units.

349

Produce a dissertation by the end of May in the second year (c 6,000 words) on a topic related to their ministry chosen by the student and agreed with the Course Director. Guidance will be given in designing a dissertation proposal at the appropriate point.

Submit all pieces of coursework and dissertations in accordance with the regulations of Cliff College. All written work must gain a pass grade using the marking regulations and criteria of the College in order for the diploma to be awarded.

Wherever and whenever possible, attend regional tutorial meetings. Such meetings reinforce learning, encourage reflection, and offer mutual support to students in the preparation of the required assignments and dissertation.

Be allocated a local tutor who is available to offer help regarding any aspect of the course, monitor progress and mark work. Where practicable, course members are also informally linked to past graduates of the course who reside in their region. This provides opportunities for guidance, advice and encouragement.

Be expected to commit sufficient and reasonable time to the course requirements. An average of at least six hours a week, for (at least) thirty weeks in each year of a course, is suggested.

### ENTRY REQUIREMENTS AND ADMISSIONS PROCEDURES

Diploma Course members will normally:

(a)     be a former student of a course with a standard at least equivalent to that of GCE 'Ordinary Level' in English and/or Biblical Studies,

OR

(b)     have completed in-service training courses relating to ministry to a level deemed appropriate by the sponsoring church.

OR

(c)     have successfully completed a recognised course in some aspect of Ministry and have several years relevant work experience.

The applicant must also satisfy the sponsoring church that they have:

(a)     a genuine interest in and commitment to a process of reflection on their work through issues raised by the course

(b)     a desire to work at the intellectual and academic issues arising from undertaking the course

350

(c)    a concern to integrate and apply insights arising from the course to their own ministry and the wider context within which they work.

(d)    an ability to reflect on their work experiences in an open, critical, constructive way, which will enhance their professional and personal development

Candidates will be expected to provide a reference supporting their application from the leader of their sponsoring church.

**INCLUSIVE DATES OF THE RESIDENTIAL TEACHING PERIODS**

**2002   Friday 19$^{th}$ July - Thursday 1$^{st}$ August inclusive**
**2003   Friday 18$^{th}$ July - Thursday 31$^{st}$ July inclusive**
**2004   Friday 16$^{th}$July - Thursday 29$^{th}$ July inclusive (To include ceremony for first graduates)**

**SUMMARY OF COURSE OUTLINE/TIMETABLE**

To be finalised in association with the local church(es). The questions of Leadership, Justice, Reconciliation and Peace and the concern about Aids are high on the Agenda alongside reflections on 'Doing Theology' in a cultural context. Some of these topics are covered in the SPCK International Series of study books which will be used throughout the course.

COURSE STRUCTURE: PROPOSAL FOR THE IDIAMM. (INTERNATIONAL DIPLOMA IN APPLIED MINISTRY & MISSION)

Course Structure (Undergraduate Level 2):-Students must take all modules.

| Module Assessed | Credit | Study | Block |
|---|---|---|---|
| Christian Initiation and Spiritual Renewal x Dist. Learning Module | 10 | 1 year | 1 |
| Reconciliation and Ministry Portfolio-equiv 3,000 words | 10 | 1 year | |
| The Renewal and Ministry of the Church x 3000 word assignment | 10 | 1 year | 1 |
| Old Testament and Mission x Dist. Learning Module | 10 | 1 year | 1 |

| | | | |
|---|---|---|---|
| Spirituality and Personal Development | 10 | 1 year | |
| Refl. Journal (3,000 words) | | | |
| The Qualities & Skills of Church Leadership | 10 | 2 year | |
| Portfolio of competencies | | | |
| Equiv. of 3,000 words (portfolio 60% | | | |
| Appraisal 20% presentation 20%) | | | |
| The Context of the Church's Mission | 10 | 2 year | 1 |
| x 3,000 word assignment | | | |
| Evangelism in the context of AIDS | 10 | 2 year | |
| Refl. Journal (3,000 words) | | | |
| New Testament and Mission | 10 | 2 year | 1 |
| x Dist. Learning Module | | | |
| The Renewal of Christian Worship | 10 | 2 year | |
| Portfolio (3,000 words) | | | |
| Research Project | 20 | throughout | 1 |
| x 6,000 words | | | |
| | 120 | | |

COURSE ORGANISATION AND MANAGEMENT

The Course Director is **Revd Dr Martyn D. Atkins, BA** and the administration will be within Cliff College.

The Course Coordinator and Leader is **Revd Richard Jackson, BD, MA,** Associate Tutor at Cliff College

Visiting lecturers with expertise in subjects relating to the course and with experience of living and working in cultures other than their own will work in partnership with local colleagues designated by the sponsoring body to provide input into each of the residential teaching weeks.

The Course Leader, Revd Richard Jackson, will be the contact person for those offering particular expertise and after consultation with associates will have final responsibility for choosing a balanced team to deliver the Course.

Our hope is that lecturers will be released, encouraged, supported, funded, and seconded by their employing authorities for this work for a period of not less than four weeks. The plan is for visiting lecturers to arrive in the country a few days before the two-week residential allowing time for settling in, acclimatisation and Course Team liaison.

After the concentrated two-week residential, members of the team will relax, explore and conduct some Seminars in the Provincial Areas. No lecturing fees will be paid, but the visiting lecturers will have provided or be reimbursed for all expenses associated with travelling, accommodation, and food.

The Cliff College Course Management Team will use the experience of Theological Education by Extension and of the Open Learning Centre (now based at Cliff College) to overcome the difficulties experienced by ministers and prospective students who have limited or no access to books. It is hoped that the generosity of sponsors and the support of SPCK with its eminently suitable International Study Guides will make it possible for us to provide both some books and prepared materials linked with the course for home study.

## THE COURSE STAFF TEAM

In addition to visiting lecturers, the course will be supported by a consultant staff team, which includes:

**Revd Paul Ashby,** Director of Studies and Lecturer in Old Testament at Cliff College.
**Rt. Revd Cyril Ashton,** Bishop of Doncaster,
Author of *Threshold God, Church on the Threshold, Servant Spirit, Serving Church, and A Faith worth Sharing.*
**Dr Timothy Chester,** Formerly Public Affairs Officer *of* Tear Fund
Author of *Awakening to a world of need.*
**Revd Philip Clarke,** National Director of Evangelism for the Methodist Church. Author of *Jesus at Tesco.*
**Revd Prof Kenneth Cracknell**, Research Professor in Theology & Mission, Brite Divinity School Texas.
Author of *Justice, Courtesy & Love* and *Towards a New Relationship.*
**Revd Prof. David Dunn-Wilson,** Retired Lecturer with experience of living and lecturing in many cultures.
**Revd Chris Edmondson,** Vicar of St Peter's, Shipley
Author of *Strategies for Rural Evangelism*
**Bishop John Finney,** author of *Finding Faith Today, Recovering the Past, Church on the Move, The Well-Church Book and Understanding Leadership.*

**Mrs Susanne Garnett,** Social Studies Tutor & Open Learning Centre Director, Cliff College *author of Christian Aid materials including, Alliances for Survival, People Power, and Global Perspectives on Christianity.*

**Revd Dr Peter Graves,** Methodist Minister & Chaplain at the University of Cambridge.

**Revd Peter Meek,** URC Minister in Buxton

**Revd Howard Mellor,** Principal of Cliff College.
Author of *The Good News Works.*

**Revd Dr Brenda Mosedale,** Medical doctor and Methodist Minister in Norwich

**Revd Peter Phillips,** Senior Tutor and Lecturer in New Testament at Cliff College.

**Prof Andrew Walker,** Kings College, London
Author of *Telling the Story, Different Gospels* and *Enemy Territory*

**Ian White MA,** Cliff College Staff,
Author of *In His Footsteps – Young People and Pilgrimage.*

**Revd Dr Nigel Wright,** Principal of Spurgeon's College, London,
Author of *The Radical Evangelical* and *The Radical Kingdom*

**Revd Dr Canon Timothy Yates**
Author of *Christian Mission in the Twentieth Century*

PATRONS OF THE PILOT PROJECT IN SIERRA LEONE

| | |
|---|---|
| **Bishop J. C. Humper** | **United Methodist Church** |
| **Bishop A. F. Kulah** | **Principal, Theological Hall** |
| **Bishop J. O. Lynch** | **Sierra Leone Church** |
| **Rt Revd F. S Nabieu** | **Methodist Church Sierra Leone** |

APPLICATIONS AND GENERAL ENQUIRIES

Will be channelled through the local church(es) authorities. In practice it is expected that most students will be nominated from those churches participating in the National Christian Council.

FEES

There will be an initial £50 non-returnable registration fee payable to Cliff College for the two-year course. This registration fee should be accompanied by a completed application form and a passport-sized photograph. It is expected that the student and/or their sponsoring body will pay this nominal fee by the end of May, prior to the first residential week.

The student/sponsoring body will be responsible for the student's accommodation (though there will be limited availability on site for those attending from the provinces) and feeding. It will be possible for the local church(es) to provide one main meal per day. All expenses related to the production and the delivery of the IDIAMM Course are expected to be met through the generous donations of our sponsors.

SPONSORS

A number of church bodies led by the World Church Office of the Methodist Church in the United Kingdom have expressed an interest in undertaking the funding of this pioneering project.

*A final list of those sponsors which may include the Irish Conference of the Methodist Church and the United Methodist Church and hopefully other denominations will be included here. Any surplus monies beyond the necessarily speculative budget may be utilised in expanding/extending the scheme.*

**PROPOSED (GUESS-TIMATE) BUDGET FOR TWO YEARS**

EXPENDITURE                                                         £

STAFFING

| | |
|---|---:|
| Visiting Lecturers x 3 people x 2 years: Return travel to SL | 6,000 |
| Co-ordinator/Leader x 2 visits x 2 years: | 4,000 |
| Insurance, Medicals, Visas, Yellow Fever, Antimalarials etc. x 4 x 2 years | 2,000 |
| Honorarium (including local Staff Team Members) £200 x 8 x 2 years | 3,200 |
| Visiting Staff Team Misc. (Meetings, Office Admin Costs) | 2,000 |
| | 17,200 |

ACCOMMODATION AND FOOD

Related to above staffing-depend on availability of a suitable 'church' Residence that can be 'done up' (possibility being explored) or 'nightly' payment at the inflated levels that have been prompted by the influx of Non-Government Organisations funded by Aid Agencies. The latter is the more likely outcome for this pilot scheme.

| | |
|---|---:|
| Visiting lecturers x 4 x 4 weeks x 2 years | 4,000 |
| Co-ordinator/Leader x 1 x 2 weeks x 2 years | 1,000 |
| | 5,000 |

Will depend upon decisions made about local requirements, number of
students and possibility of subsidised books from SPCK. If only half of the Methodist Ministers in SL take advantage of this IDIAMM's Course that will give us thirty students, before other churches nominate their own participants.

The local church(es) will subsidise the course by providing free use of the Theological Hall and arranging accommodation/feeding for the students.

If we budget for 100 students receiving just five books each without Subsidy and a similar number of Course Notes (5) based on Open Learning Centre (OLC) costs.

| | |
|---|---|
| Books (SPCK-International Study Guides) | |
| Average Cost £8 x 100 students x 5 | 4,000 |
| Course Materials (Some specially produced) | |
| Average Cost £16 x 100 " x 5 | 8,000 |
| Misc. readers, reports, photocopying etc. | 2,000 |
| | 14,000 |

**CLIFF COLLEGE INTERNATIONAL LEARNING CENTRE SET-UP**

| | |
|---|---|
| Capital costs-Office | 2,000 |
| Secretarial | 2,000 |
| Staff costs | 4,000 |
| | 8,000 |
| **CONTINGENCIES** | 5,800 |
| | £50,000 |

*N.B Much has been learned through practical experience and later development of the programme, but the original figures are noted here for historical integrity.*

ARRANGEMENTS MADE

What follows is a brief summary of the progress that has been made towards implementing this pilot scheme for Sierra Leone in association with Cliff College and funded largely through the World Church Office of the British Methodist Church.

## Sponsors

The outline proposals have received the unanimous backing of the Theological Hall in Freetown and the Christian Council of Sierra Leone. Bishops J. C. Humper (United Methodist Church); J.O.Lynch (Sierra Leone Church); A. F. Kulah (Principal, Theological Hall); and the Rt. Revd F.S. Nabieu (President, Methodist Church Sierra Leone & Chairman, Board of the Theological Hall) are enthusiastic about the Project and have graciously agreed to act as patrons. Revd Vidal Kamara-Cole, MA has been appointed as the Sierra Leone co-ordinator for the project.

## Course Outline

In consultation with the churches in Sierra Leone, Cliff College has produced a draft Prospectus covering the subjects required and meeting the academic course standards of a University two-year part-time course at Level 2. The possibility of University validation (as well as Cliff College validation) for a level 2 course is being explored. *(Note-Cost of £250 per student for British University validation was deemed prohibitive. Course and ITC has continued to be Cliff College validated.)* Help with Study Skills and Research Methods will be given throughout the course. Modules for the IDIAMM have been outlined to include:

A provisional Prospectus and a Course Booklet have been prepared. Module specifics outlining Aims, Learning Outcomes, Required Reading and Distance Learning Materials will be agreed **with guidance from the subject tutors by 31st March**. The checked and finalised IDIAMM Course Booklet will be produced by **mid-April.** A provisional timetable has been produced for the two Residential Weeks taking place from Friday, 19th July through to Thursday 1st August 2002. This residential will introduce the modules for year one. Both Staff and Students will complete evaluation forms at the end of the 'Residential' and the project/process will be reviewed in the light of experience.

STUDY BOOKS AND RESOURCES

The following SPCK International Study Guides (at a much-reduced cost) (linked to module numbers) will be used by tutors and provided free to students as the basic books for the course. Other books required by course tutors will be added to the list as funds are made available.

| | | £ |
|---|---|---|
| Baxter Margaret Link 1/2 | Jesus Christ: His Life and His Ch. | 2.95 |
| Bowen Roger Link 2/1 & 3/1 | So I Send You | 3.20 |
| Bowen R Link 1/2 | A Guide to Romans | 4.15 |
| Brown David Link 3/2 & 4/2 | A Guide to Religions | 3.70 |
| Hargreaves J Link 1/2 | A Guide to St Mark's Gospel | 4.15 |
| Hargreaves J Link 1/2 | A Guide to Acts | 5.40 |
| Hinson David Link 1/1 | The Books of the Old Testament | 3.10 |
| Hinson David Link 1/1 | History of Israel | 3.15 |
| Hinson David Link 1/1 | Theology in the Old Testament | 4.50 |
| Parratt John Link 4/1 & 5/1 | A Guide to Doing Theology | 3.50 |
| Parratt John Link 4/1 & 5/1 | A Reader in African Christian Theol | 2.90 |
| Taylor Harold Link 5/1 & 2/2 | Tend My Sheep | 3.50 |
| NRSV Bible | | 5.00 |
| | +p&p | 49.20 |

Priority if funds available-add three books on Church History @ £9.35

358

Cliff College All course resources from Certificate through to Postgraduate level.

Open Learning Centre Courses

TEE College SA (Megan Norgate) South Africa Distance Learning Material already produced based on SPCK ISG's.

Awaiting set of masters that we can reproduce on payment of royalty if suitable for our purpose.

Bayley Anne One New Humanity: The Challenge of Aids (Out of Print, but we have permission to copy and use with appropriate acknowledgement.)

Mildmay Centre resources HIV/AIDS

Econi Study Pack Christian Response to Justice, Peace Reconciliation etc. from Northern Ireland setting. Link 4/1

All Study Guides, Books, Residential Course Lecture Notes, & Distance Learning Material will be ready by the beginning of May for delivery by (Irish Church Container?) reaching Freetown early July.

### STAFFING

An ecumenically balanced and well-qualified team of lecturers with appropriate subject/overseas experience has been recruited. They are at work already preparing level 2 materials suitable for students working in English as a second language.

Revd Richard Jackson: Methodist, Co-ordinator & Cliff College Tutor-formerly Sierra Leone.

Revd Dr Dennis Cooke: Irish Methodist Principal Edgehill College

Mrs. Susanne Garnett: Lay Anglican, Cliff College Social Studies formerly Christian Aid.

Revd Dr Walter Klaiber: United Methodist Presiding Bishop, New Testament scholar

Revd Dr Michael Thompson: Methodist, Old Testament, Circuit Minister-formerly Ghana.

Mr. Keith Phillips: former VSO Sierra Leone, 'At own expense.' Available for admin/teaching role.

Arrangements are in hand for visas and flights bookings. Accommodation has been booked at Jahovey House in Freetown. After the 'Residential' most of the visiting lecturers will travel 'up-country' to view the working environment of the students and provide regional seminars for local churches.

The Sierra Leone Tutorial team is being put together by the co-ordinator and Theological Hall Tutor Revd Vidal Kamara-Cole.

From the 20 Jan - 3 Feb 2003 two-day Regional Groups to encourage and monitor the progress of students will be organised and staffed by the Co-ordinators. All students will be required to be present and will be expected to make some form of academic presentation at these groups.

A UK based **Consultant Staff Team** from mixed backgrounds/denominations is in place.

STUDENTS AND FUNDING

The course is being limited to 100 students who are being designated by the Church Leaders of the different denominations associated with the Christian Council of Sierra Leone.

Each student will complete an application form (already produced and being distributed) which will be countersigned by their immediate supervisor and approved by the national church leader.

Forms will be returned to the Sierra Leone Co-ordinator by early April so that numbers can be finalised in advance of the transit of books/materials.

Each student, on the two-year course will be expected to attend the 'Residential Weeks' (two a year); the Regional Groups (one a year); and produce course work to the likely deadlines of 30/9; 31/11; 31/1; 31/3; 31/5; with the final piece of work being a 8,000 word dissertation on a topic that relates to the course and their own ministry. A register of attendance will be kept.

Graduation for successful students is planned to take place at the end of the second of the second year of the course on Saturday 31$^{st}$ July 2004.

FUNDING

The Methodist Church (UK): World Church Office has approved the proposals and is funding the major part of the provisional budget by allocating £20,000 per annum for two years. The Methodist Missionary Society (Ireland) has pledged £10,000 (and help in kind) over the two years and further funding is being sought.

We are receiving some help in relation to the provision of course books at reduced cost from SPCK. 'Feed the Minds' have given a grant of £2,500 towards the cost of Books and Distance Learning materials. Other Christian publishers have been approached seeking additional books free or at cost to supplement what we can make available to students with no access to local libraries and few books of their own.

Further comments/suggestions/offers of assistance/finance (payable Cliff College ILC) will be welcomed by:
Revd Richard Jackson Co-ordinator, International Learning Centre,
Cliff College, Calver, Hope Valley, Nr. Sheffield S32

ARRANGEMENTS: NOTES MADE-TO BE ACTIONED BY THOSE INVOLVED

TRAVEL

Arrival at Lungi-Anyone with authority, to welcome and shepherd group and/or additional baggage through customs/by road/helicopter for personnel. N.B. Formal invitation letter from CCSL for visa purposes. Travel arrangements for visiting team: from Jahovey House & in Freetown. Outside of course hours. Up-country after residential two weeks- ?seminars.

THEOLOGICAL HALL

Any refurbishment required, (especially toilet facilities), books for library.

Equipment Available: OHP & Screen: Pens/chalk for boards: ?TV/Video in situ: Tape Recording Equipment & tapes: Photocopier? Computer ? Printer? Scanner? Paper? Library arrangements- availability of books. Student accommodation/rooming list

Question? Role/Status/attendance of current Theological Hall Staff & Students.

SL STAFF TEAM

x 4 + co-ordinator Vidal Kamara-Cole designated. ? Visiting speakers

Students x 100 designated (Breakdown of Church affiliation, current work location & responsibilities)

Signing in on arrival-Registration Form returned with Full names, addresses, telephone numbers, e-mails, mini CV passport photo etc.

(RJ to produce introductory letter outlining the course with Application/Registration Form (produced) & e-mail to SL for distribution.)

TIMETABLE/TIMING

Venues for lectures (lecturer moves-students remain) Tutorials for each student. Timetable requirements:

For prayer arrangements of SL Co-ordinator with balanced input to Course.

for 4.00 pm slot with visiting speakers and students being interviewed for CCSL catering arrangements: lunch & including morning break.

Evaluation forms for completion by staff and students at end of course. Set date/time for review with SL Church Leaders & team of tutors (UK & SL) at end of residential. Review arrangements for visiting team post-residential in terms of up-country seminars etc.

MARKING/ASSESSMENT ARRANGEMENTS

Moderator/External Examiner.
Deadlines for different aspects of course and production of work.
Dissertation to be received by $31^{st}$ May in the second year of the course.
Timing and Staffing of Regional Groups (? 20 Jan - 3 Feb 2003)
Preliminary look at: $2^{nd}$ year diploma/graduation ceremony-suggest-Saturday, $31^{st}$ July 2004
External validation at level 2 with Sheffield University/Open University/SL
Level 3 progress and/or postgraduate diploma/MA for capable students.

### BUDGET

Plans to supplement the £20,000 allocated by World Church Office (UK).
? Irish MMS contribution
? UMC-USA contribution
£50 per head registration for designated students-arrangements for payment in SL.
CCSL to approach British Council in SL ref possible funding especially on Aids, Justice aspects.
Feed the Minds Application Form to finalise with request coming from SL.
Scripture Union contacted re possible support through books/literature.
Personal Donations received from individual donors-fund raising events.

### PERSONAL NOTES:

Course Video & Photographs
Articles for publicity, UK & SL
Purchase Notebook/Laptop Computer
Transport of Books/Distance Learning Materials in good time.

**FLIGHTS**

Now two flights per week with Sierra Leone Airlines/Monarch-return dates decided. Flight times:
L/GTW Monday & Thursday 21.30 Arrive Freetown Tuesday & Friday 04.10
Freetown Tuesday & Friday 22.30 Arrive L/GTW Wednesday & Saturday 05.10
Cost with Key Travel: 6 Weeks Excursion rate £650+£45 Tax; Visa £45
*Note to contact Monarch ref possibility of 'cheap' additional baggage for transport of materials.

**STAFFING AND TUTORS**

PROPOSED Visiting team: (15th Jul to *13th August 2002)
Revd Richard Jackson: Methodist,
Co-ordinator & Cliff College-experience Sierra Leone.
Mrs. Susanne Garnett: Lay Anglican,
Social Studies Lecturer @ Cliff College & Christian Aid.
Revd Dr Michael Thompson: Methodist,
Old Testament, Circuit Minister-experience Ghana.
*(Revd Dr Walter Klaiber: United Methodist Church, Germany, Presiding Bishop, New Testament
*(Medical wife Dr Annegret travelling.
will visit UMC sponsored projects). 19/7 to 5/8
Mr. Keith Phillips: former VSO SL at own expense. Available for admin/teaching role.
Revd Dr Dennis Cooke: Irish Methodist,
Principal Edgehill College, Belfast 15/7 to 5/8
Prof Andrew Walls: Methodist-Aberdeen-
Visiting lecturer worldwide. 23/7 to 5/8

POSSIBLE visiting team (14th July to 12th August 2003) to be made up from:
Revd Richard Jackson: Methodist, Co-ordinator & Cliff College-ex SL
Cliff College Tutor: to be arranged (Award of Diplomas Ceremony, Saturday 31st July 2004)
Revd Dr John Cree: Anglican, Former Tutor Theological Hall SL
Revd Stuart Clarke: Methodist, Former Tutor Theological Hall SL

Revd Dr Sahr Yambasu: Irish Methodist, Sierra Leonean,
Former Principal Theological Hall, SL
* United Methodist Church, Germany

**SIERRA LEONE TEAM:**

Revd Vidal Kamara-Cole: Methodist,
National Co-ordinator & Theological Hall
Revd Dr Leopold Fuller, Baptist-Lecturer at Fourah Bay College
Revd Canon Emerson Thomas, Anglican-Lecturer at Theological Hall
Revd David Cole, Methodist Supt Zion & Lecturer Theological Hall
Mr Samuel Forde, Methodist, Lecturer at Theological Hall

**DISCUSSION ON ARRIVAL OF WORKING TOGETHER IN PARTNERSHIP TO DELIVER
THE TWO-YEAR COURSE:**

Pre-course preparation-meet together 17/18th July. Team briefing on
SL 'etiquette'. (FSN to arrange)
Delivery of 'first residential 2002' largely with visiting team. Discuss
delivery of second residential
Post residential arrangements, support for students, marking,
supervision, examinations.
Arrangements for January 2003 Regional Groups 21/1 to 31/1 and
accompanying SL Tutor(s)

**FUNDING**

£20,000 per annum received from the Methodist World Church Office
in London
Funding £5,000 per annum and help in kind received from the
Methodist Missionary Society (Ireland)
* Funded by the United Methodist Church, Germany

**THE COURSE STAFF TEAM**

In addition to the Course Director Revd Dr Martyn Atkins of
Cliff College and the visiting lecturers, the course will be supported by
a staff team from different backgrounds/denominations, who have
agreed to act as Consultants and Patrons from the churches in Sierra
Leone.

**TO BE ARRANGED BY/FOR STAFF**

**(Please check that you, if it is your responsibility, have taken the
appropriate action on the following)**

Flight bookings (RJ)

Arranging passports and visas (RJ) Insurance (Personal)

Medical check-up & inoculations

Purchase anti-malarials:-individually on prescription

First aid kit to be prepared (RJ)

Accommodation. bookings SL-New arrangements being made

Feeding for all meals/costs/arrange   ? Any special diets for visitors or personal medication

Transport arrangements in SL (FSN)

## Arrangements for the International Diploma in Applied Ministry & Mission (IDIAMM COURSE)

Provisional Course Booklet. Module specifics being prepared with Aims, Learning Outcomes, Required Reading list-recognising book availability limited and Distance Learning Materials to be agreed with guidance from the subject tutors.

Produce checked and finalised IDIAMM Course Booklet with revised referencing (10.1) mid-June.

SPCK International Study Guides to be used by tutors and provided by us free to students as the basic books for the course. Additional books and materials will be supplied free to students and will arrive by container from Ireland, which will leave on Monday, 10th June.

VISITING LECTURERS PLEASE TAKE SPECIAL NOTE

Our copy-printing machine at Cliff College struggled with over-heating when running off my 10 Study Skills Lecture Notes: 10 x 2 double sided sheets x 110 (for students + lecturers). The thought of having to do the same with five lots of 110 student hand-outs in the rainy season humidity of Sierra Leone horrifies me. If you have access to a good copy printer and can run off your own hand-outs x 110 to carry with you-fine. If not, please make sure that I receive master copies at Cliff College soon so that I can have them run off and make some arrangements to have them delivered to SL in time. My hand-outs in a cardboard box weighed in at 13 kilos on the bathroom scales! Our baggage allowance is 30 kilos-if you can take them within your baggage allowance, it will leave you extra space to bring souvenirs/presents back. I headed up my own lecture notes as follows:

# CLIFF COLLEGE INTERNATIONAL LEARNING CENTRE

## INTERNATIONAL DIPLOMA IN APPLIED MINISTRY & MISSION

### STUDY SKILLS LECTURE 1 - STUDYING WITH CLIFF COLLEGE

It would be good, but is not absolutely essential to have a similar pattern of heading for all the lecture note hand-outs on the course.

SCHEDULE (DATES) PRESENT WORK TO SL TUTORS FOR MARKING

**2002**
Sep 30 OT Assignment (Study of ISG's for year-end exam)
Nov 30 NT Assignment (Study of ISG's for year-end exam)
**2003**
Jan 21/31      Regional Groups (2 days in areas to be decided)
Jan 31   Becoming the Church (Assignment-3,000 words)
Mar 31  Being the Church: Spirituality (Journal-3,000 words)
May31  Being the Church: For the world: Reconciliation
        (Portfolio equivalent 3,000 words)
**Jul 17  Morning Examinations (OT & NT modules)
        9.00-10.30: 11.00-12.30**
Jul 18-31      Residential
Sep 30  Joining the Church-Initiation & Renewal-Distance Learning
Nov 30 Being the Church: Evangelism-Assignment 3,000 words
**2004**
Jan 21-31      Regional Groups
Jan 31  Being the church in the World: Contextualisation-Min. Project
        incl. 'Aids' initiative)
Mar 31  Being the Church: Worship (Portfolio-equivalent 3,000 words)
        Being the Church: Ministry (Portfolio of competencies-
        equivalent 3,000 words)
May 31 Completed dissertation 8,000 words.

KEY BOOKS PROVIDED FOR STUDENTS

## IDIAMM COURSE IN SIERRA LEONE (2002-04)
Baxter M., Jesus Christ: His Life and His Church (London: SPCK, 1987)
Bowen R., So I Send You (London: SPCK, 1996)
Bowen R., A Guide to Romans (London: SPCK, 1975 Revised 1996)

Brierley P. & Wraight H., Atlas of World Christianity (Hmpshr: Hunt&Thorpe 1998)
Brown D.A., A Guide to Religions (London: SPCK, 1975)
Foster J., The First Advance (London: SPCK, 1972 Revised Frend W.H.C.,1991)
Foster J., Setback & Recovery (London: SPCK, 1974)
Foster R., Streams of Living Water (London: Harper Collins, 1998)
Hargreaves J., A Guide to St Mark's Gospel (London: SPCK, 1974 Revised 1995)
Hargreaves J., A Guide to Acts (London: SPCK, 1990)
Hinson D., History of Israel (London: SPCK, 1973 Revised    1990)
Hinson D., The Books of the Old Testament (London: SPCK, 1974 Revised 1992)
Hinson D., Theology in the Old Testament (London: SPCK, 1976 Revised 2001)
MacCormack J., Thoughts from a Warmed Heart, (Blfst: Colourpoint Books, 2002)
Mellor H. & Yates T. (Ed) Mission and Spirituality (Cliff College Publishing) 2002
Parratt J., A Guide to Doing Theology (London: SPCK, 1996)
Parratt J., A Reader in African Christian Theology (Lndn: SPCK, 1987 Rv'd 1997)
Taylor H., Tend My Sheep (London: SPCK, 1983)
Terhoven K., Back to Basics (Ilkeston: Moorley's 1995)
Thomson A., New Movements (London: SPCK, 1976 Revised 1990)
Todd S.K., Keep Going, (Dublin: Columba Press, 2000)
Carson et al Ed New Bible Commentary
Marshall et al Ed New Bible Dictionary
Wright & Ferguson Ed New Dictionary of Theology
Alexander & Rosener Ed New Dictionary of Biblical Theology

NRSV Bible

**SL Staff Team**

National Co-ordinator Vidal Kamara-Cole organising as per timetable visiting speakers etc.

Students x 100 designated (Breakdown of Church affiliation, current work location & responsibilities)

Application Forms should have been returned with Full names, addresses, telephone numbers, e-mails, mini CV passport photo etc. Each application authorised by the head of the church. Registration for the course will take place on Thursday, 18th July and daily attendance records will be kept.

# AN ALTERNATIVE EXPERIMENT IN SL

(Translated from the German by one of our students, Andy Profitt and edited for Cliff Today, this is how the United Methodist Church in Germany wrote up their lecturers' reflections on the initiative in their 2002 yearbook.)

Translation from UMC Germany Year Book pp 157-159

## THE THEOLOGICAL HALL, FREETOWN, SIERRA LEONE

The "Sierra Leone Theological Hall" with the "Church Training Centre", has its seat in the capital Freetown and is the central ecumenical place of training. The Theological Hall was founded in 1975 by the United Methodists, Anglicans and a second Methodist church, and offers a theological education to more than 150 students from 14 protestant denominations. There are various courses on offer. Around one third of the students are women, and around half the students want to go into ordained ministry.

In order to go into the ministry a three-year degree programme at the Theological Hall is needed. Studying by distance learning is available, where students take part in a TEE (Theological Education by Extension) programme, which involves learning at home, examinations at one of six regional centres, and an intensive month-long course at the Theological Hall once a year. A diploma can be obtained in 1 or 2 years. Lay people can obtain a certificate after one year's training preparing them for children's work or other services in the church. Five full time teachers lead the institute, and are supported by many part-time workers. In addition to their regular lessons they lead weekend courses, retreats and workshops.

Overseas workers were forced to leave the country because of its unsafe situation. The state of war, continuing since 1990 culminated in the desertion of the site between May 1997 and February 1998. The library in particular was severely damaged; a major part of the books went missing. One student was killed when rebels captured the city again on 6 January 1999. A lecturers two children were taken away by the rebels. Accommodation for 20 students was destroyed by fire and other buildings were damaged. The psychological effect on students and teachers has shown itself, amongst other things in that they become ill more often. The impoverished churches that support the project cannot make money available to pay for repairs.

How are the supporting churches and their partner churches in Europe and the USA dealing with the situation? Money won't solve the basic problem, and money is being made available- for example by British Methodists for re-obtaining literature. The local management are not giving up the hope that the institution can be maintained. A shift in the emphasis of education into the area of distance learning is being planned, however this means that more skilled teachers will be required in the regions, such people do not exist at the moment, and therefore the education of the educators is the highest priority. This will not be achieved without support of staff from overseas.

However can we send theological lecturers from abroad for three to five years (with families) into this country which continues to be at risk? British Methodists have taken on this challenge. In co-operation with the management at the Theological Hall they have created a plan for the development of a sort of theological "shuttle-service". It is soon likely to become reality. In order for this to happen there is a need for willing young theologians, former workers in Africa and other people with theological qualifications to go to the Theological Hall for a short period (expected to be yearly for 3 years for a maximum of 4 weeks) to teach intensive course modules from a pre-determined teaching plan. The central qualification for this, as written in the project's outline: "flexibility, adaptability, and a sense of humour".

### THE INTERNATIONAL DIPLOMA IN APPLIED MINISTRY AND MISSION (IDIAMM)

This initiative is a part of the programme of the "International Diploma in Applied Ministry and Mission" (IDIAMM). Target groups are people in (Methodist) partner churches world-wide, who have no theological further education available to them, and who want to study to gain basic knowledge for church service, or those who have been employed in church service for many years and need a theological refresher course. A pilot project has been planned, looking at Sierra Leone, which will begin in summer 2002, and will be completed in July/August 2004. Because it is unlikely that state recognition of academic achievement will be available in the near future, the project is offering a diploma, awarded by a British Bible college. A framework for the course modules already exists along with a management team in England, and an achievement committee including the Theological Hall Management in Sierra Leone, the Christian council in the country will be named as having overall control of all of this.

On the basis of this concept lies British experience in theological education, which is the setting in which modules are awarded by distance learning. Looking at the demands of this programme (entry qualifications and final examinations) it has been made clear that through courses at the Theological Hall this must be complemented. Students who take this course can build upon it, and go on to specialise further in theological education, and gain further qualifications for their future church work. Students are offered the opportunity to be educated in their own home context, in order to contribute to the achievement of peace and safety in their own land.

**APPENDIX 7A (2003) -DRAFT JOB DESCRIPTION: HALF-TIME COORDINATOR**

# (PRODUCED 20$^{TH}$ SEPT: MINOR-REVISIONS 19$^{TH}$ OCT 2002; (Redrafted 2009 Appendix 10E )

ADMINISTRATION: includes all office/computer work related to:

Preparing and keeping under review the concept that is the ILC
Revising and applying the concept to specific situations like Sierra Leone
Planning with others everything from dates the 'Residentials' to provision of student materials
Responding to daily emails, letters, and telephone calls relating to every aspect of the project.
Relating to Cliff College, World Church (& other organisations) Staff & Committees
Keeping up-to-date with current political and economic situation in SL
Briefing and de-briefing regarding the area with which involved and providing focus for action
Becoming transit conduit for 'SL recovery materials' in UK for onward transmission from Ireland
Liaising with possible contributors of staff/materials e.g. UMC Germany & TEE, South Africa
Keeping in touch with all interested parties, including future prospects
Keeping up to date all files and filing as a resource and justification for the Project
Convincing others that they should fund, support or take part in this innovative project

ACADEMIC: IDIAMM includes maintaining academic standards:

Discussing, evaluating, amending and producing all Course and Module materials.
Reading for ideas on 'Distance Learning' programmes 'successes' and 'failures'.
Pursuing possibilities of practical courses relating to HIV/Aids, Justice/Reconciliation etc.
Reviewing the books appropriate to the Course and evaluating suggestions (in light of budget)
Commissioning and producing 'Distance Learning material relevant to the Course.
Providing a Course Booklet covering Regulations, Referencing and all the requirements for university level 2 academic courses.
Responding to tutor suggestions re modules in light of 'Applied' intention of the Course
Copying for students and keeping copies of all lecture notes/materials used on the Course
Producing, circulating and amending all blank forms used for the Course from Application, and Marking through to Evaluation. Checking and analysing all completed forms.
Preparing and revising timetables and practical provision for the delivery of the course

Delivering the two week July 'Residential Course' in the context of a four week stay in SL

Assessing progress and providing encouragement through two week January visit for 'Regional Groups' and supervising/moderating the work produced by students and marked locally in SL

Pursuing possible University validation of Course locally or internationally at reasonable cost

**PERSONNEL: includes relating personally to everyone involved here and in SL:**

Making and maintaining contacts with possible tutors willing to serve with the ILC

Recruiting ecumenical staff support team in the UK e.g. Bishop Cyril Ashton, Prof Andrew Walker, Dr Tim Chester et al

Planning and preparing tutors and other helpers for participation in the 'Residentials'

Obtaining personal information and CV's for possible Academic validation purposes.

Arranging with participants inoculations, insurance, visas etc. and booking flights

Coping with last minute complications, re-booking, flights hotels etc.

Arranging accommodation, feeding and hospitality and first aid kit for the visiting team.

Leading (this time a team of 8 people) for four weeks in July and arranging hospitality.

Linking each with their local counterpart in presenting and marking their module

**SPONSORS: includes organisations, groups and individuals offering support:**

Soliciting funds, books and other materials from a variety of organisations and church bodies.

Completing the required forms for organisations like 'Feed The Minds' and providing the required information for the World Church Office and MMS Ireland.

Arranging transfer of books and other materials to Ireland for onward transport to SL

Arranging release from the docks and secure distribution in SL

Reporting back to all organisational and individual donors in ways appropriate to them.

**PARTNERS: includes everyone associated with us in the local setting:**

Developing relationships with key people in the Christian Councils of partner churches.

Liaising with local church leaders, tutors and the local coordinator

Linking with the Principal and staff of the Theological Hall in Sierra Leone

Working at enhancing the work of the Theological Hall through provision of resources/staffing

Working through the possibilities of 'exchanges' with the Theological Hall in SL

Responding to enquires from prospective partners/enthusiasts and assessing possibilities

Assessing and supporting the continuing work of the local coordinator and tutors

**ACCOUNTS: includes everything from budgeting to petty cash reimbursements:**

Raising the necessary funding from churches, organisations and concerned individuals

Accounting in detail for every aspect of income and expenditure which eventually passes through the Cliff College books

Arranging and checking payments for all major expenditure on books, flights etc.

Paying and claiming back all personal expenses of team members here and in SL

Preparing and adjusting budgets.

Arranging collection of and accounting for student enrolment fees

Providing detailed accounts for Cliff College, World Church and Sponsors

**PUBLICITY: includes personal, preaching and paper contacts:**

Preparing initial proposals and regular reports on the progress of the ILC

Producing and sorting digital pictures for use with publicity and newspaper articles

Writing reports and articles for a variety of Committees, Synods, publications and individuals

Interviews for Radio in Sierra Leone

World Church services/events already scheduled in the UK

Responding to many requests for further information about everything from 'missing persons in Sierra Leone' to links with former 'missionaries' who want 'to help' in some way.

**MISCELLANEOUS: includes everything overlooked in the above summary:**

Everything not covered above that an innovative pioneering project of this kind requires!

Richard Jackson (Revd)
Cliff College International Learning Centre
19<sup>th</sup> October 2002

OF INTERNATIONAL DIPLOMA IN APPLIED MINISTRY AND MISSION

2002 96 responses out of 99 students = 97% response: Independent summary shown below:

**PROGRAMME**

Excellent–28% V Good–41% Good–22% Satisfactory–9% Poor – 0%

This programme is the first of its kind in our country
Excellent, we cannot afford to travel abroad or attend any normal college to get a degree.
An opportunity to gain theological learning which I have never been fortunate to have. Learnt a lot–2 Very interesting Quality learning Rich in subject matter content–3
Timely inspiring and appropriate Well planned and co-ordinated– 8
Timetable is very intense–16 Timetable overloaded every day Finish earlier each day–7 Start later, e.g. 9am as some have to travel-11
Need to extend length of teaching session so not as intense, max 5 lectures a day – 9 Appreciated the breaks – 16 Need more breaks - 3
Sundays to be free    Saturday to be free/half day - 3
Each lecture should be 1 hour long to allow time for lecturer to summarize.
Some inefficiencies with invited lecturers arriving late - 3
Scheduled Devotion was only Methodist and not other churches

**COURSE**

Excellent–59% V. Good–36% Good–5% Satisfactory–0% Poor–0%

Taught in a way all can understand – 7        Rich – 9        Challenging
Motivating and inspiring – 2 Very encouraging     Very educating – 3
Thought provoking – 2        Well selected/structured – 5
Able to learn a lot in a short time     Continuity between the contents
Gives insight into deeper thinking of ministry and mission
Spoke to the areas where we were lacking – 3
Would like hand-outs for all lectures–5 Appreciated Suzanne's booklet
It will have a positive effect on my ministry / relevant / equipping - 28

Course will not only increase our academic status but will definitely equip us to meet the challenges and needs of present day Sierra Leone
Good preparation for an advanced course – 2

SPEAKERS

|  | Excellent | V. Good | Good | Satisfactory | Poor |
|---|---|---|---|---|---|
| Richard Jackson | 72% | 27% | 1% | 0% | 0% |
| Michael Thompson | 69% | 30% | 1% | 0% | 0% |
| Walter Klaiber | 40% | 45% | 12% | 3% | 0% |
| Andrew Walls | 47% | 35% | 13% | 4% | 1% |
| Susanne Garnett | 55% | 41% | 4% | 0% | 0% |
| Dennis Cooke | 69% | 28% | 2% | 1% | 0% |
| Invited Speakers | 6% | 18% | 48% | 25% | 3% |

All of high standard – 11  Presentation very good – 8
Motivating lectures. All tutors excellent command over their lectures, full of wisdom, modesty and care for each student in the class
Lecturers are so wonderful and are blessed with the gifts and graces of teaching. All tutors understanding, approachable, encouraging – 5
Classes a bit too overcrowded, gain more if smaller. Lecturers cultivated the interest of the student with student's active participation
Lecture notes a great help, would like them for all lectures – 8
Would like Andrew Walls notes when available – 3 Would like time for questions. Despite English being our second language we were able to understand - 8
Walter Klaiber- difficulties with accent – 5 Andrew Walls soft voice difficult to understand when $2^{nd}$ language – 12
Dr Cooke's presentation on reconciliation was very helpful - 2
Invited speakers (from agencies) disappointing, didn't go into enough depth - 8
First invited speakers (from agencies) did not prepare well – 9
Invited speakers came (late in the afternoon) when we were all tired–2
Thanks to God that Richard has the wonderful skill to keep the whole programme under control
Thank God Prof Andrew Walls was able to take us to most parts of the world in 2 weeks

Lecturers made us reflect not only on what the scripture had to tell us but to look at it within our own context and find out how best we can be able to cope with the different situations in the Ministry.

**LIBRARY & BOOKS MADE AVAILABLE**

Excellent–58% V. Good–32% Good–6% Satisfactory–4% Poor–0%

Students were not able to use the library–4 Library needs improving, equipping to cater for the great demand it has–6

Books we received were very good, current, well chosen for the course, useful– 43 Essential for us to pass the course 3

Thanks to God for these precious gifts–8

Appreciate the books/Thanks-12

Especially liked bible commentary and bible dictionary-2

Need a good English dictionary to help with the coursework/assignments etc. - 11

Look forward to supply of the other books and notes - 6

Books came at right time-I would not have go money to even buy one of these books - 5

I wasn't expecting the quantity of books received, covering nearly all the areas we had received lectures on

The books supplied have become the start of the library we lost during the incursion  - 5

Very happy to receive all the books, since I lost all my reading material because of the war.  My house was burnt down. Recovering those books is a spiritual blessing. God bless you.

Book materials provided is the first of its kind in our history.

The books are a legacy, not only of use to course but long term – 12

Still a need for more text to enable students to do more research

Arrangements should be made for the library to be made available even 3 times a week during 'residential' classes        Need time to use the library/read the books - 5

**GENERAL ORGANISATION & ADMINISTRATION**

Excellent–36% V. Good–41% Good–15% Satisfactory–6% Poor–2%

Commendable – 4     Very helpful     Effective and efficient

Encouraging and accommodative    Very good interaction and accessibility to information

Some lapses in communication in preliminary arrangements – 5

Classes interchanged smoothly with ease and understanding – 8

Would have liked revised timetable – 2     It was stated that the course was residential, but this was not so and gave difficulties and disappointment – 7

No proper arrangement for food, this needs looking into for next time – 6

No tea/coffee was served during the coffee/tea break this should have been explained to us - 2

More attention has to be paid to the administrative sector of the course in future - 2

The course would not have been possible without the very good organization and administration

Please be informed of Methodist Synod dates

The assessment and evaluation of church service report was not properly monitored

Seminars (outside agencies) not well organised

Don't only focus on Methodists for conducting services

Need public address system for larger groups

Chapel not suitable for lectures/too many students in one room – 3

Richard Jackson a very good administrator and head of the team

Students' problems dealt with as quickly as possible.

**WEEK OVERALL**

Excellent–29% V. Good–55% Good–13%Satisfactory–3% Poor–0%

Good opportunity for learning – 14    Very intensive – 11    Great for a pioneer programme

Excellent and well spent – 2            Time of reflection – 2 Sometimes a bit boring - 4

Grateful to God for being able to participate in this course – 2

All my expectations met – 2            Good    preparation    for    future courses

Chance to meet with old friends and make new ones – 7

Interaction with lecturers good – 4    Went by too quickly, hope for longer period together

Too little time for interaction and to develop interpersonal relationships

Some students were learning under great stress, no food, no money for our travelling and no accommodation – 2

         Transportation was a problem

Tea biscuits and even lunch mentioned in the booklet, but didn't see any of these – if not available don't mention them          Venue quite good but classes too large

Lunch to be served to students (even if have to pay)/ cafeteria system needed – 27

Provide tea and biscuits/snacks – 3        Facility for drinking water - 2

Course be Residential/accommodation at the Hall for students – 23

More arrangements should be made for our brothers and sisters from the Provinces – 10

Provincial pastors should be given lodgings by their course authorities

Why can't we go up to the Provinces next year?  Each church member lodge one, then hold classes in churches and have lunch only.

Encourage local churches to look at our feeding and accommodation with some amount of priority and seriousness – 4

Ensure correct information re accommodation/food is sent to students

Medical facilities be available – 2

Stop all mobile phones during lectures Less talking during lectures

People in other offices to be told to moderate their voices while lecture in progress

Extend length of course, two weeks is too short – 17

Need a day off each week

Finish day at 1600 hrs – 2      Shorter lecture periods – e.g.40 mins

Evening programme of entertainment, sports or social event

More time to share ideas and testimonies - 3

Students able to use library at breaks-Monitor library books properly

Set up special library for the course   Improve on the buildings – 3

Too crowded/ divide class – 7        More reading materials - 2

Notes to be given out to students or hand-out with references prior to start for all lectures - 5

Give resource material to students on day of registration - 3

Resident lecturers be given some chance to take classes as a means of familiarisation to students of other churches and institutions

Give opportunity for students to proceed to England to carry on with other courses - 3

Have a notice board at the door of the coordinators office so as to facilitate information flow

Advanced information concerning churches to go to on Sundays

Advertise the course more widely so get more students from other denominations

Other churches should be allowed to conduct devotions

Methodist pastors attend worship services in other churches

Let it be continued – 3

IDIAMM SL students (Names deleted and random numbering inserted to preserve confidentiality.)

Initial marks and dissertation themes as at Jan 2003

| | | | OT | NT |
|---|---|---|---|---|
| 000 | Baptist | FTWN Vine Mem. | 58 | ? |
| | Diss-Awaited | | | |
| 001 | Methodist | BUNUMBU | 35 | ret |
| | Diss-Reconciliation in Dodo Kotuma | | | |
| 002 | Methodist | FREETOWN Koidu | 58 | 70 |
| | Diss-Case study of responses of Aberdeen Road Camp amputees to TRC | | | |
| 003 | Methodist | FREETOWN Wesley | 55 | 60 |
| | Diss-Impact of charismatic churches on MCSL in the Western District | | | |
| 004 | Methodist | FREETOWN Zion | 50 | 40 |
| | Diss-Impact of Christian education on Sunday School of Ebeneezer MC | | | |
| 005 | W.A.M. | FREETOWN West | 50 | ? |
| | Diss-Taking care of aged. Case study of King George VI home | | | |
| 006 | Anglican | FREETOWN St.Andrews | 55 | 58 |
| | Diss-Foundation of the Parish of St Andrews, Leicester by the CMS | | | |
| 007 | W.A.M. | FREETOWN South | 55 | 55 |
| | Diss-Awaited | | | |
| 008 | A.M.E. | WELLINGTN N. Zion | 45 | 53 |
| | Diss-Establishment of American Episcopal Church in SL | | | |
| 009 | Methodist | FREETOWN City Mission | 40 | 65 |
| | Diss-The pastor and his mission in SL | | | |
| 010 | W.A.M. | FREETOWN Wlbrfce | ? | ? |
| | Diss-Awaited | | | |
| 011 | Methodist | KAILAHUN | 45 | 45 |
| | Diss-Types of marriage ceremonies among the Kissi tribe of Lalehun, Penguia | | | |
| 012 | Methodist | YORK | 55 | 50 |
| | Diss-Church attendance & giving in Brunswick Methodist Church, York village | | | |
| 013 | W.A.M. | MOYAMBA | 40 | 40 |
| | Diss-Why more people becoming Christians than joining Islam in Moyamba | | | |

| 014 | Methodist | FREETOWN Balmer | 55 | 45 |

Diss-Impact of rebel war on MCSL

| 015 | Methodist | FREETOWN | 55 | 50 |

Diss-Investigation of work of Peace & Civic
Education Desk of MCSL

| 016 | Pentecostal | WELLINGTON | 40 | 40 |

Diss-Religious significance found in crowning
of Paramount Chief in Kono

| 017 | Methodist | SEGBWEMA Daru | 55 | 48 |

Diss-Origins of Christianity in town of Daru,
Eastern Province SL

| 018 | Anglican | FREETOWN St.John Ev. | 48 | 46 |

Diss-Awaited

| 019 | U.M.C. | MOYAMBA | 40 | 40 |

Diss-Obstacles to acceptance of Gospel in
Gendema, Moyamba District

| 020 | Anglican | KISSY | 60 | 53 |

Diss-Children in the Bible compared with children in SL today

| 021 | Methodist | FREETOWN Zion | 40 | ? |

Diss-MCSL and HIV/AIDS prevention

| 022 | A.M.E. | FREETOWN Bp Campbell | 45 | 50 |

Diss-Impact of Pentecostal churches on membership
of AME church

| 023 | Anglican | MURRAY TOWN | 45 | 46 |

Diss-Awaited

| 024 | Methodist | JIMMI Sumbuya | 55 | 50 |

Diss-Expce of Liberian refugees in Jimmi Bagbo camp
Nov 2001–Oct 2002

| 025 | Methodist | JUBA Gibraltar | 65 | 65 |

Diss awaited

| 026 | U.M.C. | FREETOWN | 45 | 55 |

Diss-Evangelism and ethnic diversity in SL

| 028 | Methodist | SONGO Ribbi | 48 | 40 |

Diss-Future of Bethel Methodist Church, Songo

| 029 | Lutheran | FREETOWN East | 40 | 40 |

Diss-Traditonal ways of worship in SL

| 030 | Methodist | WILBERFORCE | 55 | 50 |

Diss-Development youth work in Wilberforce Circuit

| 031 | Methodist | TIKONKO | 55 | 44 |

Diss-Hist of Tikonko Circuit 1970-2002

| 050 | Methodist | FREETOWN Zion | 55 | 45 |

Diss-Awaited

| 051 | Deeper Lifer | FREETOWN Eastern | ? | ? |

Diss-Awaited

| 052 | U.M.C. | FREETOWN | ? | ? |

Diss-Establishment of Jarwlee Lewis UMC in Freetown

| 053 | Methodist | MURRAY TN. Hstg 50 | 45 |

Diss-Effect of Secret Society membership on
church participation of young

| 054 | Methodist | BO Town | 55 | 45 |

Diss-The foundation of St. Phillips Evangelical Church, Ftwn

| 055 | Methodist | WELLINGTON | 60 | 43 |

Diss-Innovations in MCSL Sunday worship and
their impact on congregation

| 056 | Methodist | KAINKORDU Sandaru | 40 | 40 |

Diss-The concept of God and gods among the Konos of SL

| 057 | Methodist | FREETOWN Wesley | 55 | ? |

Diss-Hist Warren Memorial Methodist Church,
Krootown Rd 1980-2000

| 058 | Methodist | SEGBWEMA | 60 | 70 |

Diss-Awaited

| 059 | Anglican | FREETOWN St. John's | 45 | 45 |

Diss-Awaited

| 060 | Anglican | FTWN Lumley | 50 | 43 |

Diss-History of St Charles Parish Church, Regent, Freetown

| 061 | Methodist | KENEMA | ? | 60 |

Diss-Assessment of MCSL mission drive in pre-war rural SL

| 062 | U.M.C. | FREETOWN Western | 45 | 40 |

Diss-Ahmadiyah Muslim mission and its impact in
SL 1960-2000

| 063 | Methodist | KENEMA Jojoima | 60 | 45 |

Diss-Awaited

| 064 | Catholic | FREETOWN St.Anthony | 55 | 50 |

Diss-Conflict resolution and reconciliation in post-war SL

| 065 | Methodist | WILBERFORCE | 45 | 55 |

Diss-The role of MCSL in post conflict reconstruction in SL

| 066 | Lutheran | WELLINGTON | 40 | ret |

Diss-Pastoral leadership and administration in
the Lutheran church

| 067 | U.M.C. | MAGBURAKA | 45 | 40 |
|---|---|---|---|---|

067 U.M.C. MAGBURAKA 45 40
Diss-The impact of war on the women of the
Tonkolili District of SL

068 U.M.C. BO 48 45
Diss-Trad beliefs in existence Land/River spirits
in Mende/Sherbro lands

069 Anglican WELLINGTON Trin. 50 43
Diss-Why is the message of the sermon forgotten so quickly?

070 Anglican FTWN Pademba Road 55 70
Diss-Effect of evangelism on the Anglican Chch in Ftwn

071 Methodist FREETOWN City Mission 55 58
Diss-What should be the mission of the church in SL today

072 Lutheran FREETOWN Lumley 49 40
Diss- Response of amputees to the 'Amputee
Trust Fund' of Ev Lutheran Ch

073 Latter Day St FREETOWN 40 40
Diss-History of Church of Jesus Christ of Latter
Day Saints in SL

074 Methodist FREETOWN Zion 40 40
Diss-Role of CCSL and the Inter-religious Council
in reconciliation process

075 W.A.M. MOYAMBA 40 40
Diss-The growth and development of Levuma Church

076 Lutheran WELLNGTN Kaimapo 40 ?
Diss-Awaited

077 Methodist SEGBWEMA 35 ret
Diss-Study of people in the 'Lebanese Displaced
Persons' Camp, Kenema

078 Methodist KAILAHUN 41 40
Diss-An experience of exile

079 U.M.C. MOYAMBA 48 48
Diss-Influence of Pentecostal movements on a
church in the Moyamba District

080 Methodist WILBERFORCE 45 45
Diss-Role of traditional music in the community
church Lalehun, Penguia

081 Methodist KOIDU 48 45
Diss- Examination of burial ceremonies in the Kissi tradition

082 U.M.C. WELLINGTON 45 48
Diss-Awaited

**SUMMARY**

Assignments passed

OT-95 NT-85

Assignments not received

OT- 2 NT-10

Assignments with marker

OT- 2 NT- 0

Assignments failed, returned for resubmission

OT- 0 NT- 4

Dissertation themes awaited

16

**CLIFF COLLEGE**            **96 (Rev'd 30/11//2002)**
Final Figures for 2001/02 and Draft Budget for 1.9.2002 - 31.8.2003
**TUTORIAL – ILC Head of Department & Budget Holder: Richard Jackson**

**Budget: Actl-31.8.02: Bdgt 31.8.03**

| INCOME: | | | |
|---|---|---|---|
| GAD Donations - ILC | 500 | 50 | 50 |
| Non-GAD Donations for ILC | 500 | 538 | 500 |
| Grants for ILC (Methodist-WCO) | | | |
| *Approved x 2 years | 20,000* | 15,000 | 15,000 |
| (Methodist WCO-tfr to MCSL Cliff a/c) | | 5,000 | 5,000 |
| (Mthdst WCO-Grant ½ time coordinator) | | | 12,000 |
| (Mthdst-MMS Ireland)*Approved x 2 years | 5,000* | 10,000 | nil |
| (UMC-Germany)     *Applied for increase | nil | 1,895.86 | 7,000* |
| Grants for ILC (Feed the Minds-Literature) | | | |
| * Appd & rec'd 2$^{nd}$ year | 2,500* | 2,500 | 7,500* |
| Others (Air fare donated) | 1,000 | 695 | 100 |
| #Christian Council SL in MCSL Cliff a/c) | nil | 500 | nil |
| #Registration Fees (£50 x 99 stdnts x 2 year | | | |
| in MCSL Cliff a/c) | 5,000 | 4,950 | 3,500 |
| Misc | nil | 14.10 | Nil |
| **TOTAL INCOME** | **34,500** | **41,142.96** | **50,650** |

| EXPENDITURE: | | | |
|---|---|---|---|
| Stationery - ILC | 500 | 552.92 | 600 |
| | | | |
| CCILC Administration, Registration etc. | 8,500 | 8,788 | 6,000 |
| Coordinator (1/2 time) | | | 12,000 |
| ILC – WCO to MCSL CCILC a/c | | | |
| (incl. salary £500 P/T SL Co-ordinator) | 500 | 5,000 | 5,000 |
| lLC - Sundry Expenses | 3,000 | 712.66 | 3,000 |
| ILC - Visiting/External Staff Costs | 12,000 | 6,724.57 | 12,000 |
| ILC - Course Materials/Publications | 9,500 | 8,922.98 | 12,000 |
| Contingencies | 500 | nil | 50 |
| # MCSL CCILC expenditure (See below) | nil | 8,892 | nil |
| **TOTAL EXPENDITURE** | **34,500** | **39,593.13** | **50,650** |
| **Surplus/Deficit** | **0.00** | **1,549.83-** | **0,000** |

# **METHODIST CHURCH SIERRA LEONE (MCSL) A/C – SUMMARY:**
CLIFF COLLEGE INTERNATIONAL LEARNING CENTRE ACCOUNT#

| World Church Office Transfer | 5,000 | Theol Hall Rfrbihmnt | 2,173 |
|---|---|---|---|
| Registration Fees paid or pending) | 4,950 | Accommodation | 5,157 |
| Christian Council of SL-Donation | 500 | Misc | 1,562 |
| | **10,450** | | **8,892** |

387

A (2005) WEB-SITE HISTORY OF THE METHODIST CHURCH IN CUBA

The Cuban Methodist Church began with the missionary work of Methodist men and women from Florida who came to Cuba by the end of 1883 with the mission of preaching the gospel. During the first years, the work extended and consolidated. Many preaching fields were opened and the church grew so much that, in 1959, the Methodist Church was the largest one in Cuba. The mission on the island was part of the Florida Conference.

From that year on, the church's membership decreased drastically as part of an exodus out of Cuba or out of the church, caused by the political changes that had taken place. In the 80's the Cuban Methodist Church got involved in a powerful movement of growth and development which has made it a vigorous, living church with a prophetical message for today's Cuba. The Methodist Church enters the 21st century after having always shown a testimony of consecration. All over the country, from West to East, we have churches where our congregations meet to give thanks to the Lord of History. The main characteristic of the Cuban Methodist people is their total dependence on God even in the most insignificant things. Amidst limitations, God's support is seen every moment, providing His people with all they need.

Nowadays there are 215 churches and more than 700 missions, 190 pastors and a membership of more than 17 000 people.
Some interesting data (6/05):
Official members: 17 000
Average attendance: 30 000
Visitors: 40 000
Women: 6 500
Young people: 5 300
Children: 3 200

This is a very young church. The group that ages from 1 to 30 years represents more than 70 % of the total congregation. There was low average attendance until 1980. In 1987 there was an explosion in attendance and many people came to God, so much that more than 90% of the current church came after that date.

## THE CUBAN CHURCH'S MISSION

The main mission of the church focuses on the testimony of thousands of Cuban Methodists who are aware of belonging to God and called to minister to the Cuban people. So evangelism, service, and prayer are the centre of this church's life.

A special stress is made on training ladies and young people, the strongest groups in the Methodist Church. At national and local levels, they are trained for vigorous leadership.

## SERVICES TO THE COMMUNITY

Several ministries are carried out to assist elderly people, like the Methodist Elderly Home located in Havana, which serves around 40 older people. Several local churches have plans to supply food and health care for the elderly and ministries to special people, like deaf and with motor and mental needs. "So walk in love, like Jesus loved us." This is the spirit that encourages Methodist people to approach pain, needs, sickness, and despair. Praise God who has raised a sensitive, active and always serving people of priests.

## NEWS

The 38th Annual Assembly of the Men´s Methodist Fraternity will be held from October 20 to 23 at Canaan, the Cuban Methodist Camp. Under the slogan "Men who fence in and fulfil God's purpose," 362 delegates from all over the island will reflect on 2 Timothy 3:17 "for the man of God to be perfect, fully prepared for all good works." One of the topics that will be analysed is "The father's authority at the present time," which will be developed by the Christian Center for Family Orientation. In addition, there will be two festivals of talents and a revival service. The closure will be in charge of Bishop Ricardo Pereira Díaz.

## PROJECTS: CUBAN METHODIST PROJECTS YOU COULD SUPPORT:

Development of the children's ministry
Training courses for pastors and lay leaders
Work with specific groups such as elders, special people, and others
Development of leadership skills among ladies and young people
Evangelism
Opening of new pastoral fields and missions
Rebuilding of churches and manses
Canaan camp

## (EVALUATION SHEET – REGULAR USE (AMENDED) NG JULY 2006) (*Compressed in size from A4 for book*)

**Do not put your name on this sheet**
**(Please tick a box and comment as honestly as you can on the following.)**

**The Programme (Timetable for the two weeks)**

| EXCELLENT | VERY GOOD | GOOD | SATISFACTORY | POOR |
|-----------|-----------|------|--------------|------|
|           |           |      |              |      |

Comments:

**The Course so far (Subjects taught over the two years)**

| EXCELLENT | VERY GOOD | GOOD | SATISFACTORY | POOR |
|-----------|-----------|------|--------------|------|
|           |           |      |              |      |

Comments:

**Speakers/Visiting Lecturers-Presentation, Content and Lecture Notes (alphabetical order)**

|                   | EXCELLENT | VERY GOOD | GOOD | SATISFACTORY | POOR |
|-------------------|-----------|-----------|------|--------------|------|
| Albert Beah       |           |           |      |              |      |
| Nicola Garnham    |           |           |      |              |      |
| Audrey Hensman    |           |           |      |              |      |
| Richard Jackson   |           |           |      |              |      |
| Janet McCall      |           |           |      |              |      |
| Malcolm McCall    |           |           |      |              |      |
| Invited Speakers  |           |           |      |              |      |

Comments:

**Suggestions for books to be made available through the library and/or with personal copies**
Comments:

**Library books and access**

| EXCELLENT | VERY GOOD | GOOD | SATISFACTORY | POOR |
|-----------|-----------|------|--------------|------|
|           |           |      |              |      |

Comments:

**General Organisation & Administration for the course**

| EXCELLENT | VERY GOOD | GOOD | SATISFACTORY | POOR |
|-----------|-----------|------|--------------|------|
|           |           |      |              |      |

Comments:

**Catering Arrangements**

| EXCELLENT | VERY GOOD | GOOD | SATISFACTORY | POOR |
|-----------|-----------|------|--------------|------|
|           |           |      |              |      |

Comments:

**The Week overall (impressions)**

| EXCELLENT | VERY GOOD | GOOD | SATISFACTORY | POOR |
|-----------|-----------|------|--------------|------|
|           |           |      |              |      |

Comments:

**Any suggestions, ideas, improvements**

Thank you.      Coordinators:      Okon Ekerendu/Richard Jackson   July 06

A PERSONAL BRIEFING PAPER ON THE PAST, PRESENT AND POSSIBLE FUTURE OF THE CLIFF COLLEGE INTERNATIONAL LEARNING CENTRE (CCILC) SUBMITTED SEPTEMBER 2009 BY REVD RICHARD JACKSON IN RESPONSE TO A REQUEST OF MR MICHAEL KING (WCO) AS AN 'EXIT STRATEGY' FOR THE PIONEER AND CURRENT, (BUT AGEING!) COORDINATOR OF THE CCILC.

THE PAST

The CCILC was established in 2001, initially as a response to the church training/resourcing needs of post-conflict Sierra Leone. With the support of the World Church Office (WCO) of the UK Methodist Church a training programme was drafted that would allow students to achieve a Cliff College validated 'International Diploma In Applied Ministry & Mission' (IDIAMM) by 'distance learning'. At the invitation of The Christian Council of Sierra Leone (CCSL) and the Methodist Church Sierra Leone (MCSL) a highly successful programme was piloted in Sierra Leone (2002-4). Following a pattern established at Cliff College, students attended six residential weeks over two years, where teaching and lecture notes were provided by highly qualified visiting lecturers. They then worked under local tutor supervision; reading (with many books supplied free); completing assignments; doing research and applying what they learned to their local situation.

The primary funding for the programme of £20,000 per annum provided through the UK Methodist Church was supplemented by grants for books and resources solicited from SPCK; Feed The Minds; The Langham Partnership; MMS (Ireland); UMC (Germany) and personal donations. We found that with a budget of around £40,000 per annum this pioneering ecumenical venture was able to deliver a two-year programme of training to 99 students (of whom 73 graduated) and resource every student with books valued at £700. A follow-up programme requested by MCSL incorporated the work being done with Local Preachers and Women Workers in Sierra Leone by Revd Gilbert & Mrs Sylvia Hall, and during three visits we gave further training in administration to ordained ministers. Also we funded some IT equipment and training for MCSL Conference Office Staff.

Experience gained was utilised in November 2005, when at the request of the WCO and the Cuban Methodist Church, Revd Dr Martyn Atkins (then Principal of Cliff College) and Revd Richard Jackson, the International Coordinator of CCILC learned and shared an enriching experience whilst contributing to the 'Distance Learning' programme of training for Methodist pastors in Cuba.

## THE PRESENT

The Head of the Methodist Church Nigeria (MCN) made contact with the CCILC in November 2004. His Eminence Sunday Mbang having been told about the success of the pilot programme in Sierra Leone invited us to be involved in a similar partnership with Nigeria. This invitation was linked with the culmination of their restructuring programme and the comment, "recently our Conference approved repositioning Methodist Church Nigeria for the 21st Century and evangelism was put as the key to achieving this dream". In Nigeria we were encouraged to emphasise the 'Applied' aspects of the programme, with students' learning particularly from worship experiences in New Generation Churches (Pentecostal/Spirit churches!). All students were to be challenged to plant new churches; organise community projects; train vernacular evangelists etc. and analyse the progress made as part of an 'Applied Evangelism Portfolio'.

Once again, with £20,000 per annum primary funding provided through the UK Methodist Church Scholarship And Leadership Training (SALT) advisory group and other sponsorship, all of the 139 Methodist students (largely evangelists and pastors) who began the programme in Nigeria in 2006 were resourced with lecture notes, books and practical training that will enhance their ministry for many years to come. 108 students graduated with an IDIAMM Diploma in 2008. MCN's own evaluation of the programme led them to make a request for a further two-year programme for up to 150 of their ordained ministry and deaconesses to be trained during the period 2008-10.

With WCO funding in place, a total of 134 specially selected students were enrolled for this second programme. 125 are continuing on the second year of the course from July 09.

Additionally in July 2009, the team were asked to share in and contribute to a three-day 'Episcopal Training Consultation' for the 60 Bishops of MCN. A book containing typical ILC lectures was prepared and introduced to the participants. This generated some very positive testimonies as to the impact of the CCILC programme. MCN have asked that these programmes continue beyond 2010.

## THE FUTURE

It is my view as the pioneer and current coordinator of the proven CCILC programme that we are now at the stage where decisions need to be made about the future of the CCILC. This briefing document alone cannot justify its continuation, but detailed information, regular reports and reviews (which can be made available) have been supplied to sponsors/interested parties since the inception of the programme in 2001. There appear to be three options opening up before us:

1. The CCILC concept of 'doing training there' at the invitation of and in partnership with national churches has served its purpose and it should be phased out by 2012.
2. The CCILC concept has proved its worth. It should continue as an established World Church Office (SALT) programme with annual funding for a half-time coordinator's appointment. It would then respond to requests and provide (as at present) training with primary funding allocated through SALT for specific approved programmes.
3. The CCILC concept has now developed sufficiently from being an innovative/pioneering project to justify its inclusion as a continuing Mission and Ministry in the World Church Programme under the direction of a WCO funded half-time member of staff based at Cliff College. Applications could be assessed before funding requests were made through SALT.

PERSONALLY, (AS MIGHT BE EXPECTED), I WRITE IN SUPPORT OF THE THIRD OPTION ON THE GROUNDS THAT:

1. There is a demand within our partner churches for properly resourced and practical training. This is evidenced by the many (as yet unmet!) requests that have been received.
Limited funding is available for cross-cultural scholarships. A small percentage of that funding invested in training much larger numbers in their home environment has proved its worth in giving practical 'on the job' training to personnel there and in resourcing mission.

2. It has been demonstrated that where designated primary funding is made available through the UK Methodist Church, that money is multiplied through other agencies and donations; additional resources can then be channelled to our partner churches.

3. The regular training work of colleges overseas is revitalised as local lecturers' partnering visiting lecturers share lecture notes/information whilst delivering the CCILC programme. In addition, for Nigeria alone over £20,000 in further funding has been generated by lecturers from the UK to improve college facilities (water supplies, accommodation etc.)

4. Cliff College has the background, expertise and resources to become the focal point for sharing with our partners overseas in delivering, academically recognised, but practical courses of training for church workers of all age groups.

5. With a little more organisation at the centre, we can utilise the (wo)manpower resources from every District/Circuit/College of the UK Methodist Church to provide short-term residential training overseas for many aspects of the churches' developing work. The popular approach of organising independent 'building' teams to work overseas is not usually as productive in the longer-term as providing training.

6. A funded ILC appointment within a college dedicated to training would relieve the pressure on WCO by becoming a clearing house sharing expertise (and possible exchanges/partnership etiquette!) among the increasing number of bilateral UK District/Partner Church relationships being developed.

7. The recurring cost to the church of a half-time appointment would be £25,000 per annum. A similar amount could be set aside for approved projects, which might include short-term exchanges with the UK. £50,000 per annum in all. (About 1/7 of the current SALT budget)

**(Names of visiting lecturers up to 2014 added to complete listing)**

**Core Team (Organising, leading teams & lecturing on a variety of subjects at different times in several countries)**

**Jackson Revd Richard MA BD** International Coordinator of CCILC (Ret'd) Methodist Minister & PG Tutor
**McCall Revd Dr Malcolm BA MA** Methodist Minister (Ret'd) Shetlands, missionary teacher & Naval Chaplain
**McCall Mrs Janet BA (Hons)** Methodist LP, Teacher in Africa; French & English as second language skills
**Phillips Mr Keith CQSW** Anglican, VSO in Sierra Leone Social Worker in Child Care field-Logistics/admin.

**Invited Trainers/Lecturers (many contributing to more than one CCILC programme from 2002-14).**

**Atkins Mr James BA(Hons)** TV Production Experience of filming: Sierra Leone, Sri Lanka & Nigeria
**Atkins Revd Dr Martyn BA** Cliff College Course Director Principal Mission/Evangelism-Then and now
**Baxter Mrs Margaret BA(Hons) PGCE** Anglican Trainer Author-Adult Learning
**Beah Revd Albert, MA BA** Sec of Conf to the MCSL Particular expertise in Community Development
**Blake Revd Dr Chris MA BSc** Principal of Cliff College; Pastoral & New Testament
**Bolas Revd Pamela BA (Hons)** Mthdst Minister, Leicester Involved in HIV/Aids awareness and Counselling
**Burns Major Alan MA** Salvation Army Officer Particular responsibility for evangelism in Norwich area

**Clark Revd Peter MA PGCE** Methodist Minister Former Mission Partner overseas, Dev & Social Work
**Clarke Revd Phil MA BA** Methodist Supt., Former Director of Evangelism, Cliff College & Methodism
**Claye Mr Michael** Communication Camera & DVD production assistant
**Cooke Revd Dr Dennis BA BD MTh** Methodist

College Principal, Belfast; Reconciliation following Conflict
**Cree Revd Dr John** Anglican Rector Chorley
Being the Church in the World: Contextualisation
**Dunn-Wilson Revd Prof David BA MA BD PhD**
Methodist Mission Partner & College Lecturer: Church History

**Emery-Wright Revd Dr MDiv BA** Methodist Minister,
Lecturer in Missions, Cliff College, Youth Work Research
**Ensor Revd Dr Peter MA** Methodist Minister
CC Director of UG Studies: Lecturer in New Testament
**Eze Very Revd John MA** Nigerian Methodist Minister,
Cliff College Graduate, Mission & Evangelism
**Garnett Mrs Susanne MA, MEd** Anglican
Cliff College Lecturer-Spirituality in Ministry

*{Garnham Capt. Nicola (late) MA BSc Salvation Army Officer
Lecturer at William Booth College in London}*

**Gibson Dr Jenny** Hospital Doctor
Long term missionary in Africa-Responding to HIV/Aids
**Habib Revd Dr Usman MA** Postgraduate Research Student; Nigerian
Lecturer on New Generation Churches
**Hall Mrs Sylvia** Methodist LP Formerly Nigeria & MCSL,
Teacher & Network Leadership, Lay Trainer
**Hall Revd Gilbert** Methodist Minister, Formerly Nigeria & MCSL,
Chair of District (retired), Lay trainer
**Härtner Revd Prof Achim MA** United Methodist
Prof of Evangelism at Reutlingen Seminary, Wp & Preaching
**Härtner Mr Lukas** United Methodist from Germany; Youth &
Logistics
**Hensman Mrs Audrey MA** Methodist Local Preacher
Former Social Worker-NT Evangelism

**Jackson Dr Carole** Methodist Conf. Medical Committee;
Psychiatrist-special interest in adult learning disabilities
**Jackson Chris MEng (Hons) ACGI AMIMechE**
Camera/Video Producer with team in Nigeria
**Kirk Mrs Janet MA (CQSW)** Methodist Local Preacher; Social
Worker with training experience

**Kirkwood Revd Cameron MA (CNAA)** Methodist Supt Minister, Brixton, London Community & Mission
**Klaiber Revd Dr Walter** Presiding Bishop UMC Germany; Church & Mission Theology - NT
**Mellor Revd Dr Howard (Then)** Principal of Cliff College Mission Lectures & graduations
**Morris Revd Dr Heather** Irish Methodist Director of Ministry, Edgehill Theological College, Belfast (Born in Nigeria)

**Okegbile Revd Dr Deji MA** MCN Presbyter; PhD Research Student Lecturer on Fresh Expressions of Church
**Olabimtan Revd Dr Kehinde BTh MTh** Baptist Minister-Lagos: Lecturer in West African Church History
**Parker Miss Amy BA (Hons)** Student Liaison, Evaluation and Promotion, Marketing Expertise
**Parker Mr Douglas** IT Lecturer; Cameraman on training visit to Cuba
**Richardson Revd Dr Neil MA BA MLitt** Former Principal & President of UK Conf-NT Lectures & graduations
**Skuce Revd Dr Stephen MPhil BD** Irish Methodist Minister Cliff College Dean of Studies & CCILC Director
**Smith Revd Dr Jennifer BA MPhil** Methodist Minister Lecturer Wesleyan Holiness & Mission, Politics and Religion
**Stapleford Mr Mike** IT Assembly & Computer Training Community Development projects

**Thompson Revd Dr Michael MA BD** Methodist Minister Former Missionary SL, Religion & Mission Theology – OT
**Todd Revd Kenneth BA, BD, MA** Irish Methodist Minister, Past President of Conference & Mission Partner SL
**Walls Prof. Andrew** Methodist Missionary Statesman Church History and Mission in Africa
**Worrell Mr Peter** Methodist LP Ret'd violinist with Halle Orchestra; Lecturer on Worship & Adult Learning
**Yambasu Revd Dr Sahr** Sierra Leonean Methodist serving in Ireland West African Church History

*NB Whilst our thanks are being expressed to the people listed above we want to pay tribute to the leaders of churches, coordinators, resource persons-lay and ordained, lecturers/Principals in Sierra*

*Leone, Cuba and Nigeria for their hospitality and encouragement. With unfailing good humour they have supported the ILC programme as an add-on to their ongoing responsibilities and helped us, as visiting lecturers, in countless different ways. As visitors we are welcomed during our brief visits, but it is the day to day work of student supervision undertaken so graciously by our partners in this enterprise that has produced such successful outcome(s). Those listed above want to say, thank you to our friends for their partnership in this programme which has enhanced our ministry! We are pleased that we have been able to reciprocate with hospitality for some of you visiting the UK and by raising funds for projects/resources that build upon our relationship.*

**APPENDIX 10C: 300+ PAGES: BOOKLET OF LECTURES**

Delivered by some of the above lecturers as part of the ten module CCILC programme and distributed at the Episcopal Consultation.

***N.B. For later courses most of these lectures were included on CD's that have been distributed to leaders, lecturers and trainees involved with us in the programme.***

# (IN NO PARTICULAR ORDER)

**1. What contribution does the partner church make to the programme?**

*National churches have provided venues for teaching and lecturers (some UK scholarship trained partners) that have supervised/given guidance to the students. Also, they have paid for internal travel/flights, food and accommodation for the visiting team(s).*

**2. Why is the course not validated by a recognised University?**

*The cost of validation by a UK university would be prohibitive for the large numbers of students enrolled on our courses. Overseas validation has not been properly explored, but if either route was taken, we must recognise that it would lead to much more administration and much reduced flexibility in tailoring courses appropriate to the situation.*

**3. Having begun as an ecumenical programme why is it now restricted to Methodists?**

*The original intention was to develop an ecumenical programme. Despite the verbal support of the Archbishop of Canterbury, repeated efforts to enlist the cooperation of CMS; USPG; and the UMC foundered, with reasons given unique to each organisation. Visiting lecturers are recruited from many denominations. The UMC in Germany and its ecumenical partners supported the work in Sierra Leone by providing lecturers and funding. MCN (like many other churches in Nigeria) is so large that specific training needs (outside of shared ministerial training at Emmanuel College, Ibadan) are dealt with denominationally.*

**4. What do lecturers from a declining church in the UK and Europe have to offer to growing churches overseas?**

*We need to remind ourselves that many of the traditional churches overseas are not growing because they are finding it difficult to leave behind imported structures and ways of worship that do not appeal to the younger generation. Despite a declining church, we continue to be comparatively rich in human, financial and information resources. Lecturers recruited, most with previous experience of serving overseas, have easy access to the latest thinking/practice on most topics. These lecturers/trainers have communicated that thinking in ways that can be assimilated by pastors/students living and working in differing cultural environments. The students have translated those ideas and made practical use of them in their own rapidly changing world in ways that will feed through into the World Church.*

**5. How are the travelling lecturers funded?**

*Roughly 60% of the WCO (SALT) grant expenditure is related to lecturers travelling from the UK. The UK/European lecturers give their services free, but out-of-pocket expenses are refunded. Some have solicited grants or paid for everything themselves. Expenses related to travel within the UK, the cost of Flights overseas, Insurance, Visas, Inoculations, Anti-malarials etc. make up the larger part of that expenditure. We do provide a small honorarium and travel expenses for indigenous lecturers/supervisors.*

**6. Could the ILC be located somewhere other than at Cliff College?**

*Yes, the concept is not copyrighted and every denomination should have one! Nevertheless, the God-given vision has flourished in the Cliff College environment with good reason. Traditionally, Cliff College is a lay training college with strong links with our partner churches overseas. Recent years have seen the development of University of Manchester validated 'distance learning' programmes at diploma through to doctorate level. These 'in-service' training courses on many aspects of church work have attracted both ministers and lay people of many denominations to do further training at Cliff. CCILC has made use of college resources/expertise to maintain academic standards and produce practical training courses. The academic network and contacts with graduate practitioners in mission have helped us recruit the trainers used. Above all, Cliff College and Methodism have provided the vouched for integrity that pioneering programmes need to attract funding/resources.*

**JOB DESCRIPTION:** (See Appendix 7A-2003) **Based on current experience! This Revision: September 2009**

ADMINISTRATION includes all office/computer work related to:

Preparing and keeping under review the concept that is the ILC

Revising and applying the concept to specific situations like Sierra Leone, Cuba, Nigeria etc.

Planning with others everything from dates of the 'Residentials' to provision of student materials

Responding to daily emails, letters, and telephone calls relating to every aspect of the project

Relating to Cliff College, World Church (& sponsoring organisations) Staff & Committees

Keeping up-to-date with current political and economic situation overseas

Briefing trainers regarding the area with which involved/providing focus for preparation

Becoming transit conduit for programme information and usable materials

Liaising with possible contributors of staff/materials e.g. UMC Germany & MMS (Ireland)

Responding to requests and keeping in touch with all interested parties, including future prospects

Keeping up to date all files as a resource and justification for the project

Convincing others that they should fund, support or take part in this innovative project

ACADEMIC-IDIAMM includes maintaining academic standards:

Discussing, evaluating, amending and producing all Course and Module materials.

Studying to improve 'Distance Learning' programmes-'successes' and 'failures'.

Pursuing possibilities of practical courses relating to HIV/Aids, Justice/Reconciliation etc.

Reviewing the books appropriate to the Course and evaluating suggestions (in light of budget)

Commissioning and producing 'Distance Learning' material relevant to the Course

Producing Course Booklet covering Regulations, Referencing, and Modules for academic courses

Responding to tutor/partner church suggestions Revising modules in light of 'Applied' intention

Photocopying for students and keeping copies of all lecture notes/materials used on the Course

Producing, circulating and amending all blank forms used for the Course from Application, and Marking through to Evaluation. Checking and analysing all completed forms.

Preparing and Revising timetables and practical provision for the delivery of the course

Delivering the two week Jan/July 'Residential Courses' during a three week stay twice a year

Supervising/moderating the work produced by students and marked locally by tutors

Pursuing possible University validation of Course locally or internationally at reasonable cost

**PERSONNEL**-includes relating personally to everyone involved here, in Sierra Leone and in Nigeria:

Recruiting ecumenically for experienced and qualified visiting staff/trainers support team

Making and maintaining contacts with possible tutors willing to serve with the ILC

Planning and preparing tutors and other helpers (here and there) for participation in 'Residentials'

Obtaining personal information, photographs and CV's for possible Academic validation purposes.

Arranging with visiting tutors recruited: inoculations, insurance, anti-malarials etc.

Soliciting invitation documents required for visas from Partner church authorities and Cliff College

Receiving passports/organising visas through personal visits to the London High Commission(s)

Booking flights, coping with last minute complications, re-booking, flights, hotels etc.

Arranging accommodation, feeding and hospitality and first aid kit for the visiting team

Leading team of up to 10 people for January/July residentials and arranging hospitality

Linking each visitor with their local counterpart in presenting and marking their module

SPONSORS include organisations, groups and individuals offering support:

Soliciting funds, books and other materials from a variety of organisations and church bodies

Completing the required forms for organisations like 'Feed The Minds'

Providing the required information for the World Church Office and MMS (Ireland)

Arranging transfer of books and other materials to overseas centres

Arranging release from the docks and secure distribution in overseas centres

Reports-Reporting back to all organisational/individual donors in ways/forms requested by them

PARTNERS include everyone associated with us in the local setting:

Developing relationships with key people in the Christian Councils of partner churches

Liaising with local church leaders, tutors and the local coordinator

Linking with the Principal and staff of the centres being utilised

Working at enhancing the work of the Colleges through provision of resources/staffing

Working through the possibilities of 'exchanges' with the colleges overseas

Linking up tutors with possible avenues for further study and channelling applications

Responding to enquires from prospective partners/enthusiasts and assessing possibilities

Assessing and supporting the everyday work of the national coordinators and college tutors

ACCOUNTS include everything from budgeting to petty cash reimbursements:

Raising the necessary funding from churches, organisations and concerned individuals

Accounting in detail for every aspect of income/expenditure passed through Cliff College accounts

Arranging and checking payments for all major expenditure on books, flights etc.

Paying and claiming back all personal expenses of team members here and overseas

Preparing and adjusting budgets, balancing the books!

Providing detailed accounts for Cliff College, World Church and Sponsors

PUBLICITY includes personal, preaching and paper contacts.

Preparing initial proposals and regular reports on the progress of the ILC

Producing and sorting digital pictures for use with publicity and newspaper articles-ILC DVD

Writing reports and articles for a variety of Committees, Synods, publications and individuals

Interviews for Radio and TV overseas

World Church services/events scheduled at churches/events in the UK

Responding to many requests for further information about everything from 'missing persons in Sierra Leone' to links with former 'missionaries' who want 'to help' in some way

Writing up and re-writing the success story that is the CCILC

MISCELLANEOUS includes everything overlooked in the above summary:

Facilitating related enterprises: Zonkwa College; Mary Archer Champness; College development

Hospitality for visitors/students from overseas and relationship building through their families here

Everything not covered above that an innovative and continually developing pioneering project of this kind requires!

Richard Jackson (Revd) (Retired!!!)
Coordinator, Cliff College International Learning Centre
September 2009

# CLIFF COLLEGE INTERNATIONAL TRAINING CENTRE (CCITC)
# IN PARTNERSHIP WITH
# THE METHODIST CHURCH NIGERIA (MCN)
### (Sponsored by the Methodist Church in Britain & Ireland)

## INTERNATIONAL CERTIFICATE IN METHODISM, LEADERSHIP & MISSION (ICIMLM) (2nd-19th April 2013)

After 170 years of Methodism and 50 years of autonomy, the Methodist Church Nigeria is growing as it responds to its own (2006) Mission Statement:

"TO CONSISTENTLY WIN MORE SOULS FOR CHRIST, TO DEVELOP SPIRITUALLY FULFILLED MEMBERS AND REMAIN VERY ACTIVE IN SERVING HUMANITY."

During the past six years at the invitation of the MCN Leadership, Cliff College, through its International Training Centre has shared in the further training for 'Ministry & Mission' of several hundred Evangelists, Priests and Presbyters in Nigeria.

As a follow up to the autonomy celebrations being held this year in Nigeria, a further partnership programme for training lay leaders is being piloted in three arch-dioceses during 2013. In addition, this growing church wants to give its 'Episcopal Leadership' numbering more than 70 bishops the opportunity to share in a programme of training at Cliff College and some cross-cultural exposure to British Methodism and our common Wesleyan Heritage by visiting the UK (at its own expense) shortly after Easter in 2013.

This brief draft is intended to introduce the thinking behind the proposed programme to those who are likely to be involved in some way (at home or overseas). There is much still to be approved/agreed by the parties directly concerned but putting this on paper will allow everyone time to reject, correct, adapt, or suggest alternative arrangements during the next few weeks.

The current leaders of MCN: The Prelate, His Eminence Dr Sunday Ola Makinde; the Secretary of Conference, Rt. Revd Dr Raphael Opoko; and the Bishop of Evangelism, Rt Revd Dr Sunday N Onuoha; want this programme to be organised as a structured spiritual retreat and training programme for the Episcopal leadership of MCN. The programme will build on the work done together during an 'Episcopal Training Consultation' enjoyed by many of us in Lagos in July 2009. Our hope is that the planned training programme at Cliff College backed up by a second week visiting Districts will provide an enriching experience and benefit everyone who chooses to be involved in some way.

The overall theme for the whole programme is likely to be: LEADING BY EXAMPLE, which has been a continuing theme of our training programme. This theme will feed into the further training programme planned for Lay Leaders in Nigeria also in 2013 which is likely to major on Team Leadership. Both Episcopal and Lay Leaders will have received in advance of these training programmes their own personal copy of the CCITC Training DVD and CD of 'Ministry & Mission' resources distributed in August 2012.

**Required Pre-preparation by Participants (submitted by 31/12/2012) should include:**

Submission of a detailed (Arch-) and Diocesan Report analysing the past five years with statistical details.
Share a paper outlining the Diocesan leader's personal vision for mission in their own (Arch) diocese.
A personal (confidential) Spiritual Journal kept from 01/01/2013 'Tuning into Wesleyan Spirituality.'
Completion of 'Application Form' with CV outlining experience in Church life and leadership.
Payment through MCN of £500 non-refundable deposit payable to Cliff College by 31st Dec 2012.

**Personal travel & other arrangements (for post-Easter 2013):**

**Tue, Apr 2**  Travel overnight Lagos to London (Wednesday a.m. onward to Cliff College)

**Wed, Apr 3**   to Tues April 9 @ Cliff College: Orientation-Lectures:
'Leading by Example'
with lecturers recruited for sub-themes under:

Scriptural Leadership;                  Wesleyan Leadership;
Organisational Leadership;              Spiritual Leadership;
MCN Leadership for Today & Tomorrow.

We plan to include also in the Cliff College programme:
A group visit to Epworth.
An Open Day Sat and/or Sunday for former missionaries in Nigeria,
visiting friends of MCN and the burgeoning Nigerian Diaspora.

**Wed, Apr 10**
Travel to British and Irish Districts (2 Bishops to a District) Yet to be
agreed and arranged.
Personal discussions with Chairs, Ministers and Lay Leaders in
Districts.
Introduction to Chaplaincies; Fresh Expressions and other District
Projects related to mission.
Visit Methodist Heritage Sites and Sights of interest in District.
Worship & Preaching possible by District arrangement personally with
MCN visitors.

**Tue, Apr 16**
Travel to London for WCR Consultations/Debriefing; Visit Wesley
sites; Family time!

**Fri, Apr 19**   Return day-time flight to Lagos.

2013 June    Submission of paper (3,500-4,000 words) on: Forward
Together: What action should we take to apply what has been learned
and stimulate church growth in our own (Arch)-Diocese?

2013 July    Presentation of Cliff College:

INTERNATIONAL    CERTIFICATE    IN    METHODISM,
LEADERSHIP & MISSION (ICIMLM)
to those who have fulfilled the above requirements relating to the
whole programme.

*Acting for the leadership of the Methodist Church Nigeria, MCN have designated the Bishop of Remo, Rt. Revd Babatunde Taiwo as their national coordinator for this 'Episcopal' programme. He will liaise with Revd Richard Jackson, Coordinator of CCITC at Cliff College. When approval has been received for this outline programme and invitations issued through the appropriate church authorities Bishop Taiwo and Revd Jackson will issue a further communication giving some indication of the next steps that will be required by all of us who will be associated with this exciting (ad)venture.*

As indicated already, the planning for this proposed visit, which will do so much to build upon the excellent relationships already enjoyed by British & Irish Methodism with the Methodist Church in Nigeria, is in its very early stages. If approved as outlined, it is likely to be late in September before we can circulate further information. In the meantime, we look forward to receiving your comments and further suggestions as soon as possible so that, if as we anticipate approval is given for the practical preparations to begin, we may move forward quickly with the many arrangements necessary that will help turn this inspired vision of the leader of the Methodist Church Nigeria into a reality.

# CLIFF COLLEGE INTERNATIONAL TRAINING CENTRE (CCITC)

## (INTERNATIONAL DIPLOMA IN APPLIED MINISTRY AND MISSION) IDIAMM
## (INTERNATIONAL CERTIFICATE IN METHODISM, LEADERSHIP & MISSION) ICI-MLM
## (INTERNATIONAL CERTIFICATE IN LAY LEADERSHIP- Level 1) ICI-LL1

The developing programme of the Cliff College International Training Centre is our response to specific requests being made by partner churches overseas for shared further training programmes (in-country) that will help to meet the needs of growing churches in West Africa. Following the success of the IDIAMM programme in providing further training in 'Ministry & Mission' for evangelists and the ordained ministry in Sierra Leone and Nigeria we have been asked to share in providing a practical programme which will help senior leaders (both ordained & lay) to build into their roles and responsibilities a 'teamwork mentality'. The expectation is that this realistic recognition of roles and responsibilities and the training given will generate further spiritual and numerical growth in and through the life of the church in the community.

*N.B. A proposed programme in outline (ICI-MLM) for post-Easter 2013 has been submitted already in relation to the Episcopal Leadership of the Methodist Church Nigeria (MCN). (See separate paper introducing ICI-MLM)*

This second paper will share some preliminary thinking about the INTERNATIONAL CERTIFICATE IN LAY LEADERSHIP-Level 1 (ICI-LL1) which is scheduled to begin with a pioneering pilot scheme in 2013 for enrolled 'Lay Leaders' from three major MCN Archdioceses focussed on: Lagos; Sagamu; and Umuahia. This training will be made available largely, but not exclusively, to Lay

410

Leaders. Our plan is that some sessions will bring together the Lay and Ordained Leadership of the Archdiocese (& Dioceses) to encourage working together as a team.

After discussions with the MCN leadership about local custom and secular responsibilities for lay people it was agreed that the pilot programme of training for each Archdiocese would consist of a long weekend in late January/early February 2013, beginning early on Friday morning and ending on Sunday evening:

**i.e. 2013: Jan 18-20 (Sagamu); Jan 25-27 (Umuahia); Feb 1-3 (Lagos).** This will allow for travel between centres for visiting trainers (and perhaps for a mid-week evening training extra for other groups within travelling distance). The intention is to repeat this pattern with the same group of leaders in June/July 2013.

**i.e. 2013: June 28-30 (Sagamu); July 5-7 (Umuahia) July 12-14 (Lagos).** Between the training events in Jan/Feb and those of Jun/July 2013 all Lay Leaders participating will be required to apply some of what they have been learning to their local situation and to write up their experiences in a format that can be shared, discussed and acted upon at the subsequent training event.
A post Jan/Feb 'Lay Leadership' training programme review with MCN leaders

**i.e. 2013 (?4/5$^{th}$ Feb) at the MCN Conference Office in Lagos** will provide an opportunity for shared reflection on the progress being made with this programme (and possibly finalising details for post-Easter 2013 Episcopal Retreat).

The content of the training to be given on Level 1 of this programme has yet to be worked out in detail, but we are working towards harmonising it with what has been shared with so many of the ordained ministry over the past 6 years through the IDIAMM programme. Hopefully, it will also fit well with what is being planned for the 2013 'Episcopal Retreat'. Participants in all programmes will have a common and shared foundation having been given their own copy of the ITC-DVD and the associated CD with lecture notes relating to the 'Ministry and Mission' programme. Obviously, further resources specific to their role as lay leaders will be made available to those who enrol from the Archdiocese for the Jan/Feb-June/July training events. What those resources will be will depend to some extent on the funding made available but also upon further conversations/consultations with those who are likely to take part in the programme. Some suggestions about 'content' of the programme outlined below have been shared with us already in conversation with the leaders of MCN.

## 1. SPIRITUAL RETREAT

If a 'Spiritual Retreat' is a requirement for those who are ordained and have senior leadership roles in the life of the church, then it must be built into any Church Lay Training programme. When a church has set itself some church growth goals, it must also help its lay people as well as its ministers to reflect upon those 'church' situations where growth is taking place, whether they are New Generation/Pentecostal or Traditional churches or indeed Methodist! We may discuss whether it is growth that changes the church or church changes that promote growth, but you cannot hope to have one without the other. Growth and change are inextricably linked, but on the whole it is the lay leadership rather than the ordained ministry who have to cope (sometimes quite literally) with the 'fall-out' when changes take place or church growth becomes the focus of our worship as well as our witness.

## 2. WESLEY AND HISTORIC METHODISM

A concern has been expressed by the leadership of MCN, but shared through many others, both lay and ordained elsewhere, at the shallow grasp of historic Methodism, its theology and how it affects our understanding of, and response to, the 2006 Constitution of the Methodist Church Nigeria. Whilst culturally the Methodist Church in Nigeria, as in other parts of the world has developed an indigenous (colourful!) identity it has flourished within a largely hierarchical society in community and political life.

With less formal/structured but growing New Generation, (Pentecostal) styles of leadership proliferating there is a real pressure for the traditional main-line churches to be seen to offer an alternative style of leadership which will pay more than lip service to the concept of the 'Priesthood of all Believers' and will be evidenced by 'Humility in Serving'. Modelled in church life and translated into the political sphere, it may be a concept that will do much to break down barriers, enrich our understanding of democracy and promote 'working together' in national life.

### 3. ACCOUNTABILITY, ACCOUNTS AND ADMINISTRATION

The MCN leadership continues to promote 'transparency' as fundamental to good governance in the church as well as in the political arena. Much 'less good' governance in church and state, particularly in relation to the care and use of funds can be traced back to the lack of training and supervision. Unfortunately, many priests, presbyters and lay leaders who joke about it, help to give administration a bad name. (The improvements made, in and for the community, by the 'administration' of the present governor of Lagos is a contemporary illustration that can be viewed by all!)

Even in the church, many make excuses or blame others for their own failings because they simply cannot be bothered to learn to do the right things in the right way to achieve a proper and 'transparent' outcome. Some cloak their inefficiency with an 'unredeemed spirituality' which seems to suggest that the Charismatic Spirit of God is not a Spirit of Order (See 1 Cor.14 especially v32). Our hope is that further teaching about administration and basic accounting that recognises the importance of the 'ministration' that gives meaning to the word administration will provide motivation backed by minimal competence, that will reduce, if not eradicate the suspicions about some in leadership that do harm to the church fellowship.

### 4. TEAMS AND THEIR LEADERSHIP

In the church our leadership model is Jesus Christ. Leaders that exemplify leadership are unhappy with committees that talk a great deal but do not commit themselves to disciplined action. How should we organise ourselves as followers of the Lord Jesus Christ, under the guidance of the Holy Spirit to do what God wants us to do as the Church? 'Changing world: Changing Church' has to become more than the title of a book.

As we respond to the issues and expressed needs highlighted above we have the beginnings of a practical training programme for MCN Lay Leaders in thoughts about 'Lay Spirituality'; Methodism and the MCN Constitution; Administration as Ministry; Teams and Their Leadership. We feel sure that many people reading this, both in the UK and overseas, will have exciting contributions to make as we prioritise input for our first phase of Lay Training. For the second phase we may begin to look at meeting needs of the different generations; of insider and outsider. Or perhaps something along the lines of: Know yourself; Know your church; Know your Community; Know your Mission. MCN and CCITC will welcome any emailed thoughts and materials relevant to the content of the proposed 'Lay Leadership' programme.

Our standard practice of having the national church share the cost by providing accommodation, the venue and in-country travel for the visiting team through their training levy keeps expenditure down. Nevertheless, realistic budget figures extracted from earlier programme costs indicate that the primary funding required (and to be sought from Church funding agencies) to run this pilot Lay Leadership training programme for 300 lay leaders in Nigeria (100 at each Archdiocesan Centre) is £20,000.

As with all such initiatives and pilot programmes, flexibility and a sense of humour will be the key to the success of this further experiment in 'Doing Training There in Partnership'. This brief presentation is intended to introduce this new enterprise to those who will have direct involvement in it and to encourage a positive practical response from those who may be willing to sponsor the project with funding and resources. Thank you in anticipation of a positive response in supporting this expanding programme.

CLIFF COLLEGE INTERNATIONAL TRAINING CENTRE (CCITC) 2001-14

(VAT-Value Added Training: worth much more than 20%-Why?)

We have made available to those concerned, detailed reports, DVD's, and positive evaluations which show how the work of the International Training Centre has developed over the past thirteen years. As the pioneer and coordinator of the programme my intention in this personal conclusion is to argue that what has been achieved through our own publicised **"Programme for the 21$^{St}$ Century" of 'doing training there in a partnership'** is in harmony with much of mission thinking about world church relationships appropriate for the coming years.

VISION FULFILLED

*Since 2001 Partner Churches overseas have invited us to engage with them in their further training programmes for the:*

*Reconstruction* (physical, social, spiritual) of devastated churches and communities in post-conflict Sierra Leone

*Restoration* of historic ties between Cuba, their Wesley heritage and the 'Mother Church of Methodism'

*Repositioning* of the church with an intentional focus on applied mission and evangelism in Methodist Church Nigeria

*Reinforcing* of the structures and training of the small, but growing church in Uganda.

*Realisation* of their dream in visiting UK Methodist Heritage Sites and 'Walking where the Wesleys' walked".

One unexpected outcome accompanying our response has been experienced in the renewal of long-forgotten relationships. Relationships forged by missionaries in the past, have been fertilised in the present as we have lived and worked together in the programme. Apart from expertise in a specific subject and usually, but not always, some experience of cross-cultural mission, we have asked everyone

415

associated with the programme to be flexible and to share a sense of humour. Even those people who have previously served overseas have gained a fresh understanding of 'The Young Church in Action' as it makes its way in the contemporary world. Our partnership 'there' has enriched us all in ways that provide much more than 20% Value Added Training (VAT) in the exchequer of world mission.

Networking together with all of our partners and sponsors both here and overseas we have learned to respect the 'invitation' and the intention of the national church leadership. Their testimony suggests that we have earned their respect by our willingness to be at one with them as we have matured together through a two-way:

Fellowship of faith(s) growing through biblical insights, Friendship and spiritual awareness:
Meeting of minds through sharing and training for Mission in differing cultural contexts:
Hospitality of the heart by meeting and learning from each other how to interpret the 'Home' environment:
Concern for creation generated in a caring community through respect and care for each other's needs.

*From an income averaging £40,000 per annum* (=cost of 2-3 UK scholarships or one mission partner being supported for one year) provided by sponsors and donors CCITC has networked relationships nationally and internationally, denominationally and ecumenically, *as we have:*

**Learned** through cross-cultural experiences shared by more than 60 visiting lecturers from Europe and West Africa
**Received** hospitality and returned hospitality overseas and at home with everyone hosting 'friends' rather than visitors
**Enlisted** sponsors/supporters/book agencies to provide discounted books, resources, and funding for special projects

**Utilised** available (wo)man power resources and expertise, at no cost, other than expenses, for lecturing/ training visits

**Responded** to enquiries about materials and access to resources, from churches in Africa, Asia, The Caribbean etc.

**Exchanged** information/resources with countless colleges /university tutors in Sierra Leone, Cuba, and Nigeria

**Resourced** with materials: trainees/lecturers receiving free-books retailing at up to £700; College libraries updated

**Shared** in projects improving accommodation, water supplies, libraries, at colleges in Sierra Leone and Nigeria

**Trained** using in tandem, qualified, local college Tutors/Trainers (small honorarium paid) with visiting lecturers

## FULL CIRCLE IN MINISTRY (*1969-2014*)

IN CONCLUSION, TO SUMMARISE SOME OF WHAT HAS BEEN SHARED IN THIS BRIEF
HISTORY:

1. A VERY PERSONAL REVIEW

1969-79     My wife, Dr Carole Jackson and I served as Mission Partners in Sierra Leone.

1979-2000   Circuit Ministry: Bristol; Bramhall, Stockport; Ashton-under-Lyne

1979-2000   Stayed in touch with SL, through the traumas of the 1990's-Blood Diamond!

2000        Posted to Cliff College as Postgraduate Tutor.

2001   Return to post-conflict Sierra Leone as delegate to MCSL Annual Conference.
       Vision for Cliff College International Training Centre jotted down on aeroplane 'sick bag'! & 'Doing Training There in Partnership' with our partners overseas.

2005 Sept 'Retirement' Sale Cct & 'The Avenue Methodist Church'

**2002-4 SL** (Post Conflict) **The Methodist Church Sierra Leone (MCSL) and Christian Council of Sierra Leone (CCSL)** at their College in Freetown Two-year pilot ecumenical training project in Sierra Leone for 99 church leaders-MMS Funded. Lecturers recruited for four lecturing 'Residentials' and £700 of books supplied to each trainee.

**2004 SL** **73 students graduate with a: Cliff College International Diploma in Ministry And Mission (IDIAMM)**

**2005 Oct NG** Advance preparation for Methodist Church Nigeria (MCN) IDIAMM course.

**2005-Nov CU The Methodist Church in Cuba & FLET training in Camp Canaan, Santa Clara.** Trainers travel with Revd Dr Martyn Atkins to support growing Methodist Church in Cuba. Shared in providing in-service 'distance' training for 100+ Trainee-pastors and spouses on Wesley, Methodism & Mission. Learned lessons, later shared elsewhere in Africa from a growing 'indigenous' Methodist Church

**2006-7 SL** **MCSL 3 training visits on Leadership & Administration,** (SALT funded) replacing IT equipment & giving training to Conference Office staff and key leaders, plus Local Preachers' & Women Worker training: March & Oct. 2006; Feb. 2007 Rebuilding Relationships through post-conflict reconciliation and re-building programme for manses, schools, hospitals etc.

**2006-8 NG** **Two-year programme for 139 Church Leaders (Lay & Ordained)** with four lecturing 'Residentials' Umuahia MTI (in the east) and Sagamu MTI (in the west) Books provided. (SALT funded) Focus on applied aspect in relation to re-positioning of MCN

**MCN Zonkwa MTI  (in the north)**
Shorter programme & resourcing

**2006-08 NG   Programme: Total of 108 trainees graduate with a: Cliff College International Diploma in Ministry And Mission (IDIAMM)**

**2009-Jul-NG Training Programme with 59 Episcopal leaders** in Lagos. Lecture Notes (300 pages) & Books supplied.

**2009-Nov SL** Follow-up Retreat for Ministers & Lay Training Conferences in Sierra Leone.

**2008-10 NG   Two-year programme for 134 Church Leaders (Lay & Ordained).** with 4 'Residentials' and books. SALT funded

*Sample outline of regular two-year IDIAMM course for information, shown for 2008-10, as follows (Course booklet available)*

| *Event* | *When?* | *Where held & Attendees* |
|---|---|---|
| Res 1-UM | 1-16 Jul 2008 | **Umuahia MTI** 77 trainees |
| & | | enrolled on the two-year course |
| Res 1-SG | 1-16 Jul 2008 | **Sagamu MTI** 57 trainees |
| | | enrolled on the two-year course |
| Res 2-UM | 6-13 Jan 2009 | **UM** Level 2 qualification: |
| Res 2-SG | 13-20 Jan 2009 | **SG** Level 2 qualification: |
| Res 3 | 1-15 Jul 2009 | Umuahia & Sagamu Residential |
| Res 4-UM | 5-12 Jan 2010 | Final Residential & Submissions |
| Res 4-SG | 12-19 Jan 2010 | Final Residential & Submissions |

*Graduation 07 July 2010*          **Umuahia  76  graduating** from 77 trainees in Jan 2009

*Graduation 17 July 2010*          **SAGAMU 53 graduating** from 57 trainees in Jan 2009

**2008-10 NG** Total of 129 trainees graduate with a: Cliff College International Diploma in Ministry And Mission (IDIAMM)

**2009 NG** 14-16 JUL **EPISCOPAL TRNG CONSULTATION**
The Prelate, Secretary of Conference and 59 Bishops in attendance at Lagos venue. Several of the (new) bishops have completed or been involved in the IDIAMM two-year programme. MCN bishops have begun planning for a fraternal 'training in mission' visit to the UK in 2013/14

**2010-12 NG** **Two-year programme for 162 Church Leaders (Lay & Ordained)** with 4 'Residentials' and books

**2012 NG** Total of 141 trainees graduate with a: Cliff College International Diploma in Ministry And Mission (IDIAMM)

2012 May (MCSL) & Aug (MCN)  **'Refreshing Training' & DVD updating resources** of former trainees undertaken in both Sierra Leone & Nigeria in association with attendance at their Church Conferences.

**2013 UK** **April 23 to May 10 EPISCOPAL TRAINING RETREAT & UK HERITAGE TOUR**
**MCN Funded:** Privileged to host 47 Episcopal Leaders and facilitators from the Methodist Church in Nigeria at Cliff College; in the UK Districts of the Methodist Church; and on a tour of Methodist Heritage sites.
**(2014 08 Presentation of International Certificate in Methodism, Leadership and Mission (ICI-MLM) to Episcopal visitors on completion of 'Forward Together' submissions.)**

**2013-Oct. SL** Part 1-Effective Management & Administration Course. Part 2-follow later in 2015 (Subject to Ebola controls!)

**2013-14** Two-visit training programme for Nigerian Lay Leaders (Nov 2013 & Feb 2014 books & resources provided.

**2014 Feb NG 83 MCN Lay Leaders graduate with International Certificate in Methodism, Leadership and Mission (ICI-MLM)**

2014 June UK Nigerian Lay Leaders Retreat at Cliff College and UK Heritage Tour

**2014 Aug UG** Revd Dr Malcolm McCall and 'Path-finding Programme' in Uganda
2014 Aug NG Richard Jackson British Delegate to: Methodist Church Nigeria Conference in Port Harcourt.

The bare-bones of this unique and pioneering partnership programme in training cannot do more than give a snapshot of what has been a mutually enriching programme. Quite rightly it is described elsewhere as VAT (Value Added Training) for everyone who has been involved in it.

## READ INTO THE TITLE WHAT YOU WILL BUT: 'GOING AND GROWING' WORKS FOR ALL OF US!

Lightning Source UK Ltd.
Milton Keynes UK
UKOW06f0006140116

266329UK00016B/91/P